SO VAST
SO BEAUTIFUL
A LAND

Louisiana and the Purchase

by Marshall Sprague

MONEY MOUNTAIN
MASSACRE: THE TRAGEDY AT WHITE RIVER
NEWPORT IN THE ROCKIES
THE GREAT GATES: THE STORY OF THE ROCKY MOUNTAIN PASSES
A GALLERY OF DUDES
THE MOUNTAIN STATES
SO VAST SO BEAUTIFUL A LAND

SO VAST
SO BEAUTIFUL
A LAND

Louisiana and the Purchase

MARSHALL
SPRAGUE

LITTLE, BROWN AND COMPANY — BOSTON — TORONTO

FIRST EDITION

T 05/74

Library of Congress Cataloging in Publication Data

Sprague, Marshall.
    So vast, so beautiful a land; Louisiana and the
Purchase.

    Bibliography: p.
    1. Mississippi Valley--History--To 1803.
2. Louisiana Purchase. I. Title.
F352.S75   973.4'6   73-21943
ISBN 0-316-807664

*Published simultaneously in Canada
by Little, Brown & Company (Canada) Limited*

PRINTED IN THE UNITED STATES OF AMERICA

For the Little Ones

SUSANNA JANE

and

EDNA FRANCES

Acknowledgments

IN PREPARING THIS STORY of how the vast drainage area of the Mississippi River came to be discovered by Europeans and then absorbed by the United States I was blessed to have at my disposal the new Charles Leaming Tutt Library at Colorado College in Colorado Springs. In addition to the beauty, good cheer and comfort of this place, its research facilities were perfect for my needs, especially its complete files of periodicals of the nation's historical societies and all official documents from the start of the republic that Tutt has available as a government depository. I wish to express my thanks and appreciation to the Tutt staff for their superb reference and research assistance, especially to George V. Fagan, Kee K. Deboer, Rosemae Wells Campbell, Jean S. Casey, Giovanna R. Jackson and Irene Vasloff. If Tutt didn't have on hand what I wanted I usually found it in the Colorado and Western History Department of the Penrose Public Library, also in Colorado Springs, where I could count on the help of Margaret G. Reid, Brenda Hawley, Kay DeFries and Norman Sams. For special maps and microfilms of ancient London and New York newspapers I had only to drive a few miles north to the U.S. Air Force Academy Library, directed by Claude J. Johns, Jr.

I was most pleased to have the permission of Edith Friedlander, of the Frederick Ungar Publishing Company, to use Frederick C. Green's vivid description in his *Eighteenth-Century France* of the rue Quincampoix in Paris during the "Mississippi Bubble" madness of 1719. Virginia Mc-

Connell allowed me to reprint Governor Bienville's report of the Mallet expedition to Santa Fe in 1739 that was published in *The Colorado Magazine* of September, 1939.

Of the hundreds who helped me thread my way through nearly three centuries of Louisiana events, I offer particular thanks to Dumas Malone, Thomas Jefferson's biographer, and George Dangerfield, the biographer of Robert R. Livingston. During the several summers that my wife and I spent roaming around Louisiana, we were instructed by Wildey Mitchell of Duluth, Minn.; James Taylor Dunn of the Minnesota Historical Society, St. Paul; Marvin Melick and Isadora Veigel of the Mankato (Minnesota) Regional Library; Sepp and Annemarie Hoedlinoser of Marquette, Michigan; Gus Wolhowe of Verendrye, North Dakota; J. R. Murray, president, Hudson's Bay Company, Winnipeg, Manitoba; Charles Le Barge and Burt McClelland of Samuel de Champlain Provincial Park, Ontario; Carl Johnson of Fremont, Nebraska; Mildred R. Anderson of Lindsborg, Kansas; George Davis of Peoria, Illinois; Geraldine Turley of Lamine, Missouri; Evelyn Coates of the Missouri State Museum, Jefferson City; Captain Ernest Wagner, skipper of the *Delta Queen* during our trip down the Mississippi from St. Louis to New Orleans; Amos E. Simpson, Glenn R. Conrad and Flossie Montgomery, all of the University of Southwestern Louisiana, Lafayette; Louise R. Fisher of the Iberia Parish Library, New Iberia, Louisiana; Faye B. Crain of the West Texas State College Library, Canon, Texas; and the Nelson Pearces of Bellview, New Mexico, who directed us to the nearby ultimate source of the Red River; also James Freeman, U.S. Army Corps of Engineers, New Orleans; and Jim Johnston, State of Louisiana Department of Commerce and Industry, Baton Rouge.

This account has emerged under the patient prodding and friendship for the past fifteen years of Ned Bradford of Little, Brown. I am thankful once again for the help of my long-suffering typist, Maxine Whitworth. Of course I could not have written a line of the book without the constant guidance and gentle policing — sometimes not so gentle — of my kindest of critics, my wife Edna Jane.

Contents

TWO: THE PURCHASE

Illustrations

MAPS

Chronology

1541   Hernando de Soto: discovers the Mississippi River; explores from Tampa Bay, Florida, across the Mississippi to central Arkansas.
Francisco Vásquez de Coronado: from the Upper Rio Grande to Kansas.

1658–1660   Médard Chouart, sieur des Groseilliers, and Pierre Esprit Radisson: to the Upper Mississippi from Lake Superior.

1673   Père Jacques Marquette and Louis Jolliet: down the Mississippi from the Great Lakes to the Arkansas River.

1680   Père Louis Hennepin: the Upper Mississippi from the Illinois River past the Falls of St. Anthony to the Mille Lacs area.

1680–1687   René Robert Cavelier, sieur de La Salle: from the Great Lakes down the Mississippi to its mouth (1682); by sea from France to Matagorda Bay and East Texas (1684).

1687–1690   Alonso de León: through East Texas to the Red River area.

1699   Pierre Le Moyne, sieur d'Iberville: the Mobile Bay area and up the Mississippi to the mouth of the Red River.

1700   Pierre Le Sueur: *sailed* up the Mississippi from the Gulf of Mexico to the mouth of the Minnesota River, and up the Minnesota as far as the Blue Earth River near present Mankato.

1712–1724   Etienne Véniard, sieur de Bourgmond: to central Kansas and up the Missouri River to above present Omaha, Nebraska.

1714–1716   Louis Juchereau de St. Denis: East Texas, from Natchitoches on the Red River to the Rio Grande.

1719   Jean-Baptiste Bénard de La Harpe: eastern Oklahoma.
Claude Charles du Tisné: eastern Kansas.

1738–1743   Pierre de La Vérendrye and sons: from the Lake Winnipeg region of Canada via the Souris River to the Mandan villages on the Upper Missouri River and west to the Big Horn Mountains.

1739–1741   Pierre and Paul Mallet: from Kaskaskia in Illinois to Santa Fe via the Missouri and Arkansas rivers; returning to New Orleans via the Canadian River.

1762   November 3. Secret treaty of Fontainebleau. Louis XV gives westside Louisiana and New Orleans to Spain.

1763   February 10. Treaty of Paris. Great Britain wins eastside Louisiana (except New Orleans) from France and the Floridas from Spain.

1768   August 17. Spain takes over the administration of westside Louisiana and New Orleans from France.

1779–1781   Governor Gálvez of New Orleans occupies for Spain lands north of West Florida to and beyond the Yazoo River.

1783   January 20. Treaty of Paris. Great Britain returns the Floridas to Spain and gives trans-Appalachia (eastside Louisiana) to the United States.

1794   November 19. Jay's Treaty. Great Britain agrees to evacuate her forts in the American northwest.

1795   October 27. Pinckney's Treaty. Spain accepts the 31st parallel as the north boundary of West Florida and agrees to give the United States free navigation rights on the Mississippi River and right of deposit at New Orleans.

1800   October 1. Secret Treaty of San Ildefonso. Spain agrees to return westside Louisiana and New Orleans to France but Charles IV does not ratify the treaty until October 15, 1802.

1802   October 16. The Spanish intendant Morales suspends the American right of deposit at New Orleans.

1803   April 30. Napoleon sells Louisiana to the United States for $15,000,000.
        December 20. The transfer ceremony is held at New Orleans.

1818   October 20. Convention of 1818. The United States and Great Britain agree to the 49th parallel as the northern boundary of Louisiana from the Lake of the Woods west to the Continental Divide. The Oregon country is put under joint occupancy.

1819   February 22. The Adams-Onís Treaty. The United States and Spain agree on the southwest and western boundaries of Louisiana. Spain sells the Floridas to the United States in exchange for payment by the United States of up to $5,000,000 in the spoliation claims of American citizens.

Prologue

THE TRANSACTION took place in Paris on April 30, 1803. By paying fifteen million dollars to France on easy terms, the feeble and infant United States acquired the largest and most valuable river system on earth. The land area of the new republic was doubled by the addition of the entire westside drainage of the Mississippi plus the New Orleans delta region. Later surveys showed that the extent of the westside drainage was a million square miles.

The size of the Purchase was reduced to 883,072 square miles in 1818–1819 after practical boundaries were agreed upon by the United States and by the owners of adjoining properties: Spain in the southwest and Great Britain in Canada. Even so, the reduced Purchase area was larger than the combined size of present-day Spain, Portugal, Italy, France, both Germanys, Holland, Belgium, Switzerland, England, Scotland, Wales, Northern Ireland and Ireland, which contain altogether 860,438 square miles. Thirteen of our largest western states have been carved out of it, starting with the state of Louisiana in 1812 and ending with Oklahoma in 1907.

The dimensions of the Purchase as implied vaguely in the Treaty of Paris (1803) were theoretical since only bits of the vast hinterland had been explored by Europeans even after three centuries of trying. Louisiana was understood to end in the remote west at "the height of land" — which was, in modern terms, the Continental Divide in the Rocky Mountains beyond Denver, Colorado. In the far north, the Purchase ended at the unknown source of the Mississippi (actually at Lake Itasca some two hundred and fifty airline miles north of Minneapolis). In the tropical south it ended at the Red River more or less — the same Red River that marks the boundary today between Texas and Oklahoma but which was known in 1803 only in the vicinity of Natchitoches, Louisiana.

It would be difficult to present a balanced account of the people who had a hand over the years in this momentous development. The men who explored the wilderness and those who took part in making the Purchase happen were too colorful for that. Among the insuppressibles was René Robert Cavelier, sieur de La Salle, who found his way from the Great Lakes to the mouth of the Mississippi in 1682, claimed the whole country for France, and gave it the handsome name of Louisiana, honoring his monarch, Louis XIV, the Sun King. La Salle, touched by the idealism that would flower with Voltaire and the *philosophes*, dreamed of the great valley as a paradise where Frenchmen could find the freedom and the opportunity that were denied them at home. That dream displeased the Sun King, who did not care for even a little freedom among his subjects. As a result, La Salle's career ended in failure and personal tragedy.

Other venturesome men, Frenchmen and Spaniards, had no better luck with the province through the eighteenth century. There was the pirate, the sieur d'Iberville, who survived the ice floes of Hudson Bay and the hurricanes of Mississippi Sound only to die of fever near Havana in mid-career. The gay duc d'Orléans, patron saint of the provincial capital, turned the royal resources of France over to his Scotch friend, John Law, in 1719, and watched most of them melt away in Law's Mississippi real estate scheme. The heroic Pierre de La Vérendrye and his sons exhausted their strength, spirits and financial resources exploring the upper Missouri region against the odds of an indifferent French bureaucracy. The charming duc de Choiseul protected Madame de Pompadour from younger rivals for Louis XV's love and persuaded Charles III of Spain in 1762 to accept westside Louisiana as compensation for losses that he had sustained as an ally of France against Britain.

Near the end of the Purchase story, two gentlemen of special glamor appeared. One was Napoleon's foreign minister, Charles Maurice de Talleyrand, famed in history as the craftiest, most dissolute and most corrupt of European statesmen. Talleyrand matched wits with President Jefferson's envoy in Paris whom the Frenchman judged at first to be a guileless farmer from up the Hudson. But Talleyrand found himself losing out to the farmer when he tried to persuade Napoleon not to sell Louisiana. The wily American was Robert R. Livingston, the ranking plutocrat of Dutchess County and head of one of the oldest and most powerful dynasties in New York State.

Thomas Jefferson, many-sided, endlessly provocative and inspiring, was more than colorful. From the time of his childhood below the Blue Ridge of Virginia, he seemed to be part of the rhythm, the gusto, the dynamics of the movement of Americans westward toward the mystic Mississippi. His career as author of the Declaration of Independence, governor of Virginia, minister to France, secretary of state, vice president and finally president in 1800, proceeded with a fixed conviction — that the land and its independent farmers were the keys to national wealth, political stability and the ideal for the republican government he had in mind. He never crossed the Alleghenies himself, but he saw the exuberant effect that the wide-open country of Ohio, Kentucky and Tennessee had on the tens of thousands of Americans who did cross after the Revolution, and even on those who stayed behind, knowing that they could cross if they wanted more freedom than they had in the seaboard states.

The Louisiana Purchase was the totally unexpected climax of Jefferson's hopes. It occurred at a moment in history when the citizens of the United States were by no means certain whether to continue their dubious and expanding experiment in freedom and democracy or resign themselves to becoming satellites of England with leanings toward monarchy. Possession of the empire which had caused France and Spain so much grief and which England hoped to win right up to the War of 1812 raised the United States to world power overnight. At the same time, it set its people permanently on a course that would lead them in no time at all to the Pacific Ocean.

ONE

THE DISCOVERY

1

Phantom River

It was the morning of April 9, 1682, on the Mississippi delta and one can be sure that the humid air smelled of crayfish and brine, even as today. On the left bank of the broad brown river a few miles above Head of Passes was a cluster of battered birch-bark canoes. Above the canoes, gulls and egrets floated about looking down on what to them was a very strange sight. Near the canoes was a wooden pole to which had been nailed a handmade coat of arms of the king of France. Sixty-odd people, dressed and undressed, milled around the pole. Half of them were French explorers. The rest were Indian employees that the explorers had picked up in the Illinois country — Abenaki and Mohegan refugees from King Philip's War in New England with their wives and children.

The shirts and pants and moccasins of most of the Frenchmen were in bad shape. They had had little else to wear since their departure from Montreal six months earlier. But one of them wore fine clothes that had been carried in a trunk all the way down the Mississippi for this occasion — a ceremonial scarlet coat trimmed with gold lace, knickerbockers of Rouen linen, silk stockings from Lyons, buckled shoes. The man, slight of build, had a striking, austere face. His name was René Robert Cavelier, sieur de La Salle; his age was thirty-nine. Three days before, he had achieved the first stage in an epic dream of empire by discovering the mouths of the Mississippi below Head of Passes.

After his Frenchmen had chanted the Te Deum, shouted *Vive le Roi*

3

and fired their muskets at the misty willows across the bayous, La Salle stood before the royal coat of arms and raised a hand in a gesture for silence. Then he began to read the proclamation that he had prepared in the precise French phrasing of his Jesuit-trained youth in Normandy. The translation:

In the name of the most high, mighty, invincible, and victorious Prince, Louis the Great, by the grace of God King of France and Navarre, Fourteenth of that name, I, this ninth day of April, one thousand six hundred and eighty-two, in virtue of the commission of his Majesty, which I hold in my hand, and which may be seen by all whom it may concern, have taken, and do now take, in the name of his Majesty and of his successors to the crown, possession of this country of Louisiana, the seas, harbors, ports, bays, adjacent straits, and all the nations, peoples, provinces, cities, towns, villages, mines, minerals, fisheries, streams, and rivers within the extent of the said Louisiana, from the mouth of the great river St. Louis, otherwise called the Ohio, as also along the river Colbert, or Mississippi, and the rivers which discharge themselves thereinto, from its source beyond the country of the Nadouessioux as far as its mouth at the sea, or Gulf of Mexico, and also to the mouth of the River of Palms, upon the assurance we have had from the natives of these countries that we are the first Europeans who have descended or ascended the said river Colbert; hereby protesting against all who may hereafter undertake to invade any or all of these aforesaid countries, peoples, or lands, to the prejudice of the rights of his Majesty, acquired by the consent of the nations dwelling herein. Of which, and of all else that is needful, I hereby take to witness those who hear me, and demand an act of the notary here present.

This exultant naming and claiming of Louisiana — and "also to the mouth of the River of Palms" (Rio Grande) — was the high-water mark of La Salle's career. His notion of what he was claiming was grandiose enough. The fact was grander than anything he or any other European could have imagined in 1682. The Mississippi drainage would turn out to be the richest and one of the largest on earth, stretching from the Alleghenies to the Continental Divide in the Rockies and from Canada to the Gulf of Mexico. But La Salle was not the inventor of Louisiana. The chain of events that created it and drove him to give his life in a desperate struggle to make it French began two centuries earlier when Columbus jolted the world into modern times by landing on San Salvador Island. For many decades after 1492, the Mississippi valley was unknown to Europeans, a nameless white space of nothing on maps, a terrestrial mystery. To earn their keep, royal cartographers collected the gossip of travelers overseas and widened Louisiana gradually as a fantasy of peninsulas and archipelagos, mountain ranges and bays and oceans curving south from the north part of Asia to join the known lands of Mexico, Peru and the rest of Spain's metal-rich American possessions.

The first approach of record to the mystery was made in 1519 by the Spanish explorer Alvárez de Pineda, when his ships from Jamaica in the West Indies coasted around the shallow, treacherous north shore of the Gulf of Mexico. Pineda had no great interest in Louisiana itself. His hope was to find the mystic Strait of Anian leading from the Gulf of Mexico through the unknown land to the South Sea (the Pacific Ocean) — a short ship route that Spanish merchants could use to trade with the merchants of China and the Spice Islands. Such a route would eliminate the greedy middlemen of Venice and Marco Polo's interminable overland route from Venice to Shangtu. It would eliminate also the need to repeat Ferdinand Magellan's long voyage around South America (then in progress), Vasco da Gama's swing around South Africa, and the malarial portage across Panama that Vasco Núñez de Balboa had pioneered in 1513.

This Strait of Anian shows what the science of exploration was up against in those days. Perhaps Anian was Bering Strait, which on successive maps had worked its way from Alaska far to the south because the Spaniards wanted it so badly to run from the Gulf of Mexico through California to the South Sea. In his search for Anian, Pineda logged a few of the hundreds of rivers and bays of the north shore of the gulf, discovering the mouth of the Rio Grande — more lagoon than river — on his way to Tampico on the Pánuco River and Veracruz, where Hernando Cortez had landed recently to conquer Montezuma. Pineda may have seen the delta of the Mississippi but he did not mention a delta in his report. He mentioned Bahía de Espíritu Santo, which was Mobile Bay perhaps, but who knows? In the years ahead, the Spanish would apply the name Espíritu Santo to nearly every bay and lagoon on the Gulf of Mexico from Tampa in Florida around the twelve-hundred-mile crescent to Matagorda Bay on the Texas coast.

Some years after Pineda's voyage, the Holy Roman emperor, Charles V of Spain, set up the province of Florida and claimed for himself whatever might be found between the Gulf of Mexico and the North Pole. Charles's

5

claim was based on an act of his grandparents, King Ferdinand and Queen Isabella in 1493. They had persuaded that spectacular sinner, Pope Alexander VI, to issue a bull giving them title to all land (that is, land as yet unclaimed by other rulers) lying west of a north-south line some 360 nautical miles west of the Cape Verde Islands. Unclaimed lands east of the line — in Africa, India and so on — went to Portugal. A year later, at Portugal's insistence, the line of demarcation was moved further west, being placed this time at about 1,300 nautical miles west of the Cape Verde Islands and the Azores (the new location gave Portugal some territory in the New World — Brazil). The pope based his right to hand out empires on an old Middle Ages idea that was later exploded by the Protestant Reformation. The idea held that Jesus Christ was king of the world and issued orders on its government to be enforced by the pope, his agent. Any Christian ruler who questioned a papal bull was liable to excommunication. Charles appointed a man named Pánfilo de Narváez as governor of his mystical Florida and Narváez sailed from Cuba in 1528 with three hundred Spaniards to begin colonizing the new territory by building a capital for Florida somewhere on the shores of the Gulf of Mexico. Disaster followed disaster as Narváez and his men learned how hard it was to survive in that swampy land of hostile Indians and on that terrible gulf of hurricanes, calms, fogs and shoals. The handmade boats of the remnant eighty colonists may have floated westward from Florida past one of the delta mouths of the Mississippi because they spoke of "fresh water that ranne into the Sea continually and with great violence." Their boats were wrecked at last on the Texas coast in Galveston (Espíritu Santo) Bay and they died of starvation one by one until only three Spaniards and a Negro slave were left, including the treasurer of the Narváez expedition, Alvar Núñez Cabeza de Vaca. These durable four spent eight years as captives of Texas Indians and as naked desert rats tramping through Texas and New Mexico to sanctuary at Compostela near the Gulf of California. It was an incredible odyssey.[1] North America would not be crossed again until Alexander Mackenzie's party of fur traders crossed Canada in 1793 and that of Lewis and Clark made it across the continent through Montana in 1805.

For all their travels, Pineda and Narváez and Cabeza de Vaca did not help the muddled geographers much to clear up the Mississippi mystery. For one thing, Spanish officials had a steadily growing fear of distributing information about what their explorers were doing on the Gulf of Mexico.

They were afraid that other Europeans would find ways to reach their rich mines, particularly those in the mountains of the present province of Nuevo León a hundred miles or so south of the Rio Grande. Besides, all explorers of that era were handicapped because they could determine only latitude by using their astrolabes on the sun and stars. They could not determine the longitude of a place with any practical accuracy. They needed a reliable timepiece to do that, and such a chronometer would not be available until the 1760's. They knew that the world was round, but they had only dead reckoning and compasses to help them guess how far around. And how could one reckon accurately on a sailing ship that moved fast and slow in all directions at the whim of the wind? And the vastness of the New World was so far beyond their experience, which was based on distances in Europe, that they could not imagine it.

The mystery for two centuries of the shape of Louisiana and the whereabouts of the mouths of the Mississippi derived in part from this navigational failure. Many river mouths of the Americas were known early because they could be spotted as mouths from ships far out to sea and they could be approached safely. Columbus's friend Vicente Yáñez Pinzón charted the estuary of the Amazon, the largest river on earth by volume, in 1500. But the Mississippi, the longest river if measured from the source of the Missouri, was hard to spot from any distance offshore, in spite of the discolored water issuing from its mouths. There were three main mouths below Head of Passes and hundreds of bayou channels that looked like mouths. The river's muddy water ran from the mouths into the gulf through the thumb-shaped delta thrusting a hundred miles out from the mainland — a delta lying so low in the gulf as to be imperceptible from offshore except at close range and in the absence of the fogs that hung around it so much of the time. This thumb-delta was remarkable but not unique. The Volga, the longest river in Europe, has something like it — an estuary of many mouths projecting seventy-one miles out into the Caspian Sea.

When La Salle discovered — rediscovered is a better word — the main delta mouths of the Mississippi in 1682, he determined their latitude with some accuracy. Thereafter mariners on the Gulf of Mexico could coast offshore from east to west between the 27th and 28th parallels knowing that they wouldn't run afoul of the hidden delta and its labyrinth of mud lumps, shallows, sandy points and shell islands. But without knowing the delta's exact longitude, a sailor had to have dumb luck to stop at one of several right places on his east-west course to enter a proper mouth. After the Narváez tragedy of the 1520's, Spanish explorers dreaded that north shore of the gulf. Their homes in Cuba or in Mexico City were far, far away. If they wrecked their ships on shoals in that uncharted wilderness they would never get home again. They would starve to death trying to find the right overland trails, or they would wind up as bones in the garbage dump of some cannibal Indian camp.

It is perfectly true that the Spaniard Hernando de Soto, discovered the Mississippi River in 1541. But he did not find it anywhere near its obscure mouths. He discovered it eight hundred miles above the delta, and in such a limited, once-over-lightly way that Louis Jolliet and La Salle and other Frenchmen had to discover it all over again much later. De Soto, one of Pizarro's officers in the conquest of Peru, sailed from Cuba with a force of 620 horsemen and footmen and a packet of fine intentions — to explore Narváez's "Lands of Florida," to find tons of gold and pearls and that Strait of Anian route west to California and China, and, maybe, to establish colonies, if they had time. All those Spanish conquistadores under the great emperor Charles V were bitter rivals in their race to get pieces of American wealth. They kept an eye on one another. De Soto's spies in Mexico City had told him that the viceroy of New Spain, Antonio de Mendoza, was hot on the track of the legendary Seven Cities of pure gold somewhere north of Mexico in a region called Cibola. De Soto surmised that the Strait of Anian to the South Sea had to run through Cibola and he intended to get to the gold of the Seven Cities ahead of Mendoza's explorers. During 1540, de Soto left his ships at Espíritu Santo (Tampa) Bay on the Florida coast and began chasing gold rumors all over the Deep South, murdering hordes of Choctaws and Chickasaws and losing hundreds of his own soldiers in skirmishes and from disease.

Meanwhile, Viceroy Mendoza had selected General Don Francisco Vásquez de Coronado as his Seven Cities explorer. This second army was almost as large as that of de Soto. Coronado left Compostela west of Mexico City with the same ends in view that de Soto had and he headed toward the same unknown region of Cibola in the north. It is probable that both de Soto and Coronado supposed that that part of the American continent was on the order of Mexico — a few hundred miles wide from ocean to ocean — from the North (Atlantic) to the South (Pacific) Sea. Coronado had a naval arm to explore the Gulf of California, which was called Mar Vermejo (Vermilion Sea) because Baja California was thought to be an island. A detachment of his land army had the thrilling experience of discovering the Grand Canyon of the Colorado. Coronado himself found the Seven Cities of Cibola, and then he found the Continental Divide near present Grants, New Mexico. The Seven Cities were a bitter disappointment. They were poor Pueblo Indian villages of red sandstone that looked splendid and rich from a distance, as everything does in New Mexico's golden sunshine.[2]

Early in 1541, after setting up headquarters at a salubrious spot called Tiguex in the cottonwoods of the Upper Rio Grande near present Albuquerque, New Mexico, Coronado met a slave of the Pueblo Indians whom he called the Turk "because he looked like one." The Turk, perhaps a Wichita Indian, was a persuasive trickster who impressed everyone by talking for hours at a stretch with the Devil, who lived in a pitcher of water. The Turk told Coronado all about two fabulous kingdoms to the east, Thegayo and Quivira. Quivira, corresponding to present Kansas, was his homeland, rich in gold, he said. Thegayo bordered it on the south. Beyond Quivira was a great river — the Mississippi, of course — "in the level country which was two leagues [five-and-a-half miles] wide, in which there were fishes as big as horses [alligators] and large numbers of very big canoes, with more than twenty rowers on a side, and . . . they carried sails, and . . . their lords sat on the poop under awnings, and on the prow they had a great golden eagle."

Lured by the Turk's glowing tale, Coronado headed eastward from the Upper Rio Grande toward Quivira and the big fish of the "great river" just when de Soto's army headed westward toward the same Mississippi from the piney uplands of present Alabama. Neither explorer knew where the other was out there in the wilds, but it does no harm to pretend that a race ensued between them to be the first European to set foot on the Mississippi drainage that La Salle would name Louisiana. Their routes are given on the accompanying map.

Each of the conquistadores was in his forties, and they were as different as night and day. The brutal de Soto was a tough, smart peasant from Estremadura who rose to wealth and power by colonial enterprise and by buying a wife with a title. As governor of Cuba and of Florida, he was his own boss in America. His method of controlling the Indians along his course was to shoot them or starve them or wear them out in slave labor —

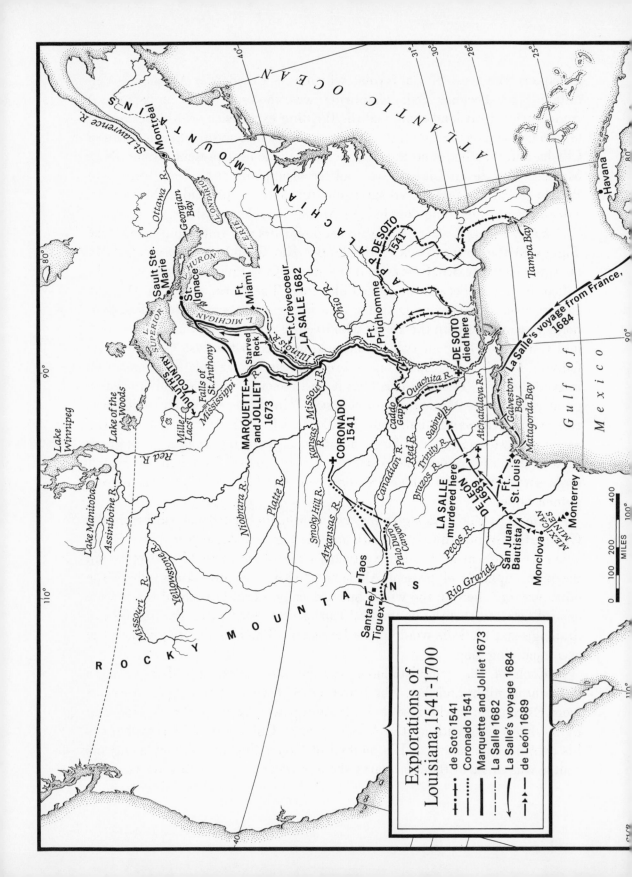

Explorations of
Louisiana, 1541–1700

┼─ ┼─ ┼	de Soto 1541	
· · · · · · ·	Coronado 1541	
────────	Marquette and Jolliet 1673	
─ · ─ · ─	La Salle 1682	
⟶ ⟶	La Salle's voyage 1684	
▶─▶─▶	de León 1689	

ATLANTIC OCEAN

APPALACHIAN MOUNTAINS

ROCKY MOUNTAINS

Gulf of Mexico

St. Lawrence R.
Ottawa R.
Montréal
Georgian Bay
L. Huron
L. Ontario
L. Erie
L. Superior
Sault Ste. Marie
St. Ignace
L. Michigan
Ft. Miami
Ft. Crèvecoeur
LA SALLE 1682
Starved Rock
Illinois R.
Ohio R.
Ft. Prudhomme
DE SOTO 1541
DE SOTO died here
Havana
Tampa Bay
La Salle's voyage from France, 1684

Lake Winnipeg
Lake Manitoba
Lake of the Woods
Assinniboine R.
Red R.
SIOUX COUNTRY
Mille Lacs
Falls of St. Anthony
Mississippi R.
MARQUETTE and JOLLIET 1673
Missouri R.
Kansas R.
Platte R.
Niobrara R.
Smoky Hill R.
Arkansas R.
CORONADO 1541
Canadian R.
Red R.
Caddo Gap
Ouachita R.
Atchafalaya R.
Galveston Bay
Matagorda Bay

Missouri R.
Yellowstone R.

Taos
Palo Duro Canyon
Santa Fe
Tiguex
Rio Grande
Pecos R.
Brazos R.
Trinity R.
Sabine R.
LA SALLE murdered here
DE LEÓN 1689
Ft. St. Louis
San Juan Bautista
Monclova
MEXICAN MINES
Monterrey

MILES
0   100   200   400
100°

110°   90°   80°   90°   80°
40°   31°   30°   28°   25°

In 1541 Hernando de Soto and his army discovered and crossed what would be called the Mississippi River at a point some eight hundred miles above its mouth, below present Memphis. (Courtesy of the Missouri Historical Society)

Shortly before de Soto crossed the Mississippi, Coronado and his "Chosen Thirty" became the first Europeans to set foot on terrain of the future Louisiana Purchase: at Palo Duro Canyon of the Red River in the Texas Panhandle. (Courtesy of the artist, Ben Carlton Mead, and the Panhandle-Plains Historical Society)

a process of systematic inhumanity that they never forgot or forgave. De Soto was driven by the same greed for gold and status that had driven Cortez and Pizarro, who were natives also of those harsh Estremadura uplands. Coronado, on the other hand, was a cultured Salamancan of noble birth. He was conservative and relatively humane, and he lacked drive because he had everything he wanted. He had a sense of duty to his Catholic God and to his emperor and he did what Viceroy Mendoza asked him to do without much zest, shooting and burning Pueblo Indians along the Upper Rio Grande only if necessary and yearning to get the exploring job done and return home to his bride, Doña Beatriz.

De Soto stepped on the Mississippi drainage first. As Coronado was leaving his Upper Rio Grande headquarters for Quivira, de Soto crossed a divide to the Yazoo River and then stood on a low bank of the broad Mississippi near present Clarksdale, Mississippi, some seventy-five miles downstream from the Chickasaw Bluffs of Memphis. Coronado's turn to reach a bit of Louisiana came a few weeks later, after he had ordered most of his army back to the Upper Rio Grande. On May 29, 1541, while de Soto's carpenters were building barges stout enough to get his army across the immense river, Coronado and his "Chosen Thirty" rode into that stunning red gorge of embroidered willows, mulberries, grape vines and rose bushes that we call Palo Duro Canyon, in the Texas Panhandle. The source stream that he found running through the canyon was the Red River, the Mississippi's most southern tributary. Coronado could not have divined the importance of that stream as an international boundary in the centuries ahead.[3]

So there they were — two clusters of Spanish animation crawling along different parts of future Louisiana with their glinting helmets and coats of mail and arquebuses and trumpets and high boots. But they were just human beings in the heat of that summer so long ago, much the same as people today. They got weary and quarrelsome and longed for home and were proud of their adventuring and were thrilled by strange sights of the trail to tell their children about later — huge herds of buffalo, prairie-dog towns, roadrunners, or a rose-breasted grosbeak in the dogwood. As de Soto moved his men west into Arkansas after getting them over the Mississippi, he grew fretful over false rumors of gold and was ungallant toward the brown "wives" that the Indian chiefs assigned to him to temper his cruelty and to aid his slumbers in the villages of central Arkansas. He led the way across the St. Francis and White rivers through the humid languor of June, always arguing that gold or the Strait of Anian would be found on the other side of the next hill. Meanwhile, Coronado's eastering Chosen Thirty met no one as they crossed the sandy fingers of the Canadian and North Canadian rivers. They endured the shimmering dry heat of western Oklahoma and admired the stunning sunsets. Those high treeless plains were so flat that some of the soldiers found themselves able to stand on their heads and see the horizon through the legs of distant buffalo. On June 29, 1541, the Chosen Thirty waded the Arkansas River at a ford (today's Ford, Kansas, east of Dodge City), some 650 miles from where de Soto was crossing the same Arkansas near present Little Rock. In mid-August de Soto followed trails to Caddo Gap in pine-fragrant foothills west of present Hot Springs, Arkansas. He looked at the imposing Ouachita Mountains ahead that blocked his path to the Strait of Anian and he gave up the quest to find a route to China about the same time that Coronado gave up his gold quest in Kansas 370 miles northwest of de Soto's position at Caddo Gap. Coronado had reached the center of the kingdom of Quivira. But Quivira's golden capital, as described by the Turk, did no more for him than the Seven Cities of Cibola had done. It was just a huddle of straw villages of the Caddo Indians.[4]

The heartsick Coronado had the Turk strangled for luring him to nothing and led his Chosen Thirty back to the main army at Tiguex on the Upper Rio Grande as autumn came along. He survived being kicked in the head by one of his horses and spent much of 1542 being carried on a litter as he returned his tattered force to Compostela, and himself to Doña Beatriz in Mexico City, never more to roam. De Soto faced a much more bitter defeat after wintering his army in a red-soil clearing on the Ouachita River below present Hot Springs. Of his 620 men who had begun their exploration at Tampa Bay, only 320 had survived the human and vegetable perils of Louisiana. They had worn out or eaten most of their horses. They were short of the arms and gunpowder that they would need if the Indians they had treated so atrociously came at them in revenge. They broke camp in March, 1542, and terror seized them as they asked de Soto how they would reach the Gulf of Mexico and, if they reached it, what would they do for boats to carry them over a thousand miles of water to Cuba? De Soto had no answers. That may have been one reason why he came down with a fever and died near the junction of the Mississippi and the same Red River that Coronado had seen at Palo Duro Canyon far upstream a year before. De Soto died in the prime of life, at the age of forty-six.

Captain Luis de Moscoso assumed command. Remembering the

Narváez shipwreck, he planned to avoid the dangers of the gulf by setting out on an Indian trail that was rumored to lead overland for no great distance to the Mexican port of Tampico on the Pánuco River down the coast from the mouth of the Rio Grande. He led his men up the Red River through the Shreveport area into East Texas and then perhaps as far as the Trinity River near present Dallas, where legend has them bumping into an escaped Indian concubine of one of Coronado's officers, Juan de Zaldivar. The girl links the rival expeditions in a nice romantic way, if she existed, but she did not know where Tampico was or anything else about Texas geography. So Moscoso and his soldiers trudged back to the mouth of the Red River, where they had planted the body of de Soto in a tomb fashioned out of a hollow log. They passed the winter of 1543 making seven crude boats out of river timber, launched their craft in July, floated three hundred miles down the Mississippi and out one of those delta mouths into the gulf. They steered their clumsy craft slowly and warily around the Texas coast and somehow did reach Pánuco harbor and Tampico. Then they hiked over the Sierra Madre Oriental to Mexico City.

The de Soto expedition had little to show for its four years of toil and terror and death — no gold, no pearls, no Strait of Anian. Moscoso brought back to the geographers of Spain only a vague idea of where his men had been in Louisiana. They were too busy staying alive to observe much. Moscoso's sketchy report, and Coronado's, did spread by slow degrees a belief in Europe that North America must be a lot more than a mere peninsula or archipelago. Coronado's naval arm proved that Mar Vermejo was really a gulf (California). His army spotted the Colorado River and the Continental Divide, and showed the way to the Spanish New Mexico that delights us still. But the reports of both expeditions were absurdly misconstrued by mapmakers and filed so carelessly in the Archives of the Indies in Seville that Spanish officials had a very hard time finding them when they needed them later. In their preoccupation with dreams of quick wealth, the explorers did not dwell on the real potential of the Rio Grande and Mississippi drainage areas. Nor did they bother to consider geographical possibilities — that Coronado's beautiful Upper Rio Grande might be the same unprepossessing stream that Pineda found flowing into the Gulf of Mexico; that Coronado's Arkansas in Quivira was the same river that de Soto crossed near Cáddo Gap; that Coronado's trickle of a Red River emptied into the Mississippi where de Soto's turbulent career wound up in a hollow log. Moscoso's dramatic exodus from one of the delta mouths was forgotten, and the great Mississippi returned once more to the status of a phantom river in a phantom land.

The discoveries of Columbus brought revolutionary changes to Europe between his day and that of La Salle two centuries later. The mere thought of all that space imbued people wedged in Europe's steaming corridors with wild dreams of fortune and freedom. At the same time, the Italian Renaissance was producing a new kind of zest for living. Advances in printing stimulated reading and enlarged mental horizons. As world trade expanded over the new sea routes to India, Africa and the Americas, a nascent capitalism and mass production caught on. Some ruling classes began to suspect that commerce and industry were more profitable to them than gouging the peasantry on their lands and they encouraged ambitious commoners to take up shipping and colonial enterprise.

France and England kept up with these changes toward materialism, putting aside the supernatural faith of the Middle Ages and international unity based on the power of the pope. Spain's rulers did not keep up, and got the usual punishment of the old-fashioned. After the death of Charles V in 1558, Spain fell rapidly from her eminence as the most powerful nation in Europe, leaving the field to France and England, with Holland caught in the abrasion of their rivalry. A fatal blow to Spain was the defeat of Philip II's Invincible Armada in 1588. Thereafter, Philip III and Philip IV, pathetic weaklings, wasted the enormous mineral wealth that came to them from the mines of Mexico and Peru in futile efforts to sustain the degenerate papacy and the Hapsburgs of Austria.

All the while, the Reformation was dividing Europe into Catholic and Protestant camps. The Lord vented no special wrath on the heretical Protestants, and rulers lost their fear of excommunication by the pope. In particular, the rulers of France and England forgot all about that 1493 bull of Pope Alexander VI and sent hordes of explorers to trespass on the North America that he had given to Spain and to claim anything that they found by right of discovery. Their pirates raided the West Indies and seized tons of Spanish silver and gold all along the Spanish Main from Panama through the limpid Caribbean to the Bahamas. Still, Spain hung on to most of her possessions south of the Rio Grande and banished the ships of her rivals from her Gulf of Mexico. The ban was observed somewhat more from fear of the gulf's notorious hurricanes than of Spanish reprisal. As a result, the Mississippi River that de Soto had barely seen in 1541 came to be approached not up from the open sea of the south but down from the remote interior of the far north. This slow and laborious process came about from the pursuit of a new approach to an old dream. The French and English were as fascinated as Pineda had been by the idea of a direct route to China. But instead of seeking a Strait of Anian from the banned Gulf of Mexico, they searched northward for what they called the Northwest Passage to the South Sea — another strait, perhaps, or two rivers meeting at a low divide in the unknown continent. They probed many of the inlets of the North Atlantic coast, even the icy wastes of Hudson Strait and Baffin Bay — blind alleys all. The rivers were especially frustrating, notably the James, Potomac, Susquehanna, Delaware, Hudson, Connecticut and Penobscot. They looked so promising in their bays but most of them turned out to be navigable for only a few miles inland to tidewater. Beyond that, they were not much more than creeks, ending soon at the forested barrier of the Appalachians.[5]

The glorious exception was the grand and beautiful St. Lawrence. In 1535, Jacques Cartier, a French navigator from Saint-Malo in Brittany, was sure that he had found the Northwest Passage when he sailed around Newfoundland by the Strait of Belle Isle and discovered this extraordinary waterway. His ships and longboats ascended a thousand miles from the Gaspé into the interior of a wilderness that he called Canada, an Iroquois word for "village." He was stopped at a wide, two-mile stretch of white-capped rapids in that lovely world of forests and clearings just beyond the river-isle of present Montreal. The forest site and rapids would be known later as Lachine, in derisive honor of young La Salle's original plan — before he caught the Mississippi bug — to continue up the St. Lawrence in his search for that same road to Cathay. But nothing came of Cartier's exploration in the sixteenth century because France was busy with her religious wars. Meanwhile, in 1578, England's illustrious pirate, Sir Francis Drake, searched for the Northwest Passage from west to east — that is, from the North Pacific to the North Atlantic. His pirate ship *Golden Hind* rounded South America and sailed up the coast of California almost to Puget Sound before he gave up the search and turned back to anchor in Drake's Bay near the Golden Gate. Somehow, he did not notice the mouth of the Columbia River and neither did anybody else until the Boston skipper Captain Robert Gray reported it in 1792. How would history have unfolded if Sir Francis had explored then this closest thing to a practical Northwest Passage?

In reaching Lachine Rapids, Jacques Cartier made a giant, if accidental, stride toward Louisiana. The pace of the approach to the mystery quickened after 1585, when Sir Walter Raleigh's people landed off Roanoke Island — the first of a host of English adventurers, riffraff, ambitious yeomen, Puritans and aristocrats to occupy a strip of Atlantic coast from the Carolinas to Penobscot Bay.

Cartier's successor on the St. Lawrence, and Canada's first governor, was a superb explorer and colonizer with the lilting name of Samuel de Champlain. He was born at Brouage on the Bay of Biscay. As a young man he sailed the Caribbean with the Spanish, proposing away back then a canal across Panama "to shorten the voyage to the South Sea by more than 1,500 leagues." Champlain wanted to colonize Virginia but he thought that the English were there already so he helped to organize L'Acadie instead, in 1603–1604, on La Baie Françoise (Fundy) just above Penobscot Bay. Part of L'Acadie became Nova Scotia later — one very big bone of contention in the long struggle of England and France to possess North America. From L'Acadie, Champlain cruised to Cape Cod and then up the St. Lawrence as far as Lachine Rapids. He was impressed by the promise of fur trade with the Iroquois, Hurons and other St. Lawrence tribes and he began setting up snug villages of stone and log cabins for French traders and merchants along the bright chill of the river — the origins of Tadoussac, Quebec, Trois Rivières, Montreal. In 1609, his questing birch-bark canoe took him up the Richelieu River south from the St. Lawrence. Perhaps his heart leaped when he gazed on that sapphire gem, Lake Champlain, the first white man to do so. Near the site of Ticonderoga, he helped Algonquins and Hurons to crush an Iroquois band — an unfortunate act that began a permanent Iroquois-English alliance against the French from the Hudson River–Lake Champlain line all the way west to the Mississippi.

Champlain pushed closer to the Upper Mississippi, still as a searcher for the Northwest Passage, in 1615. The Iroquois and Hurons were always talking about "the big water" out west beyond the lakes of the St. Lawrence drainage, so he pointed his canoes that way from Lachine Rapids, but not on up the St. Lawrence. Instead, he paddled and portaged up the ancient Ottawa River route of the Hurons and down the French River to become the first European to see one of the Great Lakes — the placid cobalt expanse of

17

Georgian Bay (he named it Mer de l'Eau Douce, or Sea of Sweet Water). That was part of Lake Huron, but Champlain and his companions did not risk the trip across the rough open water to Manitoulin Island and the main Huron. They threaded south through the Georgian Bay isles, trailed over-land past Lake Simcoe to Lake Ontario, and had another scrap with the Iroquois at present Lake Oneida in New York, getting beaten this time. Champlain returned from Lake Ontario as he had come, the long Ottawa River way, rather than risk capture and torture by these strange, fierce people on the paddle down the St. Lawrence from Lake Ontario to Lachine.

Time had slipped along. By 1623, Canada's first governor was feeling his fifty-six years. He assigned his next Northwest Passage excursion to his interpreter, Etienne Brulé, who pushed around Lake Huron to discover the east end of Lake Superior at Sault Ste. Marie. Brulé, an overbold explorer, ended up being eaten by the Hurons. Eleven years after his Superior trip, Champlain's old friend Jean Nicolet, a *coureur de bois* from the village of Trois Rivières, continued from Huron through the Straits of Mackinac, which are spanned today by a spectacular five-mile bridge from St. Ignace to Mackinaw City, Michigan. Beyond the Straits, Nicolet found Lake Michigan, and then he paddled up Green Bay to a Winnebago village near the mouth of the lovely Fox River. That was far west of Quebec and Trois Rivières, and Nicolet concluded that the South Sea had to be very near. Furthermore, the Winnebagos, a new tribe to him (they were Siouan), seemed so much like Chinese that he greeted them with proper ceremony in a Chinese robe — "all strewn with flowers and birds of many colors." The name Green Bay came much later — an English corruption, perhaps, of the French Grande Baie. The Winnebagos called it something that was trans-lated into Baie des Puans. They themselves were the Puans (stinkers) and their homeland, Nicolet gathered, was a salty marshland on "the Big Water" three days travel farther west — some one hundred and fifty miles. One reached it by hard paddling up the winding Fox past Lake Winnebago to its source, sluggish with wild rice, then portaging a mile and a half through the woods, and floating down the west side of the low divide on a river known later as Ouisconsing to "the Big Water."[6]

"The Big Water" had to be the South Sea. Or was it? Nicolet was too busy trading with the Winnebagos to cross the divide to find out. But it was crossed at last to the region of western Wisconsin and Minnesota by a pair of French fortune hunters during several spectacular trading trips that they made between 1654 and 1663. Their names were Groseilliers (gooseberry bush) and Radisson (radish) and historians are unsure of what about them is fact and what is hot air generated by the youngster, Radisson, who had a promoter's gift of gab and a mania for intrigue. In any case, they were remarkable men, who changed the entire focus of European thinking about North America and Louisiana in particular. They went west from the St. Lawrence, not to find any chimerical Seven Cities of solid gold or a passage to China that would take them through the unknown land with all possible speed. Their interest was in the unknown land itself, and how it might be used to enrich themselves and posterity. They were the first to start breaking the freeze of ignorance about the Mississippi that de Soto and Moscoso and Coronado and all the explorers after them had failed to thaw.

Médard Chouart, sieur des Groseilliers, was born in Meaux near Paris in 1621, joined Jean Nicolet and other professional nomads at that hotbed of exploration, Trois Rivières, in 1641, and acquired enough gooseberry land there from the king to take on a Canadian version of the French landowner's title, "sieur."[7] He was a lay worker for a time at the Jesuits' Huron mission near Georgian Bay, and somewhere along he way he married a sister of Pierre Esprit Radisson, a rash Breton boy of fifteen in 1651 when he left Saint-Malo for Trois Rivières seeking excitement. Saint-Malo had been Jacques Cartier's hometown too — a good place to leave, like the rest of impoverished Brittany, if a youngster wished to amount to anything. Radisson found excitement soon, when some Mohawk Iroquois kidnapped him and he spent many months with various Iroquois bands in two sessions of captivity as a kind of house pet. He claimed to have enjoyed all sorts of strange sights — sea serpents on Lake Ontario, a unicorn with a five-foot horn sticking out of its forehead, a colony of three hundred hungry bears. Before his second escape, he became inured to watching ingenious forms of Iroquois torture — female captives forced to eat their own barbecued children, males having their nails pulled and teeth smashed out, their thighs seared and sliced like roast beef, and "their stones cut off for the women to play with." The Huron and Algonquin victims of the torture behaved as stoically as possible during their long days of pain because they might be turned loose to die in peace if they were brave enough.

Back home at Trois Rivières, Radisson told Groseilliers startling things that the Iroquois had told him — hints of a big river (the Ohio) rising south of Lake Ontario that flowed a long distance to some salt sea;

hints of another big river "that divides itself in two" west of Nicolet's Green Bay; hints of profitable canoe routes for fur traders from Brulé's Lake Superior north to Hudson Bay. Groseilliers may have made a trip without his brother-in-law to the Winnebagos at Green Bay in 1654. Four years later, according to some agile unscramblings by students trying to make sense of Radisson's scrambled chronology, the pair led a party of *voyageurs* and Hurons up the old difficult Ottawa River trade route to "the delightsomest lake in the world." That was Lake Michigan. They called it Lake of the Staring Hairs because many of the Indian refugees from Iroquois fury whom they found there wore crew cuts. The explorers wintered at Green Bay and crossed the low Fox-Wisconsin divide to trade with the Sioux — but to trade on the Mississippi River, not on the shores of Nicolet's imagined South Sea. They spent a second winter in what must have been Illinois, so salubrious and fertile that they dreamed of southern France. To reach Illinois, they could have crossed the divide from the source of the Chicago River, which flows into Lake Michigan, to the Des Plaines branch of the Illinois, which flows into the Mississippi. This divide was so low that waters of the Des Plaines at flood stage leaked into the Chicago and on into Lake Michigan.

But one can't tell exactly where they crossed from Radisson's story of that 1658–1660 "voyage," which was written in London years later in his, or somebody else's, weird English. It is easier to guess what happened to the two men on their 1661–1663 Lake Superior "voyage." They portaged past the mile-long rapids of Sault Ste. Marie to Whitefish Bay, and paddled during that fall of 1661 along Superior's "wondrous coasts" where Nature was "so pleasant to the eye, the spirit and the belly." They saw raw copper at Au Sable Point and found the Huron Islands as full of gulls as they were when President Theodore Roosevelt created the Huron National Wildlife Refuge in 1906 to protect them. They continued west nearly to the end of Superior — farther west than St. Louis would be — to Chequamegon Bay. Here, at the picturesque site of present Ashland, Wisconsin, they built a small trading fort and guarded it with a burglar alarm of little bells hung on a string. Typically, the careless Radisson went swimming naked and watched a squirrel gallop off with his breechclout. He chased the beast half a mile before he could recover his modesty.

It is surmised that the explorers hiked south from Chequamegon through forests of pine and birch out of the St. Lawrence to the Mississippi drainage. They nearly starved to death through a brutal winter with some

Chippewas at Court Oreilles Lake. Then they snowshoed down along the rushing St. Croix to the sandstone bluffs of the wide blue Mississippi itself and made camp just west of it on Prairie Island downstream thirty miles from present St. Paul. Groseilliers, who was subject to epilepsy, rested there through the summer of 1662 while Radisson roamed around the prairie with the Sioux, who made obscure allusions to the Missouri branch of the Mississippi, and a "big water" — the Pacific — far beyond that. He reported seeing white pelicans and antelope and buffalo and Sioux houses of buffalo hides and "such knives as we have had" — Spanish knives passed up the big river by Indian traders from a salt sea. What sea? Coronado's Mar Vermejo in California? De Soto's Golfo de México? The two Frenchmen returned to Chequamegon Bay, met some Crees in the fall and traveled with them north toward the James Bay arm of Hudson Bay, perhaps by Lake Nipigon and the Albany River. Some students think that they reached James Bay. Trading was good along their trail and they arrived back in Quebec in July, 1663, with a huge flotillla carrying furs that were much better in quality and quantity than those being gathered around the St. Lawrence, the supply of which was already beginning to peter out.

And here a mistake occurred of the kind that French rulers and their agents would make time after time until Napoleon made the final blunder that inspired this narrative when he sold the richest empire on earth for a song to Thomas Jefferson. At bottom, the fault was in the French political system — the predilection of the Bourbons, from Henry IV on, toward absolutism, centralized government and the divine right of kings.

Louis XIII and Louis XIV could not grasp the fact that their pioneer colonists in La Nouvelle-France (New France) had to be let alone to succeed, had to be free to make something of their wilderness without interference from officials who made decisions in terms of European, not Canadian problems. Stanley Vestal put it succinctly when he wrote, "In those days the French monarch conducted his affairs according to a charming system; he sent one man out to do something and sent two others along to keep him from doing it." And there was another difficulty. Louis XIV, ensconced in the Louvre with Madame de Montespan and other expensive luxuries, could not visualize the pioneering process, the value to his estate and his subjects of land discovery and land development overseas on a long-term basis. He was inclined to dwell instead on New World matters of more immediate cash value, such as the seizure of those fabulous Mexican mines near the Gulf of Mexico that Spain guarded so nervously.

When Groseilliers and Radisson, weary but jubilant, turned up in Quebec with their discoveries and their fur treasure, Baron Dubois d'Avaugour, the governor of Canada, did not honor them as brave heroes. He did not reward them for geographical achievements of priceless value to France. With the king's cut of fur profits in mind, and those of the Quebec middlemen, he threw Groseilliers in jail for a spell and fined the pair twenty-four thousand francs for trading without a license.

The result? Groseilliers and Radisson went back to France and protested these insults at court without effect. Then they went across the Channel and turned over all their knowledge to Charles II of England. That monarch was as inept a creator of colonies as Louis XIV in the way he handled his English settlers along the Atlantic, but he had the good sense to receive the French renegades cordially and to put them on his payroll. He listened to stories of their travels with intense interest, having just won New Netherlands (New York, Fort Orange, the Hudson River valley) from the Dutch by the Treaty of Breda in 1667. The explorers explained to him how French expansion west from the St. Lawrence into the fertile Mississippi valley and north to Hudson Bay could be blocked forever if England could win control of the Great Lakes and the fur trade routes south from Hudson Bay to Superior, Huron and Ontario, and on down the Mohawk and Hudson through friendly Iroquois country to New York. They stressed the value of the Hudson Bay area as being far superior to the St. Lawrence in its fur wealth. And England could assail La Nouvelle-France further by pressing northward from Boston and westward from Newfoundland.

Their evaluation so impressed King Charles that he took a new interest in the military and fur-trade advantages of his Hudson River outpost at Albany — the new name for Fort Orange, which he had just acquired from the Dutch. And the king supported his cousin Prince Rupert in 1670 when Rupert and other "noblemen and gentlemen" formed the Hudson's Bay Company and sent men to Hudson Bay that Henry Hudson had claimed for England in 1610, and on south to James Bay, where they built a log fort. Here they began trading with the Indians for beaver pelts to make great floppy hats for the aristocrats of the era.[8]

But Frenchmen on the St. Lawrence paid little attention as yet to English activities on Hudson Bay. The French were looking west toward the Mississippi, not north, particularly since the arrival in 1665 of Louis XIV's new intendant, or fiscal watchdog, Jean-Baptiste Talon.

2

The Mist Rises
—a Little

HISTORICALLY, Talon's office as royal watchdog was a product of that leaning toward absolutism which led the Bourbons to seize the fiefs of the nobility and turn them into provinces of their own. As a sop to the pride of the shorn nobles, the kings appointed many of them to govern the royal provinces. But the noble governors had a habit of intriguing to regain their dukedoms and counties and so the kings began to send out bright young commoners to keep an eye on their activities. After the ministry of Cardinal Richelieu during the reign of Louis XIII, these intendants had acquired as much power as the governors, and sometimes more.[1]

The commoner Talon dressed as showily as any blue-blooded courtier but there was much more to him than his love of foppish clothes and powdered curls flowing down over his shoulders. He had been picked for the intendant job by his friend and mentor, Jean-Baptiste Colbert, the king's chief minister, because he was a shrewd economist and an able administrator. Colbert instructed him to find out why the private St. Lawrence monopoly, The Company of New France, which Richelieu and his friends had set up in 1627, and the king's Company of the West Indies, which had replaced it in 1663, lost so much money and why they had attracted less than 4,000 settlers while New England alone swarmed with 80,000 Englishmen.

When Talon arrived at Quebec for work in 1665 he was very much aware of the three-pronged English threat to seize Canada. He planned to meet it by claiming all the Great Lakes — all the St. Lawrence drainage — formally for Louis XIV. One of these lakes, Lac du Chat (Lake Erie later) was guarded by the ambushing Iroquois and remained unexplored, though everybody knew where it was. In 1666–1667 the Iroquois problem was eased when a force of French regulars so cowed the Mohawk tribe of Iroquois that the nation as a whole permitted the French villages on the St. Lawrence to trade in peace for a while.[2] Meanwhile, Talon mulled over the Groseilliers-Radisson tales about their "great river" and found himself possessed by an imperial dream far more ambitious than the English Charles II's dream of seizing Canada and Hudson Bay for furs and fish. In Talon's alert mind, the Mississippi, more of a tantalizing phantom than ever because of the tales, had assets that seemed certain to speed up the colonial development of La Nouvelle-France. If, he thought, the river was as big as it seemed to be, it must drain a vast valley stretching from Lake Superior southward to some Spanish-controlled sea. Its climate must be equable and it was bound to be an agricultural paradise that would attract a great many more Frenchmen than the beautiful but chilly St. Lawrence area with its short-season fur and farm production. The occupation of such a Garden of Eden in the South, Talon felt, would strengthen the French economy and naval power, pin England in the narrow belt between the Alleghenies and the Atlantic coast, and block any northward advance of the Spaniards, if they would try to expand their colonial empire northward from the Gulf of Mexico, on the grounds that the land was theirs by Pope Alexander VI's bull of 1493.

First, Talon had to know whether Radisson's river flowed to the Gulf of Mexico or to the Gulf of California. In 1668, he sailed to France to get permission from Minister Colbert to find out. Before leaving Quebec, he ordered a check on Radisson's account of seeing raw copper somewhere on the south shore of Lake Superior. If the copper story were true, Talon would need an easy ship route to carry the ore from Lake Superior to the St. Lawrence and on to France — a route to replace the laborious, portage-plagued canoe route that Indians had been using since the beginning of time from Lake Huron up the French River and down the Ottawa to Montreal. The man he chose to do the checking was a new kind of Frenchman, a native-born Canadian. Members of this new breed were as free as the wind and proud to be French but the process of their thinking was much less rigid than that of those who had grown up in Europe under an absolutist regime. Talon's French Canadian was Louis Jolliet, the twenty-three-year-old son of a Quebec wagon master of the Champlain era. Jolliet, an able, prudent Jesuit-trained trader from Trois Rivières, made the hard paddle up the Ottawa with its many portages and on to the Jesuit log chapel at Sault Ste. Marie. He found the mission priests there full of speculation about Radisson's big river and about the buffalo Indians of the prairies and their portable skin tipis, so different from the longhouses of the eastern Iroquois. The river had a name now. Some Illinois Indians taught the Jesuits to call it Messipi — an Algonquin word meaning great.

The black-robed members of the Society of Jesus were planning new missions in all western parts of La Nouvelle-France — known and un-known — for the conversion of the Hurons and other tribes driven from their eastern homes by the Iroquois. Father Claude Allouez had built one mission already, St. Esprit, on Lake Superior's Chequamegon Bay, where Radisson had almost lost his breechclout. He planned another, St. Francis Xavier, near the Green Bay Winnebagos and Pottawatomis. Jolliet was pleased to find the Sault Ste. Marie chapel managed by a frail, ebullient Three Rivers friend of his, Jacques Marquette, who was about to take charge of Allouez's St. Esprit mission. Jolliet was fond of the gentle Père Marquette, as who wasn't? Marquette was a holy man unconcerned with the worldly ambitions of his militant order — a man of such selfless charm that the warmth of his bold and loving spirit still pervades the Michigan country. He was twenty-nine years old when he arrived in Quebec in the summer of 1666 just as another young man as adventurous as himself arrived in Montreal: René Robert Cavelier, sieur de La Salle, aged twenty-two.

This René Robert Cavelier was baptized on November 22, 1643, in that busy supply center of New World exploration, Rouen, down the Seine a bit from Paris. The year was marked by great political change. Cardinal Richelieu had died the previous December, five months before the un-mourned death of his flyweight king, Louis XIII. Louis XIV, aged five, replaced his father on the throne of France in May, 1643, to begin what turned out to be the longest, most powerful and most glittering of absolutist regimes, all seventy-two years of it. To this day, when people want to be ostentatious, they go to Louis XIV's Versailles for ideas on how to go about it. The Rouen Caveliers lived on the same enthralling rue de la Grosse Horloge that tourists stroll along today on their way to the ancient cathedral of Notre-Dame. As a child, René Robert had walked a few blocks to Rouen Bridge to watch the parade of boats gliding toward the English Channel — some loaded with hardware, trinkets and brandy for the Indians in Canada. He had dreamed of floating down to Le Havre himself and hiring on a seagoing ship of Colbert's enlarging merchant marine. His preference was for one of the whalers, cod boats or traders' brigs that had been shuttling the North Atlantic for a century and more. It took only a month or two to cross that turbulent ocean to L'Acadie or to the Grand Banks off Newfoundland. The Cavelier family, like most of the Gallican Catholics in Rouen, ate quantities of delicious cod from Banc Vert and Banc aux Baleines on their many fast days.[3] Or La Salle could dream his way far up the St. Lawrence where his older brother, Abbé Jean Cavelier, was a lay priest at the Seminary of St. Sulpice in Montreal. His aim in that more exciting dream was to find what all those other explorers had failed to find: the Northwest Passage to China.

The family name, Cavelier, was not a misspelling of the word *cavalier*, implying knighthood and nobility. La Salle's lineage was not quite so exalted. Though his merchant father Jean was richer than many nobles, he stood a rung beneath them on the French social ladder. But nobles were not so important any more under these absolutist Bourbons, and Jean was a businessman with royal connections at the Louvre. And he owned a country place, a seigniory near Rouen called La Salle. That is why the Cavelier men added "sieur de La Salle" to their name. "Sieur" signified a Frenchman of property, if not of nobility.

Jean Cavelier's son grew up to be on the slight and wiry side, of medium height, shy, ambitious, temperish, deadly serious. He did not care for close friends, male or female. He spent his teens at the College of Jesuits six blocks from his home, now called Lycée Corneille. He had a nodding acquaintance with Pierre Corneille, Rouen's great poet, who had been a protégé of Cardinal Richelieu's.

At the College of Jesuits, La Salle read many of the annual Jesuit "relations," those excellent reports of what the members of the Society of Jesus were up to along the St. Lawrence in the way of missions and exploration. He may have planned to be a Jesuit teacher himself, but he took no final vows after his novitiate. Perhaps he was influenced by his brother,

Abbé Jean, who deplored Jesuit schemes to oust the priests of rival orders from Canada.[4] Besides, the younger Cavelier was a loner. He longed to be on his own solitary road to greatness. He was out of the Jesuit order by 1666, when he moved down the Seine from Rouen at last and caught one of those fast-sailing ships to join Abbé Jean on the St. Lawrence. He arranged a living in Montreal by getting a land grant from the Seminary of St. Sulpice. The grant was up the rapids of the St. Lawrence eight miles above Montreal and it got the nickname Lachine in short order because La Salle talked so much at first about going to China from there by finding the Northwest Passage. He built his palisaded Lachine headquarters and soon fur traders, priests, merchants and Indians were stopping to share his bread and brandy and to pass on the same gossip about the big river in the west that Intendant Talon was hearing in Quebec.

Within a year, La Salle knew everybody in La Nouvelle-France — for all its vastness, it was that kind of a closely knit community. Quite probably, Louis Jolliet stopped at Lachine on his canoe trip to find copper on Lake Superior and told La Salle of Talon's wish to have the Mississippi explored. But La Salle became more intrigued during that winter of 1668–1669 by the old Radisson story of another big waterway rising south of Lake Ontario. Some Seneca visitors at Lachine called it Ohio — "beautiful river" in Iroquois — and they claimed that one could float down it to a salt sea in eight or nine months. In the spring of 1669, when the ice went out of the St. Lawrence, La Salle canoed to Quebec and got official permission to look for the Ohio at his own expense, provided he joined some Sulpician priests in Montreal. These priests wanted to have a try at pacifying the Seneca Iroquois, who were spreading terror among tribes in the Ohio country. To finance his exploration, La Salle sold his Lachine lands back to the Sulpician Seminary and to several Montreal merchants.

La Salle's party of fourteen men in four canoes and a party of seven Sulpicians in three canoes left Lachine on July 6, 1669, coasted the beautiful south shore of Lake Ontario to Irondequois Bay at present Rochester, New York, and ascended the Genesee to some Onondaga villages of the Iroquois where they hoped to find Senecas to guide them to the Ohio. At one village, the Senecas staged a show for them — six hours of torturing, burning and eating a young Ohio Shawnee tied to a stake. La Salle was sickened by the spectacle, though he may have recalled that Europeans could be just as cruel — in his own town of Rouen, for example, the English had tied a

This old engraving of La Salle by Waltner conveys something of the quality of that lonely, romantic, driven explorer, who gave his life to bring to France a great river empire with no help worth mentioning from his king. (*Courtesy of Tutt Library, Colorado College*)

The rapid penetration of Louisiana by way of the Great Lakes would have been impossible if the French had not mastered that miracle of Indian transportation, the birch-bark canoe. The clumsier elm-bark canoe was useful also.
(*From Lahontan's* New Voyages to North America)

nineteen-year-old girl to a stake and burned her alive for hearing voices. While with the Senecas, he found that he had an affinity for Indians and their way of life, and an ear for their language. He developed a tolerance for, if not quite a gourmet's appreciation of, their *sagamite* — pounded Indian corn boiled with smoked whitefish. He even began to form in his own mind the outlines of an Indian policy that was to prevail in principle, though limpingly, among the successive governments in North America to modern times. These savages, he thought, must be persuaded to stop fighting among themselves, submit to the rule of their Great Father, Louis XIV, give up title to their lands, and consider themselves lucky to be able to accept the blessings of French civilization. If they had to fight, it should be in alliance with the French, and not with the English at Fort Albany.

Aside from the torture incident, La Salle was enjoying his first real venture into the wilds. For months he had studied the skills of travelers like Jolliet — food gathering, path finding, the use of medicinal herbs, crude surgery, the ability to be comfortable anywhere in any weather — and he came to find beauty in these skills as instruments of freedom and self-reliance. He was entranced by that miracle of transportation among north-ern Indians, the light canoe made of birch bark from the paper birch or canoe birch (*Betula papyrifera*) that was common throughout most of the St. Lawrence drainage. He discovered the exquisite pleasure of launching his canoe in lake or stream, leaving behind the rough forest trail with its tiresome frictions and perils, and gliding almost without effort through new waters along new shores with something wondrous apt to appear around the next headland or bend — moose, caribou, eagle, loon. He had learned how to make one of these miracle boats in a few hours out of strips of birch bark sewn together with tamarack root and made waterproof with pine or balsam gum. It would be twenty feet long and two feet wide. It weighed only fifty pounds, and yet it could carry half a ton of supplies and trade goods. It was so fragile that canoeists always stepped into it barefoot or wearing soft deerhide moccasins. At the same time, it was as safe from attack, as sturdy under assault by moderate winds and waves, as speedy and as luxurious as any calif's flying carpet.[5]

Since La Salle and the Sulpician priests could find no one to guide them from the Iroquois villages on the Genesee to the Ohio, they went hunting for a guide back on Lake Ontario. They paddled toward the west end of the lake and past a stream mouth that seemed to emit a sullen roar. They were hearing the sound of Niagara Falls ten miles up the Niagara River. In late September, 1669, they reached an Iroquois village at present Hamilton, Ontario, and here La Salle bought as his guide a young Shawnee slave from the Ohio country named Nika. Just then, Louis Jolliet and his *voyageurs* strode in from the woods carrying their canoes. Jolliet had found no copper on Lake Superior but he had found something of greater importance — a new water route from the Great Lakes at the south end of Lake Huron into Lake Erie by using what we call Lake St. Clair and the Detroit River. The distance from Sault Ste. Marie on Lake Superior to Montreal by way of Lake Erie would be a good deal longer than the troublesome Ottawa River passage but it would involve only one portage — around the great falls in the middle of the short Niagara River connection between Lake Erie and Lake Ontario. Jolliet added that a lot of work would have to be done to make the Niagara Falls portage commercially practical.[6]

Jolliet told the Sulpicians that the western country was thick with unconverted Indians — news that prompted the priests to split off from the Ohio-bound La Salle, who was getting tired of sharing the leadership with them anyhow. The priests left the Iroquois village to winter on the shores of Lake Erie and to try Jolliet's ship route to Lake Huron. In that project, they lost their portable altar and gunpowder on the Detroit River, but they found sanctuary with Père Marquette at Sault Ste. Marie.

Meanwhile, the La Salle party and the Shawnee guide Nika made a second attempt to find the Ohio, approaching it this time from Lake Erie. And then, incomprehensibly, all of them dropped from sight for a year and more. Some students say that La Salle reached the Ohio during the winter of 1669–1670. If so, one can guess that he took one of the ancient Indian trails leading to it — perhaps the Le Boeuf Creek–French Creek trail south from Lake Erie near present Erie, Pennsylvania, through the site of Waterford to join the Allegheny branch of the Ohio near Oil City, and on to the actual Ohio at Pittsburgh. From there, he is said to have floated six hundred miles down the river past the sites of all those modern places — Wheeling, Marietta, Huntington, Cincinnati — to a stretch of fast water called the Falls of the Ohio (Louisville, Kentucky). And then he could have returned up the Scioto or Muskingum through the charming Ohio hills back to Erie and the St. Lawrence during 1670–1671. The trouble with these guesses is that La Salle himself never claimed to have made such a long and perilous trek when he arrived in Quebec in 1672 to report his adventure to officials.

He made no statement as to precisely where he had been. He said merely that his men had deserted him somewhere south of Lake Erie and that he and Nika were lucky to get back alive.

The explorer reached Quebec discouraged by the poor results of his Ohio trek and impoverished by the cost of it. But he was taken in hand by a man as determined as himself, and one to whom he was strongly attracted, for all their differences of personality. Louis de Buade, comte de Frontenac, had just been appointed governor of Canada (Jacques Duchesneau was replacing Jean-Baptiste Talon as intendant). Romantic, headstrong, fiery, vain as a peacock, and fifty-two years of age, Frontenac had come to the wilds to mend his shattered fortunes after having enjoyed the most effete sort of court living. He was reputed to be a low-born Basque, but his father had served so well in Louis XIII's household that the king gave the boy his name and made him his godson. In his youth, Frontenac had led troops for various European rulers, had eloped with a wayward beauty, Anne de la Grange, who was a member of the king's household in the Louvre, and had lost Anne's love when she became attached first to a militant female named Madame de Montpensier, Louis XIII's niece, and then to Mademoiselle d'Outrelaise, with whom Anne maintained for years a famous Paris salon. The latter pair were called Les Divines. In 1652, the comtesse de Frontenac and Madame de Montpensier (in full finery, the tale goes) directed troops at Orléans during an episode in the Fronde revolt of nobles against Louis XIV and his land-grabbing absolutism. The revolt was led by Louis II de Bourbon, prince de Condé, who happened to have a strong interest in the future of La Nouvelle-France. The king put down the Fronde revolt and pardoned Condé, partly because he was a Bourbon relative of his but mainly because he needed his military talents. Though the comtesse de Frontenac refused to live with her mercurial husband, she was proud of him. Both she and the powerful Condé pulled wires at court in his behalf, and their influence could have been a factor when Louis XIV sent Frontenac to rule Canada as governor in the fall of 1672. Gossip had it that the king did so also because his current mistress, Madame de Montespan, held tender feelings toward the count.

Like Condé, Frontenac did not admire the absolutism of his monarch. He believed that strict royal supervision was bad for Canadian enterprise, and especially bad for certain secret and illegal trading enterprises of his own whereby he hoped to become solvent again. For a year or two, the count

31

put La Nouvelle-France under a liberal government, until Colbert caught up with the slow mail service between Paris and Quebec and put a stop to it. This "three estates" government put power in the hands of a combine of nobles, priests and commoners that was as treasonably un-absolute and decentralized as England's combine of king, lords and commons, trending toward parliamentary rule. Frontenac removed some of the royal red tape that had alienated Groseilliers and Radisson. He enraged the Jesuits, whom he could not stand, by favoring their Recollet rivals, by permitting the sale of liquor to the Indians who traded with the Jesuits and by meddling generally in the way the Jesuits managed the Indians. He enraged the Montreal merchants by hiring La Salle early in 1673 to build a fort for him on Lake Ontario to intercept fur trade from the north that the Iroquois were diverting to the English at Albany. Of course, the count's Fort Frontenac would catch this English trade and prevent it from reaching Montreal. Frontenac learned from La Salle and from Jolliet of the necessity of a practical portage around Niagara Falls between Lake Ontario and Lake Erie if France was to keep the English out of the Great Lakes. To solve this problem, the count commissioned La Salle to build supply boats on both Ontario and Erie and to build a good portage road around the steep drop of the Falls.

The Jesuits and merchants agreed that these measures could have results that would be very bad for their interests. And they were deeply disturbed when Frontenac took up Talon's idea of finding where the Mississippi debouched. If it led west to the South Sea, France would have a Strait of Anian to exploit by way of the St. Lawrence, the Great Lakes and the Mississippi. If it led south to the Gulf of Mexico, Louis XIV would demand that Spain open her private sea to French ships so that his colonists could develop the Mississippi empire from the mouth northward as well as from the Great Lakes southward. In either of these river plans, priests and merchants saw the worst of threats to their local interests. Already their agents were at work in Paris, for they did not intend to be bypassed on the St. Lawrence by the governor and his henchman La Salle.

Before Intendant Talon's recall, he had chosen Louis Jolliet to conduct the Mississippi exploration, and Frontenac confirmed the choice. Jolliet picked Père Marquette to accompany him, remembering the priest's wish to carry the vision of his Blessed Virgin Immaculate to the Illinois Indians. After Marquette had done his missionary stint at Chequamegon Bay, he had served Huron and Ottawa Indians briefly on that green cliff-walled isle, Michilimackinac. Then he had moved to the north shore of the Straits of Mackinac, where he built a mission church of alder poles and named it for St. Ignatius Loyola, the Spanish founder of the Jesuit order. The church stood on the site of today's town of St. Ignace. It was a strategic as well as a beautiful spot. Sault Ste. Marie and the east end of Lake Superior were fifty-odd miles north of it. Lake Huron's cobalt waters lapped its sand canoe beach, with Quebec a thousand miles further east by way of the Ottawa, or twelve hundred miles by way of Lake Erie and the Niagara. Westward was the sparkling, deceptively placid blue of Lake Michigan. Across Lake Michigan, Father Allouez's St. Francis Xavier and the trading settlement around it stood up the Fox a little near the head of Green Bay 160 miles away. And Green Bay was where one took the leap into the great beckoning beyond.[7]

In the winter of 1672–1673, Jolliet picked up five expert *voyageurs* at Sault Ste. Marie and joined Marquette at St. Ignace in early spring. On a crisp, radiant mid-May morning, Jolliet's two canoes with the seven explorers grated off the beach, passed through the Straits of Mackinac and entered the white-capped waters of Lake Michigan, with gulls wheeling in the soft wind around them (see the map on page 10). The contrast was utter between this tiny homespun party — all that the Europe-oriented Louis XIV was willing to pay to find a new world — and the futile glittering battalions of de Soto and Coronado that Charles V had sent out more than a century before. The two canoes carried the bare bones of need — corn, dried meat, compass, guns and powder, Marquette's small portable altar, beads and buckles to please the Indians. The leader in charge was Jolliet, big, tireless, indestructible, his mind absorbed in the logistics of canoe travel. The party's mood was set by Marquette's mood — joyous with expectation, acutely curious and observing, his heart bursting with love for the Blessed Virgin who had given him "the grace of being able to visit the Nations who dwell along the Mississippi River." They visited Indian friends along their route — Menominees on upper Green Bay, and Mascoutens, Miamis and Kickapoos on the Fox. In early June, they toiled up the Fox through wild-rice lagoons and clouds of teal and "bustard" (the Canada goose) to the wide, sandy Wisconsin (Marquette's Meskousing) and on June 17 slipped into the majestic blue-green current of the Mississippi. Marquette named it Rivière de la Conception. Jolliet called it Rivière de Buade, honoring

Frontenac's family. They coasted the steep shores of Iowa and were startled by Indian footprints at the sandy mouth of the Des Moines River. Here was a test of their courage. Hostile Indians could put all seven of them through the long agony of torture that had appalled La Salle on the Genesee. Marquette could be brave quite easily because the Blessed Virgin was always with him and he had no fear even of a ghastly dying. Perhaps the others drew valor from his repose. Jolliet and the priest left the *voyageurs* with the canoes, followed the footprints some miles up the Des Moines and found hundreds of Indians in three villages. They were friendly Illinois, who honored them with ceremonials that reminded Marquette of the opening of the ballet in Paris. After several feasts, the hosts sent them on with a calumet (French for "reed pipe") — the Indian passport and mark of welcome — so that tribes below would be more inclined to treat them well.[8]

They floated on down the great waterway past the grassy prairies of Illinois, observing in a rising tide of wonder huge turtles, catfish almost big enough to damage their canoes, dragons painted on a cliff, and "a monster with the head of a tiger." Marquette described herds of buffalo — "pisikious" — in an essay that has hardly been improved on in three centuries. "The head," he wrote in small part, "is very large; the forehead is flat, and a foot and a half wide between the horns, which are exactly like those of our oxen, but black and much larger. Under the neck they have a sort of large dewlap which hangs down; and on the back is a rather high hump." The mouth of the Missouri, an exciting sight still, must have been far more so when that little group passed it in their fragile canoes. "I have seen," Marquette wrote, "nothing more dreadful. An accumulation of large and entire trees, branches and floating islands, was issuing from the mouth of the river Pekitanoui, with such impetuosity that we could not without great danger risk passing through it." *Pekitanoui* was an Algonquin word for "muddy."

At this point in his diary, the priest dropped a few casual comments confirming Radisson's tales, answering Talon's questions and stating some truths about North American geography. "Pekitanoui is a river of considerable size, coming from the northwest from a great distance. . . . I hope by its means to discover the Vermilion or California sea. Judging from the direction of the course of the Mississippi, if it continues the same way, we think that it discharges into the Mexican gulf." This passage was at least a start toward visualizing the actual relation of the Missouri's drainage to the

Columbia's — the relation Lewis and Clark would discover some day at Lemhi Pass in Montana. Marquette's "California sea" was the wrong relation, but he had good reason to be inaccurate. The Columbia was not even a rumor in 1673, so he assumed that any westering continuance from the source of the Missouri beyond the Continental Divide had to be the only known river out that way, the Río del Norte (Colorado) that Coronado's associate Alarcón had found emptying into the Gulf of California. By the phrase about how the "considerable" Missouri came "from the northwest from a great distance," Marquette would seem to have ended all further dreaming of a South Sea just west of Green Bay. And in his own mind he widened the North American "archipelago" by many hundreds of miles, though his enlarged conception was still far short of the truth.

The Mississippi began its erratic curving as the men moved around the giant *S* short of the mouth of the Ohio. The Indian had told the Europeans to call the Ohio "Ouboukigou" — "Oubache" and "Wabash" later. Marquette noted that it "flows from the lands of the East" but he did not suggest that it might be the same beautiful Ohio that La Salle had explored, or tried to explore, in 1670–1671. They began fighting mosquitoes as the now-brown Mississippi bore them past the Chickasaw Bluffs above present Memphis and on to the maze of islands and bayous in the seventy-mile wriggling stretch between the mouth of the St. Francis (Helena, Arkansas) and the Arkansas itself that we saw last with de Soto's weary army. In this tedious, humid meander they felt themselves emerging suddenly from the wilds. They met three groups of almost "civilized" Arkansas Indians living in bark cabins, eating fat dog from wooden plates, raising corn and watermelons, and owning guns, cloth, hatchets, knives and beads that they had bought in trade for buffalo hides. ("They know nothing of beaver," Marquette explained. "Their wealth consists of the skins of wild cattle.") It appeared that these European articles had been passed up to them from Spanish traders on the gulf ten days downstream and "from Europeans who lived to the East" — English traders who had crossed the Appalachians from Virginia or the Carolinas to do business with Chickasaws and Choctaws.

In mid-July at the large Akansea village on the west bank of the Mississippi near the mouth of the Arkansas, Jolliet and Marquette agreed that they had gone far enough. They knew for certain now that the river flowed into the Gulf of Mexico, not into the Gulf of California. They were

35

tired, Marquette especially, as he was suffering from chronic dysentery. The Akansea villagers (they were Quapaws) told them that the river below was infested with hostile Indians who still despised white skins, remembering tales of de Soto's cruelty. The gulf, the villagers said, was only a couple of days journey downstream. The Frenchmen thought that if they continued, they might be captured by Spanish patrols at the river's mouth and imprisoned in Mexico City for trespass. They had not come so far and learned so much to spoil everything by taking unnecessary risks. Their plain duty was to get back to Frontenac with their information.

So the seven explorers headed north against the current from Akansea on July 17, 1673, toiled past the mouths of the Ohio and the muddy Missouri, and turned up the Illinois River in mid-August. Marquette found that Radisson's admiration for that region was more than justified. The priest wrote, "We have seen nothing like this river that we enter, as regards its fertility of soil, its prairies and woods; its cattle, elk, deer, wildcats, bustards, swans, ducks, parroquets, and even beaver. . . . We found on it a village of Illinois called Kaskas[k]ia, consisting of seventy-four cabins. They received us very well, and obliged me to promise that I would return to instruct them. One of the chiefs of this nation, with his young men, escorted us to the Lake of Illinois (Michigan) whence, at last, at the end of September we reached the Bay des Puantz, from which we had started at the beginning of June." Their route from the Illinois was up its Des Plaines branch to the site of today's Joliet city and on to Lake Michigan by the Chicago River.

All together, from Green Bay back to Green Bay, the little band of seven men traveled 2,750 miles in those four months of 1673. They lifted out of the mist of rumor 1,100 miles of the Mississippi's total length of 2,560 miles. Among other things, they found that whereas the Fox-Wisconsin route was a good way to reach the Mississippi from Lake Michigan, the route up the slow-moving Illinois was easier for canoeists moving from the Mississippi homeward to Lake Michigan. Marquette spent the winter of 1673–1674 at Green Bay nursing his dysentery. He made it in the following year to Kaskaskia as he had promised, but the effort broke down his health completely. On May 19, 1675, he reached the end of his short life — he was only thirty-eight — dying of exhaustion "with a countenance beaming and all aglow."

Jolliet wintered at Sault Ste. Marie and prepared there a map of the exploration. On his map, Frontenac's name was given to both the Mississippi River and to Lake Ontario. The Mississippi Valley was labeled La Colbertie and the Illinois River was named La Divine after Frontenac's countess. It was politic to honor one's patrons.

In the fall of 1674, Jolliet arrived in Quebec and reported to Governor Frontenac that he had explored La Colbertie with Marquette and found it to be a vast valley of incalculable richness both for agriculture and mining. The governor was jubilant over the report but he was angered just then by a dispatch from Minister Colbert to the effect that Louis XIV was opposed to further Mississippi exploration. The jealous St. Lawrence merchants and the Jesuits had convinced him that their fur trade and established local businesses were more important to him in terms of royal revenue than the vague possibility of a colonial empire on the Mississippi — some day. Colbert implied further that his influence at court was waning. The Sun King — how he loved that name "Le Roi Soleil," which put him at the center of the Universe! — was looking for quick results to solve his budget problems. He was losing patience with Colbert's drastic fiscal reforms and his program of slow worldwide commercial expansion. Instead, the king was supporting two purely European projects that left very little money for anything else. In Colbert's opinion, both projects were disastrous to the French economy. Billions of francs were being spent in a confused war promoted by the king's war minister, the marquis de Louvois, against the Dutch. More hundreds of millions were being poured into a vast agglomeration at Versailles, where workers toiled away at Louis XIV's glittering offices and salons, his lodgings for his courtiers and their ladies, his acres of orange trees and gardens. The palace at Versailles was designed to replace the Louvre as the most awesome seat of centralized power on earth — a proper demonstration of the divine right of kings.

Colbert's dispatch was a blow to Frontenac but he was too absorbed in the promise of the Mississippi to let self-serving people on the St. Lawrence put a crimp in the dreams that he and La Salle had inherited from Talon. La Salle had completed construction of Fort Frontenac above the Thousand Islands on Lake Ontario (the site of Kingston). He was developing a large trade of dubious legality there for Frontenac and himself because of the post's strategic position in relation to the Great Lakes fur trade. News of the trip of Jolliet and Marquette down the Mississippi reached him at a time when he was beginning to enjoy his success as a trader. But their adventures and achievements restored his old desire to be a great explorer, to do for France on the Mississippi what Columbus and Cortez and Pizarro had done for Spain in winning a vast empire below the Rio Grande.

The questions that Jolliet and Marquette answered about the big river convinced La Salle that he had no time to lose. The guns and hardware that Jolliet had found in the hands of the Akansea Indians showed that Spaniards and Englishmen were closing in on the river. La Salle's first task would be to follow the Mississippi down to its mouth. Then, he would organize the Illinois and other Indians of the Mississippi valley into fighting units under his control to offset the power of the Iroquois and their trading alliance with the English at Fort Albany. He would build a string of forts to hold the river for France and to protect trading posts that would deal in buffalo hides and other valuable products that Marquette had noted — products that would bring Louis XIV far more in royal revenue than the Canadian fur trade.

Frontenac was just the kind of adventurer to fall in with La Salle's grandiose plans, and he began pushing them at once. The shortsighted attitude of the king toward exploration had to be changed, of course. To that end, the count sent La Salle to Paris in November, 1674, with letters of recommendation to Colbert and to the prince de Condé. The trip was at least useful. Louis XIV refused to finance or to permit exploration but he showed tacit approval of La Salle's past activities by bestowing on him "the title and quality of nobility" — royal recognition of "the good deeds he performed in the land of Canada."

Back at Fort Frontenac, La Salle worked to raise exploration funds through larger trade profits while waiting for the governor's next move. As the profits reached an unusual 25,000 francs a year, the jealous Montreal merchants plotted to block both the profits and La Salle's Mississippi plans — bribing his servants to put poison hemlock in his salad, for instance, and accusing him of keeping two concubines for his own use at the fort. And there was the attempt of a Quebec tax official's wife to seduce him in her guest room while her husband took notes at a keyhole on the progress of the blackmail scheme. The explorer refused to behave improperly. Finally, in the fall of 1677, Frontenac packed him off to Paris once more to present his plans to Colbert's son, the marquis de Seignelay, a rising young official at the Louvre. This time, La Salle proposed to pay all the costs of his explorations and Seignelay won the king's consent. On May 12, 1678, Louis XIV issued a five-year royal patent permitting La Salle to find the mouth of the Mississippi, to build forts on the river, to sell parcels of land around the forts as he was permitted to do at Fort Frontenac, and to monopolize the sale of buffalo hides throughout the Mississippi valley.

However, the king made no mention of allowing him to start colonies beyond the St. Lawrence. The merchants were protected by his order "to carry on no trade with the savages called Ottawas, or with other tribes who bring their peltries to Montreal." No matter. La Salle's future was on the Mississippi, not the St. Lawrence, now. With the royal grant in his pocket, he rode from Paris to his native Rouen and borrowed several hundred thousand francs from relatives and friends on his prospects. Back in Canada, in September, 1678, he went to work with the energy of one releasing a decade of frustration. He was thirty-four years old. The romantic idealism of his Northwest Passage days was combined with a great deal of practical experience in the Canadian wilderness. First off, he sent fifteen *voyageurs* ahead by way of St. Ignace and Green Bay to find a headquarters for his expedition in Marquette's Illinois country. He put a host of craftsmen and laborers — French, Flemish, Italian, Indian — to making small freight boats on Lake Ontario and to taming the Niagara River by means of a twelve-mile road around Niagara Falls. He built Fort Condé near present Fort Niagara to protect his portage road from the Iroquois.

Through the severe winter of 1678–1679, his workers hauled anchors and cables, small cannon and lumber, from the Lake Ontario end of the portage road to the Lake Erie end at the mouth of Cayuga Creek above Niagara Falls. There the wooden ribs of a sailing ship of forty-five tons were filled out by slow stages. La Salle named her *Griffon*, honoring the armorial seal of the Frontenacs — forepart of an eagle, rear of a lion. At her prow, he placed a crude griffon figure. She was launched in mid-spring while the workmen cheered and a handful of Recollet priests sang the usual thanksgiving Te Deum.

The *Griffon* was a small homemade craft but its presence on the remote surface of Lake Erie had the effect of a miracle. For La Salle the tiny ship was a vital link in his design to conquer the Mississippi. On August 7, 1679, while the king was busy raising funds to pay for the costly European conquests of the marquis de Louvois, La Salle and thirty-three companions boarded the *Griffon* and watched her sails fill as a fresh breeze pushed her westward on Lake Erie. Four days later she turned up the Detroit River and stopped briefly at a small trading post that La Salle had set up recently. Then she crossed Lake St. Clair and the glossy grandeur of Huron, where she met the test of a storm. She paused at Père Marquette's St. Ignace, moved into Lake Michigan in September, and anchored off Washington Island at the head of Green Bay. Here La Salle's men loaded her with $12,000 worth of contraband furs for delivery and sale at Fort Frontenac to help the explorer to pay some of the more pressing bills of his expedition — contraband furs in calculated violation of the terms of the king's patent. After delivering the furs at the Niagara portage, the *Griffon* was instructed to wend its way westerly again and meet La Salle's party at the Chicago end of Lake Michigan with supplies for the winter in Illinois and materials for building a large river boat there.

When the *Griffon* sailed east from Green Bay for St. Ignace and Lake Erie, La Salle and his men left also in eight canoes that he divided into two groups to explore the west and east shores of Lake Michigan. Most of his men were of the careless, undisciplined brigades that would be pushing the unknown off maps of western America during the next two centuries. Some were outlaws lately arrived on the St. Lawrence from France — murderers wanted in Paris, deserters from troops in Flanders, youngsters fleeing from broken homes, peasants driven from their land by Louis XIV's tax collectors. Their manners and speech were crude. Their wardrobes were of the simplest — coarse woolen cloaks and knee britches, breechclouts, blanket leggings, moccasins and other Indian deerhide garb, black felt hats or crimson caps. They slept on rush mattings under evergreen shelters. Boiled Indian corn was their staple food, though they ate plenty of wild game in season — turkey, deer, "bustard" (the Canada goose), duck, bear. Their lives were hard but they were sustained by the joys of adventure, self-reliance, freedom. They were not easy to handle. Many of them had tendencies to mutiny or to desert to the nearest Indian camp and Indian girl. Young Radisson had explained why the Indians were so attractive — how the adoring Menominees of Lake Superior had made "Caesars" of Groseilliers and himself, "which admired more our actions than the fools of Paris to see enter their King and the Infanta of Spain, his spouse."

La Salle was too tactless and abrupt to manage such unruly subordinates. He left that chore to his second in command, Chevalier Henri de Tonty, a Neapolitan nobleman whose father, Lorenzo, had created the "tontine" principle of term life insurance still used today. Tonty, then thirty years old, had grown up in the same royal milieu that had produced Frontenac. He survived eight years of French military service and had his right hand blown off by a grenade in Sicily. A gloved iron hook replaced the hand and Tonty learned to do marvelous things with it. His friend and patron, the ubiquitous Louis II de Bourbon, prince de Condé, infected him with his own enthusiasm for Canada and passed him along to his other protégé, La Salle, in Paris, with the request that La Salle take him on his Mississippi tour. Tonty typified the sensitive young blueblood of his time, critical of the king's absolutism, bored by court society, and yearning for a more flavorsome life. He found peace and fulfillment in the Canadian wilderness, and La Salle became his god of all. Tonty was utterly trustworthy, brave, capable and calm under stress — a good balance for his leader's high-strung disposition.

To give his project religious sanction, La Salle had along three Recollet priests in gray robes, cowls and sandals, all from Spanish Flanders. One of them, Gabriel Ribourde, was sixty-five years old and so feeble that he had to be lifted in and out of his canoe. Father Zenobius Membré was La Salle's diligent reporter. The third friar, Louis Hennepin, had the appearance of being just another earnest saver of souls. Actually, he was a professional adventurer as well, who would become the first of those vivid travel writers of the seventeenth and eighteenth centuries who revealed so much of western America to Europeans — at times through the literary device of pretending to have been there.

Hennepin was born in Ath, Belgium, in 1640. After his training, he contrived to find much priestly work to do in English Channel grog shops so that he could listen to sailors talking about his favorite subject, travel in America. Though theoretically a Spaniard, he was the sort of roving continental who changed nationality often. After serving as chaplain to a Dutch unit at Seneffe, he became French and had his order send him to Canada, where he tried to make Catholics of the Iroquois at Fort Frontenac. He helped Tonty to build the *Griffon* and was the first man to describe Niagara Falls. Nobody since has used a finer flush of hyperbole. Sample: "Betwixt the Lake Ontario and Erie, there is a vast and prodigious Cadence of Water which falls down after a surprizing and astonishing manner, insomuch that the Universe does not afford its parallel." Hennepin was a brilliant man, immensely curious and observant, but La Salle grew weary of his bombast

41

and vanity. On the *Griffon* riding to Green Bay, Hennepin made it clear to La Salle that he considered himself co-commander of the party, and the mastermind behind the whole Mississippi plan.

After the two groups of canoes had coasted the shores of Lake Michigan, La Salle's employees gathered at the mouth of the St. Joseph River near Chicago, where St. Joseph, Michigan, stands now. Here La Salle built a log fort and named it Fort Miami to please the Miami Indians, whom he hoped to add to the Illinois bands in his anti-Iroquois league. On a wintry December 3, 1679, the thirty-three Frenchmen paddled their canoes up the St. Joseph, struggled across the dreary Indian portage (South Bend, Indiana) to the Kankakee and floated down that prairie branch of the Illinois to the milder climate and more attractive setting of the Illinois itself. They passed on their left the tawny, flat-topped eminence called Starved Rock. Just beyond it they found the spreading meadows of Marquette's big Kaskaskia village — Utica, Illinois, today. It was deserted, so they continued downstream. Early in January, 1680, they came upon many Illinois Indians camped on both sides of the river below Lake Peoria. Near the Indians, on a wooded rise above the left bank of the Illinois, La Salle put up a second log fort in that supply line of empire that he proposed to stretch three thousand miles all the way from Fort Frontenac through the Great Lakes and down to the mouth of the Mississippi. He called his second fort Crèvecoeur (heartbreak) — perhaps recalling Condé's siege of the Dutch at Crèvecoeur in 1672.

The melancholy name fitted the state of his spirits. During that bleak January and February of 1680, signs of trouble ahead kept multiplying — signs that were all the more distressing after the joy and hope he had felt when the *Griffon* was launched in August. The *Griffon*'s fate headed the list of his worries. Couriers from St. Ignace reported that she had not arrived there from Green Bay. He had to assume that she had perished in a gale on Lake Michigan, and that her crew and cargo of furs had gone down with her — or, worse still, that she had been hijacked by rival traders. La Salle's creditors at Fort Frontenac were bound to hear of the loss and would put claims on all his properties. He would have to return there at once to raise new money and order new supplies before he could continue down the Mississippi. Tonty would have to hold his men together during his absence. Already they were grumbling about back pay and seven of them had deserted to the Indians. La Salle was distressed also because the Indians around the fort expressed bitter opposition to his Mississippi plans and seemed to distrust his motives. When he talked of joining them in an alliance against the Iroquois, they hinted that he was really their enemy who was arming the Iroquois secretly for their destruction. Such a notion must have come to them from agents of his St. Lawrence enemies — Montreal merchants, Jesuits, even Intendant Duchesneau at Quebec. Duchesneau had been critical of Governor Frontenac and of La Salle ever since he had replaced Talon as the king's agent.

La Salle's worries were genuine, but there was a touch of paranoia in his preoccupation with some of them. He had moments when he imagined that Father Hennepin might be able to replace him as leader of the expedition. And he suspected a man who was not even along of planning to reach the mouth of the Mississippi ahead of him. This man was an adventurous young noble named Daniel Greysolon, sieur Du Lhut (Duluth). He was a friend of various Bourbons (including Louis XIV), a French cousin of Tonty, and a relative-by-marriage of Pierre Esprit Radisson. Duluth had fought with Condé at Seneffe and met Father Hennepin there. He had come to Canada in the middle 1670's to find the Northwest Passage and had worked up a social and business relationship with Governor Frontenac that was much like La Salle's. At the time that La Salle was launching the *Griffon* on Lake Erie, Duluth was exploring the beautiful Mille Lacs country of the Sioux Indians west of Lake Superior. He had Frontenac's permission to claim the Upper Mississippi region for France before the English could get down to claim it from Hudson Bay, and before the Spaniards could find a way to reach it "from the South Sea."

Before La Salle left Crèvecoeur on his emergency run to Fort Frontenac, he instructed Hennepin and two expert woodsmen, Michel Accau and Antoine Auguel, to see what they could find *up* the Mississippi above the mouth of the Wisconsin, where Jolliet and Marquette had begun their epic trip downstream. The three men were to ascend the river as far as they could and return to the St. Lawrence by way of the Wisconsin-Fox portage to Green Bay. It was astute of La Salle to make this assignment. Hennepin might be able to learn what Duluth was doing up there and he could help the cause of Mississippi exploration by penetrating unknown upper portions of the river while La Salle was repairing his finances at Fort Frontenac.

Besides, the egotistical priest was beginning to get on La Salle's nerves.

3

The Paths of Glory . . .

THERE IS IN HENNEPIN COUNTY, Minnesota, a large and lively city which, as Francis Parkman wrote, "by an ingenious combination of the Greek and Sioux, has received the name of Minneapolis, or City of Waters." One can stand in the center of this city on Hennepin Avenue Bridge looking west up the shopping boulevard, Hennepin Avenue, toward a triangle of land under the Basilica of St. Mary. The triangle contains an imposing statue of Father Hennepin himself, created in 1930 by Fred A. Slifer. Just below Hennepin Avenue Bridge is Third Avenue Bridge and, below that, the river flows past Hennepin Island and disappears as such in the dams and apron, canals and remnant mill races that produce hydroelectric power for the Northern States Power Company. At the foot of these structures, in an angle on the river's left bank formed by the Tenth Avenue Bridge and the Stone Arch railroad bridge, is Lucy Wilder Morris Park. The park contains a bronze marker where Hennepin is said to have first seen the Falls of St. Anthony and to have named them for the Paduan holy man to whom he applied for protection during the adventure that would inspire Minnesotans in another two centuries to honor Hennepin's name above all others.[1]

His adventure began at Fort Crèvecoeur and ended at Green Bay eight months and two thousand miles later. On February 29, 1680, the Flemish priest and his two French companions loaded their canoe with trade goods, guns, calumets, and also his notebooks, portable altar, silver chalice and embroidered chasuble that he wore while saying mass. They said goodbye to La Salle and to Henri de Tonty and headed down the Illinois River toward the Mississippi 175 miles below. By mid-March, as spring brightened the land, they were paddling north up the clear blue Mississippi, unsullied as yet by the muddy riot of the Missouri. The grassy prairies of Illinois were on their right, the woody hills of Missouri and Iowa on their left. They passed bits of alluring wilderness that would become sites of Mark Twain's Hannibal, of Keokuk where the Des Moines River came in, of Burlington high on its bluff with a superb upstream view, of Davenport and Rock Island and Dubuque. In early April they glided through the chains of islands above the mouth of the Wisconsin. They thought of themselves as discoverers now, for they believed that no European had explored the Mississippi above that point. And, on April 11, the drama of their journey was heightened when they were captured near the mouth of Black River by a party of Sioux Indians — the same "Issati or Nadouessiou" that Daniel Greysolon, sieur Du Lhut, had done business with when he had crossed overland the summer before from Lake Superior to their Mille Lacs homeland. In modern terminology, they were the Santee Sioux tribe of the huge Dakota group that would include Sitting Bull's Teton Sioux of the northern Great Plains and the Assiniboines above them in the Saskatchewan River valley of the Hudson Bay drainage. All these Sioux were the western power equivalent of the eastern Iroquois. Hennepin's Issatis were the ancestors of those Minnesota men who would perpetrate the bloodiest of American Indian uprisings — that of the Santee Sioux in 1862.

For the next few weeks, the three captives traveled north up the Mississippi in separate Issati families who held each one of them in a kind of loving custody — not so loving at times when the chiefs debated whether to split their skulls open with tomahawks to see what the brains of white gods looked like, or whether to use them as contacts to enlarge the Issati trade with *coureurs de bois* like Duluth. The Issati groups entered the widening of the river known now as Lake Pepin. Hennepin named it Lac des Pleurs (Lake of Tears) because "the Indians who had taken us, wishing to kill us, some of them wept the whole night, to induce the others to consent to our death."[2] They noticed Lover's Leap rock tower where the legendary Sioux maid Winona cured her lovesickness by jumping off. They passed the mouth of the St. Croix and seemed to know that it was the standard canoe route to Lake Superior — the one Groseilliers and Radisson used if they actually reached the Mississippi during their 1661–1663 "voyage." Just

45

Hennepin's map of "Northern America" was mostly guesswork. He placed the Illinois and the Wisconsin rivers in proper relation to Lake Michigan, but his Mississippi starts near Hudson Bay and its mouth appears on the Texas coast. (Courtesy of Tutt Library, Colorado College)

short of present St. Paul, the Issatis gave up canoe travel and tramped with their prisoners 150 miles further north through the great pine region of present Mille Lacs County to Mille Lacs Lake (Hennepin's big Lake Buade — practically an inland sea). At Mille Lacs the priest was only a hundred straight-line miles from the source of the Mississippi, though he did not know it.

Hennepin spent May and June on a Mille Lacs islet as a "son" of the family assigned to keep him, living mainly on wild rice and whortleberries. He took notes on Issati behavior and used them two years later in suburban Paris when he wrote *Description de la Louisiane*, the first of two self-glorifying books about his Canadian experiences. The book's Indian ethnology may seem trite today because thousands of writers since have repeated so much of it. But his views were delightfully fresh to seventeenth-century Europeans. He discussed the dependence of the Sioux on buffalo for food, clothing and shelter, and dwelt on their pilfering habits, and their love of all-night dancing, feasting and lamentation at the top of their lungs. He explained how they painted their bodies and wore porcupine quills and feathers in their black hair dripping with bear grease. He told of their elaborate burial rites, their superstitious deism and how they liked to carry around the bones of dead friends in sacks — one sack being made out of Hennepin's chasuble. He spoke of their steam baths and how they ordered him to copy them in entering one of these hot-rock saunas with no clothes on, "but I merely concealed my nakedness with a handkerchief." He admired their method of diapering their children "almost in the same way as women in Europe [do]," and he praised their health: "The Indians are very robust, men, women and even children are extremely vigorous; for this reason they are rarely sick, they know nothing about treating themselves delicately, hence they are not subject to a thousand ailments which too great effeminacy draws down on us. They are not gouty or dropsical, gravel or fever-vexed, they are always in movement, and take so little rest, that they escape maladies which beset most of our Europeans for want of exercise." But he deplored their aversion to washing, their continual belching, their habit of making love publicly if so inclined, their casual marriages, their lack of table manners and their insouciant "breaking wind before all the world without caring for any one." And he thought it graceless of them to try to convert him to their savage ways when he was risking his life to bring to them the blessings and enlightenment of his.[3]

Early in July, 1680, Hennepin got respite from his islet prison and the whortleberries by joining a group of Issati buffalo hunters as a helper. The hunters took the Rum River water route from Mille Lacs south to the Mississippi and moved downstream to the short portage around a "cataract," as the priest wrote, "which I called the Falls of St. Anthony of Padua. This cataract is forty or fifty feet high, divided in the middle of its fall by a rocky island of pyramidal form." Hennepin had an escape plan — to work south with the hunters and slip away from them up the Wisconsin and down the Fox to complete his summer's work for La Salle at Green Bay on Lake Michigan. By this time, Michael Accau and Antoine Auguel were as tired of the priest's overweening manner as La Salle had been, and avoided him when they could. Even so, his escape plan for the three of them was developing nicely at the foot of Lake Pepin in late July when astonishing news arrived. Five Europeans were reported to be paddling down the St. Croix toward them. Hennepin remembered La Salle's instructions to see if Duluth planned to poach on his terrain. He returned up the Mississippi with the Indians to find out who these strangers were and what they were about.

They turned out to be Duluth and his men, sure enough. The noble-

Douglas Volk depicts Father Hennepin in a pious mood before the Falls of St. Anthony. They would vanish two centuries later beneath the hydroelectric structures of Minneapolis and St. Paul.
(Courtesy of the Minnesota Historical Society)

man had wintered at an exotic spot on the north shore of Lake Superior, the mouth of the Kaministiquia River, and left Superior to lay out a canoe trade route by way of the Bois Brulé and St. Croix rivers to Mille Lacs for the benefit of his silent partner, Governor Frontenac, and himself. And he bore in mind the count's order — to watch for trespassing Englishmen and Spaniards. Hennepin and Duluth met near the mouth of the St. Croix and grew cordial after each man realized that the other was on proper business. Perhaps they discussed the battle of Seneffe, an event of another planet, another age, or so it could have seemed to them on this remote river bank with their feathered Issati friends. Meanwhile, the Indians became ecstatic over having eight gods in custody. They insisted that everybody return to Mille Lacs to celebrate an event without parallel in their lives. At Mille Lacs the feasting and dancing, the belching and calumet smoking, went on until the guests of honor were exhausted. In late September they were allowed to leave. They reached Green Bay safely by way of the Wisconsin and wintered with the Jesuits at St. Ignace (Michilimackinac).

In the spring of 1681, Father Hennepin paddled on east over Huron and Erie to La Salle's Fort Frontenac and canoed down the St. Lawrence to Montreal. Here, Francis Parkman wrote, Count Frontenac looked out of his window one frosty morning and "saw approaching a Recollet father whose appearance indicated the extremity of hard service; for his face was worn and sunburnt, and his tattered habit of St. Francis was abundantly patched with scraps of buffalo-skin." The count took Hennepin in, cleaned him up and fattened him and sent him along to Quebec, where Duluth had already arrived to defend himself successfully against Intendant Duchesneau's charges of illegal fur trading. Paris was still far away but the priest arrived there in the summer of 1682. Louis XIV gave him permission to write a book and soon he was scratching away at his *Description de la Louisiane* in the convent at Saint-Germain-en-Laye.

Altogether, Father Hennepin explored some three hundred new miles of the Mississippi for La Salle between the Wisconsin and Mille Lacs during the summer of 1680. That was no great feat compared to Marquette and Jolliet's in 1673, when they explored eleven hundred miles of the river from the Wisconsin south to the Arkansas. But Hennepin's Louisiana book (it appeared in France in 1683) created wide interest in the still-phantom Mississippi. It presented the same patronizing attitude toward La Salle that Hennepin had assumed on the *Griffon*. La Salle, the priest implied, had had something to do with the expedition, but not much since it was all Hennepin's idea. The book made such a hero of the priest in the minds of readers all over Europe that he was inspired to write another that would make him still more heroic. In 1697, he published *Nouvelle Découverte d'un très Grand Pays, situé dans l'Amérique*, containing much material from the first book. For good measure he added to his new text a purely imaginary account of how he had *descended* the Mississippi from the Illinois with Accau and Auguel, discovered its mouth, and *then* returned upstream to spend that summer of 1680 with the Issatis — an impossibility in the two months of March and April that had elapsed between the time of his departure from Crèvecoeur and his arrival at Mille Lacs. But nobody minds a liar if his tale is well told. The second book, translated into many languages, was a publisher's dream. It was probably the most popular adventure story ever written up to then. Because of the dazzling light it threw on the Upper

49

Mississippi, its bumptious author deserved to become a Minnesota immortal, with his statue on Hennepin Avenue.

But one should note, in fairness, that Daniel Greysolon, sieur Du Lhut, did far more than the priest to open up that splendid northern region before he completed his twelve years of exploring. And yet Duluth's fame in Minnesota is small compared to Father Hennepin's. Few citizens outside the membership of the St. Louis County Historical Society know why the place was named Duluth back in 1856. Of course it was Duluth's own fault that he failed to match Hennepin's celebrity. He never got around to writing a best-seller eulogizing his achievements, real and imagined.[4]

Meantime, La Salle's main task remained undone — the exploration of a thousand miles of the Mississippi from the Arkansas south to that shadowy mouth somewhere on the Gulf of Mexico. For a decade, this stubborn, imperious, lonely man had fought for his dream of a great river empire against the apathy of his king, the opposition of Canadian merchants and Jesuit priests, and the hostility of the wilderness in all its forms — bad weather, famine, the fury of the Iroquois, the awful distance from place to place. Soon after Hennepin left Crèvecoeur for the Upper Mississippi, La Salle left with four *voyageurs* to meet the crisis that the *Griffon* disaster must be causing at Fort Frontenac. To save some five hundred miles of circuitous Great Lakes paddling, the men broke trail overland from Fort Miami on the St. Joseph across the swamps and pinelands of southern Michigan. Their lives were threatened along the way by hostile Indians, but they made it to the Detroit River and so on by canoe to Frontenac — a thousand miles in sixty-five days.

The situation that La Salle found at his trading post in early May of 1680 could not have been worse. Creditors held his property, and word came that a ship from France filled with supplies for his proposed Mississippi forts had sunk at the mouth of the St. Lawrence. Once again Governor Frontenac came to La Salle's rescue with more funds. But in August, messages from Henri de Tonty revealed that most of his Crèvecoeur men had mutinied, destroyed and looted the fort, and left the Illinois to destroy and loot Fort Miami. Tonty added that the Seneca tribe of Iroquois were gathering to attack the Illinois villages. La Salle prepared to return to Crèvecoeur but was delayed by a scarcity of men to make a party. His enemy, Intendant Duchesneau, it seemed, was draining off the labor supply at Quebec. He got away at last with twenty-five men, passed the charred remains of Fort Miami, and arrived at the Illinois villages during the bleak days of December, 1680 (see the map on page 10).

What he found was horror, indescribable and utter. The dozen villages that lined the Illinois River for eighty miles between Starved Rock and Crèvecoeur had been thriving places when La Salle had left them in March. He had visualized their seven thousand residents then as the core of the Indian alliance that would thwart the Iroquois and open the Mississippi for his French colonists and the rich trade in furs and buffalo hides that would come down to them from the Sioux country. But the Iroquois had struck in September, as Tonty had predicted. The Illinois had fallen before them and fled across the Mississippi. La Salle found the twelve villages totally destroyed, swarming with buzzards and filled with the smell of death. The fire-blackened meadows and cornfields were strewn with mutilated corpses that the Iroquois had dug up from the burial grounds. Crèvecoeur was a ruin and La Salle saw no sign of what had happened to Tonty and the Recollet priests, Zenobius Membré and the feeble Ribourde. Downstream near the mouth of the Illinois he found relics of an Iroquois victory celebration — the half-eaten bodies of Illinois women still bound to torture stakes.

That was the perspective of tragedy and defeat through which La Salle saw his great river for the first time. He could have seen it from that spectacular bluff above the mouth of the Illinois in present Pere Marquette State Park near Alton, looking across the curve of the Missouri, and across the prairie where St. Louis today crowds along the Mississippi west of its beautiful Gateway Arch. The view of that junction of three great waterways is wonderfully moving, but La Salle may have been too depressed to feel much of anything as he looked at it.

He had reached a bitter end. His sane course was to stop striving, return to Fort Frontenac and resume his easy career as a trader. But he could not stop. It was not just a matter of loyalty to his backers, who had loaned him more than half a million francs. His mind and will had one direction, one inflexible purpose. For him this second bitter end was merely a time to begin his third attempt. He turned his canoes around and moved with his men back up the Illinois and Kankakee to Fort Miami, which he rebuilt during January, 1681. Through the winter, he planned a much more powerful anti-Iroquois alliance, to include the Illinois, Miamis, Shawnees, and a number of Mohegan and Abenaki refugees who had filtered west to the St. Joseph after King Philip's futile war against the New England Puritans. The new alliance and new plans to explore the Mississippi were putting him in debt still further. In May, he left for Montreal, where the faithful Frontenac bailed him out once more, partly with funds derived from Duluth's illegal trading. On the way to Montreal, La Salle was cheered when he found Tonty and Father Membré in good health at Michilimackinac. By a miracle they had survived the September attacks of the Iroquois, though other Indians had murdered Father Ribourde as they fled from the big Illinois village near Starved Rock to Green Bay.

During the summer of 1681, La Salle untangled his affairs without interference by Intendant Duchesneau. His five-year contract with Louis XIV would not expire until May 12, 1683. By its terms, his buffalo-hide monopoly, rights to explore the Mississippi, to build forts and to sell land around them had more than a year to run. In early fall, as he led a flotilla of canoes westward toward the Illinois, he could close a letter to his cousin, François Plet, one of his Paris backers:

This is all I can tell you this year. I have a hundred things to write, but you could not believe how hard it is to do it among Indians. The canoes and their lading must be got over the portage, and I must speak to them continually and bear all their importunity, or else they will do nothing I want. I hope to write more at leisure next year, and tell you the end of this business, which I hope will turn out well: for I have M. de Tonty, who is full of zeal; thirty Frenchmen, all good men, without reckoning such as I cannot trust; and more than a hundred Indians, some of them Shawanoes, and others from New England, all of whom know how to use guns.

By February, the flotilla had left the Illinois and started down the Mississippi. La Salle called it La Fleuve Colbert, following Marquette's usage.[5] The exploring party had settled down to a total of fifty-four people, including a strong high command — La Salle, Tonty, the reporter Father Membré, and a French Canadian of means, Jean Bourdon, sieur d'Autray. Twenty-three of them were whites; eighteen were Abenaki and Mohegan Indians from New England and from Maine. Ten of these men brought their wives and three children along in a tradition of western exploration that would continue through the days of Sacajawea and her baby Little Pomp, who would accompany the Lewis and Clark expedition. As La Salle's party passed the boiling muddy mouth of the Missouri, Membré made notes that revealed a somewhat clearer notion of that stream's importance (he called it the Ozage) than the notion Marquette had held nine years before:

It is full as large as the River Colbert, into which it empties, troubling it so that from the mouth of the Ozage the water is hardly drinkable. The Indians assure us that this river is formed by many others, and that they ascend it for ten or twelve days to a mountain where it rises; that beyond this mountain is the sea, where they see great ships; that on the river are a great number of large villages, of many different nations; that there are arable and prairie lands and an abundance of cattle and beaver. Although this river is very large, the Colbert does not seem augmented by it; but it pours in so much mud that from its mouth the water of the great river, whose bed is also slimy, is more like clear mud than river water, without changing at all till it reaches the sea, a distance of more than three hundred leagues, although it receives seven large rivers, the water of which is very beautiful, and which are almost as large as the Mississippi.

Membré's comment shows again how hard it was for Europeans to grasp the scope of North America. He interpreted correctly what the Indians told him, except sizes and distances. His "a mountain" would turn out to be the Rocky Mountains; his "the sea" was the Pacific Ocean; his "great ships" belonged to those rare California coasters, Cabrillo and Ferrelo (1542–1543), Sir Francis Drake (1579), and Vizcaíno (1602–1603), none of whom tried to explore the mystery of North America from west to east, whereas so many after Columbus had pushed into it from east to west. The "large villages" were those of the ancestors of Osage and Kansas tribes — Poncas, Mandans, Blackfeet and so on — along the Missouri. The "seven large rivers" flowing into the Mississippi below the Missouri were the Ohio, Yazoo and Big Black from the east, the St. Francis, White, Arkansas and Red from the west. But Membré's "ten or twelve days" up the Missouri "to a mountain where it rises" would have put people traveling in a hollow-tree Indian pirogue no further than present Kansas City, with 2,700 miles to go to the actual source of the Missouri at Red Rock Mountain in western Montana. His "more than three hundred leagues" to the Gulf of Mexico — 825 miles — was not too far off. The length of the lower Mississippi in all its curves below the Missouri is around 1,800 miles.

La Salle's birch-bark canoes, getting a bit battered now, floated on south below the mouth of the Missouri, keeping in the deeps of the brown current as it moved outside the bends from one side of the mile-wide river to the other. If La Salle recognized the mouth of the Ohio as the same stream he had visited from Lake Erie in 1670, he did not say so. At the third Chickasaw Bluff, some miles above present Memphis, one of La Salle's hunters, Pierre Prudhomme got lost for six days. While looking for him, a search party met two Chickasaw Indians living in the vicinity. They carried English articles that bore out Marquette's earlier impression that the Chickasaws were being reached by English traders from Virginia and the Carolinas. Near the Third Bluff out of the river's flood range, La Salle built a supply stockade and named it Fort Prudhomme to console the lost hunter for his six days of anxiety.

On March 13, the travelers reached the silted mouth of the Arkansas and the Quapaw village of handsome, cordial Indians that Marquette had admired. The mood of the Europeans was one of tension — eagerness, wonder, curiosity, fear of capture by the Spaniards. The white men thought that the Gulf of Mexico had to be very near the Quapaw village. Marquette's account had put it only two days downstream. But Marquette must have erred. They paddled on for two days, and then for two weeks, and still no hint of salt water. La Salle found himself stunned by the extent of the empire he was creating. Upstream behind him, his river had flowed through more than a thousand miles of fertile country too beautiful for words, swarming with buffalo and other game — a country ten times larger and richer than all of northern France from Brittany to Lorraine, from Picardy to Orléans. Now, the river was carrying him through a totally different world — a lotus land as heavenly as Provence and as tropical as the isles of Martinique and Guadeloupe that France had seized from Spain in the Caribbean. The Mississippi, besilvered at dawn and glowing red at sunset, was becoming narrower and deeper, its channel winding past swamps and bayous and crescent lakes and cypress forests wreathed in moss. It was held between bright green banks guarded by flocks of egrets and herons and hungry alligators.

The explorers learned to feast on alligator meat, and Father Membré noted with astonishment that this awesome monster began life in a small egg, as tamely as a chicken. They floated by the high bank that is now part of Vicksburg and paused near present Newellton in Tensas Parish, Louisiana, to visit some hospitable Taensa Indians. These were a caste-conscious crowd wearing clothes made of mulberry bark and living in a neat ceremonial town of adobe lodges, sacred perpetual fires and a temple to the sun girdled with the skulls of slain enemies. Below this town, the travelers crossed the river to call on a similar tribe, the Natchez Indians, who occupied the top of that dramatic bluff where so many lovely antebellum houses stand now in present Natchez. They called next on a Coroas village near Natchez, and then, on a misty March 31, they passed the mouth of de Soto and Coronado's Red River without seeing much of it. La Salle named it the Seignelay. Perhaps the Red's strong spring current deterred him from paddling up it a few miles to look around. If he had done so, he would have found a curious thing. Half of the Red flowed into the Mississippi. The rest flowed on south, and he might have guessed the fact that it flowed to the gulf parallel to and west of the Mississippi — today's vagrant Atchafalaya River. When La Salle heard of this Red River oddity later, he misconstrued the description of the Atchafalaya to mean that the Mississippi below the Red River reached the gulf in two channels.

After another hundred miles, the explorers found themselves ducking a shower of arrows sent their way by a battalion of Quinipissa Indians from their eastside village near Lake Pontchartrain just above present New Orleans. And then the river swept them along the silent shores past what is now the picturesque bustle of Metairie and Gretna, Canal Street and the Vieux Carré, and on around an enormous bend (English Turn).[6] Suddenly, the river water was brackish, and then salty, for they were moving out the bewillowed ninety-mile Mississippi delta into the gulf — a world of sky and of land so eerily flat that distant trees seemed suspended above the horizon. And, on April 6, 1682, it was all over. They had come to the end of the line at the watery hub called Head of Passes. These passes cut the river in slivers so that its brown water rushes into the gulf through three main canal-like mouths, three narrow fingers of sand and mud ten miles or so long. For three days a crew under Tonty explored the middle finger, South Pass. D'Autray's men paddled around Pass a Loutre eastward. La Salle moved out Southwest Pass with the gulls screaming overhead until he could take in all the blue gulf, frightening in its emptiness, and try to realize that his long search was over.

What he thought of what he saw has to be surmised from what little he knew about that part of the world. He had only the haziest notion of where he was on the gulf in longitude west of France, west of Montreal, west of Spanish Cuba, west of French Martinique. The twistings of the

Mississippi had prevented him from keeping any sort of track by dead reckoning. What he knew was based mainly on a guesswork map that Nicolas Sanson had made for Louis XIV in the 1650's. That map led La Salle to believe that Pineda's indented Bahía de Espíritu Santo (Mobile Bay?) was a bit east of the Mississippi's mouth. He supposed that Coronado's Quivira — if he had heard of it at all — and New Spain's mysterious outpost, Santa Fe, were not too far away in the West. The Sanson map suggested to him that Tampico on the Pánuco River, presumably a gateway to Spain's Santa Barbara silver mines in northern Mexico that Louis XIV had been eyeing with envy for years, was in the near southwest yonder of the gulf — 275 miles at most from where he stood (900 miles actually). That put Sanson's Rio Grande — the Río de las Palmas that Pineda had discovered in 1519 — still closer to him.

Using his astrolabe, La Salle determined secretly that the tip of the Mississippi delta was near the 29th parallel of latitude — secretly because he guarded his findings of late to keep them from rival explorers. But he did not know that it *was* a delta thrusting ninety miles into the gulf. It was too wide and too flat and too wrapped in steamy mist for him to be able to see that. There were no distinguishing landmarks — no hill or bluff or grove of tall trees — nothing to guide a navigator seeking one of the mouths by sea. This absence of landmarks made him understand why, as he came down to the mouths, he had seen no sign that Spaniards or any other Europeans had ever managed to find their way into the Mississippi from the gulf. He concluded that the Spanish articles found among Indians upstream must have reached them through traders from Santa Fe beyond Quivira in the west, and not from the gulf.

La Salle seems to have assumed that the Spanish king had a right to claim the Rio Grande as the northern border of Spain's American empire, based on Pineda's discovery of that river. And now it was France's turn to do some claiming, based on La Salle's discovery. And so, on April 9, he arranged the ceremony on the river bank near Head of Passes which we described at the start of this book. Garbed in his scarlet coat, he read his proclamation on his conquest of Louisiana to the wooden post bearing Louis XIV's coat of arms and to his assembly of ragged Frenchmen and naked Indians.

The proclamation contained plenty of braggadocio. La Salle was claiming regions that neither he nor any other European knew anything about. To make sure that he claimed enough, he went beyond the stupendous Mississippi drainage with the phrase "and also to the mouth of the River of Palms" — meaning the Rio Grande. That brought in all of present Texas and half of present New Mexico. Of course, he had not actually "acquired" any of these areas "by consent of the nations dwelling herein." But he believed that his claims would stand up, as indeed they did with some authorities for many decades — even into Thomas Jefferson's time.

This claiming and naming of Louisiana was one of history's least publicized events. Louis XIV was not particularly impressed when La Salle told him about it in detail two years later. Talk of the Mississippi valley and its alleged potentials by La Salle, Frontenac and Talon had bored the Sun King for a decade and more. What really interested him in 1682 was the spending of billions of francs wrung from his despairing peasants to support an army that could add a few more acres of Europe to the 200,000 square miles of his kingdom of France. And he enjoyed also pleasing his vanity and asserting his divinity by moving his huge bureaucracy and his elegant court from the Louvre to Versailles while his workmen — 36,000 of them at times — toiled to get his palace ready for its grand opening in May.[7]

4

———∽———

. . . Lead But to the Grave

THE UNEXPECTED VASTNESS of what La Salle saw of the Mississippi valley brought commensurate changes in his plans for developing it. He had plenty of time to think about them. As he pushed upstream toward the remote St. Lawrence and Montreal, he came down with a fever brought on partly from eating what he thought was dried alligator meat until he found it was dried Indian. He spent forty days recovering in the Chickasaw Bluff stockade at Fort Prudhomme while Henri de Tonty went on to Michili-mackinac to prepare a report for Governor Frontenac on the expedition's success.

Convalescing at Prudhomme, La Salle perceived that the Mississippi and the colonies and industries that it would attract could not be supplied properly by craft like the *Griffon* and birch-bark canoes portaging to Mississippi tributaries from the Great Lakes. Most of the supplying would have to be done directly from France up the Mississippi, a bypassing of the St. Lawrence that the Montreal merchants had feared all along. In addition to forts on the Illinois and below, La Salle would need a colony of French-men on the Mississippi not far above its mouth to protect Louisiana from intrusion by enemies from the sea.

As La Salle saw it, that river port would be the keystone of a circular imperialism sustained by and sustaining the marquis de Seignelay's fleet of new three-masted merchant ships — a ten-thousand-mile trade route tying ports in France to L'Acadie, the St. Lawrence, Great Lakes, Mississippi, and France's growing empire of Caribbean islands. The marine circle would have many advantages. It would deter Spaniards in Santa Fe out beyond Quivira from moving eastward down the Arkansas and Red rivers to trade with Louisiana Indians. It would break Spain's domination of the Gulf of Mexico. It would expose her Santa Barbara mines in Mexico below the Rio Grande to the threat of seizure by France. It would make it easier for Frenchmen to open the Iroquois-infested region of Ohio and to hold English colonists to their Atlantic tidewater.

But more than these obvious things, La Salle had in mind that England had two hundred thousand colonists in New England and in Virginia, as compared with a mere twelve thousand Frenchmen in Canada. The incalculable mineral and agricultural wealth of Louisiana would be the lodestone to correct this imbalance. A spectacular new era of growth and prosperity at home and abroad would develop as colonists poured into Louisiana and exchanged its infinite variety of raw materials for the finished products of France itself. Colbert's thwarted dream of national enrichment and power through expanded trade overseas would be realized at last.

In September, 1682, La Salle was well enough to leave Fort Prudhomme and to join Tonty at Michilimackinac. The two men and a crew of carpenters were back on the Illinois by Christmas building a replacement for Fort Crèvecoeur on top of Starved Rock (they called it Fort St. Louis). Through the winter, La Salle spent much time encouraging his Indian friends to come back to their villages from which they had been driven by the Iroquois. He was amazed at their response. As the dogwood bloomed, the rebuilt villages overflowed with returned bands of Illinois, Miamis, Shawnees, Kickapoos, Abenakis. In a letter to Minister Seignelay proposing a French colony and a fort on the Lower Mississippi, La Salle stated that the population of his Indian allies around Fort St. Louis had increased from seven thousand in 1680 to twenty thousand. There were more than enough warriors among them to help protect a colony if Seignelay allowed it to be established.

During that springtime of 1683, La Salle approached his fortieth year in a mood of hope, even of restrained jubilation. The tragedy of the *Griffon* was fading from his mind. For a stretch of weeks he saw no clouds ahead and he was almost relaxed, almost happy. But the clouds returned blacker than ever. A courier arrived at Starved Rock from Montreal and reported that the king had removed Count Frontenac from the governorship of Canada for making too many enemies, which was true enough.

La Salle's flamboyant mainstay had gone back to France already. His replacement at Quebec was a corrupt and greedy naval officer named Le Fèbvre de La Barre who, the courier said, had persuaded the king to ban further Mississippi exploration. La Barre's argument was that La Salle's colony plan was part of a plot to set up a Louisiana kingdom of his own. The courier said also that the new governor was conspiring with St. Lawrence merchants to push La Salle out of North America entirely. La Salle refused to believe it until later in the summer when he learned that La Barre had seized Fort Frontenac for some alleged infringement of the terms of La Salle's royal grant. And the governor was sending an agent to the Illinois to take over Fort St. Louis in the name of the king.

These acts created an impossible situation. La Salle's royal patent to operate in Louisiana had expired in May. La Barre had cut off his source of supplies to carry on trade with the Illinois Indians. Though a year had passed, he had received no words of praise from the marquis de Seignelay or from anyone else for discovering the mouth of the Mississippi. Only one course of action remained. He put Tonty in charge of Starved Rock pending the arrival of La Barre's agent and set out on the long, long trail to Paris by way of Quebec to have it out with the king himself. He arrived there at the year's end, took cheap lodgings on the rue de la Truanderie, the city's stamping ground for beggars, and began begging for help himself — help to get back his trading posts and to win the king's sanction of his proposed Mississippi colony to be supplied from the Gulf of Mexico. He had a colony site in mind — some 180 miles up the river near present Baton Rouge and not far below the mouth of the Red River.

The begging was dreary, degrading work for this excessively proud man. Under the strain of it La Salle grew more and more neurotically suspicious even of his friends, of Frontenac and Seignelay, of Abbé Claude Bernou, of his old patron, the prince of Condé, now retired at Chantilly. They pulled wires for him, though the man who helped most, brought to him by Abbé Bernou, was a rival in exploring. Count Don Diego Dionisio de Peñalosa Briceño y Berdugo was one of those attractive four-flushers who save the past from being a dull parade of logical events. He was a Spanish creole born in Peru who connived his way up through the Spanish colonial system to become governor of New Mexico in 1661 at Sante Fe on the Upper Rio Grande. Soon he aroused the displeasure of officials of the Spanish Inquisition by a number of acts that they considered unbecoming in a Catholic — rape, robbery, blackmailing settlers, enslaving Indian girls, and calling the church officials "damned rascals." He was recalled for trial to Mexico City, stopping on the way with his favorite concubine to look at the Santa Barbara mines. Before being exiled from New Spain in 1668, he had read an account of Juan de Oñate's expedition from Santa Fe to Quivira in 1601. He used the account, with himself as the hero in place of Oñate, when he went to London in the 1670's to urge Charles II to let him lead an English army to conquer Quivira by way of the Mississippi. Charles II was tired of foreign adventurers by then, having fired even Groseilliers and Radisson. Peñalosa moved on to Paris, where he pestered Seignelay with plans in a crescendo of grandeur to seize not Quivira but the Santa Barbara mines from a French base that he would establish on the "Río Bravo" — his name perhaps for Corpus Christi Bay and the Nueces River mouth on the Texas coast. In his latest plan, presented to Seignelay at about the same time that he was discussing his schemes with La Salle in the rue de la Truanderie, he proposed to seize all of northern Mexico via the Pánuco River with the help of French pirates from the island of Santo Domingo.

Peñalosa was almost seventy years old by then, in an era when men were lucky to reach forty. Seignelay did not trust him and did not think that such a fossil had the strength for such a project. Still, his idea of seizing the mines from a base in Santo Domingo appealed strongly to the king, particularly just now when France was at war with Spain over Luxembourg and the time seemed ripe to smash Spain's insolent hold on the Gulf of Mexico. The island of Santo Domingo — present Haiti and the Dominican Republic adjoining Cuba — was discovered and claimed for Spain by Columbus on his first voyage in 1492. It still belonged to Spain but the Spaniards were long gone from it after killing off most of the natives in the practice of what was so often their idea of good colonial policy. For a century it had been occupied by a mob of unruly French, English and Dutch pirates who lived not by the usual West Indian wealth — rum, molasses, sugar, tobacco — but by robbing Spanish ships of their American silver and gold. The pirates were called buccaneers, derived from the native word *boucan* — a process for curing the meat of wild pigs and cattle. The buccaneers were respected by the rulers of France, England and Holland because their fighting skill and their knowledge of the Caribbean were helping to appropriate choice bits of the West Indies — Jamaica, Guadeloupe, Curaçao, and so on.

In his talk with La Salle, Count Peñalosa proposed a joint effort — Peñalosa to seize the Santa Barbara mines to please the king and La Salle to

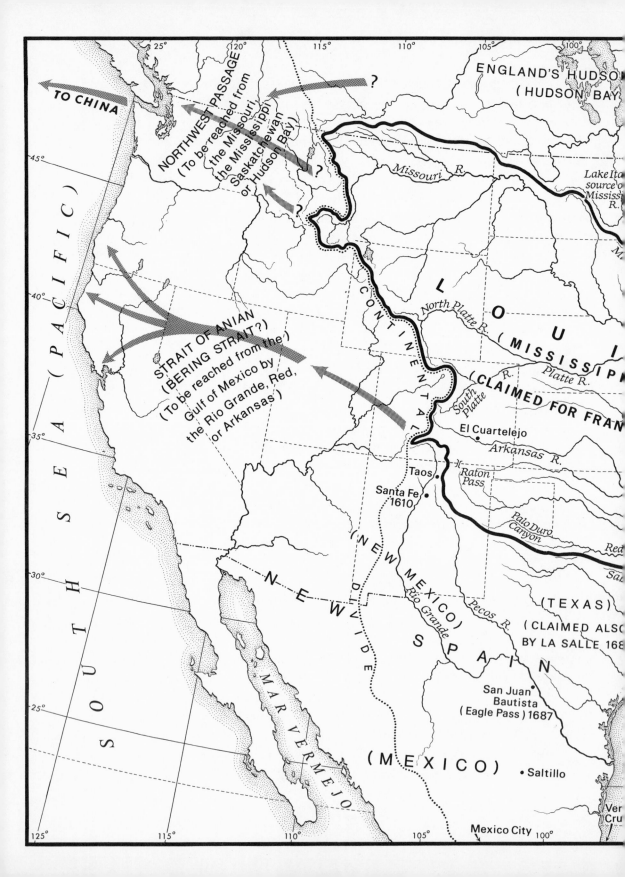

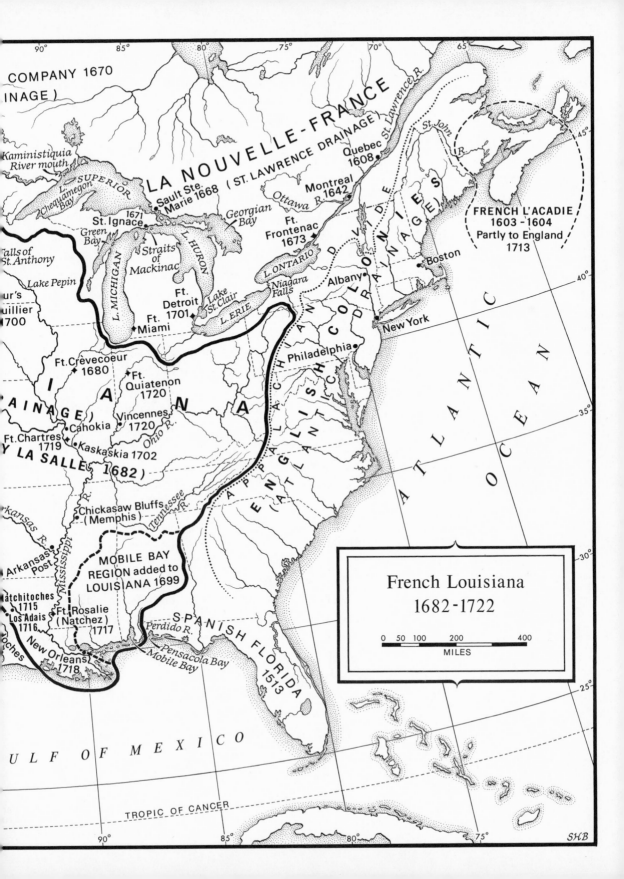

COMPANY 1670

(INAGE)

LA NOUVELLE-FRANCE

St. Lawrence R.

(ST. LAWRENCE DRAINAGE)

St. John R.

Kaministiquia River mouth

SUPERIOR

Chequamegon Bay

Sault Ste. Marie 1668

1671

St. Ignace

Georgian Bay

Ottawa R.

Quebec 1608

Montreal 1642

FRENCH L'ACADIE 1603 - 1604 Partly to England 1713

Green Bay

Straits of Mackinac

L. MICHIGAN

L. HURON

Ft. Frontenac 1673

Falls of St. Anthony

Lake Pepin

Niagara Falls

L. ONTARIO

Albany

Boston

ur's uillier 700

Lake St. Clair

Ft. Detroit 1701

L. ERIE

Miami

New York

Ft. Crèvecoeur 1680

Ft. Quiatenon 1720

Philadelphia

I A

N A

DRAINAGE)

Vincennes 1720

Cahokia

Ohio R.

Ft. Chartres 1719

Kaskaskia 1702

Y LA SALLE 1682)

APPALACHIAN

ENGLISH COLONIES

(ATLANTIC DRAINAGES)

R.

Chickasaw Bluffs (Memphis)

Tennessee R.

ATLANTIC

OCEAN

kansas R.

Arkansas Post

MOBILE BAY REGION added to LOUISIANA 1699

French Louisiana 1682 - 1722

0 50 100   200   400

MILES

atchitoches 1715 Los Adais 1716

Ft. Rosalie (Natchez) 1717

Mississippi R.

SPANISH FLORIDA 1513

Perdido R.

oches

New Orleans 1718

Pensacola Bay

Mobile Bay

G U L F   O F   M E X I C O

TROPIC OF CANCER

SHB

set up a supporting colony and fort at his chosen Baton Rouge site on the Lower Mississippi below the Red River. La Salle, the haughty lone wolf, could not abide sharing leadership with anyone, let alone an antique mountebank. He turned down Peñalosa's suggestion. But Abbé Bernou kept stressing how the king had always been fascinated by the idea of quick mineral wealth as against the slow process of colonial expansion. La Salle, pushed by desperation to compromise his integrity, combined Peñalosa's mine-seizure plan with his own colony plan in the proposal that he submitted to Seignelay and to the king in January, 1684. Though La Salle hadn't the vaguest idea where the Santa Barbara mines were in northern Mexico, he thought it politic to place them near the Rio Grande, and to place the Rio Grande even nearer to the Mississippi than his own mistaken conception of its nearness.[1] His proposal to the king comprised a fantasy in which an army of white men and friendly Mississippi and Illinois Indians would attack the mines from his new colony by moving up the Red River to the area of present Shreveport and then proceeding overland south a hundred miles to the Rio Grande — a rearrangement of geography that abolished the actual six hundred extra miles of Texas that separated the two rivers. La Salle stressed the usefulness of his red warriors by asserting that a mere six hundred Indians had "desolated" Boston during King Philip's War against the New Englanders in the 1670's.

In March, La Salle was received at the new Versailles by the Sun King himself. Some weeks later, on April 14, 1684, Louis XIV issued through Seignelay a surprising series of orders that commanded Governor La Barre to restore Fort Frontenac and Fort St. Louis to La Salle, and gave him far more than he had asked for in ships, sailors, soldiers and funds for building his Mississippi colony. By this time, the king was coming to terms with Spain and he said nothing about seizing Mexican mines, though La Salle understood that the king would not be displeased if he did so. The explorer plunged at once into frenzied recruitment of colonists and the purchase of supplies so that he could get his ships away from the Bay of Biscay port of La Rochelle before the king changed his mind. He signed up people from everywhere. There were beggars alleging to be craftsmen from the rue de la Truanderie, prostitutes from Paris and from La Rochelle, Norman farm girls seeking adventure and husbands, and a large Canadian family named Talon. Most of these people were babes in the woods with not the slightest conception of the rigors of wilderness life. The six missionary priests included Father Membré of the 1682 trip, and La Salle's stolid older brother, Abbé Jean. La Salle found a surgeon somewhere, Monsieur Liotôt. In Rouen, he picked up two young nephews, listed as "M. Moranget and Petit Cavelier," the latter only fourteen years old, and a man in his mid-thirties, Henri Joutel, whose father was gardener for La Salle's uncle. Joutel soon showed talent as a diarist. Also in Rouen, La Salle made a will bequeathing his Canadian properties to his Paris backer, François Plet. To Abbé Jean he gave a "letter of credit" (power of attorney, in effect) to act in his name if necessary.

On August 1, 1684, the little expeditionary fleet sailed from La Rochelle, pretending to head for Quebec to keep the Mississippi objective a secret from Spanish officials. It took the old Caribbean trade route for four thousand miles to Santo Domingo past Cape Finisterre, Lisbon and Madeira. The four ships consisted of the king's thirty-six-gun man-of-war *Le Joly*, commanded by an officer of the royal navy, Monsieur de Beaujeu; a three-masted storeship, *L'Aimable*, that the king had given to La Salle; a smaller three-masted "flyboat," *La Belle*, with a shallow draft for making soundings; and a two-masted ketch, *Saint François*, carrying thirty tons of gunpowder and some trade commodities for Santo Domingo's buccaneers. The ships carried nearly four hundred people — two hundred and eighty of them colonists and the rest sailors and soldiers of one kind or another. Twenty of the colonists were young women, one of whom, Madame Talon, produced a baby on the way.

La Salle had boarded *Le Joly* in an exhausted and irascible state. Nothing seemed to please him during the fifty-eight-day voyage to Santo Domingo. He bickered constantly over petty matters with Beaujeu, a Norman like himself. Beaujeu was an able and amiable officer who insisted only that his word was law on the ship by the king's order. "Do you not know," Beaujeu had written a friend in July, "that this man is impenetrable and that one never knows where one stands with him. . . . I do all I can to have his friendship; I don't know if I will succeed. . . . Never was a Norman so much a Norman as La Salle, and Normans are always stumbling blocks." There was more than a hint of mental illness in La Salle's humorless prohibition of the gay ducking ceremony so beloved by sailors as *Le Joly* crossed the Tropic of Cancer. He was furious because Beaujeu brought his warship (on September 28) to the entrancing tropical harbor of Petit-Goave near present Port-au-Prince, Haiti, instead of to his own choice,

Port de Paix, on the north coast of the island. He collapsed with fever when news came that Spanish buccaneers had captured the *Saint-François*. The fever worsened as he fretted over the misbehavior of his colonists in Petit-Goave's small but comprehensive sin quarter. Some of them deserted, and he was able to replace only a few of them with buccaneers, including a stray Englishman and a sullen German from Württemberg named Hiens. He was distressed to find that the buccaneers knew very little about the north shore of the Gulf of Mexico, though they warned Beaujeu that the shoals there were perilous during the September-March hurricane season.

On November 25, the expedition — only *Le Joly*, *L'Aimable* and *La Belle* now — left Petit-Goave to continue hunting for the mouth of the Mississippi, the last link in La Salle's imperial dream. La Salle moved out of *Le Joly* and into *L'Aimable* and, at that distance, got along better with Beaujeu. The ships coasted west off Cuba's south shore past the Cayman and Pinos islands to Cape San Antonio on the southwestern tip of Cuba near the 22nd parallel of latitude. In mid-December Beaujeu steered northwest away from the 22nd parallel into the ominous emptiness of the Gulf of Mexico. He steered on the correct assumption that the mouth of the Mississippi was in that direction some six hundred miles away near the 29th parallel, as La Salle had determined in 1682 with the help of his astrolabe. Beaujeu had learned for sure from mariners at Santo Domingo that Apalachicola Bay (in present Florida) was due north of his position at the southwest tip of Cuba.

On December 28, as the little fleet was approaching the 29th parallel, *La Belle*'s sounding crew reported shallow water of a whitish color just ahead, and then a low shore. La Salle celebrated New Year's Day, 1685, by landing there but he saw nothing like the delta mouths that he had examined on April 6, 1682. It seems probable that he landed west of the Mississippi delta near the mouth of Atchafalaya River — that defecting branch of the Red River. He discussed the question of where they were with Beaujeu and both men accepted the fatal and erroneous belief that the gulf's current had pushed them far off course *eastward* and that this whitish water flowed out of Apalachicola Bay. So they decided that they would find the Mississippi some three hundred miles further *west* (see the map on page 10).

Such was the destiny of an expedition lost in a vast sea of unknown longitudes. For tedious weeks the three ships crept on west near the 29th parallel of latitude. Crews and colonists watched for the river mouth they had already passed, dreading hurricanes and Spanish warships, taking countless soundings to avoid grounding, going ashore now and then for fresh water. They passed the mouth of the Sabine River near present Port Arthur. They passed Galveston Bay, where Narváez's boats had met disaster, and concluded that it was the Bahía de Espíritu Santo (Mobile Bay) because they had come west nearly three hundred miles from the whitish effluent of "Apalachicola Bay." They veered southwest along the Texas coast with La Salle's *L'Aimable* leading until late January when La Salle decided that they had gone far enough at latitude 28° 20″. The Mississippi *had* to be in this neighborhood — if not this channel at least that second channel west of it that he had heard about. Actually, *L'Aimable* had arrived off the thirty-mile-long sandspit of Matagorda Bay, seventy miles northward up the Texas coast from present Corpus Christi. Somehow, La Salle's pilot got the storeship past Pelican Island and through the dangerous narrows of Cavello Pass into the big bay swarming with teal and mallards, Canada geese and canvasbacks on vacation from the frozen lakes above Hennepin's Falls of St. Anthony.

L'Aimable was soon joined in the bay by Beaujeu's *Le Joly* and *La Belle*. To La Salle, all the bay region — rich oil fields today — was just so much more of his Louisiana empire that he was winning for France. As the three ships moved warily about Matagorda it was revealed to be a navigational horror of sand points, shoals and hidden inlets, though full of delicious fish, shrimp and oysters. The bleak marshy shores were covered with salt grass and forlorn clumps of trees strangled by vines and bent double by the force of past hurricanes. La Salle set up a temporary camp at the mouth of Matagorda's main stream, which he named La Rivière aux Boeufs (Lavaca River) because of the buffalo grazing along it. Later he built "Fort St. Louis" in lusher country five and a half miles upstream and moved his colonists into the fort's compound, which contained a long log dwelling for the men, a small women's dormitory and a warehouse.

Meanwhile, the careless pilot of *L'Aimable* let the storeship run aground. It split open and its cannonballs, kitchen utensils, tools and blankets were lost, though thirty hogsheads of wine and brandy and eight cannon were saved. In mid-March, 1685, Beaujeu sailed for France in *Le Joly*, taking the crew of *L'Aimable* with him. He refused to give La Salle balls for his cannon, claiming that *Le Joly* had to have them for ballast. Somewhat later *La Belle* was wrecked in the bay and the colonists under La

67

Salle's anxious care found themselves in the same straits that Cabeza de Vaca had known — stranded in a land as remote as the moon. It was likely that even Beaujeu did not know exactly where he had left them.

The inexperienced colonists, only one hundred and eighty left when Beaujeu sailed away, were helpless before the overwhelming forces of this hostile place. As the year 1685 passed into and through the year 1686 they met tragedy so often that it became the accepted order of their lives. People died regularly — some from disease, some from the arrows of the cannibalistic Karankawa Indians who prowled about Fort St. Louis and shot at the Europeans from treetops if they were out hunting. One colonist went swimming and was pulled under and eaten by an alligator. One was drowned in a fishnet. One had to have a leg amputated. Another died in agony when he was bitten by a snake. "Rattle Snake," Henri Joutel explained, "so called because it has a Sort of Scale on the Tail which makes a noise."

And still these tormented innocents at Fort St. Louis could rise above despair and find bits of happiness. Joutel reported a love affair:

When Sieur Barbier went out a Hunting, I commonly sent with him some Women and Maids, to help the Hunters to dress and dry the Flesh; but being inform'd that he us'd to slip aside from the Company, with a young Maid he had a Kindness for, and which gave Occasion to some well-grounded Railleries; the said Barbier being told I was acquainted with that Affair, came and spoke to me in private, desiring Leave to marry that young Woman. I made some Difficulty of it at first, advising him to stay until Monsieur de la Salle return'd; but at last, considering they might have anticipated upon Matrimony, I took the Advice of the Recollet Fathers and of Monsieur Chedeville the Priest, and allowed them to marry.

There was, of course, a critical shortage of Maids. Several men deserted the colony to find female companionship elsewhere. They just faded into the woods and tramped north toward the Red River some three hundred miles to the string of Cenis Indian (Caddoan) villages along the Trinity River southeast of present Dallas. Their trail from Fort St. Louis crossed the Colorado River near today's Columbus, Texas, then crossed the Brazos near Navasota and brought them to the Cenis girls in the present Nacogdoches region. Parts of this route would soon be used by Spanish soldiers crossing the Rio Grande from the mining supply town of Saltillo to challenge La Salle's penetration of what they claimed was Spanish property.

A Dutch illustrator, M. Vander Gucht, invented Texas in this sketch of La Salle's colonists landing on the shores of Matagorda Bay from the storeship L'Aimable. *The man-of-war* Le Joly *stands at anchor as two Indians attack a colonist in the background.* (*From Hennepin's* A New Discovery)

In this scrambled version of La Salle's murder, the scene is placed on Matagorda Bay instead of the Texas interior. (*From Hennepin's* A New Discovery)

The Cenis Indians were a populous and relatively sophisticated tribe. For some years they had been getting horses, hardware and European clothes from the Spanish in Santa Fe. During 1685 and 1686, La Salle made two futile trips to their villages in his determination to show that La Rivière aux Boeufs was a branch of the Mississippi, and to find, by way of the Red River, the site that he had chosen on the main stream in 1682 for his colony.[2] The trips were costly in lives and supplies. Their failure to prove anything caused mutinous muttering against his leadership, particularly by the German buccaneer Hiens, the hunter Duhaut, Jean de L'Archevêque (Duhaut's valet), and the surgeon Liotôt, whose nephew was killed on one of La Salle's trips. The dissidents were opposed also to Abbé Jean Cavelier, to La Salle's nephew Moranget, to his footman Saget and to his servant Nika, the Shawnee who had been with him ever since the Ohio trek in 1669. And perhaps La Salle deserved their criticism. As his physical condition deteriorated, as his anxiety about his people affected his judgment and impaired his ability to act, he became more aloof, more imperious than ever. He was watching the destruction of all his dreams and he was too proud to share his grief with anyone.

On Christmas Eve, 1686, the ragged colonists, wearing shoes cut crudely from buffalo hide, celebrated midnight mass. On Twelfth Night, La Salle dressed in his scarlet coat with gold braid — the only coat he had left — and led "the King drinks" song honoring Louis XIV back there in the splendor of his new Versailles. It was a valiant carrying on, for affairs at Fort St. Louis had gone beyond the point of human endurance. Henri Joutel took stock in his diary. Of the two hundred and eighty colonists who had left La Rochelle in 1684, only thirty-seven were still alive. Seven of these were women. Their remaining resources consisted of the fort's rickety buildings, seventy pigs, twenty hens, a few barrels of cornmeal, a tiny supply of gunpowder, bullets and wooden corselets to defend themselves against the Indians, and eight cannon without balls. For La Salle the time had come to forget his imperial designs and try to save the pitiful remnant of his colony. He did not know that France and Spain were no longer at war. He did not dare to cross the Rio Grande — wherever that was — to seek help from the Spanish enemy in Mexico. His only course was to go for help — to find his way over those thousands of miles north to the Red River, to the Mississippi, to the Illinois, to Michilimackinac, to Quebec, and on to Paris to get relief ships from the king.

There were shattering farewells. La Salle was especially sad to part with Father Membré, who chose to be one of the twenty left behind. The relief party of seventeen men that trudged away from Fort St. Louis on January 7, 1687, included Jean Cavelier, La Salle's two nephews, his servants Nika and Saget, and also his critics Duhaut, Hiens, Liotôt and L'Archevêque. La Salle did not dare to leave these troublemakers at the fort because he feared that they might murder the others and appropriate their property.

The weather was a torment from the start. It rained almost constantly week after week as the men slogged along north toward the Cenis villages through the cold dripping woods and prairies of East Texas, delayed by swollen streams and threats of Indian attack. Sleeplessness and hunger built up tensions among them. On March 17, while out with hunters near the junction of the Brazos and Navasota rivers, La Salle's nephew Moranget had the bad taste to tell Duhaut that he was butchering a buffalo badly. In the hunters' camp that night as Moranget slept, the surgeon Liotôt crushed his skull with an axe and went on to kill in the same way the sleeping Nika and Saget. Because of these slayings the dissidents knew that they must kill their leader too. Three days later, La Salle in his scarlet coat went searching for his hunters and was attracted to their camp area by the sight of buzzards circling over it. He spotted L'Archevêque in a clearing, approached him and asked where Moranget was. L'Archevêque answered that he was "down by the river." At that moment, Duhaut, hidden in the tall weeds, aimed his musket and sent a ball through La Salle's head. He fell and died without saying a word. The murderers stripped him of his clothes, performed some mutilations on his body, and left it to rot in the bushes near the clearing.[3]

Duhaut took forcible command of the thirteen survivors and led them on to one of the Cenis villages. As assistant commander, Hiens strutted about issuing orders in La Salle's scarlet coat. But the mutineers could not agree on what to do next. Duhaut and Liotôt wanted to return to Fort St. Louis, build a boat on Matagorda Bay and sail back to France. Hiens opposed the plan, saying that even if they knew how to build a boat he did not want to go back to Paris "only to have my head chopped off." The debate ended in May when Hiens drew his pistol and killed Duhaut. Hiens's friend Ruter shot Liotôt at the same time. These murders reduced the relief party to eleven. It was reduced further when Hiens, L'Archevêque, Ruter and one other concluded it was wise for them to retire from the civilized world and join the savages.

Late in May, Jean Cavelier acquired six horses and three Cenis Indians to guide the remnant relief party of seven to the Red River and on to the Quapaw village near the Arkansas. Besides La Salle's brother, the party included Petit Cavelier, Henri Joutel, Father Anastase Douay, a teenager from Paris named Bartholomew, sieur de Marle, and a Huguenot heretic, Teissier, who had been a pilot on the flyboat *La Belle*. None of the seven had the training to survive one of the most rugged treks in the annals of exploration. Sieur de Marle did not survive. He was drowned while bathing in a stream in July just before the party arrived at the Quapaw village on the Mississippi near the Arkansas. The six remaining paddled slowly on and on, month after month, by dugout up the Mississippi and the Illinois to Fort St. Louis at Starved Rock, where they spent the winter of 1687–1688 with Henri de Tonty.

Through all the winter, Abbé Jean, a priggish and censorious man, and the other five maintained the fiction that La Salle was alive and well at his new colony, believing that otherwise Tonty would not honor Abbé Jean's letter of credit from La Salle allowing him to draw on Tonty for money and supplies to get back to France. In the spring the six travelers continued by birch-bark canoe to Michilimackinac and then across Lake Huron to the French River and down the Ottawa to Montreal, where they took a boat to Quebec. From there they sailed for France, landing at La Rochelle on October 9, 1688. After a pause at Rouen, Jean Cavelier hurried on to Versailles to tell the marquis de Seignelay what had happened to La Salle and to ask the king to send a ship to rescue the twenty colonists near Matagorda Bay. Seignelay was not at all pleased to hear Jean's story. And he showed little interest in the plight of the twenty colonists at Fort St. Louis when he found that La Salle had failed to sally forth into Mexico to seize the Santa Barbara mines.

As for Louis XIV, he washed his hands of the whole profitless Louisiana affair. He had important things on his mind.[4]

5

Iberville's Mardi Gras

THE MAIN THING on the Sun King's mind was the trouble he got into by invading the Rhenish Palatinate in 1688. That act transformed England from a wavering ally into an implacable foe. It gave the conquering Dutchman, William of Orange, the chance to accept the English throne, to form the Grand Alliance of European powers against France, and to start the War of the League of Augsburg. The war drizzled along for eight years. Though Louis XIV won all the battles, he gained little except huge debts when the end came with the Treaty of Ryswick in 1697.

While these Augsburg armies in Europe blasted away at one another, soldiers, priests and frontiersmen carried on parallel struggles in the American wilds — officially in the north under the name of King William's War. Far to the south, Spanish officials had got their martial wind up some years earlier. La Salle and Captain Beaujeu had barely entered the Gulf of Mexico in their three ships when reports of La Salle's plans to colonize the Lower Mississippi and seize Mexican mines reached Mexico City through the medium of Spanish pirates who had captured La Salle's ketch off Santo Domingo in 1684.

Since de Soto's time, no Spaniard had bothered to explore those shallow dangerous north shores of the gulf that the pope had given to Spain in 1493. But the specter of Frenchmen forting at the mouth of the Mississippi and ready to move to the Rio Grande and into Mexico was deeply disturbing to the viceroy, the marqués de Laguna. He had still other reasons to worry about New Spain's vague northern frontier. He had heard of the plots for seizing mines that the traitor Peñalosa had been trying to peddle in the courts of England and France. And rumors came to him about a French "army" visiting Caddoan villages on the Red River. These rumors derived from a trip that La Salle's ever-loyal Henri de Tonty made with a few companions in 1686 from Fort St. Louis at Starved Rock down to the mouth of the Mississippi in search of his friend.[1] More rumors reached the viceroy about a second mercy trip that Tonty made in 1689, this time up the Red River as far as present Shreveport and on south to the Cenis villages, with hopes of rescuing La Salle's lost colonists and seizing a Mexican silver mine or two.

The viceroy moved first to find and capture the elusive La Salle and his fleet. He sent a shipload of pirates under Juan Enríquez Borroto and Antonio Romero to scour the gulf from Havana all the way around the north and west shores and on down to Veracruz. The pirates discovered Pensacola Bay on January 30, 1686, Mobile Bay in March, and then passed by one of the delta mouths of the Mississippi. They named La Salle's river Palizada — suggested, it would seem, by the odd appearance of log-shaped lumps of mud on the flats of the delta. They thought so little of the river mouth or thought it so ominous, that they did not go ashore to reassert Spain's old claim on the country. Thereafter, a storm forced them on to Veracruz with only the discovery of Pensacola Bay to show for their long voyage.

Viceroy de Laguna got more tangible results in the La Salle matter from several expeditions that he sent into the unknown wilderness of East Texas between the Rio Grande and the Red River. They were led by a capable explorer, Captain Alonso de León, from the Spanish frontier outposts of Monterrey and Monclova in northern Mexico (see the map on page 10). As de León pushed north he kept getting hints that La Salle's army (or colony, or whatever it was) was stranded on shore a bit north of the Rio Grande. Sailors coasting off Matagorda Bay found fragments of wreckage from what must have been the storeship *L'Aimable*. At a Rio Grande crossing (the ford at present Eagle Pass, Texas), de León's soldiers captured a wandering Frenchman who had deserted from La Salle's Fort St. Louis near Matagorda Bay. From this deserter, and from various Indians as time passed, Captain de León learned that La Salle had been murdered near the Cenis villages in the north, that an accomplice in the crime, Jean de

L'Archevêque, and a deserter named Santiago Grollet were enjoying life in an Indian village, and that the murderer Hiens had been killed by his friend Ruter — the fellow who had killed the surgeon Liotôt. La Salle's fearsome "army," de León learned further, had been reduced by hardship to no more than twenty colonists. Half of the twenty had died of smallpox and the rest had been slaughtered and eaten by Karankawa Indians, excepting four of the children of the Canadian Talon family and a Parisian boy named Eustache Breman. The Karankawas were keeping the children as pets.

Captain de León set up a base at Eagle Pass and called it Presidio San Juan Bautista. In 1687–1688, he made two treks from this small base northward across the Rio Grande trying to sort out the myriad trails connecting the Indian tribes of the region — tribes that included the Karankawas, Cenis and Red River Caddoans. Already de León was using the word *tejas* — an Indian word meaning "friend" — to designate East Texas and its people. At last, in the spring of 1689, he met an Indian who guided him on April 22 to what was left of Fort St. Louis. He found a plundered desolation of smashed buildings and palisades, of broken boxes and barrels, rusty cutlasses and cannon and, especially moving, a library of several hundred rain-ruined books — the colony's one cultural possession. There were the clothed skeletons of three colonists, one of them a woman, perhaps a Parisian "Maid" who had gone to La Salle's Louisiana paradise to find a better life.

Soon after de León's arrival, L'Archevêque and Grollet materialized out of the wilds and surrendered to him. Eventually, they would become Spanish enlisted men serving with New Mexican troops at Santa Fe under Governor Diego de Vargas. With the La Salle threat of conquest removed, de León and his small force spent the spring of 1690 making sure that Frenchmen did not approach the Texas region again. He explored and claimed for New Spain the East Texas terrain most of the way north to the Red River. In a side trip to Matagorda Bay, he rescued the Talon children and Eustache Breman from the Karankawa Indians and forwarded them to Mexico City from whence they were shipped to Spain. Springtime brought de León the mud and misery of East Texan rains but he and his men pushed on across the Colorado and the Brazos to the Cenis villages in the Trinity River area. At the villages, de León found the oldest Talon boy, Pierre, and also young Pierre Meusnier, confirmed Indians by now, and put them to work as interpreters.

During the summer of 1690, Spanish priests followed the path of de León's soldiers and set up the first mission in Texas, San Francisco de los Tejas, near a large Cenis settlement at the site of present Weches, just west of Nacogdoches. But these preliminaries of accession were premature. From the start, priests and soldiers squabbled over methods of administration. The Texas Indians were uncooperative, the viceroy in Mexico City was stingy, and officials in Spain were too absorbed in the War of the League of Augsburg to care. In 1693, the viceroy recalled his soldiers back across the Rio Grande and ordered the little San Francisco mission destroyed and the site abandoned. Only the French youngsters, Pierre Talon and Pierre Meusnier, stayed behind with the Indians to uphold the virtues of European man in the Texas wilderness.[2]

In the meantime, Captain de León mapped out roughly a government route through East Texas that would be known later as New Spain's frontier highway, El Camino Real. It would run from Mexico City to Saltillo and Monclova, over the Rio Grande at Presidio San Juan Bautista, and through the San Antonio and Nacogdoches areas to and beyond the Sabine River. Alonso de León is hardly a great figure in the parade of Louisiana notables but he deserves to be remembered. His El Camino Real would have a terminus beyond the Sabine that would emerge in Jefferson's day as a key point on the disputed Louisiana Purchase boundary between New Spain and the United States.[3]

While the Lower Mississippi resumed its unregarded state for a decade after the La Salle fiasco in Texas, Count Frontenac was returned to Quebec by the king in October, 1689, as governor and plunged into the task of trying to straighten out the mess that governors La Barre and Denonville had left behind in Canada. The rugged old count faced King William's War in his seventieth year, but he was ageless. His years did not affect his headlong energy nor his fiery temper nor his courage nor the freshness and audacity of his ideas. He found the St. Lawrence community still under-populated, the settlers sick with fear of Indian raids, their fur trade brought to a standstill by the Iroquois, the rival Jesuit and Recollet priests bickering among themselves, and the English — backed by one hundred thousand colonists in New England alone — poised to come at La Nouvelle-France from all directions. The Englishmen's Iroquois allies were at a peak of their fighting power and were spreading terror from Quebec to the Great Lakes.

They had just destroyed (August 4–5, 1689) La Salle's old Lachine post near Montreal and had murdered with their special awful artistry a great many Lachine residents. They were inspired at Lachine partly by disgust with Governor Denonville's treatment of them. Among other acts, the governor had kidnapped thirty-six young Iroquois — friendly Iroquois at that — and had shipped them to the Mediterranean to be chained with captive Huguenots in the king's galleys until they were worn out or died at their oars of malnutrition. Frontenac complained of this outrage to Minister of Marine Seignelay and he must have made an impression. Later when he sailed into Quebec he had eleven Iroquois along that he had salvaged from the galleys. His tactful act tempered the ire of some Iroquois bands and helped him to control them a little by threats and persuasion.

Frontenac's problem during King William's War was to contain the English to their seaboard along an interminable frontier that stretched from New York and New England to Newfoundland, the St. Lawrence, and Hudson Bay. The count was distressed to hear of La Salle's death but he took comfort in the way that the explorer's dream for Louisiana was being kept alive by Henri de Tonty and other *coureurs de bois* in the hinterland. It would be hard to exaggerate the wonders wrought by this tiny society of far-west traders and their few hundred French-Canadian employees in an association so close that most of them were interrelated by blood or by marriage. In 1686, when Tonty was returning to the Illinois from the mouth of the Mississippi, he had permitted an old Rouen friend of La Salle's, Jean Couture, to set up Arkansas Post a few miles upstream from the mouth of the Arkansas to serve the Quapaws and Chickasaws and to watch out for English traders approaching the Mississippi from the Carolinas. In 1690, Frontenac saw to it that Tonty inherited from the king La Salle's Illinois property at Fort St. Louis on Starved Rock. Because of a shortage of wood, Tonty moved that trading post downstream to Lake Peoria near the ruins of Fort Crèvecoeur.

Meanwhile, other western explorers were causing a murky kind of light to break over Louisiana's northwest, the Upper Mississippi region. Some widening of knowledge derived from the rambles of Daniel Greysolon, sieur Du Lhut, whom we saw last in 1681 squirming out of charges that he and Frontenac were trading for furs without paying proper tribute to the king's bureaucrats in Quebec. The rugged Duluth had lost none of his zest for the wilds or his skill in handling Indians. He commanded soldiers briefly at the fur-trade hub, Michilimackinac, built the strategic Fort St. Joseph on Lake St. Clair between Lake Erie and Lake Huron, and another trading post on the St. Croix River which he supplied from Lake Superior by way of the Bois Brulé River route that he had pioneered in 1680 on his way to rescuing Father Hennepin. Through the 1680's, Duluth had come to see that the furs of the Far North were finer, more plentiful and more profitable than any others. To increase the supply and to reduce the volume that English traders were getting from the Indians at their Hudson Bay posts, Duluth had worked to bring peace among the fur-gathering tribes of the Superior region — Issati Sioux and Chippewas — and among the Crees and Assiniboines who came down to him from the further northwest. To counter his English competition on the James Bay arm of Hudson Bay, he had sent in the mid-1680's his brother, Claude Greysolon, sieur de La Tourette, to build a rival post at Lake Nipigon north of Lake Superior. From Nipigon, James Bay could be reached by canoe in a fortnight's paddle by way of the Albany River.

Of all his posts, Duluth loved best his exotic and picturesque establishment at the mouth of the Kaministiquia River on the piney north shore of Lake Superior (the paper town of Thunder Bay today, near Grand Portage and the mouth of Pigeon River in the Quetico region). He had never discarded his belief that a Northwest Passage to China might be found beyond Fort Kaministiquia. His Indian friends had told him about a "Big Sea" which lay to the northwest — they meant Lake Winnipeg, of course. In any case, the Crees and Assiniboines were bringing fine beaver down to Kaministiquia from "the Big Sea." But Duluth would not live long enough to solve an epic riddle. It would fall to other Frenchmen to open the Kaministiquia and Pigeon River canoe routes to Rainy Lake, Lake of the Woods, Lake Winnipeg, the prairies of western Canada, the Upper Missouri and that greatest of topographical surprises, the Rocky Mountains.[4]

While Tonty had become top trader on the Illinois and Duluth reigned on Lake Superior in the mid-1680's, Nicolas Perrot was the equivalent white god on the Upper Mississippi. Perrot, once a Jesuit trainee on the St. Lawrence, built his rude hut of a Mount Trempealeau trading post just above present La Crosse, Wisconsin. He placed his Fort St. Antoine on Lake Pepin, and Fort St. Nicolas near the mouth of the Wisconsin (present Prairie du Chien, Wisconsin), at the end of the old Fox-Wisconsin portage from Green Bay. The Indians adored Perrot, their "Little Indian Corn," and honored him with feasts, dances, sham battles, complimentary wives and lacrosse matches.[5] Associated with Little Indian Corn was another former Jesuit from the Channel province of Artois, Pierre Le Sueur, who got the trading fever while working at the Sault Ste. Marie Mission. After some years with Perrot, Le Sueur struck out on his own further up the blue Mississippi with a post on Prairie Island that drew Issati Sioux customers from the St. Croix and from the Minnesota River that flowed into the Mississippi from the west just below the Falls of St. Anthony. Le Sueur named the Minnesota after himself: La Rivière St. Pierre.

These Frenchmen handled their thousands of western Indians so well that they persuaded them often to help Frontenac on the St. Lawrence to fend off the Iroquois — persuasion achieved by simply liking and admiring them, and also by making them dependent on the traders' supply of European goods and French brandy. An observer of the dependency process was a youth named Louis-Armand, baron de Lahontan, probably of Basque blood like his friend Frontenac. Lahontan was a caustic seventeen-year-old in 1683 when Governor La Barre made him a marine trooper at Quebec. During nine years of army service, not noticeably held down by military routine, Lahontan roamed the wilds as far west as Lake Michigan, spent a year at Fort St. Joseph, rose to the rank of captain, and got engaged to Frontenac's goddaughter because it allowed him to dine free at the governor's epicurean table. Lahontan loved his liberty. He delayed marrying the girl for months and then broke the engagement, causing Frontenac to cut off the gourmet food and give the army promotion that he had obtained for Lahontan to someone else.

Lahontan was the typical young intellectual in revolt against the status quo. He saw La Nouvelle-France and its problems as the end product of Louis XIV's restrictive and self-defeating absolutism — a nightmare land of snooping priests, strutting bureaucrats, greedy merchants, cheap status seekers, corrupt judges and shyster lawyers using the law to protect the rich and to fleece and enslave the poor. Lahontan ridiculed the attempts of the missionaries to "civilize" the Indians, arguing that the priests ought to "civilize" themselves by taking up the simple, functional, wantless way of life of the Indians. He began writing a satirical book, *New Voyages to North America*, half of which described the joys of barbarism as he had learned about them from his own observation and from experts like Pierre Le Sueur and Henri de Tonty.

The baron expressed his views in dialogues suggesting analogies to modern materialism — dialogue between himself and an imaginary Huron friend, Adario, who had been to Quebec, Paris and Versailles and found no merit in them comparable to that of any Huron village on the Great Lakes. When Lahontan mentioned the blessings and comforts brought to mankind by French science and invention, Adario replied, according to the English translation of Lahontan's book:

The More I reflect upon the lives of the Europeans, the less Wisdom and Happiness I find among 'em. . . . I know that your Prince, your Duke, your Marshal, and your Prelate are far from being happy upon the Comparison with the Hurons, who know no other happiness than that of Liberty and Tranquility of Mind: For your great Lords hate one another in their Hearts; they forfeit their Sleep, and neglect even Eating and Drinking, in making their Court to the King, and undermining their Enemies; they offer such Violence to Nature in dissembling, disguising and bearing things, that the Torture of their Soul leaves all Expression far behind it.

Adario went on to blast European food with "your Pepper, your Salt, and a thousand other Spices . . . to murder your Health." And European clothes: "You dawb your Hair with Powder and Essence, and even your Cloaths are sprinkled with the same. . . . How d'ye think it would agree with me to spend two hours in Dressing or Shifting myself, to put on a Blue Sute and Red Stockins, with a Black Hat and a White Feather, besides colour'd Ribbands? Such Rigging would make me look upon myself as a Fool. . . . And pray what harm would it do ye to go Naked in warm Weather? Besides, we are not so stark Naked, but that we are cover'd behind and before. 'Tis better to go Naked than to toil under an everlasting Sweat, and under a load of Cloaths heap'd up one above another." And Knowledge: "In your Books which are publish'd every Day, you write lies and impertinent Stories; and yet you would fain have me to Read and Write like the French." And health: "We Hurons know no such thing as your Dropsies, Asthmas, Palsy's, Gout and Pox. The Leprosy, the Lethargy, External Swellings, the Suppression of Urine, the Stone and the Gravel, are Distempers that we are not acquainted with."

Lahontan planned to keep the readers of his book awake with bawdy allusions. Of French sex life, his Huron philosopher remarked:

I have observ'd that before you pass the Age of thirty or forty, you are Stronger and more Robust than we . . . but after that your Strength dwindles and visibly declines, whereas ours keeps to its wonted pitch till

Daniel Greysolon, sieur Du Lhut, laid the basis of the fur trade of Upper Louisiana and western Canada. In 1965 this statue of him by Jacques Lipchitz was placed on the Duluth campus of the University of Minnesota. (Courtesy of the University of Minnesota, Duluth)

The Louisiana adventures of Pierre Le Moyne, sieur d'Iberville, followed a decade of freebooting from Hudson Bay to Cape Cod. (Engraving by Laguillermie from Justin Winsor's The Mississippi Basin)

we count fifty five or sixty years of Age. This is a truth that our young Women can vouch for. They tell you that when a young Frenchman obliges 'em six times a night, a young Huron do's not rise to above half the number and with the same Breath they declare that the French are older in that Trade at Thirty-five than the Hurons are at fifty years of Age. . . . This intelligence, I say, led me to think that your Gout, Dropsy, Phthisick, Palsy, Stone and Gravel, and other Distempers above mention'd, are certainly occasion'd not only by the immoderateness of these Pleasures, but by the unseasonableness of the time, and the inconveniency of the way in which you pursue 'em; for when you have but just done eating, or are newly come off a fatiguing bout, you lie with your Women as often as ever you can, and that either upon Chairs or in a Standing Posture, without considering the Damage that accrues from such indiscretion; Witness the common practice of these young Sparks . . . who make their table serve for a Bed. . . . And besides, to make some Compensation for the Nudity of our Boys, our Girls are Modester than yours, for they expose nothing to open view but the Calf of their Leg, whereas yours lay their Breasts open in such a Fashion that our young Men run their Noses into 'em when they bargain about the Beaver Skins with your handsome She-merchants. Is not this a Grievance among the French that wants to be Redress'd?

The captious Lahontan left Canada under a cloud in 1692 after a feud with his superior officer in the French part of Newfoundland. He finished writing his treasonable *New Voyages to North America* while an exile from France in Spain, Portugal and Holland. In the meantime, Count Frontenac was trying, with the inadequate troops that he had pried out of the king, to keep the English and their Indian allies on their side of the undefined borders that separated French and British North America through King William's War. Under the difficult circumstances his direction of the struggle was a miracle of management. It included outmaneuvering the Iroquois so that the Great Lakes fur trade, stalled by their raids since 1680, could resume in 1694.[6] In that latter year, he stimulated the beaver business by building a strong point, Fort Buade, at Michilimackinac, and placed in command of it a blusterous Gascon friend of his, Antoine de la Mothe Cadillac. Fort Buade's cannon and troops had the effect of helping Tonty, Duluth, Perrot and Le Sueur to pacify and to do business with the Mississippi valley Indians all the way from the Falls of St. Anthony south to Jean Couture's Fort Arkansas.

Frontenac's best officer through his frustrating war was Pierre Le Moyne, sieur d'Iberville, a member of the new Canadian aristocracy that began with Samuel de Champlain. Born in Montreal in 1661, Iberville was put together with a bit of everything good and bad, for he was handsome and conscienceless, rugged and greedy, learned and as purely buccaneer as any Caribbean pirate. He could kill a man with his fists but he had the polished airs of a Versailles dandy. Frontenac admired his fighting skill, but with reservations. Once he called him "a garrulous and presumptuous ass." Iberville's father, Charles Le Moyne, had come to Montreal from his native Dieppe in 1646 to begin a career as a St. Lawrence merchant, Indian trader and sire of at least thirteen remarkable children. He did many good deeds for the king, who paid him off in 1663 with a grant of land where the Montreal suburb of Longueuil stands now, and the ennobling title of seigneur de Longueuil. Thereafter, Charles became an opponent of everything Frontenac and La Salle tried to do to make the Mississippi valley a working part of La Nouvelle-France. Perhaps it was Charles Le Moyne's good luck to die before suffering the pain of seeing his third son, Iberville, and his much younger twelfth child, Jean-Baptiste Le Moyne de Bienville, bring about what Montrealers feared most, the creation of the royal province of Louisiana on the Mississippi to compete with the province of Canada on the St. Lawrence.

As a boy in Montreal, Iberville had heard Duluth, Tonty and other traders discussing La Salle's circular dream of empire. In 1683, after his midshipman term in France, Iberville heard La Salle himself describing his discovery of the mouth of the Mississippi and what a disaster it would be for France if England ever possessed that great central key to the continent. Three years later, Iberville was among seventy rash French Canadians who made a two-thousand-mile trek by canoes and snowshoes up the Ottawa and down Moose River to the frozen wastes of James Bay, where they seized three Hudson's Bay Company trading posts. They seized also all the loot that they could haul off — a means to quick wealth that Iberville found delightful. Back in Quebec, Iberville, now aged twenty-seven, had to distribute some of his loot as legal fees when a nineteen-year-old girl, Jeanne-Geneviève Picoté de Belestre, charged him with being the father of her unborn child. Iberville did not deny the charge, although he suggested that Jeanne-Geneviève was not exactly a one-man woman. The case was settled when the Le Moyne family put up a purse for the baby and Iberville found himself free to marry another nineteen-year-old, Marie-Thérèse Pollet, a niece of Henri de Tonty's backer, Charles Juchereau de St. Denis. Meanwhile, Governor Denonville kept young Iberville out of jail by shipping him to Versailles on royal business and by naming him commander of the James Bay posts that he had helped to take from the English.

Under Frontenac, Iberville displayed his rare talent as a warrior on land and sea. He seemed to turn up everywhere in that northern vastness, particularly if the chances of plunder were bright. He took part in the massacre and looting of Englishmen at Schenectady on the Mohawk in February of 1690. He freebooted through the winter of 1690–1691 at Hudson Bay as commander for Louis XIV and for the king's current business monopoly for Canada, the Company of the North. He pirated his way along the Atlantic coast from Mount Desert and Penobscot Bay to Cape Cod and Boston harbor in 1692. His sailors captured the Hudson's Bay Company's main post, Port Nelson, in 1649. He whipped an English squadron in 1696 off the Bay of Fundy and destroyed Fort William Henry at the Pemaquid mouth of the Kennebec River in Maine. During the winter of 1696–1697, he and his sixteen-year-old brother Jean-Baptiste de Bienville picked up a fortune in loot while his men raided a dozen English fishing villages from one end of Newfoundland to the other. Finally, just before Louis XIV and the Grand Alliance signed the Treaty of Ryswick on September 30, 1697, Iberville's naval force captured Port Nelson on Hudson Bay once more in a cataclysm of action that involved point-blank bombardments, ships colliding with icebergs and splitting amidships in sleet-laden gales, and the storming of the Hudson's Bay Company fort by French sailors howling like Indians and with cutlasses whirling.

Governor Frontenac did not learn of Iberville's Hudson Bay victory until the next spring, when mails from France informed him about it and brought the bitter news that the Treaty of Ryswick had restored the status quo in America and turned the question of who owned Hudson Bay over to the usual vacillating international commission. And so Frontenac's war years come to nothing at all. But the worn-out old fighter was too tough a spirit for self-pity. As he approached his seventy-eighth birthday, he thumbed his ample nose at his despised enemies — Jesuits, Montreal merchants, Quebec bureaucrats — when they charged that he was a paranoid tyrant, a military bungler, a bribe-taker, a philanderer, an irresponsible democrat, a slick fortune hunter, and a brandy salesman who contributed to the delinquency of the Indians. He died on November 28, 1698, beloved and honored by a great many Canadians who thought of him as their guardian angel against royal injustice and the red tape of bureaucrats. His last act was a slap at the Bishop of Quebec when he ordered that he be buried in the Recollet church rather than in the cathedral.

During the five years (1697–1702) between the Treaty of Ryswick and the start of still another unnecessary war, that of the Spanish Succession, Louis XIV worked on two schemes to save his empire from bankruptcy. One scheme was to unite the kingdoms of France and Spain by forcing England and the rest of the Grand Alliance to accept his grandson Philip, duc d'Anjou, as the new king of Spain, as directed in the will of the imbecile Charles II, who died in 1700. The second scheme was to colonize Louisiana — nothing less than a belated revival of La Salle's old, old, plan to expand and coordinate the commerce of France, the St. Lawrence, the Mississippi and the West Indies to form an economy of immense power with raw materials, finished products, transport and capitalization in perfect balance. This revival ten years after La Salle's death and with no thanks to him resulted partly from the enthusiasm of Jérôme Phélypeaux, comte de Maurepas, who, while still in his twenties, succeeded his father as minister of marine and colonies, and then as the comte de Pontchartrain. The younger Pontchartrain had drive — perhaps in outraged response to his physical handicaps. He was puny and undersized. His pockmarked face, according to the acidulous duc de Saint-Simon, was *"hideuse et dégoutante à l'excès."* He had only one good eye, walked with a limp and his buck teeth did not meet. He tried at times to distract from his ugliness by telling startling stories about bedroom antics at Versailles. To increase his power, he thought up ways to make the large marine and colonies bureaucracy even larger, with new squads of mapmakers, architects, engineers, draftsmen, oceanographers, inspectors and spies. Though few of these experts had any notion of American distances and environmental problems, they prepared bales of dossiers to guide the man whom Count Pontchartrain chose to take up where La Salle had left off in Louisiana, the hero of Hudson Bay, Pierre Le Moyne, sieur d'Iberville.

Pontchartrain assigned two fast royal frigates, *Badine* and *Marin*, and two shallow-draft Biscayan sailboats called *traversiers* to Iberville, who sailed from Brest on October 24, 1698. He had with him two hundred and

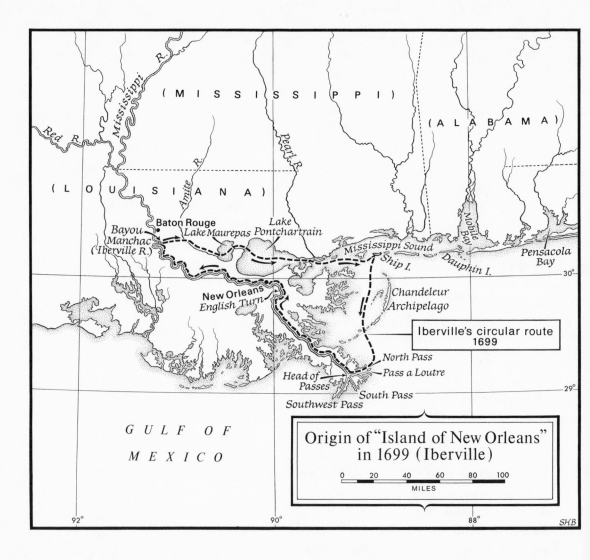

Origin of "Island of New Orleans"
in 1699 (Iberville)

Iberville's circular route
1699

eighty men, crates of gifts for the Mississippi Indians, and half a dozen
birch-bark canoes imported from Canada. His second in command was his
teen-aged brother Jean-Baptiste de Bienville. His chaplain was Father
Anastase Douay, one of the La Salle survivors. His fighting force consisted
of some sixty French Canadians who had freebooted with him through the
chill North Atlantic and who looked forward to plunder and pleasure in the
charming tropical climate of the gulf. The commander took the old trade
route to the island of Santo Domingo, now a French possession with its
buccaneers turned into respectable bureaucrats. During the voyage, he kept

a lookout for an English warship or warships that were said to have left the Carolinas recently under a Captain Lewis Banks for the mouth of the Mississippi on a mission of conquest.

After picking up some pirates and ex-convicts in Santo Domingo to use in Louisiana as colonists, Iberville sailed on past Cuba, past Pensacola Bay (Spain's preserve) and past Mobile Bay to anchor off a sand sliver called Ship Island ten miles out in Mississippi Sound from Biloxi Bay. The time was early February, 1699. The commander knew no more than Captain Beaujeu had known about the whereabouts of the Mississippi entrance from the gulf. But he was an intuitive skipper with a bolder outlook than that of Beaujeu, whose main concern in strange waters was getting his ship home to France safely. Iberville had with him a copy of Henri Joutel's journal and he remembered what La Salle had told him so long ago about the mouth of the Mississippi and about the color of the river water there, *"toute bourbeuse et blanche"* ("all muddy and white"). But mainly he relied on his skill as a sailor who had met the navigational perils of Cape Cod and the Bay of Fundy, the rock-strewn Lachine Rapids and Hudson Strait. From the Ship Island anchorage in present Mississippi Sound, he explored Dauphin Island and Mobile Bay, climbed tall oaks to look around, and conferred with some Bayogoula Indian hunters who had roamed eastward to Biloxi Bay from the Mississippi. The drawings of these Indians in the sand gave Iberville a fair idea of the great Mississippi delta — a vast sopping bog of sand and mud a hundred miles and more square through which the Mississippi flowed to the gulf in three main tropical channels, and through a thousand bayous.

On February 27, 1699, Iberville, Bienville and some forty Canadians left Ship Island to find the delta entrance of the Mississippi River (see the accompanying map). Each of their two *traversiers* had a birch-bark canoe in tow. The weather was bad, the skies leaden or rent with thunder and lightning, the warmish head winds laced with torrential rain. For days the sailboats and their canoes wallowed south through heavy seas along the bow-shaped Chandeleur Archipelago on a course designed to intercept the delta's tip projecting southeast from the mainland. On the afternoon of March 2, the tip appeared out of the mist with frightening unexpectedness. Iberville, peering over the canvas that protected him from the waves, saw that he was about to smash into a dark and "rocky" headland dead ahead (his "rocks" were the mud lumps that even today are found at the entrance of the short

North Pass segment of Pass a Loutre). Of his effort to dodge the headland and, failing that, to land on it, he wrote later:

Having held the southeast course for three hours to double a rocky point, night coming on and the foul weather continuing, so that we could not endure without going to the shore for the night, or we would perish at sea, I bore up toward the rocks in order to run ashore in daylight, to save my men and longboats. When drawing near the rocks to take shelter, I became aware of a river. I passed between two of the rocks, in twelve feet of water, the seas quite heavy. When we got close to the rocks, I found fresh water with a very strong current.

La Salle's fresh water *"toute bourbeuse et blanche!"*

So Iberville and his Canadians became the first men of record to enter the world's longest river from the Gulf of Mexico, though by the pure accident of necessity rather than by skill. Nobody cared about that. The waveless, windless peace within North Pass, where they spent the night after four days of dread and misery, was delicious, and so were the ducks they ate for supper. In the clearing morning, March 3, they sailed and oared the two boats upstream through the placid shallow water at Head of Passes. They could not find La Salle's discovery column, but Father Douay remembered that it was Shrove Tuesday and he led the men in singing a grateful Te Deum. Then he blessed the traditional French feast of Mardi Gras that followed, though the explorers had no fat ox to gorge on in proper preparation for Ash Wednesday and the abstinence of Lent. Of course they could not foresee that their feast would become the inspiration for Mobile's Mardi Gras and then, later, the more celebrated New Orleans Mardi Gras, with fat oxen beyond counting, and gay weeks of parades and dancing in the streets.

The forty men continued up the deepening river as the low banks narrowed from a mile apart to half a mile and trees replaced the rushes and reeds. They found an Indian guide at a big curve (English Turn) short of the great crescent of higher ground that would hold a beflowered metropolis, New Orleans. The guide showed Iberville the short portage from the crescent to Lake Pontchartrain (Bayou St. John) and explained how a Mississippi bayou upstream (Manchac) led to Lake Maurepas, which ran into Pontchartrain and Lake Borgne and so to Mississippi Sound and his Ship Island anchorage. Above the New Orleans crescent the men came upon the village of the Bayogoulas hunters that they had met at Biloxi. It was

This photograph of how the misty entrance to Southwest Pass looks from the air suggests the magnitude of Iberville's problem of finding a way into the Mississippi from the Gulf of Mexico. (Photo by Gasquet; courtesy of the State of Louisiana, Department of Commerce and Industry)

near Manchac Point below present Baton Rouge that they saw on the east bank a boundary marker between the territory of the Bayogoulas and that of the Houma Indians upstream — a pole stained with red (Iberville called it a *baton rouge*) and adorned with fish and bear heads. Perhaps the Canadians felt a touch of comfort here knowing that friends from Montreal had stood where they stood when Iberville found a Bayogoula chief wearing a blue French army coat that Henri de Tonty had given to him; and more comfort when a chief produced a letter dated April 20, 1686, that Tonty had asked him to deliver to the missing La Salle if he should turn up.

The Canadians watched the muddy Mississippi rise rapidly in mid-March as the snows began to melt in the north. The Manchac land about them glowed with the colors of tropical spring but the heat was oppressive to men used to freezing on Hudson Bay. Their sailboats continued north past Profit Island, False River and the Houma village near present Tunica, Louisiana. The commander was looking for La Salle's "second channel" of the river — the rumored channel that was actually the Atchafalaya branch of the Red. He gave up the search short of the Red and had his men back at Bayou Manchac on March 23.

Here Iberville showed his style as the reckless *coureur de bois*, drawn to danger by curiosity and lust for adventure. He instructed Bienville and most of the crew to return downstream and on to Ship Island in the sailboats by way of North Pass while he and four voyageurs paddled the birch-bark canoes up the tanglewood twistings of Bayou Manchac to see if it really was a short cut to Mississippi Sound. They had an Indian guide, but he deserted them. They paddled and pushed and carried the canoes on due east through the jungle cluttered with fallen trees and brush and marshes, trying not to step on alligators and even eating one as a change from their guinea-hen diet. Somehow they came to Amite River, and the rest was easy going across Lake Maurepas, Pontchartrain and Borgne. On March 31, they arrived back at Mississippi Sound and the *Badine* off Ship Island. Bienville and the others came up a few hours later in the sailboats from the mouth of the Mississippi.

The expedition's supplies at Ship Island were running low. Before sailing for France to replenish them, Iberville put his buccaneer colonists on the Biloxi shore under the command of Bienville and a family friend, Sauvole de la Villantray. He left with them some cows, pigs and a bull, and instructed them to clear land for crops and to build Fort Maurepas on a bluff of Biloxi Bay where Ocean Springs is now. He wrote a report for Pontchartrain recommending La Salle's plan for the great valley in full — colonization, a string of river forts to hold back the English, and the forging of Indian alliances. He urged the founding of missions and the development of raw materials — tobacco, indigo, rice, wheat, buffalo hides, metals. But even as he wrote he was aware of problems. The mouths of the Mississippi were extraordinarily shallow from the gulf up to and a bit beyond Head of Passes. He had found the depth of the water to be even shallower through the bypass routes to the river from the gulf at Mississippi Sound by way of Lake Pontchartrain. As things stood, it would be futile to try to set up a colony on the Mississippi right away because the skippers of seagoing ships would not want to risk using these shallow entrances to supply them.[7]

On May 3, 1699, Iberville headed his frigates *Badine* and *Marin* east from Biloxi and sailed for France. He and his crews disembarked at Rochefort two months later. Not long after his departure, the gulls and egrets at Head of Passes observed a different brand of Europeans moving up the Mississippi. Captain Lewis Banks and a few hopeful French Huguenots had arrived from the Carolinas at last in a small sloop of war to claim and colonize the country for England and an ambitious London speculator, one Dr. Daniel Coxe.[8] As it happened, Jean-Baptiste de Bienville had just finished examining Bayou St. John from Lake Pontchartrain and was floating downstream in his sailboat. Suddenly, rounding the big curve below present New Orleans, he saw the Banks sloop ahead. He drew up to it and a conference was arranged. The Frenchman and the Englishman knew of each other, since Banks had skirmished with Iberville in Hudson Bay some years before. They had a cordial or, at least, a polite talk. Banks explained his claiming mission. Bienville replied that Banks was too late to claim anything because La Salle, Tonty, Iberville, Marquette and hordes of other Frenchmen had staked out the Mississippi for Louis XIV from end to end. Banks made a few mild threats and counterclaims between sips of Bienville's brandy and then turned his sloop about and disappeared southward around English Turn. And so a Mississippi landmark got its name and an international crisis ended.[9]

Back at Versailles, Iberville found himself regarded as a national celebrity. People compared him to Spain's legendary hero by calling him "Le Cid du Canada." The king created at his request the royal colony of Louisiana and bestowed on him that supreme military honor, the Cross of St. Louis. The award recognized his work of ending the mystery of the mouth of the Mississippi, smashing the Spanish monopoly on the Gulf of Mexico, and claiming for France some seven hundred miles of coast from Mobile Bay west to Matagorda Bay. But Iberville was more than ever convinced that there was little hope for the immediate development of his plans for Louisiana. A new war was imminent in Europe. Count Pontchartrain could not give him sufficient funds to recruit colonists for Mississippi Sound and to supply those that he had already.

He returned to Louisiana briefly in the winter of 1700 and again in 1702, carrying impractical suggestions, which he ignored, from Pontchartrain's "experts" for setting up pearl fisheries at Biloxi and domesticating buffalo along the Mississippi.[10] His health was deteriorating. The splendid physique that had thrived on Hudson Bay could not endure the miasmatic airs of the hot bayous. He was leaning more and more on his brother Bienville in trying to improve the conditions of his starving colonists. But he got some things done, anticipating war with England. He shifted his provincial headquarters from the hot sands of Biloxi to Mobile Bay with its deep harbor off Dauphin Island. He put an imposing Fort Louis where the city of Mobile is now and moved most of his Biloxi colonists to a settlement near it. Though Mobile Bay was two hundred miles east of the Mississippi it was a good spot for trade with the Choctaw Indians, whom he counted on to block Englishmen trying to push down the Alabama River to the gulf from the Carolinas. He improved relations with the Mississippi Indians and he built a small blockhouse, Fort de la Boulaye, on the east bank of the Mississippi near present Phoenix, twenty-five miles below English Turn.

The War of the Spanish Succession began on May 4, 1702. The king commanded Iberville to put his Louisiana work aside and resume buccaneering as head of a French flotilla harassing the English in the Caribbean and along the Carolina coast. He had some naval victories and made dramatic plans for seizing New York and Boston. But it was all derring-do in a lost cause. He had no real support from the weary, gloomy Louis XIV, who had lost touch with reality in his old age. Though the king continued to give three glittering balls at Versailles each week, his comptroller was unable often to meet the payrolls of his fighting men, including Iberville's buccaneers.

In July, 1706, on his warship in Havana Bay, Pierre Le Moyne, sieur d'Iberville, died of a fever, at the age of forty-four — dull anticlimax to illustrious days. When news of his death reached France, his brother Le Moyne de Bienville, still in his twenties, was named by the king to carry on as governor of that troublesome province of Louisiana.

6

Chaos in Paradise

JEAN BAPTISTE LE MOYNE DE BIENVILLE had none of the flamboyance of Le Cid du Canada but he was an honest, perceptive and energetic administrator and he saw as clearly as La Salle and Iberville had seen that France had no future in North America if she failed to colonize that heartland of the continent, Louisiana. Population figures alone showed what had to be done to keep it and to make it an economic and social asset. There were 350,000 Englishmen settled along the Atlantic. France had fewer than 15,000 people in all of North America, most of them engaged in the Great Lakes fur trade or in short-season farming along a narrow belt of land bordering the St. Lawrence.

As the eighteenth century got under way, Bienville was aware of obstacles in his efforts to organize the chaotic new province that he was supposed to govern, and to relate it commercially to Canada and French islands in the West Indies. Many Frenchmen did not want Louisiana to be related. French suppliers of Irish beef to Santo Domingo dreaded the thought that Bienville might try to flood the West Indies with Louisiana buffalo beef. The Montrealers feared the potential of the great river more than ever as a rival to the St. Lawrence, and opposed Bienville bitterly in Versailles. Bienville's Mobile colony was absurdly small — eighty Europeans at most, plus a number of black slaves. He had no military force to speak of. He did not even know precisely where Louisiana ended and Canada began, though he assumed that his provincial jurisdiction ran from

None of the French pioneers tried harder than Jean-Baptiste Le Moyne de Bienville to make a success of Louisiana. He spent forty-four years at it. (Courtesy of Tutt Library, Colorado College)

Mobile and Lake Pontchartrain up the Mississippi a thousand miles to Henri de Tonty's Illinois country, and that it included La Salle's claim of East Texas from Matagorda Bay to the Red River. He presumed too that the Mississippi drainage ran no further west to its height of land near Spanish New Mexico and the South Sea than it ran east to the Appalachians — perhaps five hundred miles. The west drainage would be woodland like the east drainage to the crest of the Appalachians and would have a similar climate and rainfall. The westering rivers — the Red, Arkansas, Missouri, St. Pierre (Minnesota) — would follow the eastern pattern and would be about the same length as the Ohio.

Bienville longed to explore these western rivers, to find that still-alluring shortcut to China, to begin trade with Spanish Mexico, at both Santa Fe somewhere out there in the west and Monclova in the Mexican south. But nothing could be done while the War of the Spanish Succession was sopping up nearly everybody's money, royal and private. This lack of money was all the more frustrating because public interest in Louisiana had never been higher. Not since Marco Polo's trips to the spice-fragrant land of Kublai Khan had Europeans been so captivated by tales of a new paradise on earth where climate and scene conspired to bring joy to the spirit and health to the body, and where wealth was won merely by stooping and picking up the gold.

As we have noted, this fascination with the Mississippi basin as a new romantic environment began in the 1670's, when Pierre Esprit Radisson wrote his book about the wonderful things that he had found west of Lake Michigan. Father Hennepin's vivid *Description de la Louisiane* in 1683 filled countless readers with a longing to take off their clothes and wigs and live with an American Indian for a while. Hennepin's later book, *Nouvelle Découverte* (1697), that masterpiece of self-glorifying fiction about how he discovered the Mississippi delta two years before La Salle, brought the great valley throughout its length to worldwide attention. Also, this book showed budding authors how to get rich and famous by pretending to go somewhere new in Louisiana.

One such budding author was Louis-Armand, Baron de Lahontan. The cynical young baron found in Hennepin's technique a device to increase the sale of his own *New Voyages of North America*, which he at last got published in The Hague in 1703 after working on it for ten years while in exile. *New Voyages of North America*, you recall, slyly castigated Louis

XIV's regime by contrasting its futility with the idyllic life of his Huron Indian hero, Adario. One cannot read the series of "letters" that make up the book without concluding that the coming revolt of Voltaire and Diderot and Jean-Jacques Rousseau and the rest — the great intellectual rebellion that brought on the French Revolution — began with the thoughts of this perceptive youngster as he considered the evils of the Sun King's tired tyranny against a background of the freshness and freedom that he found in the American wilderness.

For his sixteenth "letter," Lahontan imitated Hennepin in presenting as fact an invented adventure story. It told how he left Père Marquette's old post at Michilimackinac with a few soldiers and Fox Indian guides on September 24, 1688, reached the Mississippi via the Fox-Wisconsin portage, ascended the river two hundred miles to the mouth of what he called the "Long River," and paddled up it westward for seven hundred miles, which would have put him — in fable, at least — near the Black Hills of South Dakota. Then he returned down the "Long River" to the Mississippi, floated down it to the Ohio, and got back to Michilimackinac via the Illinois on May 22, 1689 — a five-thousand-mile jaunt in five months. The baron's "Long River" resembles the Rivière St. Pierre (Minnesota) of Pierre Le Sueur, whom Lahontan had known at Michilimackinac. The Indian tribes that Lahontan described on the "Long River" — the imaginary Eckeres, Esanapes, Gnacsitares — seem to have been constructed from garbled bits of data about the western Sioux, Pawnees, Crows, Mandans and so on that Le Sueur and other traders had gleaned from sign-language talks with Indian clients at their Upper Mississippi posts. Lahontan accompanied his yarn with hints of the foolishness of European politics that remind one of Swift's *Gulliver's Travels* (1726).

And still, that sixteenth "letter" was based on fact — all the facts that anybody knew in 1688 about the northern part of French Louisiana. "Long River" derived from the yearning of traders for a stream that would unlock for them the secrets of the further west — a river that would become a reality in a few more decades as the Missouri. In describing the Great Salt Lake beyond the "Long River," the baron put it roughly in its proper position. He stated that the Spaniards of New Mexico had their Santa Fe capital some seven hundred miles from what he projected as his furthest westward advance (the Black Hills), and that was about right, too.

When Lahontan's *New Voyages of North America* appeared in 1703,

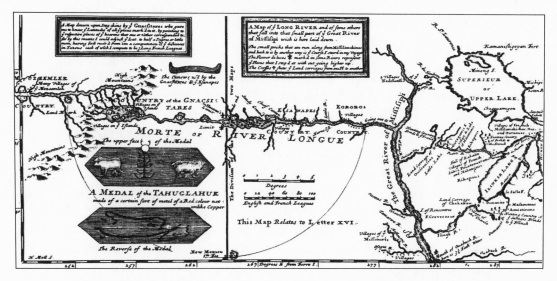

*Though the Long River was pure invention, Lahontan's map of it showed
that by 1700 Europeans were becoming aware of the vastness of the land
west of the Mississippi. (From Lahontan's* New Voyages to North America)

the comte de Pontchartrain was displeased because he saw that its popularity in Paris, London and elsewhere was due partly to its criticism of his sacrosanct monarch. Perhaps the count hoped to counteract the book's acclaim by promoting a far more preposterous adventure story that was dictated to him by an illiterate marine from Brest named Mathieu Sâgean. This marine claimed to have been born at Lachine near Montreal and to have worked for La Salle at Starved Rock on the Illinois. In the mid-1680's, Sâgean said, Henri de Tonty had permitted him and eleven other Frenchmen to paddle up the Mississippi on a more extensive mission of discovery than Hennepin's had been. Above the Falls of St. Anthony across a low divide near present Brainerd, Minnesota, Sâgean claimed to have found a stream much like Lahontan's "Long River," only it flowed south-southwest toward the South Sea — in effect a Northwest Passage at last! The Sâgean party descended this fictitious waterway some four hundred and fifty miles while their lives became just one wonder after another. Here was the land of the Acanibas governed by King Hagaren and an army of one hundred thousand men. Hagaren, Sâgean told Pontchartrain, was a great-great-great grandson of Montezuma II, the Aztec emperor of Mexico. The Acanibas were highly civilized polygamists who wore beautiful clothes made from the

97

hides of people they disliked. They had huge ears, inch-long fingernails and heads narrowed by pressure in infancy. The royal palace was full of gold idols, one of which had a gleaming garnet in his mouth as large as a goose egg. A gold female idol sat astride a golden unicorn which had a six-foot gold horn protruding from its forehead. The royal apartment was built and paved with gold bricks and the king took a new wife every day. To comfort his forlorn discarded wives, Hagaren awarded them as prizes to the winners of the army's weekly bow-and-arrow contests. The Acanibas, Sâgean added, sent their surplus gold to the Orient every six months in a caravan of three thousand oxen, receiving iron and steel in exchange. Sâgean told Pontchartrain that he did not know whether the gold caravans went all the way by land to the Orient, or whether the gold was transferred to ships at some mysterious port on the South Sea reached by his version of the Northwest Passage.

In constructing his fable, Sâgean included in it, by design or by accident, everything that Louis XIV had hoped that La Salle would find in Louisiana — easy wealth, a route to China, a promising trade potential. It was the fable of the Spanish confidence man, Count Peñalosa, all over again, only much embellished. To stress his faith in it, Pontchartrain shipped the plausible marine off to Mobile and recommended that Bienville use him as a guide to King Hagaren's golden kingdom so that Bienville could map the China passage. But Sâgean's reception at Mobile was not warm. Bienville was interested in getting colonists and soldiers primarily. And he remembered Sâgean's tall tales earlier in Montreal and knew that the marine was not a native of Lachine and that he had never got west of Lake Ontario. For Bienville's benefit, Sâgean shifted his south-southwest flowing river to the more believable Missouri, but Bienville remained skeptical and refused to set out to find King Hagaren's domain. After some weeks, Sâgean faded from the Mobile scene.

To Bienville, Sâgean was just one more time-wasting incident in the hopeless interlude of the War of the Spanish Succession. The war was only a symptom, not the root of his Louisiana problem. The root was the same old root that had defeated La Salle — Louis XIV and the centralized government that he had brought to a peak of theoretical perfection. And yet the Sun King was not a foolish monarch. In some ways he was a great one, as any visitor looking on his works today in France can see. But circumstances, often the result of the King's prodigious ego, kept pushing him into blunders. He could not resist war for war's sake. The colossal extravagance of the palace at Versailles was a blunder that he thought was necessary to enhance the image of his absolute power at home and abroad. It seems probable that if he had spent one twentieth of the cost of the upkeep of Versailles to encourage French colonization in America, the Mississippi would be a French river now and St. Louis — sidewalk cafés and all — would be the capital of an immense French empire.

In his management of his American real estate, Louis XIV continued to misunderstand the colonial process, the need to promote initiative, flexibility, freedom to solve local problems instead of dictating solutions from Versailles. His revocation of the Edict of Nantes in 1685 was a ghastly mistake, depriving French Protestants of the religious liberties that they had enjoyed since 1598. Those Huguenots who escaped the honor of his persecution fled to England and to Prussia, to Switzerland and the Carolinas — some 400,000 of them. The king banned them from La Nouvelle-France when just such large quantities of enterprising men were needed to hold the balance against the populous English on the Atlantic and the Spanish pressing north from the Rio Grande. Worst of all, Louis XIV permitted his government to slide into a blind and mindless tyranny, as oversized bureaucracies tend to do before revolution destroys them, as it would destroy the Bourbon government under his great-great-great grandson, Louis XVI, in 1789.

Through the long War of the Spanish Succession (1702–1713) Governor Bienville could only do his best to keep his colonists at Biloxi and Mobile from starving to death. He was at odds often with Catholic priests who came down from Canada to convert the Indians, and with spies from Versailles eager to catch him doing something wrong. Most of the capable French Canadians who were with him at the start wandered off in disgust to Spanish Pensacola and Santo Domingo, or joined Indian tribes to trade and take Indian wives. He could not induce the ex-pirates and Paris riffraff who remained in his tiny settlements to learn how to grow crops or to build houses or to do anything else to support themselves. They argued that the home government had sent them there and was obliged to support them. But the home government was hard put to support itself. Minister of Marine and Colonies Pontchartrain could not afford to keep his royal ships seaworthy. Even if one of them survived the voyage from France to Mobile with a cargo of food and recruits, the food was usually spoiled and the recruits dying or dead of disease.

Bienville was grateful to have the old reliable Henri de Tonty to help him at times during Tonty's visits to Mobile from his Illinois trading post on Lake Peoria. The acting governor of Louisiana (Bienville became governor after Iberville's death in 1706) could rely also on a relative of Iberville's wife, an adventurous young Canadian ex-soldier named Louis Juchereau de St. Denis. Bienville took St. Denis with him when he made improvements on the Bayou St. John shortcut portage from Lake Pontchartrain to the Mississippi for use as a commercial route for pirogues and canoes from the river to the open gulf at Mississippi Sound and to Mobile Bay. With Tonty as their guide, Bienville and St. Denis explored the Red River to a point near present Natchitoches. They passed the gulf-bound Atchafalaya division of the Red River on the way, clearing up once and for all La Salle's mistaken belief that a second channel of the Mississippi existed. Above Natchitoches their progress was blocked by the almost solid jam of driftwood known later as "The Great Raft," that extended for one hundred and sixty miles through present Shreveport to the Texarkana area. For three years, St. Denis served at Iberville's Fort de la Boulaye guarding the Mississippi passes below English Turn, but Bienville recalled him to Mobile when no enemy ships, Spanish or English, showed a desire to risk trouble in the shallows of the delta passes.

In 1702, Tonty conducted trade talks for Bienville with the Choctaw and Chickasaw Indians above Mobile and he was on hand two years later when the male colonists of the town celebrated the arrival of a ship from France carrying twenty "King's girls" escorted by a "directress" and billed as "marriageable" and "nurtured in virtue and piety, and accustomed to work." According to Francis Parkman, the "directress" was looking for a husband too, and thought that she had found a good one, Major Pierre Dugué de Boisbriant, the military commander for Louisiana, who was stationed at Mobile's Fort Louis. When Boisbriant, a cousin of Bienville's, refused to be hooked, she wrote Count Pontchartrain that Bienville had dissuaded him and added, "It is clear that M. de Bienville has not the qualities necessary for governing the colony." The "King's girls" had disappointments too, because some of the bachelors complained that they were too ugly to marry.

A sadder result of their arrival was the fact that their ship brought yellow fever to Mobile and Henri de Tonty caught it. The steadfast upholder of La Salle's Louisiana dream died in Mobile on September 6, 1704. The cohesion, such as it was, of the whole Mississippi valley from

Hyacinthe Rigaud's portrait of Louis XIV tells a great deal about royal extravagance during the king's last years. The money spent on his costume would have gone far toward properly financing a French colony in Louisiana. (Courtesy of the Louvre, Paris)

Father Hennepin's Falls of St. Anthony on down to Head of Passes had centered in Tonty's engaging personality, and in the trust he had inspired in the Indians, for nearly two decades after La Salle's death. That cohesion, Bienville came to perceive, derived from something beyond the control of European rulers and European economics. It derived from the complex workings of the huge Louisiana territory itself. At times, Versailles officials seemed aware of this intangible power and its separatist potential when they suspected that their explorers — La Salle, Duluth, Iberville, Bienville — had plans to organize the Indians into Louisiana kingdoms of their own.

Developments in Louisiana were determined mainly by the Indian trade, including the progress of French exploration which had to be financed by it. Perhaps two hundred thousand Indians all told lived in the Mississippi valley. The dozens of tribes had warred against one another long before the Europeans came — Iroquois against the Illinois, Miamis against Ottawas, Fox and Chippewas against the Issati and western Sioux, Sioux against Crees and Assiniboines of Lake Superior, Arkansas Quapaws against Houmas, Choctaws against Chickasaws. After 1700, the warring was greatly intensified as the dependency of the tribes on European goods increased. War and trade became complementary compulsions. To get more guns, ammunition, hardware, beads, rum and brandy, each tribe enlarged its production of furs, hides, ornaments and food products, trespassing on the lands of other tribes to do so. Each tribe fought for trade advantages and did its best to please the French traders of the magic wares. Some of these traders — men like Tonty and Pierre Le Sueur — risked their lives to compose differences between the jealous tribes. Many tribes maintained relations also with those official foes of the French, the English traders, who reigned on Hudson Bay, slipped into the Great Lakes from Fort Albany on the Hudson, and filtered in small numbers across the Appalachians all along the line from Pennsylvania south to the Alabama River.

This English seepage westward toward the Mississippi was nothing new. Such adventurers probably reached tributaries of the Ohio River as early as 1654, financed by the English trader Abraham Wood from his base at Fort Henry on the Appomattox River in Virginia. Wood's explorers may have ascended the James or Roanoke rivers cutting through the Blue Ridge to reach the ridge of the Alleghenies and down the New River and the Kanawha leading to the Ohio. In 1669, the governor of Virginia, Sir William Berkeley, hired a German physician named John Lederer to report on what

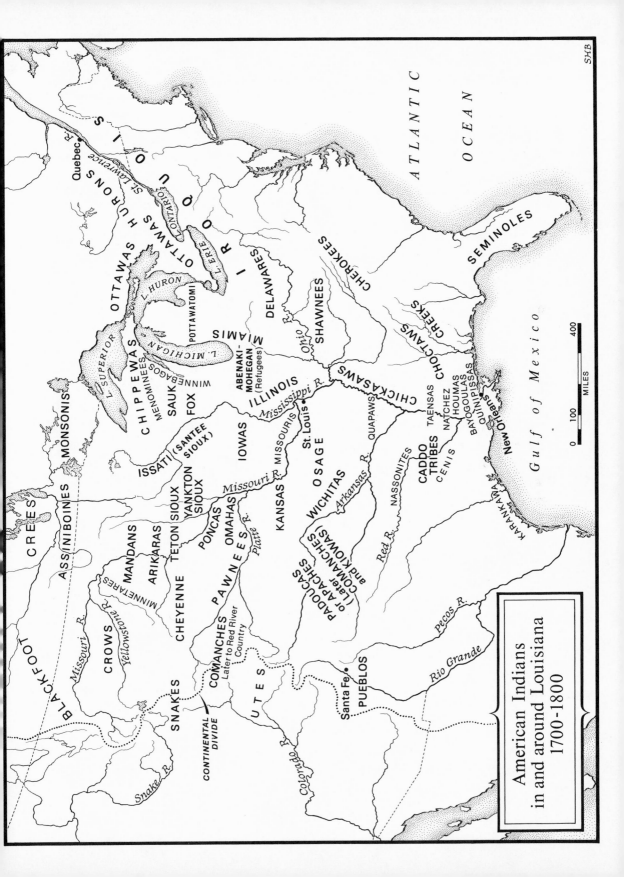

American Indians
in and around Louisiana
1700-1800

lay west of the Blue Ridge. Lederer is said to have ascended the Rappahannock and to have seen the Shenandoah valley from the lower Manassas Gap
near present Front Royal. Later, Lederer claimed to have gone up the James
River and over Goshen Pass north of what is now Lexington, Virginia, to
the Hot Springs area and beyond. He was almost the equal of Father
Hennepin in concocting whoppers. A book based on his adventures, published in 1672, had him cresting the Alleghenies and seeing leopards, lions
and peacocks along the way.

At this same time, Captain Thomas Batts and Robert Fallam are said
to have opened trade with the New River Indians. In 1673, James Needham
and Gabriel Arthur left Fort Henry on the Appomattox and hiked to the
Cherokee Indian country by way of the French Broad River and the Little
Tennessee. Meanwhile, Pennsylvania traders had made it from branches of
the Potomac and Susquehanna rivers to the Monongahela and Allegheny
tributaries of the Ohio. In 1690, Carolina traders from Charleston were
portaging from source waters of the Savannah River to the Hiwassee
branch of the Tennessee. Further south, they probed toward the Mississippi
by skirting the Appalachians through central Georgia and Alabama. As for
the Ohio itself, tradition has it that a Dutchman named Arnout Viele and
eleven companions from Fort Albany crossed Pennsylvania through Wyoming Valley in 1692 to the Allegheny River and on down the Ohio nearly to
its mouth, where they spent some months trading with Shawnee Indians.

Most of this hearsay data suggests that by 1700 the strongest pressure
of English exploration toward the Mississippi was exerted from those points
along the Appalachian frontier with the largest population — that is, the
traders pushed from eastern Pennsylvania to the Pittsburgh area of the Ohio
and from tidewater Virginia to New River and the Kanawha by way of the
James River. The English traders had better and cheaper goods than the
French but the advantage was neutralized by Indian resentment of the
English attitude of racial superiority. Although an Englishman would sleep
with an Indian girl, paying her with a few pins or an awl, it was a physio-
logical, not a social relationship. By contrast, many French traders accepted
the Indians as friends and equals. Their mixed-blood children would evolve
eventually into a special breed — the proud Métis of today's prairie provinces of Canada.

Against these trading realities of Louisiana, French bureaucrats at
Versailles imposed unenforceable rules. The purpose of the rules was to

increase royal revenues, to exclude the English from doing business in La Nouvelle-France, and to keep French settlers tied to the St. Lawrence settlements, where they were supposed to improve the king's property and increase the number of his devoted subjects by raising large families instead of running loose and free in the wilds. Even in Radisson's day, Louis XIV restricted the number of trading permits in Canada so that the *coureurs de bois* would understand that they were working for him and not for themselves. By the turn of the century, evasion of such impractical license restrictions extended even to Quebec officials who were supposed to enforce them. A good deal of the Mississippi River Indian trade had become illicit trade, with Frenchmen and Englishmen working together and conspiring to fix prices.

Much exploration unknown to Governor Bienville at Mobile or any other provincial officer was done by members of this Anglo-French underground. A typical case was that of La Salle's old friend from Rouen, the ex-carpenter Jean Couture, whom Tonty had established at Arkansas Post near the mouth of the Arkansas River in 1686. At first, Couture did business with the Quapaws and Chickasaws, and with a few Englishmen reaching the Mississippi from Carolina posts at Savannah and Charleston. To avoid legal red tape and the interminable route from Arkansas Post north to Montreal via Michilimackinac, Couture developed in the 1690's a route from Arkansas Post up the Mississippi and Ohio to the Tennessee River and up its Holston and French Broad branches. Here in the lovely Blue Ridge area near present Asheville he traded English goods that came from Charleston for the deerskins and beaver pelts of many tribes, including the Shawnees and Cherokees. Then Couture became an Englishman by adoption, working between the Carolinas and Arkansas Post by way of the Tennessee.

The Mississippi trade owed some of its stealthy growth to the fact that the Seneca Iroquois, reduced in numbers by their wars, were relaxing their policy of terrorism to hold the Ohio country. French traders, licensed and unlicensed, were traveling from Lake Erie south up the Maumee River to what would become Fort Miami and down the Wabash to the Ohio and Mississippi past the sites of the soon-to-be-built French posts, Ouiatenon and Vincennes. Bands of Catholic priests followed these traders, seeing the need for new missions on the great river if the plans of Iberville and Bienville for development downstream worked out. Among them were Father

Antoine Davion and Father F. Buisson de St. Cosmé, both from Quebec, who journeyed down below the Arkansas from Michilimackinac to start work among the Houmas, Taensas and Natchez tribes in the summer of 1699. During that same summer, the Seminary of Quebec built its Sulpician Mission of the Holy Family across the river from present St. Louis, calling it Cahokia after the Illinois Indians, who set up their wigwams near the shacks of the traders around it. Three years later, the Jesuit Gabriel Marest founded his Kaskaskia mission and trading post on fertile acres a few miles up the Kaskaskia River from the Mississippi halfway between the mouth of the Missouri and the mouth of the Ohio. Soon the priests, traders and Indians at Kaskaskia turned to farming and the place began to look like a Norman village — the first truly French colonial settlement in La Salle's Louisiana.

The Maumee-Wabash canoe route from Montreal and Lake Erie to the Mississippi was much shorter than the old Lake Michigan routes from Michilimackinac via the Wisconsin or Illinois rivers. Its use, as the Iroquois relaxed their vigilance, ended the need for Fort Buade that Antoine de la Mothe Cadillac had built for Frontenac at Michilimackinac in 1694 to serve as the western hub of the Canadian fur trade. In 1701, Cadillac built a much larger hub, Fort Detroit (Fort Pontchartrain officially), on the Detroit River between Lake Erie and Lake Huron, guarding French trade routes in all directions. Cadillac was a gifted schemer, restless, enterprising, conceited, and possessed of a hatred of Jesuits as deep as that of his friend Count Frontenac. He founded his Detroit fort and village of a hundred settlers and soldiers two centuries before his namesake, the Cadillac Motor Car Company, produced on the same spot in 1903 its first Cadillac, a buggy-shaped, topless, one-cylinder car with kerosene headlamps and a bulb horn.

For the wealthier French fur traders there were ways of getting around the king's license restrictions. Charles Juchereau de St. Denis, a former judge in Montreal and an older brother of Bienville's aide, Louis Juchereau de St. Denis, went to Versailles in 1700 and got permission from Pont-chartrain to set up a tannery for treating buffalo and deer hides at the mouth of the Ohio. The permit did not allow him to do beaver business but specified that he could take along with him eight canoes and twenty-four *voyageurs* who knew all about furs. Charles Juchereau died of fever on the Ohio within a year, and his post died with him. Perhaps he tanned a few

*After 1700, French farmhouses like this one became numerous in the
Illinois part of Louisiana near the villages of Cahokia and Kaskaskia.
(From Justin Winsor's* The Mississippi Basin*)*

buffalo hides while the post lasted and had them rafted a thousand miles
down the Mississippi and across Pontchartrain to Mobile, where no hide
market existed as yet. But the real business of Fort Juchereau was buying
furs from the Mascouten Indians and selling at least some of them to
English traders coming down the Ohio from Pennsylvania and Virginia.

Another visitor at Versailles with more elaborate schemes to avoid
license restrictions was that Upper Mississippi trading kingpin, Pierre Le
Sueur — one of baron de Lahontan's informers and still another kinsman of
Iberville and Bienville. As a business associate, Le Sueur had been watched
closely for illegal trading by the Montreal merchants all through the
Augsburg War period. On one permit-seeking trip to Versailles, he was
captured by the British on the high seas and locked up for the duration. At
last, in 1699, Le Sueur saw Pontchartrain again at Versailles and asked for
a mining, not a fur trading, permit. The Sioux Indians, Le Sueur explained,
had told him about a copper mine near the mouth of a stream flowing into
the Minnesota River a hundred miles above the Minnesota's mouth. The

stream was called Blue Earth River by the Sioux after the mountain of pure copper that was said to rise above it. Le Sueur did not bother to disclose to the king's minister that Blue Earth River had been praised by the Sioux also for its excellent supply of beaver. Pontchartrain called in one of his mining bureaucrats, a man named L'Huillier, received his approval of Le Sueur's project, and issued the permit.

Out of these maneuvers something radically new was to emerge. Anticipating a howl from Montreal that Le Sueur's mine was a cover for fur trading, Pontchartrain told Le Sueur to avoid the St. Lawrence and the Great Lakes in reaching his mine. When Le Sueur asked how that was to be done, Pontchartrain sent him to Pierre d'Iberville, who was in Paris preparing for his second expedition to Biloxi Bay. Iberville saw at once that the Blue Earth scheme was a chance to try something that had never been tried before — not by de Soto or Marquette, La Salle or Tonty. When he left France for Biloxi on his frigate *Renommeé*, he took Le Sueur with him, and also a felucca, a shallow-draft Italian craft that could sail either backwards or forwards. Le Sueur would use the felucca to ascend the Mississippi from the Gulf of Mexico nearly to its source at Blue Earth, thereby testing the feasibility of supplying the proposed French towns and raw-material industries along the twenty-five hundred miles of the river's length directly from the sea instead of from the Great Lakes.

Le Sueur's adventure began in mid-March of 1700, when he headed Iberville's felucca and two canoes loaded with trade goods and twenty-five employees upstream from Lake Pontchartrain. It was a harrowing voyage. The felucca had to be rowed and towed rather than sailed much of the time. Ten miles a day was real progress. But it gave Le Sueur experience in river navigation and a good idea of everything that had occurred on the river since La Salle's death. At Arkansas Post he ran into one of Jean Couture's English traders from the Tennessee. In mid-June above the mouth of the Ohio he and his crew met several Kaskaskia and Cahokia priests. Above the mouth of the Missouri they passed a flotilla of Sioux pursuing their ancient sport of warring on the Illinois. Near the Wisconsin they met five Canadian traders, one of whom had been wounded during a skirmish with some Green Bay Indians intent on tomahawking them and boiling them down for soup. At the river widening called Lake Pepin they passed Nicolas Perrot's abandoned trading post. With the first snow flurries of October, they reached the big terraced bend of the Minnesota River, where the Blue Earth

River flowed into it — the site of today's vegetable metropolis of southwestern Minnesota, Mankato. The golden prairie around them teemed with buffalo. Before the deep snow came, Le Sueur's hunters killed and quartered four hundred buffalo and stored the frozen meat on scaffolds within the stockade that the men built three miles up the Blue Earth River. Le Sueur named it Fort L'Huillier, honoring Count Pontchartrain's bureaucrat.

During that 1700–1701 winter, bands of western Sioux settled around Le Sueur's fort with their tall, conical buffalo-hide tipis, beaver pelts and curiosity. From their sign language, Le Sueur got fragmentary but awesome impressions of what lay in their unknown west — incredible distances, vast high, dry plains, black hills, badlands, huge mountains, strange farming Indians with light skins and roaming Indian tribes. Some of the nomads, Le Sueur learned, were riding Spanish horses that were beginning to reach them in quantity from New Mexico. In the spring, Le Sueur found near the fort the blue ore that he had told Pontchartrain about. He loaded two tons of it on the felucca and set sail down the Mississippi for France seven thousand miles away, leaving half of his men behind to await his return. Besides the legal ore, he carried thirty-six hundred contraband beaver pelts that he disposed of at posts along the river before arriving back in France.

His blue earth, unhappily, turned out to be worthless silicate of iron. Pontchartrain renewed his mine permit anyhow, as a reward for Le Sueur's feat in making it up and down the Mississippi by sailboat. But it took Le Sueur a couple of years in France to raise capital for further mining, and the amount that he was able to raise in wartime was meager. When he returned to Mobile in 1704, he found that his men at Fort L'Huillier had been frightened away from the Blue Earth region when they were caught between bands of Sioux and Fox Indians warring over who would enjoy their trade. At Mobile Le Sueur died of the same yellow fever that had just killed Henri de Tonty. Thereafter, Fort L'Huillier weathered into dust. The Sioux whom Le Sueur had cultivated in the Minnesota country for so long closed their lands and their river to Europeans and made a no-man's-land of the Upper Mississippi above Lake Pepin for more than half a century.[1]

Nevertheless, Le Sueur's pioneer round trip by felucca encouraged other sailors to try to master the endless trickeries of one of the trickiest of waterways — to become, in short, Mississippi River pilots. During the next decade, traffic by canoe, pirogue, raft and buffalo-hide bullboat grew steadily. Watching the growth, Governor Bienville knew that he must give up Mobile and Biloxi soon as ports of entry for Louisiana, and move his provincial capital west a hundred miles or so to that crescent of high ground on the east bank of the Mississippi just above English Turn. As a starter, he began marking a channel on the river through the shallows of North Pass and Pass a Loutre so that craft could ascend the Mississippi directly from the Gulf of Mexico, avoiding the awkward Lake Pontchartrain route from Mississippi Sound. Also, he placed a structure called Fort Balize nine miles up Pass a Loutre as a guide to incoming pilots.

These measures were most timely. Things were beginning to happen far away in Europe that would make them a necessity.

7

⎯✧⎯

Noble Swindler

THE WAR OF THE SPANISH SUCCESSION — with both England and France sick to death of it — came to a virtual halt in 1712, though the Treaty of Utrecht was not signed until 1713. The treaty was the final disaster of Louis XIV's interminable reign. It ended half a century of French dominance in Europe, made the English top dogs on land and sea, and tipped in England's favor the balance of colonial power in North America. One evidence of this was the treaty's assignment to England of Newfoundland and L'Acadie (Nova Scotia), which gave her easy military access to the St. Lawrence and French Quebec.[1] It gave the English Hudson Bay and its unexplored drainage area for the traders of Prince Rupert's Hudson's Bay Company to exploit. By the treaty, the five Iroquois nations were placed under British "protection." To Englishmen, this provision meant that the Ohio country where the Iroquois roamed was British territory, and not part of La Nouvelle-France as determined by La Salle's claim of 1682 to his Louisiana — the total drainage area of the Mississippi including the Ohio valley. The Treaty of Utrecht left French Canada's boundaries with New England as vague as before, a powder-keg irritant leading to the final Anglo-French contest for the continent, the French and Indian War of 1754–1763. The treaty indicated clearly in 1713 what the outcome of that final contest would be.

Louis XIV got little cheer out of the fact that the treaty recognized his grandson as the first Bourbon king of Spain (Philip V) — the succession to the Spanish throne had been the original issue of the war. Neither Philip, Frenchman though he was, nor his adopted subjects showed any interest in sharing Spain's wealth and American colonies with France. On the contrary, Spain seemed more hostile to France than in Captain de León's time, as shown by the renewed vigilance of Spanish soldiers in Mexico who were watching French activities in Louisiana both from Santa Fe in the remote west and from Presidio San Juan Bautista on the Rio Grande. The Sun King was in his seventy-fifth year when he signed the treaty that signified the collapse of his power. The humiliation was too much for him and for France. On September 1, 1715, he died in despair, with the industry and agriculture of his land paralyzed by his almost total bankruptcy. When his funeral procession rumbled through Paris on its way to the Bourbon tombs at Saint-Denis, his rioting, hungry, threadbare subjects danced ahead of it and shouted curses at his coffin instead of throwing flowers.

The king's sole legacy to Louisiana was a gentleman named Antoine Crozat, who typified the disintegration of the monarchy. In those last sad years, one small group of middle-class *bourgeoisie*, the private banking clique, managed to prosper by loaning money to the government at high interest, and by buying royal titles and lucrative offices from the king. Crozat was a ranking member of this clique. The title that he bought gave him the appellation marquis de Châtel. The lucrative office at Versailles was that of Louis XIV's counsellor of state and secretary of the royal household. Crozat's interest in Louisiana arose from the rosy tales of Hennepin, Lahontan and Sâgean, but it was a greedy interest, not Lahontan's romantic yearning for the simple life. Crozat would manage things from Versailles with his cash box, and pay others to do the pioneering.

Minister Pontchartrain paid no heed to the lessons of history. On September 14, 1712, he gave to Crozat the very same sort of private business monopoly that had failed so many times in Canada from Champlain's day on. The whole of Louisiana — from English Carolina to Spanish New Mexico, from the gulf and East Texas north to the Illinois — was turned over to Crozat to run as he pleased for a period of fifteen years. Crozat promised to recruit some colonists but he planned to get back the cost of transporting them to the Mississippi by charging them high prices for rent, supplies and licenses once they reached their paradise. The reported rich mines were his to find and exploit and he was permitted to sell a shipload of black slaves from Guinea in Mobile annually. In return for this vast monopoly, he agreed to give a fifth of his net profits to the king.

Crozat knew that Governor Bienville was not the man to direct his corporation: Bienville's heart was set on colonization for the good of France, not profits for Crozat. Consequently, Crozat had him removed (Bienville was in and out of the governorship four times during the four decades of his Louisiana career). The man that Crozat chose to replace him was that tough-minded and pompous Canadian, Antoine de la Mothe Cadillac. The new governor gave up his job at Fort Detroit and went to work for Crozat at Mobile in 1713. One of his first acts was to hire Louis Juchereau de St. Denis to organize the trading part of Crozat's Louisiana monopoly while he, Cadillac, looked after the mining part.

St. Denis, born near Quebec, raised with Bienville in Montreal, educated in France, was thirty-eight years old by this time, and still a bachelor — an impulsive and colorful man with a record of swashbuckling from Hudson Bay on south. In the thirteen years since his arrival in Louisiana on Iberville's frigate *Renommée*, he had achieved the same high standing among the Caddoan tribes of the Red River country that Tonty had held along the Mississippi. The Illinois Indians had called Tonty "Iron Hand," in friendly reference to the iron hook that he used for a right hand after his grenade accident in Sicily. The Caddoan Indians called St. Denis "Beaux Jambes" because of his shapely legs. St. Denis had encouraged the creation of a French-Spanish trading underground in East Texas similar to the Anglo-French underground in the north. In 1714, he built two small warehouses for Cadillac and Crozat on a Red River island near villages of the Natchitoches Indians. The Spanish port of entry to East Texas was Presidio San Juan Bautista on the Rio Grande, surrounded now by three missions. A midpoint on the trail between them in the area that La Salle had explored before his death was the Nacogdoches Indian village near the Trinity River.

Though Spanish officials in Mexico City and in the northern center of Monclova, Coahuila Province, had strict orders from Madrid to keep Frenchmen out of East Texas, trading went on anyhow, particularly in a new Mexican commodity that was irresistible to the French, horses and mules. A favorable factor for illegal business was the eagerness of Spanish priests for anybody's help, Spanish or French, so that they could resume the East Texas missionary work that they had given up in 1693 when they abandoned the Cenis mission, San Francisco de los Tejas. St. Denis proved to Cadillac, soon after building the warehouses at Natchitoches, that smuggling in East Texas was safe when he made a profitable foray to the Cenis Indians with a load of Crozat's brandy and hardware, laces and linen. Later that same year, he set out from Natchitoches on the Red River to penetrate into Mexico proper along the now-beaten path through East Texas toward Monclova. For transport he used a string of mules — the first pack train of record in the history of the Louisiana–Great Lakes wilderness, where traders were wont to travel on foot if water for boats was not available. One version of St. Denis's trip has it that he asked for guides at a Cenis village. The two savages who applied were light-skinned and responded to his sign language in perfect French. He found that they were La Salle colony survivors — two of the Talon brothers, Jean and Robert, who had worked back to the Cenis via Mobile after being rescued from servitude in the Spanish navy by French pirates off Cuba in 1697.

But this second smuggling trip brought problems. When St. Denis and his companions led the mule string across the shallow Rio Grande and into Presidio San Juan Bautista, they were put into hospitable protective custody by the presidio's commander, Don Diego Escalante de Ramón, himself a smuggler. Not so hospitable was Ramón's seizure of St. Denis's mule string, though the Frenchman understood that he would get the mules back after Ramón disposed of the goods. While awaiting orders from his superior at Monclova, Ramón housed St. Denis in his own home, which was decorated mainly by his beautiful seventeen-year-old granddaughter, Manuela Sánchez. As the months passed, St. Denis compromised his bachelor status by becoming engaged to Manuela. One cannot be sure whether the engagement was caused by St. Denis's love for the girl or by the muskets of two other Ramóns, her father and her uncle, who stood guard in her vicinity protecting her interests.

With the arrival of summer, Commander Ramón was directed to ship St. Denis to Mexico City, where Viceroy de Linares wined and dined him and offered him an army commission instead of punishing him for attempted smuggling. The viceroy, prompted by fear of Crozat's Louisiana activity, felt that the time had come to reassert Spain's claim to East Texas that had been neglected since Captain de León's exploration. He hoped that St. Denis, the East Texas expert, might be tempted to help him. St. Denis declined the army commission but accepted the viceroy's offer of a thousand pesos and a bay horse if he would return to the Rio Grande, marry Manuela Sánchez and escort several groups of Franciscan fathers from Presidio San Juan Bautista to the Trinity River–Nacogdoches country so that they could found new missions and start colonizing East Texas. Spanish colonization, of course, would end French aspirations to own East Texas, but St. Denis viewed the prospect realistically rather than patriotically. Antoine Crozat, after all, was pouring millions of francs into his Louisiana monopoly to make money, not to finance French imperialism. If a Spanish East Texas meant more profits for the Crozat–St. Denis post at Natchitoches, all well and good.

In the spring of 1716, St. Denis returned to the Rio Grande and married Manuela in the approving presence of her armed guard of male relatives. Since Manuela was too pregnant to travel, the bridegroom continued on alone with a large force of Franciscan priests, settlers and soldiers to guide them and to help them select their East Texas mission sites. The significant site — an international matter as it turned out — was the most easterly, where the mission San Miguel de Linares de los Adais would rise within months. The site was fifteen miles from the half-finished compound of palisaded logs on the west bank of the Red River, Fort St. Jean-Baptiste de Natchitoches, that St. Denis's workmen began building during the smuggler's residence in Mexico City. Los Adais was where the trail from Monclova and the Rio Grande presidio crossed the Sabine River–Red River divide. The divide marked the boundary of Louisiana — the total Mississippi drainage — as claimed originally for France by La Salle. The Spanish had never recognized that boundary or La Salle's later boundary either, which he put as far south as the Rio Grande below Matagorda Bay. To them, their most easterly Spanish mission, Los Adais, facing St. Denis's Natchitoches, was but a temporary frontier post until they could occupy all of the North America that the Pope had given to Spain in 1493.

In August, 1716, St. Denis was back in Mobile reporting to Governor Cadillac that he had enjoyed his trip and had acquired a wife and baby but had made no money. Cadillac reported in his turn that he had found a lead mine across the river from Kaskaskia up north, though the lead was not in paying quantities. A hot silver prospect turned out to be salted. But he had high hopes that St. Denis would recoup Crozat's mining losses with one more smuggling trip into East Texas. In the spring, St. Denis left the fort at Natchitoches and had his mules and Crozat's goods seized again by Spanish authorities while he was trying to trade with the Cenis. He took the long trip to Mexico City and protested the new outrage to his friend Viceroy de Linares. But this time the viceroy locked him up in an ordinary jail for some months and then ordered him out of Mexico and East Texas for good. Back at Natchitoches, St. Denis found that it was all over anyway as far as Antoine Crozat was concerned. The banker had just returned his fifteen-year monopoly to the king after enduring only five years of the strange intricacies of business in La Nouvelle-France. As a result of Crozat's withdrawal, Pontchartrain had removed Cadillac and reinstated Bienville as governor of Louisiana. Louis Juchereau de St. Denis was allowed to stay on as permanent commander and discreet smuggler at Fort St. Jean-Baptiste de Natchitoches.[2]

The Crozat monopoly was not a total fiasco because it served to set in motion the one serious effort that France would make to do what La Salle and Iberville had urged her to do — to colonize the Mississippi valley and develop raw-material industries there. It was a wildly colorful if bootless effort led by two remarkable men who brought a few years of flair to the downward course of this later period of Bourbon history, with its burden of bossy mistresses, corrupt royal officials and addlepated monarchs. One of the two men was Philip II, duc d'Orléans. The other was the professional gambler, John Law, a Scotsman. Their effort emerged from the usual baffling destiny-by-progeny process of European politics. Louis XV, the curly-haired "pretty boy," was five years old when he succeeded to the throne of his great-grandfather in 1715. In his will, Louis XIV had named a regency council of fourteen men to rule France until "pretty boy" reached his legal majority at age thirteen. The council would be dominated by Louis XIV's two bastard sons, the duc du Maine and the comte de Toulouse, with the duc d'Orléans as a minor member. The pious French public was enraged by the will since the two bastards were products of Louis XIV's double adultery with Madame de Montespan, and the Sun King had been making a great thing as he neared his end of his love of the Pope and his devotion to the highest virtues of monogamous Catholicism. Furthermore, the duc d'Orléans was the king's nephew, properly birthed, and had a far better right to power than the bastards. And finally, if bastardy helped to determine status, Orléans was high by association because his wife Marie Anne (Mademoiselle de Blois) was the bastard daughter of another mistress of Louis XIV, Louise de la Vallière. Thus supported by popular opinion, Orléans sat at the Parlement of Paris when the king's will came up for its approval, and had himself declared regent even before the will was read. Then he applauded the Parlement's action in annulling the will.

At age forty-two in 1715, Orléans was a brilliant and attractive courtier with a fine record of military service to his country. He was beloved as a gifted patron of the arts and sciences. Louis XIV's absolutism had infuriated him and molded him into another forerunner of the *philosophes* — as liberal and as cynical as the baron de Lahontan. Like Lahontan, he opposed everything that the establishment held to be true — God, Catholicism, the divine right of kings. He flaunted his views by heretical acts such as reading Rabelais in church during mass. He plotted to decentralize the government, as England's constitutional monarch was decentralized, by restoring the power of the French nobility that Richelieu had destroyed in the 1620's. He was a dedicated alcoholic, a zealous gourmet, an ardent gambler, a man of many loves. His mistresses were selected, or at least studied, by his mother, Charlotte Elizabeth, who described them as "good-tempered, indelicate, great eaters and drinkers." They did not have to be raving beauties. When Charlotte Elizabeth complained that some of Orléans's girls were as ugly as a mud fence, her son replied, "*Bah! Maman, dans la nuit tous les chats sont gris,*" a remark Cole Porter paraphrased lyrically in *Kiss Me Kate* two centuries later: "In the dark they are all the same."

Beautiful France, ever so abundant in natural resources, began to recover a little from the excesses of its wretched government the moment that it was relieved of the Sun King and his costly wars. Hoarded gold came out of hiding places and trade resumed with a now friendly England. Orléans had great hopes that Louis XV's empty treasury would fill with all that mineral wealth that Antoine de la Mothe Cadillac was expected to find in Louisiana. The regent was deeply disappointed when Cadillac returned to France empty-handed and Antoine Crozat resigned from his monopoly.

But a new sun was rising on Orléans's horizon. Years earlier, during his Paris visits to play faro at Mademoiselle Duclos's or Poisson's or the Hôtel de Gesvres, Orléans had become an admirer of the suave gambler John Law, who won regularly at faro and imputed his success to his mathematical mind. Law had been raised in Edinburgh and educated by his wealthy father, who was a goldsmith — a trade involving also the manipulation of interest rates and other subtle banking practices. As young Law matured, he became a student of the Bank of England's credit system by day and of lovemaking by night. He might have become a London bank official but he had a duel over a woman and killed a dandy like himself named Edward Wilson. He fled to Amsterdam and for eight years gambled and studied banking in the capitals of Europe. When he met Orléans at Mademoiselle Duclos's in 1708, he described his dream of a new kind of bank, the paper money of which would be sustained not by gold backing but by public confidence. Orléans thought even then of using Law to avert the bankruptcy that threatened Louis XIV for the lack of this very gold that Law said was unnecessary. But the Scotsman's winning ways at faro brought the Paris police down on him and he had to leave town. It was not until 1716 that Orléans, the regent by now, got him back to Paris to test his theory of substituting confidence in paper money for gold.

There was nothing harebrained about Law's scheme. It would seem elementary to today's financiers who work with a world gold supply much too small to back the money and credit needed to keep pace with modern economic growth. As part of his confidence game, Law pioneered the "in union there is strength" principle of the modern conglomerate. One starts a company, merges it with another company, and gets the second company free at the investors' expense by making them confident that the two merged companies are worth four times their unmerged value.

Law's first company was called the Banque générale. It issued its own paper money, one-quarter of which was backed by gold and three-quarters by French government bonds and the regent's word that the bonds were sound. A year later, Orléans transferred Antoine Crozat's Louisiana monopoly to John Law, and so Law had the second company in his conglomerate — the Compagnie d'Occident — known also as the Mississippi Company. He merged this one rapidly with more overseas French companies, including the Canadian fur trade monopoly, the French East India Company, and others in China, Senegal, Santo Domingo and the Barbary states. English officials were so enthralled by his financial magic that they let him have the Virginia tobacco monopoly. Law merged the whole enormous group of companies under the name Compagnie des Indes, which controlled the world trade of France. In 1718, the regent made Law's private Banque générale the government's official Banque royale, a money-printing and credit associate of the Compagnie des Indes. Since the new bank was the receiver of royal taxes Law could add still more bales of paper money to the bales that he had already printed to meet the demand that his promising mergers had created.

The "Mississippi Bubble," or "South Sea Bubble" as history would call it, developed into the most gorgeous swindle of all time. Speculators

Backed by the duc d'Orléans, the Scottish gambler John Law made his Mississippi Company the center of a gigantic confidence game—all with the best of intentions. (Courtesy of Tutt Library, Colorado College)

from the world over poured into Paris and swarmed around Law's offices in the rue Quincampoix, bidding up the value of shares in the Compagnie des Indes — doubled, tripled, quadrupled, to hit a multiple of eighteen to one during the peak period of June, 1719–February, 1720. In the words of Frederick C. Green, "High and low, prince and lackey, grand duchess and kitchen wench fought for possession of the magic scraps of paper which raised their owners overnight from poverty to wealth." Law's coachman made his millions and quit his job. "Clock loans" were common in daily trading for the shares — a quarter per cent per quarter hour. The eight-month frenzy brought the ultimate in conglomerate glory with the merger of the Banque royale and the Compagnie des Indes. When Orléans went on to appoint Law to be comptroller general of France, the erstwhile faro dealer held the wealth of the world's richest kingdom in his pocket.[3]

Law built some confidence in his activities by restoring the faith of Frenchmen in their domestic industry and agriculture. But the main bloom of wild public optimism grew out of his promotion of Louisiana. His first step was to have Governor Bienville's jurisdiction enlarged — at Canada's expense — to include Tonty's Illinois country and that part of the Ohio drainage extending up the Wabash River toward Lake Erie and the Maumee River portage. Then, to investors throughout Europe he distributed maps of his vast river valley showing probable water routes across the continent to or toward China, the location of its easily extractable gold and silver, the fine furs, the buffalo hides, the timber for ships, the mulberry groves where the silk factories would be built. The maps made clear how easy it would be to reach the Mississippi trading area from Sante Fe and other Spanish towns in New Mexico — if not by the baron de Lahontan's "Long River" then by Mathieu Sâgean's route, or by way of the Missouri River.

The busy promoter was obliged by the terms of his monopoly to send six thousand Europeans and three thousand black slaves to sites on the Mississippi granted to him for settlement, sites such as Natchez and the mouth of the Yazoo. By 1720 he had exceeded this emigrant quota. He had no trouble persuading several hundred discontented Alsatians and Palatinate Germans to leave their homes and go to a large tract, surrounding the mouth of the Arkansas, land that Orléans had obtained for Law from Louis XV. Many of Law's French settlers were forced to go to Louisiana by his private police force, an armed bunch of Paris toughs garbed in blue-silver

During much of 1719–1720, the gamblers of Europe flocked to the rue Quincampoix in Paris to buy bits of paper which John Law claimed would bring them the infinite wealth of Louisiana. (A. Humblot engraving; courtesy of Editions Robert Laffont, Paris)

uniforms and three-cornered hats. These men, nicknamed *les bandouliers du Mississippi*, emptied the Paris prisons and orphanages of crooks, prosti-tutes and waifs and sent them in chains to La Rochelle for shipment to Mobile. The results of such colonization were described a decade later by Antoine Prévost in his novel *Manon Lescaut*, about a young woman who endured the process.

Governor Bienville found real benefits for Louisiana from Law's fever-ish promotion. Funds and material arrived at Mobile from the Compagnie des Indes so that he could begin work at last on that string of La Salle–conceived river defenses against English encroachment from the east. Sol-diers in modest numbers were shipped to him from France by the comte de Pontchartrain and by the duc d'Orléans. Fort Rosalie, named for Pontchar-train's wife, was completed by 1717 on the bluff at Natchez above the Mississippi, and so was Fort Toulouse at the Alabama River forks above Mobile. Two years later, Bienville sent his cousin, Pierre Dugué de Boisbriant, a thousand miles upstream to build and to command a large post of logs and earth to serve as military headquarters for all the Illinois-Ohio-Missouri wilderness. The post was named Fort Chartres for Orléans's son, the duc de Chartres. The site chosen by Boisbriant was sixteen miles above the little pioneer French village of Kaskaskia on a grassy flat of the Mississippi's east bank, near present Prairie du Rocher, Illinois. It was only seven miles from the hills across the river where Antoine de la Mothe Cadillac had found lead deposits for Crozat.

Far to the northeast of Chartres, Fort Ouiatenon was built with John Law's funds at the junction of the Wabash and Tippecanoe to guard the route from the mouth of the Ohio to Lake Erie and Fort Detroit. A small trading post that appeared below Fort Ouiatenon would evolve into Vincennes, Indiana. All these Law-inspired developments made inevitable what Bienville had had in mind for two decades — the improvement of shipping channels from the mouth of the Mississippi at Fort Balize to and beyond the "*baton rouge*" boundary of the Bayogoula Indians. The developments made it necessary also to transfer Louisiana's capital from Mobile to Bienville's favored crescent of solid ground above English Turn. The crescent, the governor thought, was the one appropriate place for the great French port that would tie his hinterland to the outside world. In February, 1718, Bienville began plotting that part of the crescent where Jackson Square and the French Quarter are now, and named it La Nouvelle-Orléans, honoring Louis XIV's wayward regent. Four years later the crescent was an unimpressive clutter of reed-roofed huts and warehouses when Bienville moved his government there from Mobile. Time would show that the name was apt, as New Orleans took on the character that the city has to this day — a character very much like the regent — tolerant, uninhibited, hedonistic and charming.

But Governor Bienville's forts, the tiny river villages, the several thousand colonists, the slight increase in river traffic and trade, were pathetic evidences of growth measured against the high hopes of John Law's version of Louisiana, and the billions of francs that people were gambling on its success. And yet Law, nearing fifty years of age now, was something more than just another greedy, power-hungry promoter. Beneath his glittering exterior was a serious mathematician fighting for the triumph of a beloved theory — of fiscal management — and not a bad theory, at that. But he had not figured out how to control the forces that he had set in motion. He had no Federal Reserve to put brakes on credit and the money supply and public optimism. As the year 1720 began, he maintained a brash front, though he knew that runaway inflation was threatening his empire. The collapse of confidence in Louisiana's wealth began when ex-Governor Cadillac returned to Paris and tipped off stockbrokers on the rue Quincampoix that the Mississippi valley had no precious metals, or any other kind of quick wealth, that the river itself was difficult to navigate and that the marvels described by the baron de Lahontan and Sâgean were largely invented. Law's *bandouliers du Mississippi* slapped Cadillac into the Bastille with all possible speed to reflect on the unwisdom of being honest about Louis XV's colonial estate.

But the slide downhill toward financial catastrophe was under way. During the winter, Law tried to shore up the value of his bank notes by putting an embargo on gold and silver. He tried to check inflation by decreeing that the shares of the Compagnie des Indes be sold at half the market price. By midsummer of 1720 speculators were smuggling tons of gold out of France. Fifteen people were killed during riots in the Petit-Champs district near Law's Place Vendôme home as thousands of depositors tried to storm their way into the Banque royale. The end came in December, when Regent Orléans had to appoint a royal commission of inquiry to take charge of the bank and the bankrupt Compagnie des Indes. However, Orléans was able to save his faro partner from arrest and trial for fraud. On December 21, 1720, Law made a dignified exit by stagecoach from France to Holland leaving behind all but a few hundred of the two million francs that he had brought in with him when he had opened his Banque générale in 1716.

Nobody in Europe outside of France seemed to think less of Law because of the bursting of the Mississippi Bubble. He spent the last nine years of his life enjoying the fame of a man who had the genius to achieve a bankruptcy of five hundred and twenty-two million francs. Even the French seemed proud of him when he died in Venice on March 21, 1729. His rhymed epitaph in *Mercure de France* proclaimed his brilliance even if he did "send France to the Poor-house." It read:

> *Ci-gît cet Ecossais célèbre,*
> *Ce calculateur sans égal*
> *Qui, par les règles de l'algèbre,*
> *A mis La France à l'hôpital.*[4]

But the bursting bubble ruined both the power and the engaging personality of Philip II, duc d'Orléans. He turned brooding reactionary in the short period that remained before his regency ended, when Louis XV reached his majority on February 15, 1723. A week later, at the age of fifty-one, he died of apoplexy at the feet of one of his mistresses, the duchesse de Falari.

Orléans was an able and inspiring leader in his heyday. One can argue that his measures in 1715 to restore confidence in the tottering government delayed the French Revolution by three-quarters of a century. For that alone, he deserves to have one of America's most colorful cities named for him on its beflowered crescent above English Turn.

8

The Frustrations of Bienville

DURING THE SHORT LIFE of John Law's Compagnie des Indes, Governor Bienville understood only too well the magnitude of the problems that he faced in his unwieldy province. One problem was the disadvantageous terms of the Treaty of Utrecht. Another was the baffling task of finding an economy that would work in a region too vast and too complex to take orders from a few puny human beings. Hanging over all was that old portent of failure, the contrast between French and English ways of settling in North America. The governor knew that for each French settler on the St. Lawrence and the Mississippi there were still twenty-five English settlers along the Atlantic tidewater — with the ratio rising toward thirty to one. And these figures did not fully explain the English advantage. Most of the English colonists were farmers who were spreading westward along a line of frontier settlements and forts. As the line moved forward, the Indian inhabitants were forced to retreat. The English frontiersmen put the land in working shape for less adventurous farmers who would fill in behind them when they had the urge to sell out and go further west to open new lands.

This process of occupancy accompanied by Indian displacement was in contrast to what Bienville had observed in La Nouvelle-France. There the bulk of the colonists consisted of merchants and farmers occupying a small area — the narrow bottomlands of the St. Lawrence River valley. In addition there were a few hundred traders and priests roving west and south in the manner of La Salle and Marquette and Duluth — men who explored as much as they traded. The explorers buried lead plates by the dozens and held ceremonies claiming vast areas for France from Labrador to Chequamegon Bay, from Kaministiquia to Pass a Loutre. But they had no colonists to speak of to follow them and to uphold their claims. As for the Indians, they regarded the land as theirs still, even though they attended the claiming ceremonies and accepted the French king's presents.

The English settlers, Bienville knew, were belligerently self-reliant, scorning help from their homeland that many of them had left to escape persecution. They scorned also the English rigidity of rank — the once-a-chimney-sweep-always-a-chimney-sweep idea — imposed by the aristocracy, and they had only contempt for the folderol with which these lords embroidered their parliamentary government and their figurehead kings. The English settler was building a new world of his own, run by yeomen in shirt sleeves. His colonial governments, like those in Massachusetts, New York, Pennsylvania and Virginia, were wary of one another, and still more wary of taking orders from the rulers in England.

Bienville saw, on the other hand, that the French settlers were clinging to absolutism, centralized control and the divine right of the Bourbons to manage their affairs. Though life under that decaying system brought them much misery, they knew that they had a chance to be raised by their monarch to high places of power and affluence, as Talon and Colbert, Frontenac and Antoine Crozat, had been raised. With an eye on that intoxicating slim chance, the settlers, notably those of the St. Lawrence merchant class that Bienville's family belonged to, were opportunists, seeking wealth and status by obedience to the king rather than by independent initiative. They looked to Versailles for protection and guidance, and for financial aid, which they seldom got. The ambition of this class was not so much to build a French empire in America as to receive a royal grant of land, the title of "sieur" signifying their rise to pretensions of nobility, and the possibility of winning the Cross of St. Louis in lieu of cash awards that the king could not afford to give.

Even out there in the Canadian wilds, many settlers took the French court for their social ideal, borrowing money on their royal grants to defray the cost of being fashionable. Bienville saw the same shallow pattern emerging in New Orleans with the arrival of John Law's privileged *concessionaires* — favorites to whom Law gave plantation land along the river. A *concessionaire* at Natchez and elsewhere felt obliged to live like a Versailles courtier, and the conditions of that tropical clime led him to use black slaves to do all his work for him. The practice of slavery spread rapidly in the 1720's among all the French colonists on the Lower Mississippi below the Arkansas. The slave population became twice as large as that of the Europeans and had the effect of a debilitating disease, reducing the creative powers and the energy of the French to cope with the problems of their environment. Slaves caused economic problems, too, as they had to be paid for by the sale of crops that never seemed profitable enough.

But these were abstract matters. Bienville was more concerned with current events bearing on the progress of Law's Louisiana monopoly. During 1718, the governor had word from the duc d'Orléans that France was virtually at war with Spain in a squabble over Spanish infractions of the Treaty of Utrecht — the odd little War of the Quadruple Alliance of 1719–1720. This imminent war struck Bienville — and Orléans too — as coming at a propitious time to assert French claims that would put the Spanish out of East Texas and deny them fourteen hundred miles of the shore of the Gulf of Mexico in a great arc from the Rio Grande north and east past the Mississippi delta to Tampa Bay. A special objective for France would be to capture the sole Spanish settlement in that arc, Pensacola, and its fine harbor just across the Perdido River east of Mobile Bay.

La Salle had claimed East Texas for France in 1684 on the grounds that Matagorda Bay was at the mouth of a branch of his Mississippi — a claim that was weakened when Bienville and St. Denis found that the Red River was the last river, the most southern river, in the Mississippi drainage system. France had grounds to claim the Mobile Bay area because of Iberville's colonies at Mobile and Biloxi. She had no valid claim to the gulf shore east of Mobile Bay and the Perdido River short of Pensacola — a shore that the Spanish had explored many times since Ponce de León's discovery of Tampa Bay in 1514.

Bienville had nothing resembling a military force with which to implement his dubious claims but neither did his Spanish opponents in the region. He began his campaign by sending a group of convict colonists from Mobile to occupy St. Joseph Bay a hundred miles east of Pensacola on the Florida coast. They did not stay there long but news of their appearance seems to have reached the Spanish governor in charge of East Texas, Martín de Alarcón. He sent a band of soldiers, settlers and priests from his Rio Grande presidio northward as far as Los Adais to see if Louis Juchereau de St. Denis planned an East Texas invasion from Natchitoches. St. Denis showed no warlike stance, so Alarçón returned south to finish building a tiny Texas settlement, Villa de Bejar, marking the birth of present San Antonio.

When the spring of 1719 came, Bienville's patchwork army, bolstered by French naval forces, captured Pensacola, lost it to a Spanish fleet in August, and retook it in September. The governor spent the winter of 1720 getting control of the place and then sent a ship west to claim Baie St. Bernard — Galveston Bay — for France, believing that that was where La Salle had established his colony. French sailors in 1720 knew no more about the Texas coast than La Salle had known. When they missed Galveston Bay and claimed Matagorda Bay by mistake, Bienville sent out another ship. This second ship entered Galveston Bay on August 25, 1721, and its small crew held rites of French possession.

Bienville's conquests ended in the same kind of futility that Iberville had experienced in his conquest of Hudson Bay. The duc d'Orléans wanted France to own East Texas and Pensacola but he wanted even more to per- suade King Philip V of Spain to give up any claim to the French throne that he might have as Louis XIV's grandson. While Bienville was busy making a French village out of Pensacola, Philip V called an armstice in the War of the Quadruple Alliance and began discussing peace terms with Orléans. The peace talks concluded in November, 1720. Bienville did not learn what the terms were until the summer of 1721, when he was congratulating himself on his Gulf of Mexico conquests for France. The peace terms were a bitter blow to him. In exchange for renouncing his claim to the French throne, King Philip V required that France return Pensacola to Spain and give up all her claims to East Texas and the gulf coast east of Mobile Bay.

And so an obscure treaty settling a purely European matter of royal succession put an end to French expansion south of the Lower Mississippi part of Louisiana. The treaty reaffirmed the custom that the southwestern boundary of the province was on the Red River watershed between Natchi- toches and Los Adais. It implied strongly that the eastern boundary was at the Perdido River between Mobile and Pensacola. Finally, Spain retained most of her hold on the Gulf of Mexico — a strong deterrent to the realiza- tion of La Salle's dream for the free flow of French commerce between the Mississippi valley and the French ports in the West Indies.

Governor Bienville had in his makeup a good deal of his late brother's raging itch to know. At the start of Law's monopoly what Bienville wanted most to know was what lay out there in Louisiana west of the Mississippi beyond the woodland area. The itch became intolerable as more and more news reached him about that strange far west of treeless grasslands where fierce Indian tribes like the Padoucas (Apaches) and Pawnees fought each other as they roamed far and wide on Spanish horses following huge buffalo herds. Several French-Canadian traders had learned from the Indians that long shallow rivers ran down through the plains, flowing from "prodigiously high mountains," their peaks shining with snow in winter and glowing with yellow stone in summer.

The governor longed to bring peace to these Plains Indians and to make friends and customers out of them for John Law. Also he could use their knowledge of that unknown part of Louisiana to help him find a route to Spanish traders in New Mexico. With these ends in mind, he sent out two exploring parties for Law's company during 1719. One party was led by a bantam Parisian named Claude Charles du Tisné, who had won fame in Canada as an Indian fighter even though he was scarcely five feet tall. In 1715, du Tisné developed a technique of exploring along Indian trails by compass, rather than canoeing along streams, while scouting for Governor Cadillac from Mobile Bay north through present Tennessee, Kentucky and Ohio to the Great Lakes. Thereafter, du Tisné directed the building of Fort St. Jean-Baptiste for St. Denis at Natchitoches and served for some months at Fort Rosalie in Natchez.

Accounts vary as to du Tisné's route on his trek for Bienville. According to the most likely (see the map on page 131), his small party pushed up the Missouri looking for Pawnees with whom to do business. At the mouth of the Grand River near Brunswick, Missouri, the men were forced to turn back by an angry band of Missouris because, the Missouris said, the Pawnees were their enemies and would destroy them if du Tisné supplied them with guns. The party retreated downstream and flanked the Missouris on the south by ascending the Osage River to a large Osage village in present Vernon County, Missouri. From here they were directed out of the woodlands to a Pawnee town on the rich Kansas prairie that could have been near the Lindsborg spot where Coronado ended his Quivira journey in 1541. The Pawnees were as disagreeable to du Tisné as the Missouris had been. They proposed to chop off his head because he had come to them from their Osage enemies. Du Tisné urged them brusquely to chop away if they had no use for his trade goods — an act of bravery that impressed the Pawnee chiefs and caused them to call off his murder and to entertain his party by way of apology. However, they denied his request that they lead him to the Padoucas who, they said, refused to let anyone near their Arkansas River domain that stretched for several hundred miles between the Pawnees and the Spanish at Santa Fe. The Frenchmen faced homeward then and reached Fort Chartres on the Mississippi in November, 1719.

To lead his second expedition west, Governor Bienville chose Jean-Baptiste Bénard de La Harpe, a former royal bureaucrat in Brittany. La Harpe had come to Mobile recently, when Law gave him a tract of land on which to put a trading post at the Nassonite village above Natchitoches — the same village that Henri de Tonty had visited in 1689. La Harpe was a rank tenderfoot but he was an experienced reporter with training in cartography and the use of an astrolabe. He left Natchitoches with seven French companions in March, 1719, intending to explore the Red River to its source, which Bienville thought might be near Santa Fe.

The tenderfoot got his canoes safely through the swamps bordering the Great Raft mesh of driftwood choking the Red River above Natchitoches, though alligators splashed about and water moccasins spat at the men from the cypress trees overhead. On April 5, they reached the Caddoan Nassonites (at present Texarkana) and built a post that La Harpe called Fort St. Louis de Carlorette. When his messengers solicited trade with Spaniards in the Trinity River area of Texas to the southwest, the watchful Martín de Alarcón sent word back to him that Spain and France were at war and ordered him out of the Red River country. The order induced La Harpe to decide that this was no time to try to find a route to Santa Fe. Instead he bought twenty-two horses from the Nassonites and led his mounted men and pack train northwest into the lush grasslands of eastern Oklahoma around the west side of the same Ouachita Mountains that Hernando de Soto had found to be so formidable when he reached Caddo Gap on the east side.

Early in September La Harpe came upon a shallow river — probably that wayward and interminable branch of the Arkansas, the Canadian. Strung along the river was a Caddoan Indian community of, La Harpe guessed, six thousand people living in high-domed grass dwellings. The Indians were thrown into ecstasies of wonder by the sight of these pale European creatures and honored them with thirty hours of ceremonial din. When La Harpe withdrew to rest his eardrums, the adoring chiefs went along, painted his face blue, placed an enormous eagle-feather crown on his weary head and plied him with gifts. They told his interpreter tales about

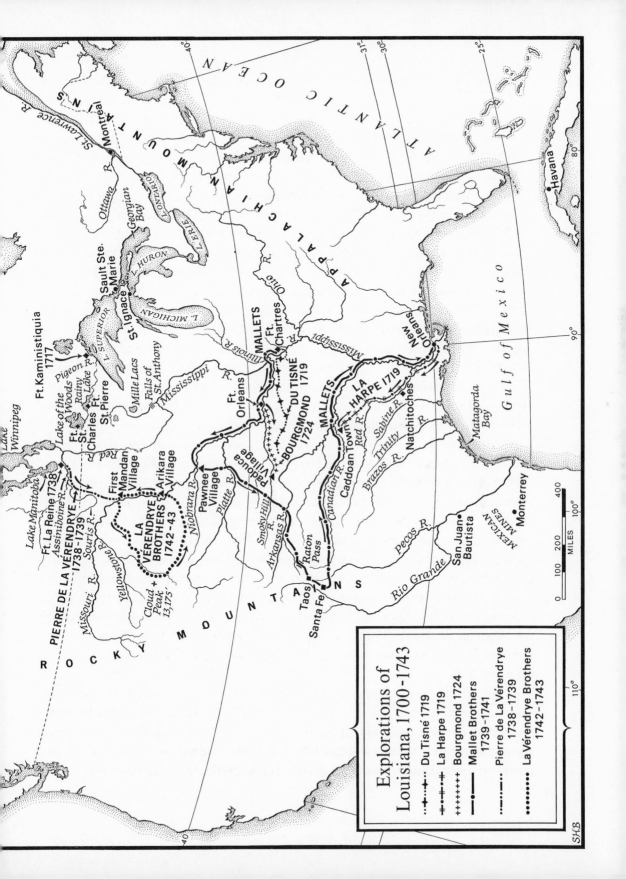

ATLANTIC OCEAN

40° · 35° · 30° · 25° · 80°

APPALACHIAN MOUNTAINS

St Lawrence R.
Montréal
Ottawa R.
L. ONTARIO
Georgian Bay
L. ERIE
L. HURON
Sault Ste. Marie
St. Ignace
L. MICHIGAN
L. SUPERIOR
Ft. Kaministiquia 1717
Pigeon R.
Lake of the Woods
Rainy Lake
Mille Lacs
Falls of St. Anthony
St. Pierre
Ft. St. Charles
Lake Manitoba
Lake Winnipeg

Ft. La Reine 1738
Assiniboine R.
PIERRE DE LA VÉRENDRYE 1738-1739
Souris R.
Red R.
First Mandan Village
Arikara Village
LA VÉRENDRYE BROTHERS 1742-43
Cloud + Peak 13,175'
Niobrara R.
Pawnee Village
Platte R.
Missouri R.
Yellowstone R.

R O C K Y   M O U N T A I N S

Mississippi R.
Illinois R.
Ft. Chartres
MALLETS
DU TISNÉ 1719
BOURGMOND 1724
Ft. Orleans
Padouca Village
MALLETS
LA HARPE 1719
Caddoan Town
Red R.
Sabine R.
Natchitoches
Canadian R.
Trinity R.
Brazos R.
Smoky Hill R.
Arkansas R.
Raton Pass
Taos
Santa Fe
Pecos R.
Rio Grande

New Orleans
Mississippi R.
Gulf of Mexico
Matagorda Bay

San Juan Bautista
Monterrey
MEXICAN MINES

Havana

400 · 300 · 200 · 100 · 0
MILES
110° · 100° · 90°

SHB

Explorations of
Louisiana, 1700-1743

Du Tisné 1719 ·+·+·+·+
La Harpe 1719 ·#·#·#·#
Bourgmond 1724 +++++++
Mallet Brothers 1739-1741 ·|·|·|·|
Pierre de La Vérendrye 1738-1739 ·|·|·|·|
La Vérendrye Brothers 1742-1743 ········

many Plains tribes, including those alluring light-colored Indian farmers on a big river in the north — the Mandans that Pierre Le Sueur had heard about at Fort L'Huillier. They stated that their own river did lead to Santa Fe but that his party could not survive passage through the hostile Padouca tribes guarding the route. Accordingly, when the ceremonies ended, La Harpe said goodbye to his exhausting hosts and led his men back through eastern Oklahoma — more attractive than ever in the crispness of October — to the Nassonites and then to Natchitoches and New Orleans.

The du Tisné and La Harpe journeys did not achieve their goals but they cast some light on Coronado's mysterious Quivira — a domain that France could claim now because her two latest explorers found at least some of it to be part of the drainage basin of the Mississippi. Accounts of their trips convinced Governor Bienville that the Arkansas and Red rivers began at "prodigiously high mountains" in Spanish New Mexico and watered vast southwestern lands that supported myriad buffalo and Indian tribes of incredible mobility through their recent mastery of Spanish horses. Neither river seemed promising to him as a highway for trade. The Red had its Big Raft blocking all watercraft. The Arkansas was shallow and winding and its mouth at the Mississippi was a maze of shifting shoals.

Meanwhile the two trips caused great anxiety in Spanish New Mexico. Exaggerated reports of them persuaded Governor Valverde in Santa Fe that a French army had set up a cannon-equipped fort among the Pawnees in Quivira. The governor was distressed already about Comanche and Ute Indians from the San Luis valley of present Colorado, who were raiding Spanish haciendas between Santa Fe and Taos. Valverde's settlers were too poor to raise forces strong enough to control these nomads. They had to be content to stay on the Upper Rio Grande and to exploit their docile Pueblo Indian slaves. They ventured no further north and east into wild Indian country than the Spanish Peaks of Colorado, Pikes Peak and the Apache community on the Arkansas in sight of these peaks — the community near present La Junta, Colorado, that they called El Cuartelejo, "The Far Quarter."

The military weakness of the Spanish settlers made them timorous and secretive about their affairs on the Upper Rio Grande, and pathologically fearful of French intrusion from the east. That was why they went into a panic during the spring of 1720, when a rumor circulated in Santa Fe that a horde of Frenchmen was poised for attack at the Far Quarter only three hundred miles away. Valverde met the crisis first by consultation about Gallic behavior with a Frenchman on his staff — the same conspiratorial Jean de L'Archevêque who had deserted to the Spanish at Matagorda Bay after La Salle's murder. Then the governor sent out a scouting party of one hundred and four Spaniards and Pueblo Indians plus L'Archevêque — all of them disguised to look like Comanches. They rode over Raton Pass under the leadership of Pedro de Villasur, and down the sandy Upper Arkansas to the Far Quarter. Finding no French army there, Villasur led his men north toward the Pawnee country along the present Colorado-Kansas border. On August 9, 1720, in the cottonwoods between the high banks of the Platte River near present North Platte, Nebraska, they were ambushed by a large band of Pawnee Indians. Villasur and thirty-three of his scouts including L'Archevêque were killed and scalped. The survivors made their way back to Santa Fe. They had to report to Valverde that his men had died for no purpose. Not a single Frenchman had been seen.

Though Bienville's knowledge of Louisiana geography was increasing, he was frustrated by the vast areas of unknown country that remained. He perceived that the prime need was a thorough exploration of the Missouri River — not just a weak thrust like du Tisné's but a major effort to develop a Plains Indian trade and a Santa Fe trade that would pay the cost of following that turbulent stream to its source. Bienville had an old friend who was uniquely qualified for such a project. Etienne Véniard de Bourgmond was one of that special breed of French Canadian, a man as enamored of the wilderness and its people as La Salle and Duluth and Henri de Tonty had been. Like La Salle, he was well educated and came from a prominent Norman family. He had arrived at Montreal in 1706 to make his fortune and went to Fort Detroit as a marine officer while Cadillac was commanding there. He soon displayed a particular talent when he wooed and won the wife of a Detroit civilian named Tichenet and fled with her by canoe down the Detroit River bound for Montreal. The enraged Tichenet and a posse of sympathizers caught up with the lovers on Lake Erie. Bourgmond was court-martialed before Cadillac, though the charge was desertion rather than stealing Tichenet's willing wife. Cadillac acquitted him. Later, Bourgmond deserted the Detroit military again, to follow an Indian girl back to the big village on the Missouri near the mouth of the Grand where her family lived. He named her La Chenette, after the flower

133

called germander in English, and he had a son by her, thus qualifying as one of the first of a long line of western pioneers who took Indian wives and sired their children.

From 1712 to 1718, the lusty ex-marine moved up and down the Missouri as a typical underground trader in illicit furs. He seems to have spent his profits financing adventurous trips far up the river. In 1714, for instance, he reported to Bienville that he had ascended the stream through Pawnee country to a point twelve hundred miles from the Missouri's mouth. That put him at the mouth of a shallow waterway that he named La Rivière du Loup, which may have been the Niobrara, or perhaps the Platte River, the largest branch of which is called the Loup River today. If he got up the Missouri to the Niobrara on the present Nebraska–South Dakota line, he would have been only four hundred miles from the Mandan villages, one of his objectives, though still a long way from the South Sea, which he was looking for also.

In 1719, Bourgmond helped Bienville in his bloodless conquest of Pensacola and then sailed for France to present at Versailles Bienville's views on exploring the Missouri. By the time that Bourgmond got through to the duc d'Orléans, John Law was bankrupt and his creditors had taken over the Compagnie des Indes. Orléans did not want to hear about any more schemes for spending money in his problem province. But suddenly, during the summer of 1721, he changed his mind. A message, dated November 22, 1720, reached him from Commander Boisbriant at Fort Chartres on the Mississippi with the startling news of Villasur's expedition from Santa Fe into Quivira. Though the massacre of Villasur and his men by the Pawnees had occurred a thousand miles west of Fort Chartres, Boisbriant placed it much closer. His message urged the regent to ship Bourgmond from Paris back to Louisiana at once to strengthen ties with the Padoucas and Pawnees and to oppose Spanish penetration of Quivira by building a fort on the Missouri opposite La Chenette's village near the mouth of the Grand.

Orléans saw the point of Boisbriant's warning. He scraped up funds from the reluctant Compagnie des Indes, collected a few bales of gifts for the Indians from the king, and sent the trader on his westering way. Though the funds were meager, Bourgmond was able to complete the construction of what he called Fort Orléans by January, 1724, with the help of his small garrison of soldiers.[1] When June came, he led eight soldiers and a large, gay, noisy crowd of Missouri and Osage Indians upstream, traveling by pirogue, raft and on horseback (their route is shown on the map on page 131). Gifts for the Padoucas were carried on pole litters called "travois" hitched to some three hundred dogs. At the site of present Kansas City, Bourgmond left the Missouri River and followed the Kansas River due west, approximating what would be in another century the caravan route of the Sante Fe Trail from St. Louis. But he was delayed for many weeks when he picked up a fever somewhere. His party did not reach a Padouca settlement until mid-October. The settlement, one of two hundred people, seems to have been on the Smoky Hill Fork of the Republican River near the site of present Ellsworth, Kansas.

It turned into a gala affair, this meeting of Frenchmen so far from home and of Plains Indians most of whom had never seen a European before. The Padouca chief produced the peace pipe and gave several banquets featuring buffalo meat and dried prunes. On October 19, Bourgmond unpacked the king's gifts from his multitude of travois and spread them on the prairie beneath a large French flag for inspection by the villagers. The variety was spectacular — rifles and sabers, axes, blankets, mirrors, knives, scissors, vermilion, awls, needles, bells, beads, rings. The gifts, Bourgmond announced, were theirs if the Padoucas would give their allegiance to the king of France, make peace with the Pawnees and all the other Plains tribes, and help him to set up a trade route to Santa Fe which, he understood, was only a journey of twelve days from where he stood. The Padouca chief agreed to each request, supervised the distribution of the gifts and gave Bourgmond seven horses in exchange for the French flag.

The explorer would have liked to continue to Santa Fe, but the season was late and his fever was still with him. He led his party down the Kansas and Missouri rivers to Fort Orléans, arriving in November, 1724. His plan was to try again to reach Santa Fe during the next summer and he was not pleased to find a letter at the fort from a Versailles official ordering him to bring a delegation of Missouri Indians to Paris "to give them an idea of the might and power of France." The official was young Jean-Frédéric Phélypeaux, comte de Maurepas, who had just succeeded his father, the comte de Pontchartrain, as minister of the marine and colonies. Bourgmond had no confidence in Maurepas's patronizing scheme but his health kept deteriorating and by spring he was glad of the chance to return to civilization.

He chose his Indian delegation with care, though he lost several of them by drowning in a boating accident at New Orleans. The remnant —

two handsome chiefs, a Metchigami and a Kaskaskia, two young Osage warriors, and an enchanting Missouri girl — created a sensation in France beyond the fondest hopes of their escort. Crowds lined the Seine and cheered them on as Bourgmond's flatboat moved up from Le Havre past Rouen and Mantes. The crowds named the Indian maid "the Daughter of the Sun," and they assumed, perhaps correctly, that she was the mistress of the irresistible Bourgmond. In Paris, high society embraced the visitors warmly, being still under the idealizing spell of the baron de Lahontan's Huron philosopher, Adario. The fifteen-year-old Louis XV and the recently widowed duchesse d'Orléans received them at Versailles, dressed them in "gold-embroidered garments" and gave them snuffboxes. Then the king arranged for them to present a war dance at the Opéra and the Théâtre Italien, and sent them hunting for stag in the Bois de Boulogne. Finally, Louis XV had the Daughter of the Sun baptized in Notre-Dame Cathedral and married to Bourgmond's staff sergeant, a man named Dubois. Before sailing for Louisiana, the guests expressed deep gratitude for all these kindnesses, though they told Bourgmond privately that the French army would not last long in their kind of woodland warfare in Missouri and they complained that "the highly perfumed Parisian courtiers smelt like alligators."[2]

They had to go home without their escort. Bourgmond was distressed to find that his health was not improving, though he remained as attractive as ever to a number of eager females, including "a very rich widow." When Louis XV awarded him the Cross of St. Louis and the title of sieur, he took the sensible course. He retired from army duty, married the rich widow and settled down to a life of ease as a gentleman farmer near Paris.

Without Bourgmond's authority and gusto, Fort Orléans could not last long. During 1726, the Indians in the area drove his small garrison of soldiers away, looted the place and destroyed it. As things developed, the demise of Fort Orléans put an end to Governor Bienville's efforts for an expanded trade up the Missouri and for further exploration of the river by way of the Mississippi. Time would show that the fort's fall marked the beginning of the end of Bienville's effectiveness as Louisiana's leader. He could not convince Maurepas that trade on the Missouri and trade with Santa Fe were essential to pay the military cost of holding the Ohio-Illinois-Missouri region. There was, Bienville argued in vain, simply no other market to be developed. Profitable commerce between Canada and the

Mississippi had failed to materialize because La Salle's portages from Lake Michigan to the Illinois remained difficult and English traders contested the Maumee-Wabash passage southward from Lake Erie to the Ohio. Fox Indians blocked traffic from Green Bay on Marquette's Wisconsin River to the Mississippi. Above the Wisconsin, the Upper Mississippi had been closed by the Sioux to Europeans since Nicolas Perrot's time.

A crowning blow to Bienville's colonial plans was the uprising of the Natchez Indians on November 28, 1729. Their complaint was against John Law's *concessionaires*, who had assumed that they could rob the natives of their beautiful bluffs above the Mississippi because of the presence of Fort Rosalie and its officers skilled in brutality. But Rosalie was undermanned. The Natchez warriors overwhelmed the garrison and went on to massacre most of the three hundred colonists. Then they destroyed their plantations of tobacco, the export of which promised to balance the provincial economy. With its tobacco gone, the struggling Compagnie des Indes surrendered its Mississippi monopoly to the king two years later.

Of course Fort Chartres was surviving below the mouth of the Missouri, and so were the two French-Canadian villages, Cahokia and Kaskaskia — forlorn vestiges of high hopes. But mainly all that was left of Louisiana for Bienville to govern through the 1730's until his retirement in 1743 was the New Orleans area westward to Natchitoches and the Mobile Bay region, where his Fort Toulouse soldiers tried to hold back the hostile Chickasaws and their English trader allies. He had time now to attend the baptisms of the delta's first French "creoles," meaning Frenchmen born in a French colony. Many of them were the children of those Paris street girls and pickpockets and paupers who had been shanghaied to Louisiana by Law's *bandouliers du Mississippi*. There was some local growth. The population of the province had risen to two thousand Frenchmen and their three thousand black slaves. The German colonists whom Law had sent to the Arkansas had settled finally on the banks of the Mississippi — "the German coast" — twenty miles or so above New Orleans.[3] Their fine vegetables had become a food staple. Brick and timber cottages had replaced the rude cabins of Bienville's crescent village. Several handsome government buildings embellished the rue de Chartres. But only ten or fifteen ships with trade goods from France and the West Indies came up the delta annually from Head of Passes. Money had no stable value. Serious problems of trade balances and shipping arose because a full cargo of finished products from

France sold at New Orleans was worth four times as much as a full cargo of Louisiana raw materials returning to France. Furthermore, export crops such as lumber and tar, furs, deerskins, rice and indigo were not in dependable supply. Bienville's attempts to grow wheat had failed utterly.

Still, the patient governor refused to give up hope. And the last decade of his long Louisiana service was not all bleakness. There was, in particular, the lift that he got from the remarkable travels of the Mallet brothers, Pierre and Paul.

9

Approach to the Rockies

WHO WERE THE MALLETS? Little is known of their early careers except that they were Frenchmen born in Canada who settled in Henri de Tonty's Illinois country and worked as unlicensed traders operating out of Kaskaskia and Fort Chartres on the Mississippi. In the winter of 1739, the two brothers were seized by a great ambition. They would do on their own what Bourgmond and the other explorers sent by the French government had failed to do. They would find their unauthorized way from Fort Chartres to Santa Fe which, they had been led to believe, lay just across the height of land beyond the source of the Missouri. They persuaded five French-Canadian friends and a "native of France" to come along, loaded their pirogue with supplies and trinkets for the Indians and pushed up the Missouri into the springtime flowering of the Great Plains. They arrived at a Pawnee village near the mouth of the Niobrara in mid-May. (Their route is plotted on the map on page 131.)

The Pawnees told them what they had begun to suspect. They could not reach Spanish New Mexico by pursuing the Missouri's northwesterly course. On May 20, the eight travelers left the pirogue behind, mounted Pawnee horses and headed southwest by compass across the undulating steppes of central Nebraska and western Kansas until they reached a wide, sandy unknown river near the Kansas-Colorado border. Here they found an Indian who knew the way to Santa Fe. He led them along a trail used by Spanish traders up the unknown river through an enchantment of magpies, antelope herds and prairie-dog towns. On a July morning they saw in the clearing mists of sunrise the blood-red spectacle of the Spanish Peaks and the great Sangre de Cristo Range of the Rocky Mountains. The trail took them past the Far Quarter southwest across Raton Pass and over the range by way of Palo Flechado Pass. From Palo Flechado the Mallets rode down to Taos and, on July 22, 1739, to Santa Fe, where the Spanish community of eight hundred families gave a festive welcome to these bronzed, bedraggled, nearly naked visitors from out of the eastern unknown. After they had been properly honored, clothed, wined and dined, Governor Gaspar Domingo de Mendoza detained them hospitably in the Palace of Governors until he could get instructions from his viceroy in Mexico City as to what should be done with them. They seemed harmless enough, but Frenchmen were Frenchmen — age-old enemies of the Crown.

Communications were slow between the two Spanish capitals two thousand miles apart. Meanwhile, one of the guests had his heart cut out "from the back" on Mendoza's order for participating in an Indian revolt. After nine months had passed, word came from the viceroy to release the seven survivors. During their long wait, Pierre and Paul Mallet had talked to many Spanish travelers and had reached certain geographical conclusions. The Rio Grande, they decided, that ran southward near Santa Fe, was the same Rio Grande that Pineda had found emptying into the Gulf of Mexico. The wide, unknown river that they had followed to the Spanish Peaks was the Arkansas. Any stream flowing east from near Santa Fe must be a branch of the Arkansas, or of the Red River, and would lead them in either case to New Orleans eventually.

On May 1, 1740, the Mallet party left Santa Fe by horseback to test the theory. They rode east over La Glorieta Pass as Coronado had ridden, across the south-flowing Pecos and on until they reached a stream flowing definitely eastward — a stream that would be called the Canadian in their honor. They followed this shallow, vagrant stream for months — first through dry, sandy lands and then through the fertile country of eastern Oklahoma. The depth of the river increased in Oklahoma so that they could turn their horses loose and take to canoes that they built of elm bark. At that time, three of the party split off overland bound for their homes in Illinois. The Mallets recognized the Arkansas by its greater size when their Canadian River flowed into it. They floated on down past Arkansas Post to the Mississippi and arrived at New Orleans in March, 1741.

The arrival of these unlicensed explorers was a complete surprise to Governor Bienville, who had never heard of them. And, as he read the journal of their travels, he found all the hopes of his youth for Louisiana flaming once more. Here in the journal were answers to questions of western terrain that had baffled him for forty years. He wrote a report of what the Mallets' discovery of a route to Santa Fe could mean to the cause of more trade for his province and sent it along to Versailles by the first ship sailing for France. While waiting for a reply, the governor sent the Mallets in September, 1741, under a naval officer, Fabry de la Bruyère, to retrace their Santa Fe route. But the Canadian was too shallow to float their canoes that fall and the Mallets returned to their Illinois homes.[1]

Nothing came of Bienville's report until nine years later, when his successor, Pierre de Rigaud, marquis de Vaudreuil, instructed the Mallets to return to Santa Fe up the Canadian to propose to Governor Tomás Vélez Cachupín the exchange of French goods — black slaves and clothing mainly — for Spanish horses and silver. The proposal amounted to smuggling, since trade with Louisiana was officially banned by the Spanish viceroy. The Mallets made it safely to the Pecos River but the old fear of Frenchmen had increased since their last visit. Soldiers seized them at the Pecos for trespassing. Governor Cachupín rejected their "bold and pernicious" proposal, declaring that by its acceptance "the commerce of New Mexico would be ruined and the province of New Orleans made more powerful." For punishment, the Mallets were sent to Spain and jailed for a time as spies.

The failures of du Tisné, La Harpe, Bourgmond and the Mallets to set up trade with Santa Fe brought an end to Bienville's hope of financing further exploration westward along tributaries of the Mississippi. Meanwhile, prospects for discovery were bright in Canada, where the paradoxical fur trade was expanding even as its peculiar nature retarded the colonial development of the St. Lawrence. Ever since 1717 officials had talked of plans to build posts westward from Lake Superior by way of Lac la Pluie (Rainy Lake) and Lac des Bois (Lake of the Woods) to produce more revenue for Louis XV's self-indulgent regime. Everyone knew by now that the richest furs were being harvested by Cree and Assiniboine Indians in regions surrounding Lac Ouinipigon (Winnipeg) beyond Lake Superior and that most of these furs were going to English traders on Hudson Bay.

Actual work on plans to intercept them began in 1726 with the arrival in Quebec of Charles de la Boische, marquis de Beauharnois, as the new governor of Canada. Beauharnois's first step was to send men to build a small Fort Beauharnois near Nicolas Perrot's abandoned Fort St. Antoine at Lake Pepin on the Upper Mississippi. His purpose was to protect his flank south of Lake Superior and the Falls of St. Anthony and to bring that region and its unruly prairie Sioux back into Canada's trading area, as in the days of Duluth and Le Sueur. Then he turned to the matter of pushing west from Poste du Nord (also called Poste de l'Ouest), a collective name for three Lake Superior posts supplied from Montreal by the old Ottawa River route to Michilimackinac and Sault Ste. Marie. The Superior posts were Michipocoton, Nipigon and Kaministiquia, lovely spots on the lake's north shore that carry the same Indian names today. Beauharnois found in command at Fort Kaministiquia two army veterans, Jacques-René Gaultier de Varennes, aged fifty, and his brother, Pierre Gaultier de La Vérendrye, nine years younger. Soon Jacques-René left Poste du Nord to fight the Sac and Fox Indians who were terrorizing the Green Bay area, and then he was ordered to garrison duty in Montreal. His recall left Pierre de La Vérendrye in command at Kaministiquia.

This La Vérendrye, forty-one years old, was the quintessential tough French Canadian, a composite of what a century of surviving the hardships of the St. Lawrence had made out of the original soft product from the bountiful land of Gaul. His father René Gaultier had come to Quebec in 1665 from Angers in the Loire country with the Carignan-Salières regiment. (Louis XIV had sent that famous troop to Canada to subdue the Iroquois and to restore his authority under Talon after Champlain's old Company of New France tottered off the Canadian stage.) When René Gaultier was assigned to the St. Lawrence hatchery of explorers, Trois Rivières, he found time to win the hand of Marie Boucher, the daughter of the pioneer governor there, and then to become a distinguished if not wealthy fur trader, Indian fighter and churchman. The Gaultiers had ten children (Pierre de La Vérendrye, born in 1685, was the youngest) before René died penniless in 1689 leaving Marie with her own brood and a dozen orphans of deceased relatives to feed. She managed it by moving to the outskirts of Montreal, where she had relatives among Iberville's Lemoyne tribe and other first merchant families.

In childhood, young Pierre de La Vérendrye asked for stories from retired *voyageurs* about French-Canadian explorers and their heroic deeds, Duluth's especially. By the age of twelve, when he joined the French army as a cadet, his mind was a storehouse of places and people that he yearned to see out in the western wilds. For sixteen years thereafter the yearning simmered while he fought Louis XIV's dreary, futile wars — three campaigns in New England and Newfoundland and three in Europe. They included the Malplaquet disaster in northern France near the end of the War of the Spanish Succession. He was one of twelve thousand French casualties inflicted at Malplaquet by Marlborough's Englishmen and he spent fifteen months as a prisoner of war recovering — never entirely — from five wounds. At last, in 1712, he made his way back to Canada, married a Montreal girl of some property named Marie-Anne Dandonneau and passed the next fifteen years as a cow-milking farmer with six children to support on a St. Lawrence island called Ile aux Vaches near Trois Rivières. During that monotonous period, the westering dreams of his childhood continued to haunt him. When Governor Beauharnois gave him the chance in 1727 to go to Poste du Nord as a trader and king's ensign, he wasted no time moving his brood to Boucherville, a family suburb of Montreal, and then pointed his canoe up the Ottawa River toward Lake Superior, seeing the road to Cathay ahead of him just as La Salle had seen it from Lachine in 1666.

La Vérendrye was more than middle-aged but his belief that an Asian passage existed out there was as youthfully strong as Jean Nicolet's had been in 1634, when he had donned his flowered robe to greet the "Chinese" at the Green Bay part of Lake Michigan. A colorful myth is hard to kill and gains strength with time as "experts" improve the original rationale. By the 1720's, Paris cartographers were declaring that the "Western Sea" designated an arm of the South Sea (Pacific Ocean). It cut deeply eastward into the North American continent at about the latitude of Golden Gate, just as the Mediterranean cut into Europe from Gibraltar. The Western Sea had to indent that way if men were to keep believing in a China passage despite mounting evidence of the continent's appalling width. A fulsome River of the West was conceived as flowing west some five hundred miles across the plains of Quivira from a salt lake near the Missouri River and the site of present Omaha to empty into the Western Sea on Quivira's west coast in the vicinity of today's Cheyenne, Wyoming. That salt lake source was thought to be near a convenient triple divide where the Mississippi, Missouri and

Rivière Rouge — the Red River of the North — were said to start in head-waters a few miles apart (one such Atlantic–Pacific–Hudson Bay triple divide actually occurs at Triple Divide Peak near St. Mary Lake in Glacier National Park, Montana). And the River of the West probably ran near Santa Fe on the Upper Rio Grande and brought within easy reach those rumored Spanish ports said to be on the Gulf of California and the South Sea. All in all, the mapmakers concocted an attractive west based on mis-interpretations of geographical fact given to men like Le Sueur and de Bourgmond by their Indian customers.[2]

After four years of mulling over these modern ideas at Fort Kaminis-tiquia — plenty of time to mull during the long winters of confinement — La Vérendrye returned to Montreal at Beauharnois's request to prepare for his western adventure, with funds loaned by nine merchant firms. The usual monopoly privileges, in lieu of royal financial help, were given to him by the young comte de Maurepas, the king's minister of colonies. La Vérendrye resembled La Salle in many ways — the same selfless dedication, iron will and skill in the sympathetic handling of Indians, the same love of that vast new world with each mile a new untrodden mile to excite wonder and test one's resources. Because of his years and the effects of his war wounds, he had none of La Salle's physical stamina. But La Vérendrye too was tor-mented by creditors, by jealous critics, by unruly Indians, by delayed supplies and by erratic fur markets. He too suffered from the cynicism of his superiors, particularly Maurepas's unshakable conviction that La Vérendrye was pocketing huge profits that belonged to the king and only pretended to explore. Maurepas, an industrious and competent bureaucrat, could be forgiven. As the son and grandson of two colonial ministers, two comtes de Pontchartrain, he knew nothing of people except those that he had observed in the corrupt royal offices and uninhibited boudoirs of Versailles. He was incapable of imagining such a phenomenon as an honest, disinterested human being.

But La Vérendrye had the moral support and comfort of four extraordi-narily devoted sons, and also the son of his sister Marie Renée, a young man of twenty-three years named Christophe La Jemmeraye. Three of the sons, the nephew and fifty voyageurs were with La Vérendrye on June 8, 1731, when he found himself clear of the red tape that obstructed such royal expeditions and left Lachine in eight big birch-bark trading canoes for Lake Huron, Michilimackinac and Kaministiquia — a twelve-hundred-mile trip.

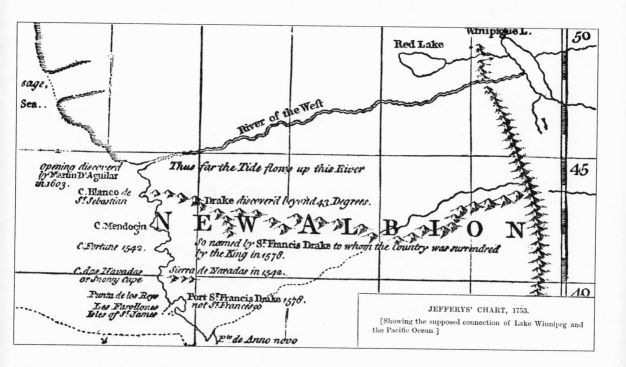

The old dream of a Northwest Passage still flourished in the mid-eighteenth century. On the Delisle map of 1752, an enormous "Mer de l'Ouest" extends into the continent as far as what is now western Kansas, within a convenient distance of both the Missouri and the Rio Grande. Jefferys' New Albion map of 1753 shows the River of the West (the Columbia) flowing eastward from the Pacific coast to pierce the Rockies short of Lake Winnipeg. (From Justin Winsor's The Mississippi Basin)

JEFFERYS' CHART, 1753.

[Showing the supposed connection of Lake Winnipeg and the Pacific Ocean.]

Each canoe carried two tons of goods and six or seven Frenchmen who cadenced their paddling with the gay songs of their native Normandy and Brittany. The eldest La Vérendrye son, Jean-Baptiste, was seventeen. Pierre was a year younger. François, the quiet and illiterate member of the family, was fifteen. Louis-Joseph, nicknamed the Chevalier, was only thirteen in 1731 and stayed home with his mother. Louis-Joseph was a serious student and was instructed by his father to prepare himself for exploration by studying mapping and mathematics.

For the next five years, setting up the string of trading posts for Beauharnois was La Vérendrye's order of business. He chose a new canoe route west — up Pigeon River from Grand Portage forty miles south of Kaministiquia, instead of struggling up Kaministiquia River as Jacques de Noyon had done when he discovered Rainy Lake and Lake of the Woods in 1688–1689. The Pigeon River route through the thick, aromatic pine forest had too many portages — thirty-two — in crossing the low divide of many ponds from the St. Lawrence drainage to Hudson Bay's. But it avoided the twelve dangerous rapids of the Kaministiquia. During the winter of 1731–1732, while La Vérendrye quelled a mutiny of some of his men, La Jemmeraye, the teen-aged Jean-Baptiste and a crew of twenty-five built the first new trading post three hundred miles from Grand Portage at the west end of Rainy Lake where Rainy River starts flowing toward Lake Winnipeg, and toward Hudson Bay a thousand miles away.

La Jemmeraye named the small post Fort Pierre for his uncle. In the spring a year later, the elder La Vérendrye himself led a canoe flotilla of Frenchmen and Monsonis Indians from Fort Pierre on west and north down Rainy River's glowing reaches to its terminus at Lake of the Woods. Cree Indians did the leading then across that placid basin spattered with islets to a lovely spot on the west shore which, the Crees claimed, was commercially strategic to hundreds of allied Indians in the area — Crees, Assiniboines, Monsonis. It was strategic militarily too, for standing off the hated prairie Sioux from the Lake Pepin country of the Upper Mississippi. Here, amid teeming game and wild rice, La Vérendrye built a quite elaborate Fort St. Charles, honoring Governor Beauharnois — a palisaded compound of bastions, a watchtower on Lake of the Woods and six lodges with fourteen fireplaces. It was situated beyond the woodlands at the edge of the Canadian prairies at about the same longitude as those du Tisné had found at the Missouri-Kansas border in 1719.[3]

146

Fort St. Charles was barely finished before the Crees were clamoring for still another post. This one, they said, should be nearer Lake Winnipeg to save Indians living west of it the trouble of making the long haul with their furs to English York Factory on Hudson Bay near the mouth of the Nelson River. La Vérendrye agreed with them and sent La Jemmeraye and Jean-Baptiste to test a water route from Lake of the Woods north to Lake Winnipeg down the Winnipeg River. The stream's spectacular rapids and falls made the route too difficult at times for trade canoes, but they found an alternative, the Red River, the Roseau River branch of which began near Fort St. Charles. During 1734, Jean-Baptiste de La Vérendrye, a seasoned frontiersman of twenty-one years by now, directed the building of an imposing Fort Maurepas on the Red River. The site was near present Selkirk fifteen miles upstream from the Red's delta mouth at Lake Winnipeg. It was twenty miles below the point in today's prairie city of Winnipeg where the Assiniboine River comes from the west into the Red River opposite the heroic bronze statue of La Vérendrye in the Winnipeg suburb of St. Boniface.

As the beaver trade lured the explorer ever westward — by no means against his wishes — his troubles multiplied. Costs increased faster than profits. Time and again he and his sons had to waste time on treks to Michilimackinac and Montreal to soothe creditors, to answer Maurepas's complaints, to speed up the delivery of goods for the Crees and Assiniboines. As every French trader knew, a shortage of trade goods and armament was a very ticklish matter in Indian relations. Having made the Indians dependent on such goods domestically and militarily, the traders had a grave responsibility to keep them supplied. Personal tragedies beset the commander. Early in 1736, his right-hand man and nephew La Jemmeraye fell ill while managing Fort Maurepas. When the ice went out in the spring, Jean-Baptiste and Pierre de La Vérendrye hurried to help him, found his condition serious and tried to carry him by canoe up the Red River back to Fort St. Charles. La Jemmeraye died on May 10, 1736, at the Red River–Roseau River junction near the cairn that marks his grave at the Manitoba village of Letellier. Some weeks later, Jean-Baptiste and twenty voyageurs left Fort St. Charles in three canoes bound for Pigeon River, Grand Portage and Michilimackinac to pick up a delayed shipment of trade goods. They camped that night on an islet in the Lake of the Woods and were attacked on the morning of June 6, 1736, by a hundred or more prairie

Sioux from Lake Pepin. The warring Sioux having failed to find their ancient enemies, the Crees, felt compelled to attack any friends of theirs. In the battle that ensued Jean-Baptiste de La Vérendrye and all his companions were killed, scalped, beheaded and mutilated. Some of the heads of the Frenchmen were wrapped in beaver skins and placed in two canoes that were set adrift on the lake. In August, the elder La Vérendrye found out about the massacre when two Monsoni Indians came across the canoes and their dismal cargoes.

The deaths of his beloved nephew and his eldest son were almost too much for the old man to bear. He was oppressed already by fiscal problems and the recurring pain of his Malplaquet wounds. The Crees became almost unmanageable in their determination to avenge Jean-Baptiste's murder by the Sioux. But new difficulties merely strengthened La Vérendrye's wish to achieve his goals — to find the River of the West, the Western Sea, the Spanish settlements. He had three sturdy sons still, Pierre, François and Louis-Joseph, the Chevalier, who had come to Fort St. Charles in 1735 after finishing his education in Quebec. The elder La Vérendrye had been promoted to lieutenant by the king and he was vastly encouraged when he discovered that the Red River area around Fort Maurepas was a crossroads for countless Indians. Some bands came from the Upper Mississippi by way of Le Sueur's forgotten Minnesota River and then on north down the Red. Some came from the remote northwest by a mysterious system of waterways that was said to rival the Mississippi — the Saskatchewan system, of course. Assiniboines arriving at the crossroads from the Assiniboine River were so numerous that La Vérendrye built two more trading posts to accommodate them during the early fall of 1738. One, Fort Rouge, was at the Assiniboine's mouth. Much the larger of the two was built sixty miles west of the Red River at the site of present Portage la Prairie, Manitoba. La Vérendrye named it Fort La Reine, honoring Queen Marie Leszczynska, the pathetic little Polish wife of Louis XV, who was finding herself lost in the eternal minuet of the king's mistresses.

From the Red River people the explorer and his men gathered much geographical information. The Assiniboines described the further west — great mountains shining like emeralds, salt seas, beaver and buffalo, rich Spanish cities and mines of gold and silver. They were especially vocal about the marvelous light-skinned Mandan Indians who lived in fine earthen houses like the French and about their six prosperous villages on a large river that, La Vérendrye concluded, had to be the River of the West flowing west from near the Missouri across Quivira to the Western Sea. When some Crees at Fort La Reine told him how to reach the Mandan villages three hundred miles away, he was more than eager to visit them.

Leaving his son Pierre in charge of Fort St. Charles, he set out from the just-completed Fort La Reine on October 18, 1738, accompanied by the other sons, Louis-Joseph and François, twenty *engagés*, a young Cree interpreter and a crowd of Assiniboine men, women and children with their domestic paraphernalia and pets (the route is shown on the map on page 131).[4] More groups of Assiniboines kept joining the caravan like excited children in the wake of a circus parade. The explorer would have preferred using canoes on the Assiniboine River, but the stream was low and there was no birch bark on the prairies for repairing canoes. Each person walked with his world's goods on his back as the party trended southwest through the pancake-flat or gently rolling open terrain from Fort La Reine around to the west side of present Turtle Mountain Provincial Park at the Manitoba–North Dakota border. That brought them to the south-running valley of a main branch of the Assiniboine, the Souris (North Dakotans call it the Mouse River), a charming tree-lined stream flowing in a deep bed through stone-specked meadows.

The caravan's pace was slow — seven weeks to cover the three hundred miles to the first Mandan village on a branch (Apple Creek) of the Missouri River eleven miles east of the site of present Bismarck, North Dakota. The simple, gentle Assiniboines lived for the fun of it, and so did La Vérendrye's French-Canadian *engagés*. All of them, red men and white, stopped often to feast, to dance, to give gifts, to kill a snake, to tease a moose, to gamble, to make love. There was no discipline. The expedition had an impromptu, helter-skelter air. After a thief made off with La Vérendrye's box of trinkets, the explorer could not be generous by giving gifts to his Indians. When his Cree interpreter vanished in pursuit of an Assiniboine girl, he had no way of understanding what his guides told him·about where he was. He was aware of a low divide when he crossed from the Souris River and the Hudson Bay drainage to that of the Missouri River but he did not suspect that he was entering a new part of La Salle's Louisiana. He had high hopes that this was the valley of the River of the West, on the Western Sea side of the Continental Divide.

In the late afternoon of December 3, 1738, the train of several hundred people made a triumphant entry into the Mandan village with a triple salvo of guns. Louis-Joseph and François led the procession bearing the white flag of the French army and the king's azure fleur-de-lis. Then came the *engagés* and the Assiniboine chiefs carrying the exhausted La Vérendrye on a leather shield, "in the fashion," the historian Antoine Champagne has written, "of ancient kings of the Merovingian period." The Mandans received their guests cordially but not without guile. To preserve their food supply after several feasts, they frightened the Assiniboine hordes into taking their large appetites off homeward by pretending that a band of prairie Sioux was approaching to kill them all. La Vérendrye observed that much of what he had heard of the Mandans was correct. They were handsome, robust, tall, graceful and courtly — as highly civilized as the Iroquois but unmartial and hospitable. They lived in spacious cabins of domed earth and dressed warmly in buffalo robes, ermine and deerskin. They were farmers and hunters. All around their fortified villages were fields for growing corn and pumpkin and melons and beans which were stored in caves for winter use. They were a tribe of average number — perhaps eighteen hundred in all. They were not notably white-skinned. Most of them were as dark as the Assiniboines, though a few had blond or white hair and blue eyes.[5]

Having lost his amorous Cree interpreter and feeling quite ill, La Vérendrye decided to return to Fort La Reine at once before the deep snows came. He found two French Canadians willing to undertake the interesting task of staying on with the Mandans to see if they could pick up some of their Siouan language — his valet Louis Renaud and an *engagé* "who could write his name." Before the explorer left for Fort La Reine he sent his youngest son Louis-Joseph and seven others eleven miles west to visit the nearest Mandan village (present Bismarck) on the presumed River of the West to check the direction of its flow. Louis-Joseph returned with puzzling news. From that east-bank village, the big river seemed to flow southward and a bit west as though it were heading toward the Gulf of California and the South Sea rather than westward toward the Western Sea.[6] The Chevalier understood also from the Mandan sign language that it arose in high mountains far to the west and that a Spanish port city stood at its mouth. It did not occur to him then that he might be on the Missouri and that the Mandans might be talking about the Mississippi's mouth at the Gulf of Mexico and Bienville's Frenchmen at New Orleans.

For La Vérendrye, the return trip from the Mandan villages to Fort La

Reine — December 13, 1738, to February 10, 1739 — was a desperate struggle to survive illness, hunger and bitterly cold weather. Thereafter he spent many months recovering his health before making the long journey back to Montreal in 1740 to placate his creditors and to counteract the lies about him that people were sending in messages to Maurepas. During his year's absence on the St. Lawrence, his sons challenged the English at Hudson Bay by pushing the La Vérendrye trading area far north from Fort La Reine and Fort Maurepas all the way to the mouth of the Saskatchewan River on Lake Winnipeg. Louis-Joseph had discovered that "grande rivière de Poskoyac" in 1739 and had ascended it to a fork where the Crees met each spring to decide whether to take their winter catch of furs to the English or to the French at Fort Maurepas.[7] To influence their decision, La Vérendrye's eldest son Pierre built Fort Bourbon at the Saskatchewan's mouth and another, Fort Dauphin, on Lake Winnipegosis, in the fall of 1741. That was about when La Vérendrye Père returned to Fort La Reine from the St. Lawrence to find his Mandan language students waiting for him. The language had been too much for them but they brought more garbled tales about the Spanish in the Southwest and about their beards, gold mines, cannon, musical instruments, devotion to people named Jesus and Marie, and walled homes in cities "near the sea of which the water rises and falls and is not good to drink."

The tales were tantalizing. Pierre La Vérendrye decided that he must try once more to solve the River of the West mystery, though vicariously through his sons, for he was too frail in his fifty-eighth year to make such a trip himself. Maurepas allowed him no funds to equip his expedition properly. On April 29, 1742, four young French Canadians and a few Indian guides left Fort La Reine on the tramp up the Assiniboine and Souris river valleys to the Mandan villages, which they reached on May 19. Their leader was Louis-Joseph La Vérendrye, the Chevalier, aged twenty-four. François, the quiet brother, aged twenty-six, was second in command. On July 23 the little squad set out southwesterly from the Mandans' big river with a band of *Gens des Chevaux* (Arikara Indians) on the first leg of their trip to the Spanish sea. The *Gens des Chevaux* passed them along in September to the *Beaux-Hommes* (Crows), who passed them along in October to the *Petits Renards* (Minnetarees), who passed them along to the *Pioyas* (Kiowas?), who passed them along to another band of *Gens des Chevaux*, who passed them along in November, 1742, to the *Gens de la*

Belle-Rivière (Cheyennes who lived on the Belle-Fourche branch of the Cheyenne River). All these "savages" treated the explorers with kindness, courtesy and generosity. Another one hundred and twenty years would pass before the Plains Indians would be goaded into responding in kind to the cruelty, injustice and perfidy of their American invaders.

The route of the La Vérendrye party was on well-known trails of Plains Indian commerce where game and water and material for shelter were plentiful. Some of the trails were changing to accommodate the greater mobility of the Spanish horses and mules that were beginning to appear among the Pawnees and other tribes on the northern plains — the same horse breeds that St. Denis had found in East Texas as early as 1714. From the site of Bismarck, the four white men hiked southwesterly past the little buttes topped with red earth of southwestern North Dakota to the multi-colored badlands of the Little Missouri. From there they moved up its Box Elder Creek branch through the short-grass vastness of eastern Montana near the site of today's lonely cow town, Ekalaka, and southward up the Powder River west of fluted Devil's Tower in Wyoming, and the Black Hills around it. Along the Powder somewhere in late November they met a band of several thousand *Gens de l'Arc* (Pawnees), who startled them with displays of many Spanish articles as well as horses and mules. The *Gens de l'Arc* told the Frenchmen that they recalled when some of their tribe had massacred Villasur's scouts from Santa Fe on the Platte River in 1720 but added that their own knowledge of Spanish affairs was slight. They gave the explorers horses to ride — something almost unique in their travels — and persuaded them to join in a westward pursuit of their enemies the *Gens du Serpent* (Snake Indians) who, they said, went to Santa Fe often to trade slaves and hides for horses. The inference was that after the Snakes had been defeated and captured, they would tell the explorers all about the Upper Rio Grande.[8]

The progress of the many Pawnee warriors and their families had to be leisurely. It was not until New Year's Day, 1743, at the Powder River–Clear Creek junction that the La Vérendryes saw low on the southwestern horizon a sparkling jumble of snow-covered summits. They were the Big Horn Mountains, which center on Cloud Peak at 13,165 feet above sea level and extend south from today's Montana border for one hundred and fifty miles. Though the Continental divide runs through the Wind River Range a hundred miles further west, the Rocky Mountains begin with the Big Horns in Wyoming for all practical and emotional purposes.

For twelve days the Pawnees and their guests ascended Clear Creek until they reached the base of the range near present Buffalo, Wyoming. As the Frenchmen gazed up at the great barrier, they may have known for certain — the first Europeans to know it — that they were seeing part of a north-south continental mountain system separating eastern from western North America. The system was exactly the opposite of what was supposed to be there. It was not a low divide like those the Europeans were accustomed to — not like the divide between Lake Michigan and the Illinois drainage or that between Lake Erie and the Ohio or the Lake Superior–Rainy Lake divide. This mountain system was higher even than the Appalachians that had penned the English on the Atlantic coast for a century. Such a barrier made nonsense out of everything European scientists had been saying about New World geography since 1492.

Furthermore, the immensity of the Big Horns forced the La Vérendryes to conclude that the Western Sea was a myth. It could not indent its way through this continental system to reach the alleged coast of Quivira. The big river of the Mandans could not flow through it either to empty into the Gulf of California or South Sea. The Mandans' river must be the Missouri River rising high in the system. If so, they were standing in French territory, in the Mississippi-Missouri drainage of La Salle's Louisiana, hundreds of miles further west than any previous estimate of how far west Louisiana extended. The Saskatchewan River that Louis-Joseph de La Vérendrye had discovered in 1739 north of Fort La Reine must start in the system too, which would make it useless to hope any longer for an unimpeded Strait of Anian or Northwest Passage anywhere south of Hudson Bay.

The brothers were distracted from these thoughts by the activities of their warring friends. To the explorers' disappointment, the Pawnees did not dare to push further into the Big Horns. When their scouts discovered an empty *Gens du Serpent* village, the whole Pawnee army retreated southeastward in a panic, fearing that the Snakes had left the village to attack their rear guard. For a time, the four Frenchmen became separated from their hosts but joined up with them in the windswept grasslands of the Cheyenne River in east-central Wyoming. Traveling by horseback was painful through February because of heavy snows and a scarcity of grass and game until the *Gens de l'Arc* moved into pleasant wooded terrain rounding the south side of the South Dakota Black Hills. In mid-March, the Pawnees passed their guests along to a band of *Gens de la Petite Cerise*

(Arikaras) who led them into their village four days later (March 19, 1743) on the big river of the Mandans. The Arikara village was near the site of South Dakota's capital city, Pierre, and here the La Vérendryes saw that the river veered definitely eastward, proving to them once and for all that it was the Missouri. Still more proof came when the Arikaras reported that a French trader called on them regularly from his post seventy-five miles below with goods that he brought up the Missouri from Fort Chartres on the Mississippi.

On a warm April day, Louis-Joseph, the Chevalier, climbed a hillock above the Arikara village and buried secretly a lead plate bearing the arms of France, signifying the claims of the nation to all lands drained by the Missouri. Later, he and François de La Vérendrye built a pyramid of stones over the concealed spot memorializing, as they explained to the Arikaras, the kind way in which the Indians received them. Soon after, the four Frenchmen departed upstream, reaching the Mandan villages on May 18. Some weeks later, on July 2, 1743, they drew up at Fort La Reine, still riding the horses that the Pawnees had given to them in November. A thankful La Vérendrye Père rushed out of the compound to greet them, having given them up for dead after their absence of one year and seventy-four days.[9]

The divine compulsion that inspired a handful of heroic Frenchmen from Champlain on to dedicate their lives to American exploration for the greater glory of France flickered out in 1743. In that year Governor Bienville retired in despair after four decades of futile striving to make Louisiana an integral part of the French empire. His vast domain, still largely unknown except along some of its major rivers, would not emerge from its doldrums under French rule. By 1743, colonization had occurred only in a small area bounded by the New Orleans delta, Mobile, Natchez, the German coast and Natchitoches — a mere two thousand Europeans and their three thousand black slaves. Meanwhile, the number of English colonists pressing ever further from the Atlantic seaboard against and beyond the crest of the Appalachians reached a million and a half in 1743. La Nouvelle-France as a whole had less than forty-five thousand Frenchmen living in North America. The distaste of the average Frenchman for pioneer life, for leaving his delectable homeland, had much to do with the failure of France to succeed on those two magnificent waterways, the St. Lawrence and the Mississippi. In addition, the harsh colonial process could not flourish under the Bourbon system of bureaucratic government — its selfishness, cynicism, extravagance, apathy and paranoid absorption in the politics of Europe.

In that same year of 1743, the elder Pierre de La Vérendrye, burdened with debt and still mourning the deaths of a beloved son and a nephew in the cause of French exploration, resigned as head of the Poste de l'Ouest in anguished protest against charges of corruption and lethargy made against him by the comte de Maurepas. Lethargy! It was the "lethargy" of his family that had unveiled the central Rockies and the Upper Missouri, established a canoe route to the Canadian prairies and beyond, opened a great fur country, discovered the Saskatchewan River, and portended the discovery of the River of the West — that presumed west-slope continuance of the Missouri — by the Boston skipper of the *Columbia*, Robert Gray, half a century later. Of course the comte de Maurepas had good reason in 1743 to deplore La Vérendrye's failure to make fur profits for the benefit of Louis XV. The king needed money desperately just then to pay for the War of the Austrian Succession. A week before the La Vérendrye brothers arrived back at Fort La Reine, the British army routed the French in a critical battle at the Bavarian village of Dettingen.[10]

The demissions of La Vérendrye and of Bienville signified that a change of life was coming to Louisiana. Another event signified something too, though nobody was aware of it in 1743 — the birth on April 13 of a son to Jane and Peter Jefferson on a tobacco farm in Virginia called Shadwell, glowing and fragrant with dogwood and apple blossoms at that time of year. The Jeffersons named the boy Thomas after his grandfather and great-grandfather, both native Virginians. Shadwell was a frontier tract on the Rivanna branch of the Upper James River. From it, the family could look curiously west beyond their low Southwest Mountains to the spot where an Indian trail led through Rockfish Gap of the Blue Ridge and across the Appalachian crest into French Louisiana.

TWO

THE PURCHASE

10

～

The Westering English

ONE OF THE LESSONS taught by history is the infinite capacity of nations to endure bad governments. Spain's wise king, the Holy Roman Emperor Charles V, took full advantage of the gold and silver that the conquistadores found in Peru and Mexico, holding the post-Columbian world in his hand until his abdication in 1556. But after the death of his son Philip II, a succession of royal idiots diverted his nation down a different road — the sad road of mediocrity. In 1743, her king was the French Bourbon, Philip V, and Spain was little more than a bargaining tool for France, whom she feared and detested — a tool cynically exploited in the ever more crucial Anglo-French contest for world leadership. Spain's empire south and north of the Rio Grande — including today's Florida, Texas and New Mexico — was feebly held and atrociously managed. Her once-superb navy could not even protect her treasure galleons in the Caribbean and Gulf of Mexico from French, English and Dutch pirates. Such treasure as escaped these harpies rarely reached Madrid. It had to be sent to European bankers to pay the national debt that had accrued while various Spanish kings, each one more inept than the one before, had tried to hold back modern times and sustain the archaic power of the pope. A low point in Spain's fall was reached in 1739, when England declared war on her for cutting off an ear of Robert Jenkins, one of England's piratical smugglers. Jenkins had made an art of misdemeanors in the Caribbean contrary to the terms of the Treaty of Utrecht. One result of the War of Jenkins Ear (1739–1742), that most explicitly named of conflicts, was apparently the upholding of England's right to punish another country for her own misconduct.

As for France, one would think that the French masses, starving, overworked, hopeless, would have used the War of the Spanish Succession (1701–1713) as an excuse to cast out Louis XIV's ruinous bureaucracy, so absorbed in its own gaudy maintenance as to have no strength left to serve the peasants who paid for it. And, if Louis XIV was a foolish monarch in his last years, his great-grandson, Louis XV, was beyond mere foolishness. This handsome, long-lashed, weak-willed "Le Bien-Aimé" was an absolute cipher for the entire fifty years of his reign.

It is true that sound measures to resume friendly relations with England and to stop warring in Europe — measures instigated by the duc d'Orléans, John Law and Cardinal Fleury — restored France to a temporary stability after Louis XIV's demise. But the amazingly durable Fleury died in his ninetieth year in 1743. Louis XV took over at the age of thirty-three and his ministers sent forth his poorly prepared armies in a dozen directions for the purpose of humbling Maria Theresa, archduchess of Austria. For his pains in this War of the Austrian Succession, Le Bien-Aimé saw the beginning of the end of French power in India that had come to him through his French East Indian Company, and he had to recognize Maria Theresa's consort, Francis I, as Holy Roman Emperor.

Louis XV's losses at this time in the American area — the parallel struggle through the 1740's that was called King George's War — seemed minor but they showed astute observers that France was no longer able to defend Louisiana, Canada and the French West Indies, the sugar isles of which were her richest colonial possessions. In the north, the war brought more French-inspired Indian raids and tragic carnage along the undefined borders of New England and it prompted the English at Albany to strengthen their alliance with the Iroquois to hold Fort Oswego on Lake Ontario. England advanced exceedingly dubious claims to the Ohio valley, too, by virtue of the item in the Treaty of Utrecht of 1713 that gave her the right to "protect" the Ohio-roaming Iroquois. To bolster these claims, colonial officials of Virginia, Maryland and Pennsylvania held a farcical conference of assorted Iroquois at Lancaster, Pennsylvania, in 1744 and "bought" from them — for the grand sum of four hundred pounds — the Ohio valley and, vaguely, any other land that might exist west of the Alleghenies.

The great blow for France in King George's War came with the fall of Fort Louisbourg on Cape Breton Island. Cape Breton was a key point in the French defense of naval approaches to the St. Lawrence and Quebec because of its location on Cabot Strait opposite Newfoundland and adjoining Nova Scotia, both possessions of England. Louisbourg was supposed to be the most impregnable fort in the world. It was captured after a long siege in June, 1745, by a mob of tattered, barefoot New England colonists armed with squirrel guns and a few light cannon. These undisciplined recruits — four thousand clerks, mechanics and farmers transported from Boston in malodorous fishing boats — acted on their own, not Parliament's, authority, inspired by bumpers of New England rum and Calvinist zeal against the papist foe. Their daring and wild energy seemed so close to madness that the five hundred French regulars surrendered out of pure awe. Oddly, the feat was as ominous for England as it was for France. It displayed the extraordinary martial gifts of the colonists, whose treasonable talk of independence was already causing worry in the mother country. The talk became louder and angrier when the triumphant New Englanders learned that Great Britain, by the 1748 Treaty of Aix-la-Chapelle, gave Fort Louisbourg back to France in exchange for the post of Madras on the Bay of Bengal in India. In other words, their heroism and sacrifice were being used by Parliament to enrich London merchants engaged in the East India trade.

Meanwhile back at Versailles, the hapless behavior of Louis XV was not deliberate. He just found himself unable to grow up. In an era of enormous political complexity, he could not cope with anything more complicated than arrangements for a hunting party in the Bois de Boulogne or the choice of a new teen-aged girl with whom to spend the night — a pastime he pursued not orgiastically but with the innocence of a boy playing at quoits. One night in 1744, a somewhat older girl of peasant origins, Jeanne Antoinette Poisson le Normant d'Etioles, began sleeping with the king against her husband's wishes and surprised the court at Versailles by continuing in his favor for a great many nights. She had been told earlier by a fortune-teller that she was destined to rule France as *"un morceau de roi."* She began to rule in 1745 when the king made her his official mistress with the title of marquise de Pompadour and she would remain in complete charge of France up to her death two decades later, at the age of forty-two.

There can be no doubt that Madame de Pompadour, that brilliant and beautiful patroness of French arts and friend of Voltaire and the *philosophes*, was one of the most fascinating of women. Her only fault seemed to be that she knew nothing about running a troubled nation and she often picked ministers as ignorant as herself. During her reign over a government that Parkman called "an animated bed of tulips" she turned French foreign policy upside down by coming to the support, for no comprehensible reason, of Maria Theresa and Austria — the exact reversal of French policy in the 1740's. The baffling turnabout would draw France into the fatal Seven Years' War against Prussia in Europe and, at the same time, against Great Britain in America — the climactic French and Indian War.

During the 1740's, Madame de Pompadour was as bored as Louis XIV had been with the costly problems and lack of progress of Louisiana and Canada, but she kept a wary eye on the comte de Maurepas, her minister of colonies. The witty count was much like the late duc d'Orléans in his administrative skills, his cynicism and his love of frivolous vice. Pompadour was jealous of Maurepas's friendship with Louis XV and called him "the torment of my life." When the social set of Paris began passing around bawdy verses about her bourgeois manners, her extravagance, her love techniques and even about her miscarriages and menstrual problems, she told the king that Maurepas had made up the verses, which may have been true, and that he plotted to poison her. The king responded in 1749 by dismissing Maurepas, whose father and grandfather, the comtes de Pontchartrain, had directed Louisiana's affairs for half a century. However, the king did not attempt to erase the names of Lake Maurepas and Lake Pontchartrain from their places on the maps of New Orleans and Louisiana.

After the resignation of Governor Bienville in 1743, his successor, Pierre de Rigaud, marquis de Vaudreuil, soon found that the recalcitrant province was producing nothing but more Indian troubles and insoluble economic problems, aggravated by King George's War. British privateers controlled the Caribbean and the Gulf of Mexico, raiding French ports and reducing by seizure the French West Indian fleet from six hundred to three hundred ships. In July, 1744, residents of New Orleans were frightened badly when three British pirate ships swept up the Mississippi from Head of Passes to the crescent town and bombarded two French merchantmen moored near the governor's mansion. The bombardment ended in the deaths of two French sailors and "a woman of quality with child" who was struck by an errant cannonball while picking peaches in her garden.

The marquis de Vaudreuil, born in Montreal, was the son of Philippe de Rigaud who had become governor of Canada soon after the death of Frontenac. The younger Vaudreuil was one of those members of the Canadian nobility who made an art of high living. In New Orleans he gathered around him a few wealthy survivors of John Law's concessionaire regime and set standards of opulence and gaiety that emulated those of Versailles. Echoes of Vaudreuil's social achievements can be heard today when the elite of New Orleans disport themselves elegantly at Mardi Gras time.

But Vaudreuil took his official duties seriously and tried hard to make the best of a hopeless situation. The old trade trouble persisted. Frenchmen in the homeland complained that dealing in Louisiana products — tobacco, rice, indigo, lumber, pitch, tar — was more trouble than it was worth because of the risks of loss that they ran because of piracy and hurricanes in the Gulf of Mexico, of spoilage and the instability of currency at New Orleans. In addition, some of these products competed with those supplied by their favored West Indian markets in the sugar isles of Martinique, Guadeloupe and Santo Domingo.

One result of this lack of support by homeland merchants was that planters around New Orleans could not make enough money to buy more slaves to improve their production, or reduce the debt owed for slaves already bought. To acquire specie — hard money — to pay royal taxes and to keep his three thousand colonists from starving, Vaudreuil had the wisdom to overlook import activity outlawed by his government. He ignored a lively market in contraband, particularly contraband arriving on enemy ships from New England and New York, the merchants of which had uses for Louisiana crops. French-Canadian fur traders at Kaskaskia, Cahokia and a few new posts up the Mississippi such as Prairie du Rocher, St. Philippe above Fort Chartres, and Ste. Geneviève, could do business with their Illinois Indians because Vaudreuil permitted smugglers to bring in the cheap English goods that the Illinois demanded.

Under these conditions, the governor could do little more than hold things loosely together, confining his management to the near hinterland, the area within the Natchitoches–Arkansas Post–Natchez–Mobile perimeter. Though he pressed a renewal of French claims into Spanish East Texas from Natchitoches across the Sabine as far as Trinity River, he made no progress whatever when it came to developing Bourgmond's Upper Missouri or the Mallets' Canadian River route to Santa Fe.[1] He lost all contact with the Illinois River area above the site of La Salle's Fort Crèvecoeur and he regarded the area as the responsibility of the commander at Fort Detroit. In 1747, Vaudreuil found Fort Chartres, Bienville's stronghold below the mouth of the Missouri, to be in such bad repair that he abandoned it and set up makeshift headquarters at Kaskaskia. He worried constantly about the lack of communication between Louisiana and Canada along the line of French forts up the Ohio and Wabash rivers to the Maumee, Lake Erie and Fort Detroit.

This worry was shared by his counterpart in Canada, the comte de La Galissonière, who became governor of the fifty thousand Frenchmen on the St. Lawrence in 1747 when Louis XV punished the marquis de Beauharnois for the Louisbourg fiasco by recalling him. La Galissonière, an alert and intelligent official whose career had been spent in the navy, had the task of protecting Quebec from naval attack. But he saw that French possession of the Ohio valley part of Louisiana was equally crucial to Canada's defense and to the preservation of her fur trade, which was dominating her economy. This meant that communications with the Mississippi and New Orleans must be vastly improved by strengthening the neglected French posts on the Maumee and the Wabash — Fort Miami, Fort Ouiatenon, Fort Vincennes. La Galissonière's policy put Louisiana in a stern new perspective. Here was some serious consideration at last of La Salle's circular imperialism, the attempt to tie Canada with the Gulf of Mexico and the French West Indies by way of the Mississippi. Heretofore, Louisiana's role in the world had been passive most of the time — that of a subtle creator of discontent, a mystic presence like Heaven above, an earthly paradise people dreamed about where they might find a better, richer, freer life. Its self-sustaining fortress design was a stimulus to such dreams — the Appalachian barrier on the east, three difficult Mississippi River "passes" guarding New Orleans, entry from French Canada only by canoe through hostile Indian lands, and no entry at all from unknown Pacific shores across the vastness of Quivira.[2] As we have seen, these potentials for freedom caused the immense popularity in Europe of romances about Louisiana like those of Hennepin and Lahontan. And they had brought nightmares to Louis XIV, who imagined in turn that La Salle, Duluth, Iberville and even the moneybags Antoine Crozat might be plotting to set up a nation of their own peopled by renegade *coureurs de bois* and *voyageurs* escaping from his tyranny and taxes into Illinois and other remote parts of the province. What was it, the Sun King had wondered, about those notoriously unprofitable wilds that turned loyal subjects into rebels?

And now, because of the British threat to the Ohio valley, Louisiana found itself thrust by La Galissonière into the forefront of international affairs. The Quebec governor was horrified to find from his agent on the Ohio that hordes of English traders were packing their goods over the Allegheny crest from Pennsylvania and Virginia and were operating mobile posts among the Shawnee, Delaware and Miami Indians for hundreds of miles downstream from the Forks of the Ohio — the site of present Pittsburgh. The agent learned that the poaching Englishmen did not hesitate to ambush and to murder French traders and that they kept telling the Indians that the Iroquois at Lancaster had appointed King George to govern them. Some of the Indians had two sets of flags, French and English, that they could fly above their villages to match the nationality of their visitors. The Indians confessed to La Galissonière's agent that they had a problem. Though the French had been their friends, even their relatives by marriage, for half a century, they were leaning presently toward the English traders. The wares and New England rum of the English were cheaper and better than the wares and the brandy of the French. The English glasses supplied to them to drink the rum were larger than French brandy glasses. The English paid more for the furs of the Indians than the French paid.

La Galissonière may have recognized ruefully from his agent's report that these English trade attractions were due to the efficiency of modern England's industrial system, and its greater vitality under the relative freedom of its decentralized government. And rum made from West Indian molasses was cheaper than brandy from French grapes because of British sea power. But the poaching had to stop. La Galissonière had to make clear to the world once and for all that the Ohio valley belonged to the king of France by right of discovery, starting with La Salle's Ohio trip in 1669.

The governor's choice for this important assignment in propaganda was a bumptious army man on the order of La Mothe Cadillac, Pierre Joseph Céloron de Bienville, who had served at Fort Niagara and other Great Lakes posts. On June 15, 1749, after announcing his intent to drive the English from the Ohio valley and open a highway to Mexico, Céloron left Montreal with a picturesque, if not impressively militant, force of twenty soldiers, one hundred and eighty French-Canadian servants of one kind or another and a crowd of Iroquois and Abenaki Indians. From Lake

Erie, the propagandists hiked and canoed to the Delaware village at the Forks of the Ohio by way of Lake Chautauqua and the Allegheny (today's town of Celoron on Lake Chautauqua honors the commander). The servants were loaded with lead plates bearing royal manifestos of possession, iron engravings of the arms of the king, ceremonial uniforms for Céloron and his officers, banners and gifts for the Ohio Indians. As the assembly floated down the Ohio through the somnolent heat of summer and then paddled up the Miami, Céloron staged frequent pageants at Indian villages and at the Logstown and Muskingum trading posts of the English, some of whom had the impudence to appear voluntarily before him to receive his order to leave the country. He nailed the king's arms to trees and buried lead plates at the mouths of dozens of streams, including the Muskingum, Great Kanawha and Scioto rivers.[3]

But, to Céloron's choleric displeasure, the colorful pageants were presented mainly to an audience of cottontails and chipmunks. The Ohio Indians ignored them utterly and refused to show up even to accept his gifts of friendship and alliance. When the party reached Fort Detroit from the Maumee and Lake Erie on October 6, Céloron had to declare that his two-thousand mile trek had accomplished none of his aims. The English were still poaching on the Ohio, the Indians declined to cooperate in driving them from the country, and no work had been done on the military road to connect Canada and Louisiana. Propaganda, he told La Galissonière later, would not do. What was needed was a string of strong new forts along the Alleghenies from Lake Erie to the Forks of the Ohio and on down to the Mississippi.

The concern of La Galissonière in Quebec and Vaudreuil in New Orleans over the westering English would have been still more acute if they had known what was on the minds of Peter Jefferson and his Virginia neighbors in that same year of 1749. The Jeffersons, the John Harvies, Dr. Thomas Walker (he was Thomas Jefferson's godfather), and the rest were a happy lot of young landed gentry out there at the fringe of western settlement where life was as fresh as a new-laid egg. Most of them appreciated the unique liberties that they had come to enjoy as Englishmen since the "glorious revolution" of 1688–1689 based on "the natural rights of man" as conceived by the philosopher of the revolution, John Locke. Though they were ruled theoretically by a remote Parliament of self-centered aristocrats and merchants under the chairmanship of a figurehead king, George II, their assembly at Williamsburg ran Virginia pretty much as it pleased and kept the royal governor in line because it paid his expenses. Everyone objected mildly to Parliament's acts of trade and navigation affecting colonial exports, but enforcement was languid and port officials overlooked smuggling as benignly as Vaudreuil overlooked it in New Orleans. Furthermore the acts were designed to serve mercantile, not political, ends — steady expansion of Great Britain, a strong navy and merchant marine, and control of world trade. The Virginians could agree with Parliament that the road to wealth, power and a higher living standard for everybody in this new Roman Empire lay in world markets rather than in fighting useless wars in Europe.

But as far as the Virginians were concerned, the colony was their property for all practical purposes, not the mother country's. For a century and more Virginians had fought for it, subdued its Indians, developed its production and created a quasi-democratic government for it that fitted the temperament of its upper class. When Peter Jefferson looked curiously west from Shadwell beyond the Blue Ridge into French Louisiana, his thoughts were quite different from what La Salle's thoughts had been at Lachine in 1666. La Salle had dreamed of imperial glory for France and, for himself, a title of nobility. Peter Jefferson's thoughts were of the fertile land off there waiting to be used for his personal benefit and that of his children — land that Virginia claimed by the terms of its royal charter all the way to the Mississippi, and on to the Pacific for that matter, even if the French had been claiming it all these years. What right had the French to Louisiana if Frenchmen refused to go there? By contrast to these French stay-at-homes, there was no end to the flood of immigrants to Virginia and to the other English colonies. In addition to the English immigrant majority, there were Scotch-Irish from Ulster, Moravians and Poles from central Europe, Dutchmen and Swedes, Germans from the Palatinate, Swiss Mennonites, and capable French Huguenots who had been forbidden by the Bourbons to settle in Louisiana or in Canada. These immigrant hordes were starved for freedom and for land. To exploit their land hunger and get rich, all a Virginia pioneer had to do was to acquire land cheaply and sell it dearly to the newcomers and then move on west to the next real estate opportunity.

Peter Jefferson's father and grandfather had moved west in this way, from Virginia's tidewater to the piedmont and on almost to the foot of the

Appalachian barrier in Albemarle County. Not that he and his neighbors were mere bundles of materialism. To them, the world beyond the Blue Ridge was as challenging to their spirit of adventure, as mystically alluring as it had been to the early French explorers. Their knowledge about what this Louisiana paradise contained was not much greater than that of Marquette and Jolliet. The Virginians had probably read the fables of Lahontan and Hennepin and seen Matthew Seutter's map of the 1730's from his *Atlas Novus* showing Quivira and the Western Sea. But they knew nothing of recent French trade secrets such as the Mallets' trip to Sante Fe or of the visits of the La Vérendryes to the Mandans and the Rocky Mountains. They believed as firmly as Duluth that a Northwest Passage must lead to the Pacific and China from Lake Superior, or perhaps from the Missouri and that the golden Seven Cities of Cibola were still waiting for them out there in the wilds.

They were better informed about Louisiana east of the Mississippi — "their" Ohio valley. They discarded John Lederer's tall tales of seeing leopards and lions and peacocks in 1672 beyond the Allegheny crest but they knew that many Virginia traders were reaching the Ohio from the Carolinas via the Tennessee River and also from the Blue Ridge by way of New River and the Great Kanawha. Other Virginians, and Pennsylvanians too, were taking trails over the crest from the Potomac at Fort Cumberland and from the Juniata branch of the Susquehanna to the Forks of the Ohio and the Logstown trading post just below.

As these pioneers on the Upper James saw it, Virginia's claims to the Ohio valley had received official sanction in the late summer of 1716 when her effervescent governor, Alexander Spotswood, led his convivial Knights of the Golden Horseshoe up the James and over the Blue Ridge at Swift Run Gap not forty miles from the future site of Peter Jefferson's Shadwell. It seems likely that Jane Jefferson told her children — she had five of them by 1749 — over and over the thrilling story of how the horseshoe knights descended into the beautiful valley of the Shenandoah River (they called it "the Euphrates") as discoverers and marked their joy at their heroism by drinking toasts and firing volleys every mile or so — toasts of champagne and other brews including Ireland's piquant cordial for conquerors, usquebaugh. Spotswood's trek was ancient history, of course. Jane Jefferson had a second, a family, adventure to relate to her children. In 1746, Peter Jefferson had spent four exciting weeks in the primeval wilderness crossing

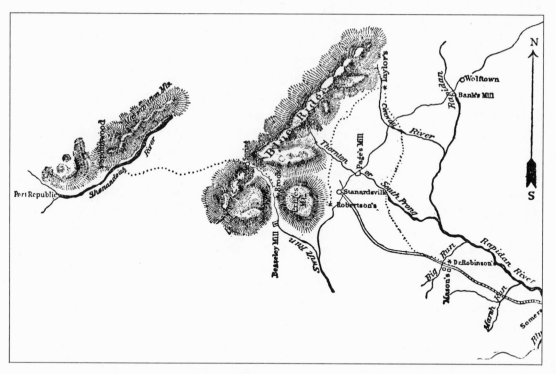

Governor Alexander Spotswood's jaunt in 1716 across the Blue Ridge, as traced on this old map, inspired Peter Jefferson and others to claim for Virginia not only the Shenandoah valley but the immense Ohio River region of Louisiana beyond the crest of the Alleghenies.
(Courtesy of Tutt Library, Colorado College)

the Blue Ridge to the crest of the Alleghenies. The royal assignment of his party was to map a southern boundary for the six-million-acre Shenandoah valley grant made to Lord Thomas Fairfax by King George II. This "Fairfax Line" ran west from the headspring of the Rappahannock to that of the Potomac over mountains and through laurel swamps and thick forests "prodigiously full of fallen timber and ivey." After surviving many perils, Jefferson reached the Potomac headspring safely, set up a stone marker and carved his initials *PJ* on a beech tree near it.

When Governor Spotswood had returned to Williamsburg at the end of his Shenandoah trek, he told the House of Burgesses in effect that he had extended Virginia's boundaries to include the Ohio valley for the purpose of "making new settlements." And so at the very time that Céloron was planting lead plates along the Ohio in 1749, the James River pioneers of

169

Albemarle County and other Virginians were deciding that the time was ripe to prepare the way for Spotswood's Ohio settlements. Peter Jefferson's friend, Dr. Thomas Walker, was especially active, having come into funds by his marriage to Nicholas Meriwether's wealthy widow. Walker gave up medicine in 1748 to become a full-time land speculator. For his Loyal Land Company, he obtained a royal grant of eight hundred thousand acres lying somewhere beyond the Blue Ridge southwest of Albemarle County. In his search for the tract, he followed an Indian trail through the Allegheny foothills near the present Virginia-Kentucky border and into a low gap in the forest which led him to two key rivers in the southern part of the Ohio drainage, the Kentucky and the Tennessee. His discovery of the gap, 1,648 feet above sea level, would compare with the discovery, by Ashley's men in 1824, of South Pass in Wyoming (the gateway to Oregon), for it would bring about the creation of the first two trans-Appalachian states, Kentucky and Tennessee, soon after the Revolutionary War. Walker named his gap Cumberland after King George II's son, the duke of Cumberland, who had recently subdued the Scots at Culloden.

Thomas Walker's rival in land development was the Ohio Company of Virginia, which received grants from King George II in 1749 totaling half a million acres along the Ohio River southwest as far as the Falls of the Ohio at present Louisville, Kentucky. The Ohio Company was organized by prominent Virginians including two tidewater aristocrats, Lawrence and Augustine Washington. At the time, their half-brother, George, aged seventeen, was getting a taste of wilderness life while surveying the Fairfax estate that Peter Jefferson had worked on in 1746. As in the case of Walker's Loyal Land Company, the Ohio Company grantees had to locate and stake their tract. For that purpose, they sent in 1750 an extraordinarily talented frontiersman named Christopher Gist and his Negro slave to inspect the Ohio valley and "to make a map of the best land." What the Virginians thought of Céloron's French pageants of possession is indicated by their instructions to Gist that "the nearer in the Land lies, the better, provided it be good & level, *but we had rather go quite down the Mississippi* than take mean broken Land."

The conflicting aims of the westering English, of the barn-storming Céloron, and of the Europe-minded Pompadour at Versailles were among the factors leading to a head-on collision between Great Britain and her allies on one side and France and her reluctant relative Spain on the other.

But the kind of impending war would be something new. Until now, the great powers of Europe had fought in Europe over European dynastic or religious issues. Now these powers faced a worldwide contention that included disputes over India, Africa, the West Indies and North America. This enlargement of scope was caused by Great Britain's determination to dominate world trade through her colonies. And it was her decision, promoted incessantly by "the great commoner," William Pitt, that the conquest of French Canada was central to this grand design — militarily because the vague Canadian border was a threat to the English colonies, commercially because if Great Britain owned Canada as well as Hudson Bay, the world's richest fur trade would be a part of her mercantilist system.

Of these collision factors, none was more disturbing to Governor La Galissonière's successor at Quebec, the marquis de La Jonquière, than the work of Christopher Gist and his black companion as they wended their way along the meandering channel of the Ohio and its branches, winning hundreds of Indians to England's side and claiming vast stretches of "good & level" land for the Ohio Company of Virginians. Gist was accompanied at times by an Indian expert as able as himself, George Croghan, who represented the Scotch-Irish fur traders of western Pennsylvania. The aims of the two scouts conflicted sharply since Gist was promoting settlement for Virginians and Croghan sought fur-rich country for his Pennsylvania traders. People were aware in the 1750's that nothing was worse for the fur business than settlers who cleared the land and drove out the beaver and other fur-bearing creatures. But the two scouts remained friends. The Ohio valley seemed big enough then for both settlement and trapping.

In the spring of 1751, Gist returned to Virginia from the Ohio country by a circuitous southward route that took him through Thomas Walker's Kentucky tract and across Cumberland Gap. In November, he returned to the Forks of the Ohio from Fort Cumberland by a shorter Will's Creek trail, one of his own divising, over the Alleghenies. The high point of his Ohio Company career occurred at Logstown near the Forks of the Ohio in June, 1752. At a meeting of Indian leaders called by himself and by George Croghan, the Indians ratified the cession to England of the Ohio valley that the Iroquois had made at Lancaster in 1744. Some months later, a few Pennsylvanians began staking out farms for themselves on the Monongahela branch of the Ohio and Governor Dinwiddie of Virginia hired a crew of men to build a stockaded fort at the Forks of the Ohio.

All these frontier maneuvers by the English were being reported in

Quebec to Governor La Jonquière, a tottering ancient of immense wealth and even greater avarice. Early in 1752, the old man could bear to hear no more threatening news. He took to his bed and died after instructing his undertaker not to waste money on expensive wax candles but to light his bier with cheap guttering "tallow dips" during the solemn requiem mass for the repose of his miserly soul. The naval officer sent by Louis XV to replace La Jonquière as governor was the marquis de Duquesne, who began vigorously to gather all the soldiers and workmen that he could find on the St. Lawrence to fortify the Forks of the Ohio region before Dinwiddie's Virginia militia got there in strength.

In choosing sites for his line of forts, Duquesne discarded Céloron's Lake Chautauqua route along the Alleghenies in favor of the Indian trail from Presque Isle — present Erie, Pennsylvania — that reached Ohio River drainage a dozen miles south of Lake Erie on the west fork of French Creek. Duquesne's first fort, Le Boeuf, went up in the winter of 1752–1753 and work proceeded on the second during the summer of 1753 at the French Creek Allegheny River junction (present Franklin, Pennsylvania). The governor named this one Fort Machault to honor a close friend of Madame de Pompadour's whom she put in briefly as minister of the marine to replace the too-witty jingle-writer, Maurepas.

While Duquesne's scouts were spying on the unfinished fort that Dinwiddie was trying to get built at the Forks of the Ohio, the Virginia governor had spies out too from Williamsburg. Their reports convinced him that it was time to send an emissary to Fort Le Boeuf to object formally to Duquesne's militancy on Ohio soil that the Indians had just ceded to English colonists at Logstown. Dinwiddie's emissary was Major George Washington, now aged twenty-one and adjutant general of the Virginia militia. Washington's guide was Christopher Gist. The pair reached Fort Le Boeuf from Will's Creek on December 1, 1753. They were greeted cordially with spots of French brandy served in small glasses by the fort's commander.

The shy fledgling, Washington, bearing no marks to suggest that the greatest of American heroes was in the process of manufacture, may have been awed by the French commander. Jacques Le Gardeur de Saint-Pierre, a renowned frontiersman, was the grandson of Jean Nicolet, the discoverer of Lake Michigan, and the son of Jean-Paul Le Gardeur de Saint-Pierre, who had explored the Upper Mississippi with Duluth. Jacques himself had built Governor Beauharnois's short-lived fort on Lake Pepin and had only just returned from Fort la Reine after two years of striving to advance the work of the La Vérendryes by finding a Northwest Passage to the Pacific from Lake Winnipeg.[4] Saint-Pierre's days were numbered, for he would lose his life eight months hence fighting the British at Lake George.

One can only imagine the private thoughts of the aging Frenchman and the young Virginia aristocrat at this Fort le Boeuf meeting. Surely Saint-Pierre would have realized how precarious the position of La Nouvelle-France had become, threatened by the British fleet on approaches to the St. Lawrence and on the Gulf of Mexico, and by massive numbers of English colonists poised along the crest of the Appalachians from Maine to Georgia. And he knew that in the midst of this crisis overseas Madame de Pompadour's ministers were absorbed in plans to defend Marie Theresa's Austria against Prussia and were wondering how France might rid herself gracefully and advantageously of her white elephant, Louisiana. Washington on his part could have been thinking about the fantastic recent growth of the English population in America — two and a half million people now — and about how the pressure of immigration would fill up the Ohio valley as quickly as he had seen the filling up of Lord Fairfax's Shenandoah valley. And from the Ohio valley these swarming English would press on in no time to the fabulous Mississippi.

Major Washington spoke no French. Saint-Pierre's English was far from fluent. How the two managed to converse is not known, but the Virginian understood perfectly what the Frenchman's reaction was to Dinwiddie's demand that the French withdraw from the Ohio. Far from agreeing to the demand, Saint-Pierre told Washington with icy politeness to get his poaching traders out of the valley at once before he was forced to drive them out bloodily with the twenty-two thousand French soldiers who, he said, were even then on the march to the Forks of the Ohio with materials and cannon for the construction of a great stronghold, Fort Duquesne.

Washington's delivery to Governor Dinwiddie, at Williamsburg in mid-January, 1754, of Saint-Pierre's ultimatum put in motion the costliest struggle in English history, the French and Indian War. At bottom, that war was a struggle between opposing ideologies, Bourbon absolutism versus John Locke's "the natural rights of man." Its immediate outcome was the final defeat of La Salle's dream of empire in North America. And later it would lead inevitably to a historic turning point in world affairs, the Louisiana Purchase.

11

France Loses an Empire

FOR NEARLY THREE YEARS, starting in 1755, the French and Indian War brought a series of ghastly defeats to the British by the French and their Indian allies at strategic points between the English colonies and French Canada. The period seemed to prove that the absolutist Bourbon government of Louis XV was much superior to England's "rights-of-man" government in directing an army. The English generals in America were confused by a welter of plans and orders from embattled Tory and Whig members of Parliament, from colonial assemblies jealous of each other, and even from King George II at such times when he could tear himself away from his mistresses and from his concern about his Hanover estates in his native Germany.

But in 1756 William Pitt, who had become the idol of the colonists, took over the British government as prime minister. Pitt was a super-imperialist, an anti-monarchist, and, for a member of Parliament, quite democratic. He still believed that the thirteen colonies were of first importance to British domination of world trade, and he argued that the huge cost of a war in America would be more than repaid in trade benefits. Inspired by his leadership, his generals conducted slashing campaigns that soon overwhelmed the French. Fort Louisbourg fell to the English in July, 1757. Soon after, the French blew up and retreated from Fort Duquesne at the Forks of the Ohio and the British built Fort Pitt on the spot. The French defenders of Fort Niagara capitulated in July, 1759. The beautiful rock city of Quebec fell in September, 1759, after a dramatic battle in which two great generals lost their lives, the English James Wolfe and the French Louis Joseph, marquis de Montcalm. On September 8, 1760, with Montreal surrounded by three sets of British troops, the governor of Canada surrendered that province to Pitt's all-conquering hordes. The surrender of Canada and the Great Lakes meant the surrender also of the Ohio valley, the Illinois country and everything else in the east sector of French Louisiana between the Mississippi and the Appalachians. The Canadian governor at the time was the marquis de Vaudreuil who had been called to Quebec from New Orleans some years before.

It was against this background of disaster that Vaudreuil's replacement at New Orleans, Louis Billouart, chevalier de Kerlérec, managed Louisiana through the 1750's. Kerlérec, a former naval officer, soon discovered what Vaudreuil knew so well, that the province was a strange and independent land that could not be made to conform to the plans of men. At first, New Orleans enjoyed a touch of prosperity. England and Spain were still friends and British privateers were allowing ships to proceed unmolested past Cuba into the Gulf of Mexico and on to Mobile and New Orleans. In 1756, Kerlérec completed an elaborate new stone Fort Chartres near the Illinois villages of Prairie du Rocher and Kaskaskia "to insure possession of the country, to make an impression on the Indians, and halt the progress of the English in our territory."

But, as the tides of war turned against France in the north, the old Louisiana troubles returned — inflation, Indian attacks, hurricanes, epidemics, crop failures. Kerlérec showed his ignorance of the Mississippi transport problem when he ordered crews from Fort Chartres in 1757 to build a stronghold near the mouth of the Ohio. He named it Fort Massiac, for the marine minister whom Madame de Pompadour had installed after the brief tenure of her friend Monsieur Machault. Fort Massiac was to be an Ohio valley center from which supplies and soldiers from New Orleans would be forwarded for the defense of Fort Duquesne and of Fort Vincennes on the Wabash. The British fleet in the Gulf of Mexico resumed blockading the mouth of the Mississippi before Fort Massiac was finished. When Governor Kerlérec tried to send a few supplies from New Orleans by keelboat a thousand miles north to Fort Massiac, he found a scarcity of oarsmen — fifty oarsmen were required to handle an eighty-foot keelboat — and a scarcity of oars, poles, ropes, provisions, sails, walking boards and everything else needed to propel such clumsy craft against the current past the rocks, sandbars, reefs, ambushing Indians and submerged trees that had always made transport on the great river mainly a downstream affair. One of Kerlérec's supply boats did reach Massiac, but in a harrowing voyage that took four months. By then the English General John Forbes and his men had occupied the ruins of Fort Duquesne.[1]

After the fall of Quebec, Kerlérec found himself answering questions about the boundaries of Louisiana put to him by Louis XV's new chief minister, the duc de Choiseul, as the minister prepared for peace talks. It was not easy for Kerlérec to determine who owned what in that part of the world. In principle if not in practice Spain still maintained that everything in North America had been given to her by Pope Alexander VI in 1493. She asserted that France and England — and Russia, too, in the Alaska region — were occupying parts of this Spanish hemisphere by her sufferance. Practically, the claim of France to the total drainage of the Mississippi both east and west of the river was beyond dispute, except for a portion of far-west terrain running a couple of hundred miles northeast of Santa Fe into Quivira where the Spanish had been trading with Apache and Comanche Indians for many years. Of course the Mississippi drainage claim was partly theoretical since nobody had found the river's source somewhere north and west of Father Hennepin's Falls of St. Anthony and south of La Vérendrye's Lake of the Woods. Nobody had found the source of a single one of the Mississippi's west branches either — the sources of the Missouri, Platte, Arkansas and Red that were presumed to be in the high mountains that the La Vérendrye brothers had seen.

As for the ownership of East Texas, Governor Kerlérec could only gather conflicting opinions for Choiseul. There had been the claim of La Salle in 1682 to the land between the Red River and the Rio Grande in addition to the Mississippi drainage. Two years later, La Salle had altered his claim by putting Louisiana's south boundary at his Texas colony on Matagorda Bay which, he said, was near the mouth of a west branch of the Mississippi. A few years later, Captain de León's Spanish soldiers had pushed up from their Rio Grande presidio to the Trinity River region and beyond to claim the La Salle country for Spain. By the 1720's, the happy smuggler, Louis Juchereau de St. Denis, was operating from the Red River deep into Texas. He was ignoring a Hispano-French boundary on the Red River divide near Natchitoches which France had accepted after the War of the Quadruple Alliance. And now in Kerlérec's time, French traders at Natchitoches acted as though most of Texas belonged to France and kept alive the old Spanish dread of a French attempt to seize her Mexican mines below the Rio Grande.

The boundary situation around Mobile Bay and Mississippi Sound east of New Orleans was just as complicated. That country, explored and claimed by Iberville in 1699, was being called Louisiane de l'Est in the 1750's, though hardly any of it was part of the eastside drainage of the Mississippi. Its rivers — the Pearl, Pascagoula, Mobile and their branches — emptied directly into the Gulf of Mexico at or near Mississippi Sound. Bienville had explored the Mobile region northward until he was stopped by hostile Chickasaw Indians above the 32d parallel of latitude near present Jackson, Mississippi, and Bienville National Forest. The land beyond that parallel was in Louisiana proper. The east boundary of Louisiane de l'Est was the Perdido River just short of Pensacola. All the empty land east of the Perdido was Spanish — part of the original Florida that Ponce de León had claimed for Spain in 1513.

Kerlérec could have supplied Choiseul with one more bit of information. The water route from the Mississippi to Mississippi Sound and the gulf by way of Bayou Manchac, Lake Maurepas and Lake Pontchartrain — the route that Iberville had explored and had found full of fallen trees and alligators — was still obstructed in 1759. It was of no practical use as an alternate route from the big river to the gulf — a route which might have threatened the status of New Orleans as the sole water gate to the Mississippi valley. Bayou Manchac (Manchac means "entrance" in Choctaw) had been named the Iberville River, though it was only a sullen backwash of the Mississippi, not a river. When the Mississippi was low, the water ran out of the Iberville, leaving a stinking marsh behind.[2]

Some French statesmen have been caricatured as paunchy, sluggish types like the old sports in Toulouse-Lautrec posters who are leering wearily at shady young ladies over a glass of cognac. Etienne-François, duc de Choiseul, was not that type at all. His lithe figure vibrated energy and youth. His small eyes flashed with intelligence. He had an ugly face, but his wavy red hair, his impudent turned-up nose, his sensuous lips, his warmth, humor, elegance, gallantry and wit drew everybody to him, including a string of delectable and notorious mistresses. He was born in 1719 into an aristocratic Lorraine family and he had served with honor in the War of the Austrian Succession. He became Madame de Pompadour's favorite in 1753 when he persuaded her to remove a teen-aged girl cousin of his from Versailles before Louis XV succumbed to the cousin's adolescent charms. The grateful Pompadour sent Choiseul to Rome and to Vienna as French ambassador and then, in 1757–1758, loaded him down with nearly every high office that the king could give — the ministries of war, marine, foreign affairs, posts and roads, and general of the army and navy. He handled these burdens through the combined Seven Years' War and French and Indian War with the greatest ease. After each day of exhausting work, he was ready to join the king and Pompadour for a few hours of strenuous royal gaiety.

It would seem that no man could stand such a pace. Choiseul not only stood it but proved himself to be the greatest minister that France had had since Cardinal Richelieu and Jean-Baptiste Colbert. His attitude toward Louisiana was based on information at first hand. In 1750, he had married a very rich fifteen-year-old girl who happened to be the daughter of Antoine Crozat, marquis de Châtel — Louis XIV's banker who had gambled calamitously on Louisiana's prospects from 1712 to 1717. Knowledge of Crozat's experience led Choiseul to regard the province as a needless drain on the royal treasury — a property that France could do without while pursuing Choiseul's long-term policy. That policy had as its purpose the rebuilding of the shattered French army and navy so that France could rise again to power and destroy Great Britain's world hegemony.

To achieve these ends, Choiseul had to have the strong support of Spain's new Bourbon king, Charles III, who had just succeeded his half-brother Ferdinand VI. Charles would develop into the best of Spain's Bourbon monarchs but he was new at the job in 1760 and overly incensed at England, whose privateers were harassing Spanish ships in the Caribbean again. In August of 1761, the wily Choiseul induced Charles to renounce his uneasy alliance with England and to join his cousin Louis XV in one of those sentimental Bourbon "family pacts" as had happened twice before when England had seemed to threaten the French and Spanish Bourbons. Choiseul was aware that Spain had fallen to the status of a third-rate power without military strength. But she carried great weight in the world, like a truculent gone-to-seed grande dame who counted because she had once ruled society. Besides, Spain had valuable colonial resources. Choiseul knew that

Though Etienne-François, duc de Choiseul, owed his eminence to the influence of Madame de Pompadour, he was the one able official in Louis XV's government. (Engraving by E. Ronjat after a portrait by C. A. Vanloo, originally published by the University of California Press; reprinted by permission of The Regents of the University of California)

The wayward Louis XV was still a handsome man in 1762 when François Hubert Drouais did this portrait of him, dimple and all. (Courtesy of the Musée de Versailles et des Trianons)

Britain's peace terms would contain demands for much territory. He hoped to meet these demands with Spanish lands rather than those of France.

The family pact obliged Charles III to join France in war against England. He did so in December, 1761. England then declared war on Spain and caused Charles great pain some months later by capturing Havana and the rest of Cuba, the jewel of Spanish islands in the West Indies. England also seized the Spanish Philippines. When Charles complained of these losses, Choiseul explained that they had the effect of weakening Britain's military strength by diffusion at a time when talks were starting to end the French and Indian War. Then Choiseul asked Charles to accept secretly, with Louis XV's compliments, the westside drainage of the Mississippi to compensate Spain for her losses. The gift included the New Orleans delta area on the east bank of the river (see the map on page 86). Choiseul knew that Charles would want that bit of east-bank land in addition to the west-bank vastness because it was the guardian of everything above it. Nobody could leave Louisiana by the Mississippi without passing New Orleans.

It is important to understand that this proffered gift was precisely the vast million square miles of land on the westside drainage of the Mississippi (plus New Orleans) that would constitute the Louisiana Purchase forty-two years later. Charles III could see its value as a buffer if the English should try to advance across the Mississippi toward Spanish Texas and New Mexico. And still he must have had strong reservations about owning it. He owned a colossal domain already — far more than he could take care of — stretching from Patagonia to Mexico, Texas, New Mexico and California. As the historian, Herbert Bolton, put it, "he felt about Louisiana as though another baby had arrived." But he was trapped by his own feelings of dynastic loyalty. In response to Louis XV's magnanimity he could only exclaim, "Oh, no, dear cousin! You are too generous!" and accept the west-side white elephant. The transfer was made official by a very secret treaty signed at Fontainebleau on November 3, 1762.[3]

While Choiseul was concocting the Fontainebleau treaty, he was working hard on the British at Spain's expense to save something for a desperate, demoralized France. England, like Spain, had a new king, George III, who succeeded his muddleheaded father in October, 1760. George III was only twenty-two years old at the time, but Choiseul perceived that this stolid, industrious young autocrat had extraordinary aims and prejudices that might be turned to the advantage of Louis XV. George had grown up despising the weaknesses of the Georges before him. He was determined to be an absolutist ruler on the Bourbon model, not a figurehead. His first step was to abolish all that "natural rights of man" nonsense by buying enough members of Parliament so that he could control the decisions of that body. His biggest problem was the demagogue William Pitt, whose great popularity as a winner of wars for world domination encouraged the unwashed masses in England and in America to challenge the prerogatives of monarchy. In the second year of his reign, George removed Pitt from the office of prime minister — a feat achieved partly by declaring that Pitt's "bloody and expensive wars" were driving Great Britain into bankruptcy. In this effort of the king to stop the commoner from winning more wars and getting more popular, Choiseul saw his chance.

By the fall of 1762, Choiseul was ready to talk peace with England and Spain. One of his main concerns was to recover the valuable French sugar islands in the West Indies — Martinique, Guadeloupe, St. Lucia, Grenada — which the English had seized. With this in mind, he had already offered the Mobile area (Louisiane de l'Est) to Britain — secretly and deceitfully, since he knew that Charles III of Spain was desperately anxious to deny the English a port on the Gulf of Mexico. To make Mobile more attractive to the English, Choiseul invented a "branch" of the Mississippi by which English craft coming down the big river could bypass New Orleans and thus be independent of French customs officials and other port authorities (Louisiana was still French officially). Choiseul's "branch" was actually the useless Iberville River to Lake Pontchartrain and Mississippi Sound.

The talks began in December and ended on February 10, 1763, with the signing of the Treaty of Paris by the duke of Bedford, the duc de Praslin (Choiseul's cousin), and a very glum Spanish delegate, the marqués de Grimaldi. The terms of the victor were probably more lenient than they would have been if the militant William Pitt had represented Britain's interest instead of George III. Britain restored Martinique and Guadeloupe to France in exchange for Canada and for all of Louisiana lying east of the Mississippi from the river's far north source down through the Ohio and Illinois valleys to Iberville River. The Mobile Bay region from the Mississippi delta east to Spanish Florida at the Perdido went to Great Britain, too. However, the English got wind of the choked condition of the Iberville and Choiseul had to guarantee that English shipping would have free use of the

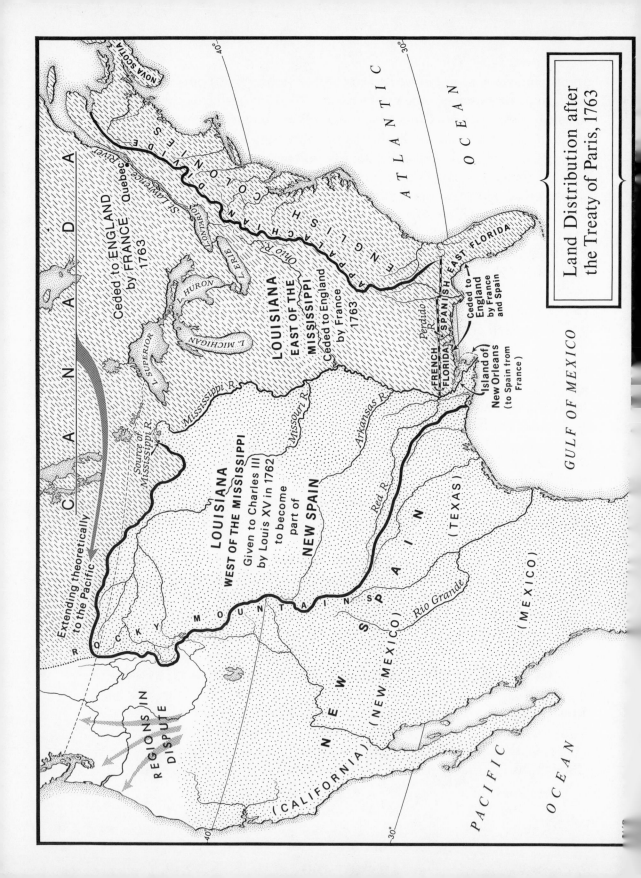

Land Distribution after
the Treaty of Paris, 1763

NOVA SCOTIA

CANADA

Quebec

St. Lawrence River

Ceded to ENGLAND
by FRANCE
1763

L. SUPERIOR

L. HURON

L. MICHIGAN

L. ERIE

Source of
Mississippi R.

Mississippi R.

Ohio R.

APPALACHIAN

ENGLISH COLONIES

ATLANTIC OCEAN

40°

30°

LOUISIANA
EAST OF THE
MISSISSIPPI
Ceded to England
by France
1763

SPANISH EAST FLORIDA

Perdido R.

FRENCH FLORIDA

Island of
New Orleans
(to Spain from
France)

Ceded to
England
by France
and Spain

GULF OF MEXICO

Missouri R.

LOUISIANA
WEST OF THE MISSISSIPPI
Given to Charles III
by Louis XV in 1762
to become
part of
NEW SPAIN

Arkansas R.

Red R.

(TEXAS)

NEW SPAIN

Extending theoretically
to the Pacific

ROCKY MOUNTAINS

(NEW MEXICO)

Rio Grande

(MEXICO)

REGIONS IN DISPUTE

(CALIFORNIA)

40°

30°

PACIFIC OCEAN

Mississippi past New Orleans to the gulf if the Iberville failed as an exit.[4] Finally, Charles III found himself obliged by the terms of the treaty to give all of Spain's Florida east of the Perdido to Great Britain as the price of getting back Cuba and the Philippines.

When the treaty was made public, Choiseul still kept secret the fact that France had given Louisiana west of the Mississippi to Spain "to indemnify Charles III for his sacrifice of Florida." He put the rosiest possible construction on the peace terms and persuaded the municipal authorities of Paris that the terms deserved a national celebration and memorial. There was a field near the Champs-Elysées between the Tuileries and the Seine, a field used for duels and *al fresco* lovemaking. In June, 1763, the field became Place Louis XV (later Place de la Concorde). In the center of it, the authorities erected an equestrian statue of Le Bien-Aimé on a pedestal with four allegorical figures at its corners — Force, Prudence, Justice and Peace. The opening festivities consisted of processions, fireworks, dancing and free wine. The noisy crowd seemed to know that it was celebrating the loss of the French empire in America and mixed its dancing with jeers at Choiseul, at Madame de Pompadour and at the king — no longer Le Bien-Aimé. Someone composed a chant about the pedestal's four female figures using names other than Force, Prudence, Justice and Peace. The names in the chant were Vintimille, Mailly, Châteauroux and Pompadour — the first three referring to the beautiful Mailly sisters who had been the king's mistresses in succession before Madame de Pompadour took him over permanently.

The bitter irony of the celebration may have depressed Pompadour. It was her last public appearance. Ten months later she died of "heart disease" at the height of her beauty and power. She was only forty-two. The equestrian statue of the king had a brief career. In 1792, the Commune changed the name of Place Louis XV to Place de la Révolution and the statue was replaced by a guillotine.

If ever a land was left to its own eccentric devices that land was the million square miles of Spain's Louisiana — the westside drainage of the Mississippi plus New Orleans — for some years after the Treaty of Paris. Until the fall of 1764 only a few officials knew that it belonged to Spain. The viceroy at Havana did not bother to replace the French acting governor, Jean-Jacques Blaise d'Abbadie, with a Spaniard for two more years, and d'Abbadie had to die to bring that about.

In the meantime, Frenchmen continued to run Louisiana after a fashion in the name of Louis XV. In the New Orleans area, smuggling had always been the stable and principal occupation of honest men. When the French and Indian War ended, it became virtually the only profitable business. The complete absence of law and order and other righteous restraints gave Bienville's crescent town a relaxed and interesting air even if business was poor and inflation rampant. The Place d'Armes was a hotbed of plotting to avoid shipping imposts. The warehouses of the river front were loaded with contraband that had come in from the whole gulf area, including Mexico's Veracruz and England's newly acquired Florida. The city's three thousand residents were of every sort of breed, creed and condition. The elite were French officials, planters and merchants, and also the many English agents of firms in New York, Boston, Philadelphia and Mobile. Black slaves from the West Indies formed the largest group and they were harshly controlled. Next in numbers were the Louisiana-grown French creoles — descendants of John Law's wealthy *concessionaires*, of Iberville's convicts, of Bienville's "King's girls nurtured in virtue and piety," of Paris prostitutes and pickpockets who had been shanghaied by Law's *bandouliers*. Along the river, Alsatian and Swiss farmers from the "German coast" hawked their fruits and vegetables. The loveliest of street girls, part Hispano-French, part Negro, flirted with sailors from every land. Indians in breechclouts stalked the streets and talked prices in sign language with French-Canadian fur traders from Kaskaskia, Cahokia, Fort Chartres and Ste. Geneviève.

Some of the French Canadians were refugees from Canada, which they had left in disgust when Montreal fell to Jeffrey Amherst's forces and Scotsmen began arriving on the St. Lawrence to take over the far-west fur trade that the La Vérendryes had worked so hard to develop. The French refugees had traveled by canoe to New Orleans along the same romantic and beautiful water route that Marquette had pioneered ninety years earlier — up the Ottawa to Michilimackinac and across Lake Michigan to Green Bay. From there they paddled up the winding Fox and down the Wisconsin to its mouth near the thriving Indian village and trading post called Prairie du Chien, and so on down the great river, the east bank of which had just become British.

In New Orleans, the refugees reported that the British had not arrived on their side of the Mississippi as yet to claim their property because of the prevailing Indian unrest. All the river tribes were disturbed by the tragic rebellion against the British army which the Ottawa chief, Pontiac, had organized in the Great Lakes region through the summer and fall of 1763. Amherst's soldiers had none of the respect for Indians that was customary with the French Canadians. When the English had occupied the French forts they had treated the tribes with contempt, had scoffed at their religion and folkways, had refused to sell them ammunition for their hunting, had raised the prices of trade goods outrageously and had let them know that they would be driven from their lands in time to make way for English colonists. Pontiac led his tribes in a futile struggle marked by hideous brutality on both sides. But the Indians were so successful for a while that the incompetent Amherst searched for any means to stop them, including a plan to infect them with smallpox. In the end, the Great Lakes Indians were defeated, not by Britain's might or genius but by a shortage of arms, food and winter clothing after they had seized and destroyed every fort in the region except Pitt and Detroit.

A thousand miles up the Mississippi from New Orleans, a second French city had its origin in this period. It derived from the activities of a Frenchman of foresight and imagination, Pierre de Laclède Liguest, who ran a small commission house in New Orleans called Maxent, Laclède & Cie. Laclède had just received a six-year monopoly of the Upper Louisiana fur trade and he began to take a special interest in the Missouri valley — the almost-forgotten valley that Bourgmond had explored into present Nebraska and had hoped to explore on and on to the Missouri's source en route to the Pacific. When Laclède heard from the Canadian refugees that the supply of beaver and otter and mink in the Lake Superior region showed signs of failing to meet the demand he decided on his life's work. To exploit his fur monopoly, he would establish a trading post in Upper Louisiana and he would develop the Missouri valley as a fur country. It had, he felt, none of the disadvantages of the Canadian northlands, the long bitter winters and complicated transport problems. He would encourage Osage, Pawnee and other Missouri River tribes to bring their furs to his post and he would float them down the ice-free Mississippi to seagoing ships at New Orleans for delivery to the furriers of Europe.

It was a large project to be undertaken by a middle-aged man of moderate means and indifferent health. But Laclède's credit was good and he had at hand to do the hard work a young assistant of unusual intelligence, drive, ambition and integrity. This sterling character was a French creole boy named Auguste Chouteau, aged thirteen. Chouteau had taught himself to read and write while he worked to support his mother. His father had vanished soon after Auguste was born. In the fall of 1763, Laclède and Chouteau loaded a thirty-ton keelboat with tools and provisions, sent it to Fort Chartres above the mouth of the Ohio for winter storage, and pushed upstream in their canoe to find a likely spot for their trading post that they hoped would shift the hub of the fur trade from Montreal and Michili-mackinac to Upper Louisiana. Laclède found his spot on a low bluff above the flood stage of the Mississippi a dozen miles below the mouth of the Missouri and across the river from the old French-Canadian village of Cahokia. In February, 1764, Auguste Chouteau, all of fourteen now, brought thirty men to the spot and bossed them in the preliminary building of Laclède's post and village. Curious Indians and French Canadians from the now-British Illinois country took an interest in the work. Traders, some of them Englishmen, began to appear from Prairie du Chien, from Green Bay, even from Michilimackinac. Laclède himself arrived during the high water of April armed with a plan of streets for his village. He named it St. Louis in honor of the great Louis XV who, he thought, still owned westside Louisiana. If he had known the truth, he might have called it St. Charles for Charles III, a name that would be applied to a nearby rival post five years later. Before the summer ended, Laclède's post was doing a lively business, thirty French families had settled in St. Louis, and a French officer was preparing to set up his Upper Louisiana command there just as soon as the British arrived to take over Fort Chartres.

Such was the realized dream of one Frenchman, so many of whom had found only heartbreak in Louisiana. St. Louis continued to thrive. Long before Laclède's death in 1778 it had grown to a town of two hundred stone-built houses and a thousand people drawing trade from England's Wisconsin and Illinois rivers as well as from Spain's turbulent Missouri. An easy grade and a wide road ran from the trading post down to a point at the river's edge. Two centuries later a graceful arch of great height would rise from the river bank near that point marking St. Louis as the gateway through which those who followed Laclède and Auguste Chouteau were propelled by manifest destiny to conquer the wilds of the Louisiana Purchase.

While St. Louis was being born, a pathetic sort of French refugee was appearing in New Orleans. These lost souls called themselves Acadians.

*Residents of St. Louis today are reminded of their
founder, Pierre Laclède Liguest, every time they
pass this statue of him by Hartley in front of City Hall.
(Courtesy of the Missouri Historical Society)*

They had been expelled by the British from their native L'Acadie (Nova Scotia) in 1755 for refusing to pledge allegiance to King George II. The most famous of them was totally imaginary, the heroine of the poem *Evangeline*, written in 1847 by Henry Wadsworth Longfellow, who had never been within a thousand miles of Louisiana. Few poems in history have been so sharply criticized. Longfellow was accused of grossly exaggerating Evangeline's woes in her lifelong search for her lost Acadian lover in Louisiana and elsewhere.[5] But the Boston poet could not possibly have overplayed the troubles actually endured by the exiles, whose ancestors had begun settling the Bay of Fundy region years before the Virginians had arrived at Jamestown.

It should be said that the English had some reason to expel them. Ever since the French cession of L'Acadie to Britain in 1713, these frugal, industrious, illiterate, intensely Catholic peasants had made no secret of their hatred of the English and they had been accused from time to time of seditious activities. Their stubborn refusal to pledge allegiance to George II during the French and Indian War was regarded as the last straw. In the fall of 1755, British soldiers herded some six thousand Acadian men, women and children together at Grand Pré and other Minas Basin points where the exiles-to-be could watch while other soldiers burned their villages, barns and farmhouses and destroyed their crops and livestock — even their pet cats and dogs. Then they were packed off on British ships down the Bay of Fundy. Those who survived the overcrowding and the grief of this *"grand dérangement"* were dumped wherever convenient — some in concentration camps in England, some in the American colonies, some in Holland and Germany for transfer to France. Nobody wanted them wherever they were dumped. The Protestant New Englanders treated them abominably because they were Catholic, though the papist Marylanders were kind to them. The mainland French deplored their lack of sophistication and refused funds to set them up on farms in France. Through the years, many hundreds of them wandered about forlornly — to French Guiana, to the West Indies, to Nicaragua and Honduras, even to the Falkland Islands near Cape Horn. A few reached Louisiana in the late 1750's. One Acadian ship missed the mouth of the Mississippi and its passengers perished when the ship sank in a storm off Matagorda Bay.

Always these homeless people sought some part of French soil where they would be welcome as Frenchmen. It was the duc de Choiseul who found such a place for them. News came to him about a group of Acadians who were dying like flies in the malarial heat of Santo Domingo. It occurred to him that people with such loyalty to France would be useful to uphold French interests in Louisiana, now that the province belonged, secretly, to Spain. He decided to try them out. Early in 1765, his agents transported two hundred and thirty of them at Louis XV's expense from Santo Domingo to New Orleans. Two more Acadian groups followed from the West Indies, bringing the total sent in that year to more than a thousand. Some of these immigrants began improving empty land for farms along the Mississippi in what are now St. James and Iberville parishes. The majority pushed west to Bayou Teche where higher prairie land was better for the raising of live-stock, which had been their specialty in L'Acadie. More Acadians arrived on the Teche each year as word got around that the outcasts had found a home.

Of course they were stunned to discover what Choiseul had neglected to tell them, that their Louisiana home was not French after all, but Spanish. The interim French governor, d'Abbadie, died on February 4, 1765. For thirteen months thereafter, d'Abbadie's French aide, Charles Philippe Aubry, kept up a pretense of a Louisiana government until Don Antonio de Ulloa arrived in New Orleans to take charge in the name of Charles III of Spain, and to conduct an official ceremony of transfer. Meanwhile the Acadians and the rest of the people who composed the society of the delta area — French creoles, West Indians, Germans, English — developed a violent aversion to becoming Spanish. As an alternative, a band of hotheads proposed the creation of an independent republic of Louisiana which would go its own way with the financial and political blessing of France and Spain. To this end, they sent an emissary to Paris to see ex-Governor Bienville, now in his eighty-sixth year, hoping that the patron saint of New Orleans would induce Choiseul to arrange an interview for the emissary with the king. The rebels were not pleased when Choiseul turned Bienville down, and they were not pleased with their first Spanish governor either.

Ulloa, aged fifty, was a literal-minded scientist, not a diplomat with a Mad Hatter's gift for managing Louisiana's Alice in Wonderland scheme of things. He had recently walked across South America to map and to measure the length of the equator. During his first year at New Orleans he applied the sensible methods of the surveyor to the task of leading his sulky subjects out of their state of anarchy into the economic and spiritual orbit of the rest of Spain's empire. Ulloa spoke no French, and few people in New Orleans spoke Spanish. The Spanish viceroy at Havana had sent him to rule without enough troops or money to enforce his decrees, which were designed to make smuggling a crime instead of the normal order of business. When the date arrived for the transfer ceremony, Ulloa and Charles Philippe Aubry thought it prudent to avoid trouble by conducting the ceremony privately a hundred miles away at the mouth of the Mississippi. There at Fort Balize the two officials drew the same sort of well-behaved audience of gulls and egrets that had witnessed La Salle's ceremony of possession in 1682. Ulloa did not announce publicly that the transfer ceremony had been held, but the news got out anyhow. When the governor continued stubbornly to issue anti-smuggling decrees and began building forts with Spanish flags flying above them opposite the English garrisons at Natchez and at Manchac, a gang of rebels staged a four-day revolution (October 29–November 1, 1768) and assumed control of Louisiana — the first colony in North America to declare its independence. Ulloa fled to Havana and then to Spain, where a furious Charles III began planning to quell the uprising. First, however, he sent Ulloa to Paris to see what his French cousin would do about his disorderly subjects. Louis XV refused to intervene.

For some time Charles III had been making remarkable progress in modernizing Spain's archaic government. He decided now to spare no expense to make Louisiana a working part of his colonial empire. In July of 1769, three thousand Spanish troops — equal in number to the entire white population of New Orleans — boarded twenty-one of the best warships in the Spanish fleet. At their head was Spain's greatest general, a professional Irish soldier named Alexander O'Reilly. On July 23, this armada moved majestically past Fort Balize into the Mississippi and anchored off New Orleans on August 17 while an awed populace watched the enormous flotilla from the waterfront. There was no sign of protest. Throughout the day Spanish soldiers in dress uniform disembarked at the levee, paraded with martial music in the Place d'Armes, and raised Spanish flags everywhere while Bienville's city shook with the boom of Charles III's cannon. Next day a suspiciously affable O'Reilly hinted at amnesty when he invited all those involved in the revolution of 1768 to a reception in the governor's mansion. But amnesty was far from the general's mind. During the drinking of champagne toasts at the reception, his soldiers arrested thirteen of the rebel leaders on charges of high treason against the Spanish crown. One of these died in jail before the trial. O'Reilly hanged six of them in public and shipped six to Havana to serve long prison terms.

While O'Reilly was cracking the whip in New Orleans he made it clear that Spain owned Louisiana and was in charge of its affairs even though the men whom he hired to run the government and to garrison the forts along the Mississippi were practically all Frenchmen. He managed also to bring trade to a standstill by enforcing the kind of decrees that Ulloa had been unable to enforce to end smuggling, particularly the smuggling of English goods, the profitability of which was growing by leaps and bounds. Fortunately for business, O'Reilly returned to Spain in 1770 and Luis de Unzaga y Amezaga arrived in New Orleans as governor. Unzaga, a wise and tolerant administrator, got trade going again by ignoring O'Reilly's decrees and any other orders received from officials in Madrid to correct the lawless ways of Louisiana's Frenchmen.

Of all those Europeans watching the pressures of international events that pushed in on Louisiana from every direction, none was more interested or better informed than the duc de Choiseul. His purpose through the 1760's remained constant: To build up the power of France and Spain on land and sea while plotting to reduce that of Great Britain and to get revenge for the humiliating Treaty of Paris. Choiseul's plots centered on encouraging the English colonists in America to revolt, which would strain Britain's military resources. In 1768, he yearned to support the New Orleans revolutionists because they might inspire the English in America to revolt also. But he did not want to offend Charles III at a time when the king was trying so hard to make a Spanish province out of Louisiana.

Choiseul's French spies in Philadelphia kept him posted on how bitterly the colonists resented being taxed without representation to pay the cost of the king's American troops. He knew about the Sons of Liberty and their widespread riots against the Stamp Act of March, 1765, and about Patrick Henry's "If this be treason" speech in Williamsburg (the audience included Peter Jefferson's twenty-two-year-old son Thomas). Choiseul kept hoping that King George's Proclamation of 1763 would become a rallying point for colonial resistance. The proclamation banned colonists from settling on lands west of the Appalachian crest and east of the Mississippi — most of that part of Louisiana that Britain had won from France by the Treaty of Paris. George claimed that the ban was necessary to pacify Pontiac's warriors by giving them lands for their exclusive use. The colonists saw it differently, especially Virginians like Dr. Thomas Walker and the Washingtons, who felt cheated of their Ohio and Kentucky land grants that they had acquired by the terms of Virginia's royal charter. They believed that George III sought to keep them east of the Appalachians, where his soldiers could suppress their mutinous tendencies toward freedom and republicanism.

In 1770, Choiseul faced a crisis that threatened war with England before France and Spain were ready for it. England and Spain developed a simultaneous interest in a rich Pacific coast fur trade region above California — the New Albion region that Sir Francis Drake had claimed for Queen Elizabeth in 1579. The two nations began squabbling over the remote Falkland Islands in South America which both of them wanted to use as way stations for their ships rounding the Horn on their way to the Pacific coast. War seemed so imminent that Spain rushed forces into the Gulf of Mexico, believing that the conquest of Louisiana would be Britain's first objective. Choiseul saw great peril to his plans in such a war. If Britain should control both banks of the Mississippi, the American colonists would be flanked all around and could not hope to stage a revolution. The minister sent word to Charles III that Louis XV would not support his war against England and he warned that Spain would be unwise just then to challenge the world's strongest power. Charles saw his point. He yielded the Falklands to Britain and the crisis ended.

In this matter, the perceptive Choiseul found a new dimension for Louisiana, in startling addition to its power over commerce between the St. Lawrence and the Gulf of Mexico. This new dimension ran west. To reach the Pacific coast by ship around the Horn took a year of a trader's time, and another year to return home. Choiseul speculated that the same journey could be made overland from St. Louis in a few weeks. Traders could ascend the Missouri to its source, cross a short portage and descend to the sea on the river that drained the other side. Here was a practical trade route to the Pacific shore of greater promise than the fabled Northwest Passage to Cathay. And, in a larger sense, it would give the possessor of Louisiana control of the continent from east to west, as well as from north to south.

But the minister knew in 1770 that Louisiana's future was out of his hands. His long service to France was nearly over. The situation was ironical. Madame de Pompadour had brought him power. Now another beautiful mistress of the king was taking his power away. Marie Jeanne Bécu, the illegitimate daughter of a Paris tax collector, rose to fame as a shill and prostitute in the comte Du Barry's Paris gambling house. Louis XV met her in 1767 and made her his official mistress as the comtesse Du Barry. Choiseul disliked her from the start, not because of her lowly origin but because she did little to make the king realize that his absolutist regime was in great danger. The *philosophes*, the middle class, the students, the clergy, the peasants, all were demanding reform and relief from the burden of this extravagant and corrupt Bourbon bureaucracy. Louis XV, aging, listless, uncomprehending, refused to listen to them.

Month by month, the king's bitterness grew against "the spirit of independence and fanaticism in my kingdom" and the manner in which his subjects "dispute with me the sovereign authority that I hold only of God." On Christmas Eve, 1770, pressed by Du Barry and her circle, he made perhaps the greatest of many mistakes when he sent these words to Choiseul, the one man in his government whom Frenchmen in general trusted and admired: "Cousin, the dissatisfaction caused me by your services forces me to banish you to Chanteloup, whither you will repair within twenty-four hours. I should have sent you much further off, but for the particular regard I have for Madame de Choiseul, in whose health I feel great interest. Take care your conduct does not force me to change my mind. Whereupon I pray God, cousin, to have you in His holy and worthy keeping."

Choiseul found some pleasure in banishment, basking in the esteem of courtiers and commoners for the rest of his life. He refused to give up his habit of living almost like a king, even though he could no longer afford it. He died of tuberculosis, at the age of sixty-six, in Paris in 1785, still elegant, witty and attractive. Not a sou remained of the vast fortune that his wife had inherited from her father, Antoine de Crozat, Louisiana's first monopolist.

12

Spain Gets a Lemon

THE WHOLE WESTERN WORLD was torn by controversy over the rights of man at the time that Louis XV completed his disintegration and died at sixty-four of smallpox on May 10, 1774, to the relief of nearly everyone. England was in turmoil as the Lord North ministry upheld George III's autocratic ideas of colonial management against the liberal views of Lord Chatham (William Pitt), Edmund Burke and Charles James Fox. Across the Atlantic, Tory New Englanders deplored the firebrand utterances of the Virginians. Louis XV's quiet, mannerly grandson, aged nineteen, ascended the absolutist throne of France with a head full of heresies about the need for a retreat from absolutism. Many of Louis XVI's courtiers at Versailles had become supporters of the English colonists of late, hoping that the cause of freedom in America might triumph so that it might triumph later in Bourbon France.

Louis XVI's eighteen-year-old queen, Marie Antoinette, was a beautiful child whose love of pleasure and craving for affection prevented her from emulating her mother, Empress Maria Theresa of Austria, as a political leader of towering integrity. Marie Antoinette's marriage to the dauphin had been arranged by the duc de Choiseul just before Madame Du Barry engineered his dismissal. The girl was shocked by the corruption that she found at Versailles but she learned the ropes by joining the raffish clique of the king's reactionary brother, Charles Philippe, comte d'Artois. Her career of expensive frivolity thereafter may have been in reaction to her reclusive spouse, who did not find the time or the inclination to treat her like a wife for seven years.

Louis XVI named as his chief minister in the spring of 1774 that old Mississippi expert, the comte de Maurepas, who had not held high office since his tiff with Pompadour in 1749. If the king had been interested he could have learned from Maurepas a lot about the recent emergence of Louisiana from the mists of the La Salle–Bienville period. The St. Louis fur trade was thriving enough to alarm the new Scottish fur crowd who had taken over from the French in Montreal. The frontier Virginians in Kentucky and Tennessee were sending large amounts of meat and flour down the Mississippi to the gulf. English contraband from the West Florida ports of Mobile and Pensacola still arrived at the wharfs of New Orleans.

The Indians everywhere worked harder to increase their gathering of furs and skins as they became more and more dependent on the guns and goods of the traders. The total number of them on the Mississippi drainage probably exceeded a quarter of a million. Among them were the many Tejas tribes in Spanish Texas; Choctaws, Chickasaws and Creeks north and northeast of New Orleans; Missouris, Osages and Pawnees of the Missouri above Auguste Chouteau's St. Louis; Fox and Sioux and many more tribes in the Upper Mississippi country served by British traders out of Michilimackinac, Fort Detroit and Prairie du Chien at the mouth of the Wisconsin. Some of these Indians were peaceful and some hostile but all were fearful of the white man's intentions and jealous of each other. (See the map on page 103.)

The comte de Maurepas could have reported that total trade for the Louisiana region had passed the equivalent of a million dollars annually — a small sum compared to the West Indian trade, but enough to meet the high cost of poling keelboats upstream as well as sending flatboats down from the Fort Pitt country. Many upriver merchants sold their flatboats for lumber in New Orleans and spent the proceeds sailing in style from New Orleans to Philadelphia or Baltimore via Havana, and so on home by stage across the Alleghenies from Fort Cumberland to Fort Pitt — a charming trek of four thousand miles. Maurepas would have known how much chaos underlay the appearance of Spanish law and order, and how French and English residents and even some Spanish officials were hatching plots daily in the cafés of New Orleans to set up a Mississippi nation of their own. All in all, Spanish Louisiana in 1774 was a fascinating place to live for those who could stand the excitement and the uncertainty.

Meanwhile at Versailles the young French monarch appointed as his foreign affairs minister Charles Gravier, comte de Vergennes, a crafty diplomat with all the élan of a cold boiled potato. In his plodding way, Vergennes followed Choiseul's policy — to try to destroy British power with the aid of a compliant Spain by helping the English colonists to revolt, as the French in New Orleans had revolted briefly against the Spanish governor in 1768. Vergennes reasoned that if the revolution succeeded, France would be able to demand from the war-weary and grateful Americans the retrocession of Canada and its fur trade. And France, he hoped, could require of her friend Charles III a share in the recovered east side of the Mississippi drainage, and some of the west side too, now that Louisiana showed signs of having value. On the other hand, if Britain should maintain her dominance, France could avoid territorial loss by putting up some of Spain's colonial property once more at the bargaining table, as Choiseul had done at Paris in 1763.

Vergennes inherited from Choiseul a rejuvenated French navy. Charles III had continued to strengthen the Spanish fleet, a process begun by his half-brother, Ferdinand VI, after the War of the Austrian Succession. Together the two fleets might be a match for the British navy, the cost of which was becoming burdensome to George III in defending William Pitt's worldwide conquests. Vergennes noted with pleasure that George III's ministers kept on exercising their talent for enraging the Sons of Liberty and other restive Americans by insisting on England's right to tax the colonists to meet the cost of controlling them.

And then came passage by Parliament of the Quebec Act in May. For a decade, Virginians had been allowed to sell land and to colonize areas in Tennessee and Kentucky south of the Ohio in spite of the Proclamation of 1763 banning settlement west of the Appalachians. But the Quebec Act flatly denied the historic claims of Virginia and other colonies to rich lands north of the Ohio by extending the old French boundaries of Quebec tremendously — to include Illinois and all the Ohio country between Lake Erie and the Ohio. To the Protestant colonists, this was insupportable. The act gave the papist Frenchmen on the St. Lawrence an absolutist government on the Bourbon model by installing a ruling council chosen by George III — precisely what the Americans condemned. It eliminated trial by jury and restored the archaic privileges and powers of the Catholic Church. In brief, the Quebec Act ignored the basis of English political and religious freedom as established in 1215 by the Magna Charta. The colonists were convinced that parliament passed it to win the loyalty of the French Canadians so that they would join the British army in suppressing any American uprising.[1]

The Quebec and other so-called "coercive" acts impelled the colonists to call a meeting in Philadelphia of the First Continental Congress in September, 1774. At that meeting, the Virginia delegates read an inflammatory instruction prepared by Peter Jefferson's lawyer-son Thomas, thirty-one now, who had grown up at Shadwell believing that Virginia's trade area would extend inevitably far beyond the Blue Ridge at least to the Mississippi. Jefferson maintained that Parliament had no natural right to rule Virginia or any other English colony. This instruction, published later as *A Summary View of the Rights of British America*, had such an impact that young Jefferson found himself elected from Virginia to the Second Continental Congress of June, 1775. A year later, as a revolutionary leader, he wrote a document called the Declaration of Independence for the representatives of "the United States of America" — an eloquent name with implications of continental grandeur. The document was based on *A Summary View*. Much of its emotional force derived from the turn of a mind nurtured in western Virginia's unshackled frontier environment. By that time, the American Revolution was well along after battles at Lexington, Concord, Ticonderoga and Bunker Hill. General Washington was lifting the morale of those in his ragged patriot army by reminding them that if worst came to worst they could retreat to the Louisiana wilderness, that mystic haven from despotism "beyond the Susquehanna, beyond the Alleghenies, beyond the Ohio."

A few weeks before the colonies declared their independence, the comte de Vergennes induced Louis XVI to deliver secretly a million francs worth of munitions to the Americans. Pierre de Beaumarchais, the French dramatist who was writing *Le Mariage de Figaro* at the time, was in charge of the forty munitions ships. Charles III of Spain followed Louis XVI's lead by agreeing to supply an equal amount of munitions to be poled up the Mississippi from New Orleans to Fort Pitt. After the rebels beat Burgoyne at Saratoga in October of 1777, Vergennes thought it was safe for the absolutist monarchies, France and Spain, to become loving bedfellows of their ideological opposite, the United States, by joining the Continental Congress in open warfare against Britain. The actual Franco-American alliance began in the spring of 1778 with the signing of two treaties, one military and the other, commercial. French and British warships had their first clash in June.

But, much to Vergennes's surprise and chagrin, Spain was in no hurry to go to war against Britain. In his sixtieth year, Charles III was a far wiser and less docile member of the Bourbon family pact than he had been when Choiseul forced him to lose Florida to Britain in 1763. While his cousin Louis XVI wavered between following the advice of the *philosophes* to be more democratic and that of most of his courtiers to be more absolute than ever, Charles strengthened his own monarchy by building public works in Spain and by improving colonial administration in the Americas. He was quick to do what England and France were doing by equipping his navy with the new chronometers, the accuracy of which allowed navigators to determine longitude by comparing the time of a given position to the time at the Greenwich meridian. By 1779, his ships seldom missed the mouths of the Mississippi as Captain Beaujeu and La Salle had missed them in 1684.

Charles's diplomacy had two motivations — his desire to get back Gibraltar and Minorca, which Spain had lost to England at Utrecht, and his determination to protect his American possessions. His fear of foreign encroachment had increased greatly after the English took Florida and after the Falkland Islands fiasco of 1770. From her Florida ports, Britain threatened Mexico, Louisiana, the Spanish West Indies and the Spanish Main seaway to Central America. From the Falklands, she threatened California and the new sea otter trading post at Nootka Sound. To meet these threats, Charles decided to organize all of New Spain north of the Rio Grande into a vast network of presidios, roads and waterways for defense and for trade. An improved Camino Real from Natchitoches on the Red River would connect New Orleans and St. Louis with San Antonio, the Spanish capital and horse market of Texas, which would be tied in turn by new roads to the silver mines of Coahuila and to Santa Fe via El Paso. To these overland designs, Charles added his intent to control the Gulf of Mexico once more by recovering Florida — especially the British forts at Pensacola and Mobile on the gulf, and at Manchac (Fort Bute) and Natchez (Fort Panmure) on the Mississippi.

The Spanish king paid close attention to the South Pacific explorations

(1768–1775) of the Englishman James Cook. When Cook's *Resolution* and *Discovery* sailed from Plymouth in 1776 on a new scientific mission to map the North Pacific and look for a Northwest Passage eastward to Hudson Bay or to the Mississippi, Charles announced through his minister for the Indies, José de Gálvez, that the Pacific Ocean was Spanish water and that the west coast of California and on north to Russian Alaska was Spanish too, having been discovered and claimed by Spaniards as far north as Nootka Sound off present Vancouver Island. Gálvez instructed his brother, who was viceroy of Mexico, to seize Cook's ships if they stopped for provisions at any of the harbors of Spain's presidios and missions that had been established lately along the California coast to challenge English or Russian claims to that region.

The firmness and energy of Charles III inspired his colonial officials to do what they could in the monumental task of bringing Louisiana and Texas, New Mexico and California, into political and economic unity. One of these officials was the rugged frontiersman Juan Bautista de Anza, who pioneered a route in 1774 from Mexico through present Arizona to Spanish California. Two years later he guided a train of some two hundred and forty settlers along that trail to found San Francisco. Anza became governor of New Mexico in 1778 soon after the return to Santa Fe of the Franciscan priests Silvestre Vélez de Escalante and Francisco Atanasio Domínguez from their epical attempt to reach San Francisco from the Upper Rio Grande through the unknown defiles of the high Colorado Rockies. They were delayed so often along the way by the hospitality of the Ute Indians that they had no time to go farther than Utah Lake near present Salt Lake City. But their journey — the most phenomenal since Cabeza de Vaca's transcontinental tramp in the 1530's — brought them the soaring scenery of the San Juan Range, wonders like the Mesa Verde cliff dwellings and the orange-purple splendor of Utah's canyon lands. It laid the basis of a pack-train route from Santa Fe and Taos to the west coast that fur traders and horse thieves would know soon as the Spanish Trail.[2] And it convinced Governor Anza that trade between New Mexico and California could be built up more easily and comfortably through the cool well-watered Rockies than by way of the burning Arizona deserts.

As he looked for unity eastward from Santa Fe, Anza observed that the hostility of the Comanche Indians was the main obstacle to trade between the Upper Rio Grande settlements and those on the Mississippi. The

Charles III was not much to look at but he was the greatest of the Spanish kings after Philip II. He tried hard to make Louisiana a working part of Spain's colonial empire. (Courtesy of the Museo del Prado, Madrid)

Comanches had swept down from present Wyoming many years earlier, driven out the Padoucas (Apaches) and taken as their homeland the Canadian River and Red River regions of the high Louisiana plains east of Santa Fe and south of the Arkansas River. They had become marvelous horsemen, using Arabian stock stolen from the Santa Fe haciendas and from Mexican rancheros below the Rio Grande. The Red River headwaters in Palo Duro Canyon that Coronado had seen in 1541 were revered by them. They prevented New Orleans traders from pushing deep enough into Louisiana's southwestern wilds to find the source of this southernmost Mississippi branch — the source that determined the boundary of that southwest corner of Louisiana as La Salle had defined it. The tactics of the Comanches were so unpleasant that travelers from St. Louis found it prudent to give them a wide berth as they developed what would become in forty years the Santa Fe Trail along routes north of the Arkansas.

Anza's first task was to subdue a Comanche band under a chief named Cuerno Verde (Greenhorn) — a band that made a habit of looting the environs of Taos and Santa Fe and carrying off Pueblo Indians as slaves. In August of 1779, the governor led a force of soldiers, colonists and Pueblo Indians in a chase of the band up the Rio Grande into the lovely San Luis valley of present Colorado, over Poncha Pass to the Arkansas River and east to the plains at the foot of Pikes Peak by a variant of the ancient Ute Pass Trail. Anza's men defeated the Comanches and killed Cuerno Verde between Pikes Peak and the Spanish Peaks below a landmark summit still known as Greenhorn Mountain. The victory was important to the development eastward of Spanish New Mexico. Of importance to geographers was Anza's recognition that he entered La Salle's Louisiana when he crossed Poncha Pass, and that the Rio Grande had to have its source short of the pass instead of in the far arctic north, as legend had it. And, on the sparkling blue Upper Arkansas, Anza was overwhelmed by the massive line of fourteen-thousand-foot peaks of the Sawatch Range, which marked the Continental Divide. What he saw was one more instance of Louisiana's endless variety to add to those enticements reported by Hennepin and Lahontan, by St. Denis and the La Vérendryes, by the Mallets, Bourgmond and Bénard de La Harpe.

While Anza dreamed of Spanish unity against British imperialism stretching from the Mississippi through New Mexico to California and

Nootka Sound, two Americans and a Spanish aristocrat conspired in New Orleans to help George Washington win his war — each one for motives that had little relation to the motives of the other two. Their names were Oliver Pollock, a Pennsylvanian from Northern Ireland; James Willing, an alcoholic remittance man who was a member of the distinguished Willing merchant family of Philadelphia; and Bernardo de Gálvez, a shrewd and ambitious bachelor in his twenties who came to New Orleans as Governor Unzaga's military chief. Gálvez was being trained by his uncle José, the Spanish minister for the Indies, to succeed his father as viceroy of Mexico. In 1777, Charles III promoted the young man to the governorship of Louisiana.

The Irish-American, Oliver Pollock, had arrived in New Orleans in 1767 with a raging desire for fame and fortune after five years in Havana as an apprentice smuggler and agent for the Morris and Willing firm in Philadelphia. Robert Morris, a signer of the Declaration of Independence who would buy the munitions for General Washington, was Pollock's particular friend. Pollock had learned to speak fluent Spanish in Havana under the tutelage of his drinking companion General Alexander O'Reilly. Partly because of this congenial relationship, Pollock had sold flour to O'Reilly's army at half price when the general had landed at New Orleans in 1769 to establish Spanish rule and to hang a few French revolutionists. Thereafter Pollock had directed for Governor Unzaga the illicit trade of the New Orleans delta area until Gálvez replaced Unzaga as governor. Pollock won Gálvez's confidence, and helped to find him a wife, a French creole whose father was Gilbert Maxent, the business associate of Pierre de Laclède, founder of St. Louis.

When the American Revolution began, Pollock believed that New Orleans was bound by the laws of gravity and economics to be the key city of an American empire based on the south-flowing Mississippi — either an empire that would be directed by General Washington and the Continental Congress or by a rival group of frontier Virginians setting up their own government in Kentucky and Tennessee. In the interests of his future prosperity and status, Pollock decided to support with money from his large fortune and with his political influence in New Orleans both the state of Virginia and the United States.

Soon after the Declaration of Independence, two American army officers disguised as traders floated into New Orleans by canoe from Fort

Pitt with orders from Congress to return to Fort Pitt with some of the ten thousand pounds of gunpowder that Charles III had offered. With official connivance, Pollock helped them to load one hundred and fifty kegs of the Spanish powder on barges and start them moving upstream at night under the noses of British spies. Eight months later the barges arrived safely at Wheeling below Fort Pitt.

It is quite possible that some of the powder wound up in the custody of George Rogers Clark, a reckless, valiant and unstable colonel in Virginia's new county of Kentucky who hated Englishmen and Indians with equal fervor. Clark was recruiting a force of woodsmen at Louisville near the Falls of the Ohio in May, 1778, on the order of Governor Patrick Henry. Some months later the colonel's foot soldiers went on to capture the British garrisons at Kaskaskia and Cahokia, and at the French town of Vincennes on the Wabash to fulfill the old expansionist dreams of Virginians like Peter Jefferson and Dr. Thomas Walker. These victories by a tiny troop of one hundred and seventy-five untrained volunteers were of enormous benefit to the shaky rebel cause. They wrecked the British plan of descending the Ohio and Mississippi from Fort Detroit and Lake Erie to seize New Orleans and cut off that important source of financial and military aid to the United States. Furthermore, Clark's success won the support of many French and Indians of the Illinois area. And it inspired thousands of settlers to ignore George III's Quebec Act and to start moving into Ohio and other parts of what the new nation would call the Northwest Territory.

While Clark campaigned brilliantly for Virginia on the Upper Mississippi, Oliver Pollock enjoyed the support of Governor Gálvez downstream around New Orleans in his volunteer job of supplying the rebels. The governor's river police guarded American craft from British seizure and allowed Pollock's privateers to sell captured British merchant ships at auction in New Orleans. Such influence caused Robert Morris to make Pollock his secret purchasing agent. He became the agent also for the state of Virginia in forwarding war goods to Clark's fighting woodsmen.

Pollock bought supplies from both friends and enemies of the United States — supplies ostensibly for Spanish use. He contracted with merchants in London and Mobile as well as in Bordeaux, Bilbao and Havana — contracts for clothing, guns, hardware, medicine, wine and everything else the Americans needed. He tried to balance his imports at New Orleans by shipping to his creditors the produce of Louisiana, Kentucky, and Tennessee — furs and tobacco, cured hams and flour, lumber and indigo. When he ran out of Spanish gold and silver to use for currency, he persuaded merchants to accept bills of credit drawn on the United States and on the state of Virginia. The bills depreciated rapidly and Pollock put up the difference from his own funds until he exhausted his specie. Then he raised more gold and silver by selling his slaves and plantations, hoping that the war would end soon and that the Americans would reimburse him promptly.

Governor Gálvez kept watch on Pollock and reported his progress to Floridablanca, Charles III's able first minister. Perfidy was an ingredient of diplomacy on both sides of the Atlantic in the late 1770's. Gálvez, like the French minister Vergennes, did not want the Americans to be too successful. He wanted them to succeed only enough to dull the edge of Britain's military ax. From his Philadelphia spies the governor learned that if the Americans won their revolution, they would demand everything that Britain had won in 1763 — Canada, eastside Louisiana and Florida, free navigation on the Mississippi and a free port around New Orleans. Absolutist France, of course, expected to receive Canada as a reward for its idealism in supporting the United States and the rights of man. Gálvez felt that Spain had a clear claim to Florida, and also to eastside, as well as westside, Louisiana. After all, that east drainage of the Mississippi had been part of La Salle's Louisiana that Louis XV and Choiseul had unloaded on Charles III with such hypocritical generosity in 1762. Choiseul had had no right to arrange its transfer to Britain a year later. But, Gálvez knew, a complication clouded these matters. In 1778, Charles III's diplomats in London were dropping hints that Spain might be willing to give up some of her American claims and drop her partnership with France if Britain would give back Gibraltar.

While Gálvez waited for Spain either to come to terms with Britain or to declare war on her, he raised an army in New Orleans composed mainly of French creoles, Acadians and Germans — an army that he hoped would be strong enough to conquer British West Florida, and even the east bank of the Mississippi as far north as the mouth of the Ohio below Colonel Clark's captured Northwest Territory. The governor planned first to attack the Natchez part of West Florida just as soon as the British forts on the Mississippi were stripped of troops to bolster those fighting the Americans up through the Carolinas. Gálvez's spy service was poor but he learned of the state of the British Mississippi garrisons through a series of events in 1778 known as the Willing Raid.

James Willing belonged to the Philadelphia Willing clan, whose members were happy to pay him an income if he would take his bibulous bad habits far away from Philadelphia. He had obliged his relatives in 1774 by crossing the mountains and setting up on the Mississippi as a merchant in Natchez. Most of his customers there were George III Tories of high moral character who had taken up plantations along the river north of the 31st parallel of latitude — the north boundary of West Florida as determined by Parliament after the Treaty of Paris. But these plantations lay in the trans-Appalachian region that George III had banned for settlement by the Proclamation of 1763. To accommodate such admirable poachers, George III had moved that part of the West Florida boundary in 1767 one hundred and fifty miles north up the Mississippi to 32°28″. The one hundred and fifty miles of Tory land between that adjusted boundary near the Yazoo River mouth at present Vicksburg and the former British boundary of West Florida above Baton Rouge at 31° were to cause trouble between Spain and the United States well into President Washington's administration.

For four years, James Willing's Natchez store survived his practice of spending his receipts on wine, women and song and never paying a bill. He feuded with the staid English loyalists who objected to his sottish ways and to his indecent comments about what he would do to Tories if opportunity offered. And it did offer, just as Willing fled to Philadelphia to escape his creditors. There, because of his presumed knowledge of the Mississippi, he was made a captain in the United States Navy by Congress with orders to deliver an agent's commission to Oliver Pollock in New Orleans and to return up the river to Fort Pitt with a cargo of Spanish arms in Pollock's keelboat *Speedwell*.

Captain Willing embarked from Fort Pitt on January 11, 1778, in a craft which he had aptly named the *Rattletrap*. His crew consisted at first of two army sergeants, twenty-four privates and a Mr. McIntyre, who seems to have been a sort of sutler in charge of the liquor supply. On reaching the Mississippi, Willing found that the small settlements on the English side of the river were undefended and deserved to be looted in as festive a manner as possible. He was joined in these gay and profitable ventures by a multilingual mob of French, Spanish and American bandits, who rushed down from St. Louis, St. Charles and Ste. Genevieve to help him plunder and celebrate. When the *Rattletrap* arrived at the bluffs of Natchez, Willing's raiders seized the handful of British guards at Fort Panmure and began their looting ritual. They picked up all the food and wine in Natchez, set fire to the houses and drove the Englishmen southward toward the Manchac trail leading to Lake Pontchartrain and sanctuary at Fort Charlotte in Mobile.

Next Willing's mob appeared at the mouth of the Iberville and captured Fort Bute. Baton Rouge and Manchac were looted and burned. The British armed sloop *Rebecca* was taken. Late in March of 1778, the *Rattle-trap* and the prize ship *Rebecca* carried the triumphant raiders — five hundred strong now — to docks on the New Orleans waterfront near the Place d'Armes. They were followed by a fleet of flatboats loaded with Tory furniture, black slaves, chickens, pigs and clothing. In a noisy ceremony, the captain presented the plunder to Oliver Pollock to sell so that Willing and his volunteers could receive their pay.

Governor Gálvez gave the sale his blessing but, as the months passed, he realized that Willing's success had been too much of a good thing. New Orleans merchants complained that his raids had ruined their upstream trade. The Tories of Natchez and Manchac soon returned home with British soldiers from Fort Charlotte to protect them. Armed British sloops arrived on the Mississippi and closed all traffic above Manchac while British warships blockaded the river mouths below Head of Passes and Fort Balize. Willing could not run the British gauntlet upstream and deliver his Spanish arms to Fort Pitt in Pollock's keelboat. As an alternative, the desperate Pollock tried to ship the arms in Willing's custody to Philadelphia by sea via Havana. But Willing's brief career as one of the first of U.S. naval heroes ended off Balize on November 15, 1778, when he was captured by the British along with Pollock's ship. That blow came as Pollock neared the end of his financial resources. He had already advanced $140,000 worth of goods to Colonel Clark on the security of Virginia's depreciated notes, and $160,000 more that he had paid for goods ordered on credit by the Continental Congress. More bad luck occurred with the start of 1779, when Gálvez told Pollock reluctantly that he was withdrawing his clandestine support of the rebel cause.

Gálvez had good reasons for this withdrawal. Washington's heroic army was having the weakening effect on Britain's military power that France and Spain anticipated. A stronger United States would not be favorable to Spain's interests in the division of American lands at the war's end. Furthermore, rumors reached the governor in May of 1779 that

Colonel Clark was planning a downstream invasion from his Fort Jefferson headquarters near the mouth of the Ohio — an invasion in conflict with the governor's own upstream invasion plans. And, in this same month of May, Spain joined France in open warfare against England when George III turned down Charles's ultimatum for the return of Gibraltar. Soon afterward, Gálvez received orders from Floridablanca at Madrid to proceed at once with the conquest of West Florida before the British had time to reinforce their garrisons and augment their naval strength on the gulf.

The sudden belligerence by the Spanish king, unexpected and unilateral, was viewed with dismay by the warring British and the Americans. Both the old nation and its infant offspring found Charles's behavior to be a serious threat to their own opposed plans for Florida and Louisiana. Minister Vergennes was dismayed too by the uncharacteristic independence of Louis XVI's partner and by Charles's refusal to join France in a military alliance with the Americans to accompany his formal declaration of war against Britain of June 21, 1779.

Early in September, the militant Gálvez conducted a picturesque flotilla of small sloops, keelboats, canoes and pirogues upstream to Manchac one hundred and fifteen miles above New Orleans. In a matter of hours, Britain's Fort Bute fell to an assault by his troop of fourteen hundred Indians and white men of many nationalities armed with every sort of weapon from tomahawks to squirrel guns. A week later, the governor put Baton Rouge under an artillery barrage. The British garrison of four hundred men surrendered in eight days. By the terms of the surrender, Britain gave up also Fort Panmure, Natchez and the land beyond to the Yazoo River boundary of West Florida at 32°28″. Gálvez had hoped to campaign on north in eastside Louisiana at least to the Chickasaw Bluffs of present Memphis. But his army was so encumbered with prisoners, captured goods and rivercraft that he ordered it back to New Orleans to extend Spanish control over Lake Pontchartrain and the West Florida mainland as far east as the Pearl River.

Late in the fall of 1779, the governor and his flotilla left New Orleans by way of Pontchartrain bound for British Fort Charlotte at Mobile. Warships carrying several hundred Spanish marines from Havana joined the fleet in Mississippi Sound. Though hurricanes battered the squadron in Mobile Bay and supplies were lost when boats ran aground, Gálvez's troops reached shore and captured Fort Charlotte on March 15, 1780. Back in New

Orleans, the governor received good news from the north. By heroic resistance, a few hundred French residents of Ste. Genevieve and St. Louis beat off a wild attack on the St. Louis presidio by a thousand Sioux and three hundred Canadians led by British officers from Fort Detroit and Michilimackinac. The attack had been organized at Marquette's old Fox-Wisconsin portage between Green Bay on Lake Michigan and Prairie du Chien on the Mississippi as a first step in the British conquest of Spanish Louisiana. During the fighting at St. Louis, George Rogers Clark posted some of his Virginians at Cahokia across the river to support the Frenchmen, but their help was not needed.

When Mobile passed into Spanish hands, the British held only Pensacola from which to exert what little remained of their authority over West Florida and the Gulf of Mexico. Gálvez knew that a thousand Englishmen defended the strong Pensacola garrison. He spent nearly a year at New Orleans preparing a force strong enough to reduce it. By the spring of 1781, he had accumulated seven thousand men — an enormous army for that part of the world. It included troops from Mobile, New Orleans and Havana, and a French naval contingent. The troops landed unopposed on Santa Rosa Island and were transported across the inlet to assault the fort. During the artillery bombardment, one of Gálvez's shells hit a British powder magazine. In the ghastly explosion, a hundred of the Fort's defenders were blown to bits.

The British surrendered Pensacola soon after. The date was May 9, 1781, five months before Cornwallis surrendered to the American and French forces at Yorktown. In that same year, Spain reached a peak of power in the Americas even greater than that achieved in the 1500's by Emperor Charles V. Because of Charles III's forthright directives, Gálvez's tactical brilliance and Anza's trail-blazing, she held both banks of the Lower Mississippi and she claimed eastside Louisiana at least as far north as the mouth of the Ohio. She owned New Spain's inconceivable vastness from Texas and St. Louis out the Missouri and over the Rockies to the Golden Gate, and north along the Pacific coast beyond Nootka Sound. She controlled the circular shoreline of the Gulf of Mexico — five thousand miles of it — from Havana and Key West to the Mississippi delta, the mouth of the Rio Grande, Veracruz, Yucatan, and back to Key West.

For his Florida conquest, Bernardo de Gálvez received his reward, becoming viceroy of Mexico and having Galveston Bay in Texas named for him later on. Esteban Miró replaced him as governor of Louisiana at New Orleans. Oliver Pollock did not fare so well. This unsung Mississippi hero of the American Revolution, whose contributions had been crucial to the victories of George Rogers Clark, was a victim of Gálvez's shift from friend of the United States to rival for territory west of the Appalachians. Pollock went bankrupt when Congress and Virginia failed to pay him what they owed him. To help him out temporarily, Congress sent him to Havana as its commercial attaché. He was greeted there by royal collectors who put him in jail for eighteen months because he owed Spain $151,696, which he had borrowed to pay for Clark's supplies.[3]

The Treaty of Paris — the general name for several agreements ending the War of the American Revolution, was signed on January 20, 1783, by Great Britain and the United States, by Britain and France, and by Britain and Spain. The American commissioners at Paris were Benjamin Franklin, John Jay, John Adams and Henry Laurens (Thomas Jefferson was appointed too late to serve). Jay and Franklin did most of the negotiating. Congress instructed them to consult with the French minister, Vergennes, before coming to terms with Great Britain but the commissioners ignored this order. The cause of their disobedience was John Jay's deep distrust of Vergennes who, Jay knew, was conniving with Floridablanca of Spain to persuade the English to return Gibraltar.

Jay had spent two fruitless years in Madrid seeking a loan for the Americans and also free navigation of the Mississippi — that is, freedom from inspection and possible seizure of cargos. Floridablanca had put him off with bland promises. Jay's disillusionment was complete when the Spanish minister ordered Governor Gálvez to proceed with the conquest of West Florida.

The Anglo-American peace treaty of 1783 turned out to be a triumph for Franklin and Jay and an unpleasant surprise for Vergennes and Floridablanca, who found that it substituted the old threat of British encroachment on Spain's Louisiana, Texas and Mexico by something potentially worse, American encroachment. The American commissioners took full advantage of rivalries among the various Europeans and at the same time got more from Great Britain than they had expected. George III was surprisingly helpful. Though he was outraged by his failure to impose his royal will on the colonists, he thought that it was best to keep the whole controversy within the family. Furthermore, he decided that cooperation with the Americans was better than forcing them further into military alliance with France, and it was the quickest way to cut the awful cost of maintaining his defeated forces abroad. Benjamin Franklin had had some hope of winning Canada and its fur trade for the United States, but he joined John Jay in accepting a compromise. Britain retained the old French Canada of Frontenac, extended indefinitely west beyond Lake Superior to the limits of British exploration.[4] The United States took the east side of La Salle's Louisiana, including the Northwest Territory — the Quebec Act extension lands — lying west of the Appalachians between the Ohio River and the Mississippi River boundary of Spanish Louisiana. In her separate agreement with Spain, Britain returned Spanish Florida — from Pensacola eastward — to Charles III, and gave him also the western French part of Florida (including Mobile) that Britain had won from France in 1763.

The Anglo-American treaty set the north boundary between the United States and Canada in the east as it runs today for the most part — from northern Maine through the Great Lakes to Grand Portage near the mouth of La Vérendrye's Pigeon River. It proceeded along the Rainy Lake canoe route past the remnants of La Vérendrye's Fort Pierre to the "northwest corner" of the Lake of the Woods near the forgotten Fort St. Charles. From this "corner" the boundary was described by the treaty as running straight to the northeast corner of Spanish Louisiana at the ultimate source of the Mississippi (see the map on page 211).

This last line was purely theoretical. The theory, as we will see soon, was incorrect. The northwest corner of the Lake of the Woods had not been precisely located and the source of the Mississippi had never been discovered. As a consequence, where that part of the boundary started or ended had no reality, nor did its length or direction.

The big blow to Spanish hopes to acquire those Louisiana lands south of the Ohio and east of the Mississippi resulted from Anglo-American acceptance of the middle of the big river from its source southward as the line separating the United States from Spanish Louisiana. The treaty put the southern U.S. boundary at the 31st parallel (running east from the Mississippi to the Apalachicola and St. Mary's rivers) — the boundary between the United States and West and East Florida. The Spanish would object bitterly to that boundary soon and would refuse to accept it. West Florida's north boundary, the angry Spanish declared, was not at the 31st

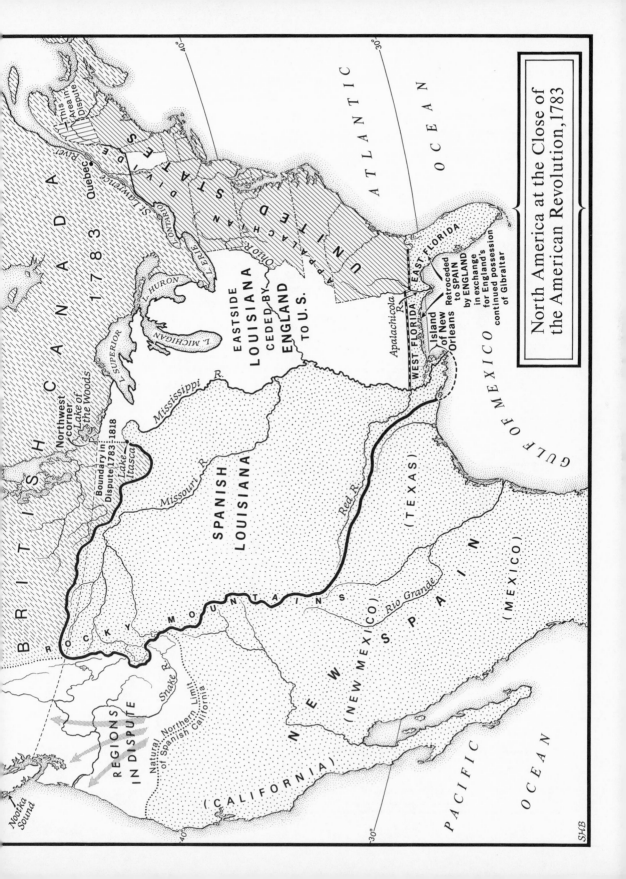

North America at the Close of
the American Revolution, 1783

BRITISH CANADA 1783

UNITED STATES

This Area In
Dispute

Quebec

Northwest
corner
Lake of
the Woods

Boundary in
Dispute 1783-1818

Lake
Itasca

St. Lawrence River

L. ONTARIO

L. ERIE

L. HURON

L. SUPERIOR

L. MICHIGAN

APPALACHIAN DIVIDE

Ohio R.

Mississippi R.

Missouri R.

EASTSIDE
LOUISIANA
CEDED BY
ENGLAND
TO U.S.

SPANISH
LOUISIANA

Red R.

ROCKY MOUNTAINS

Snake R.

REGIONS
IN
DISPUTE

Natural Northern Limit
of Spanish California

Nootha
Sound

(CALIFORNIA)

NEW SPAIN

(NEW MEXICO.)

Rio Grande

(TEXAS)

(MEXICO)

Apalachicola R.

WEST FLORIDA

Island
of New
Orleans

EAST FLORIDA

Retroceded
to SPAIN
by ENGLAND
in exchange
for England's
continued possession
of Gibraltar

ATLANTIC OCEAN

GULF OF MEXICO

PACIFIC OCEAN

40°

30°

40°

30°

SHB

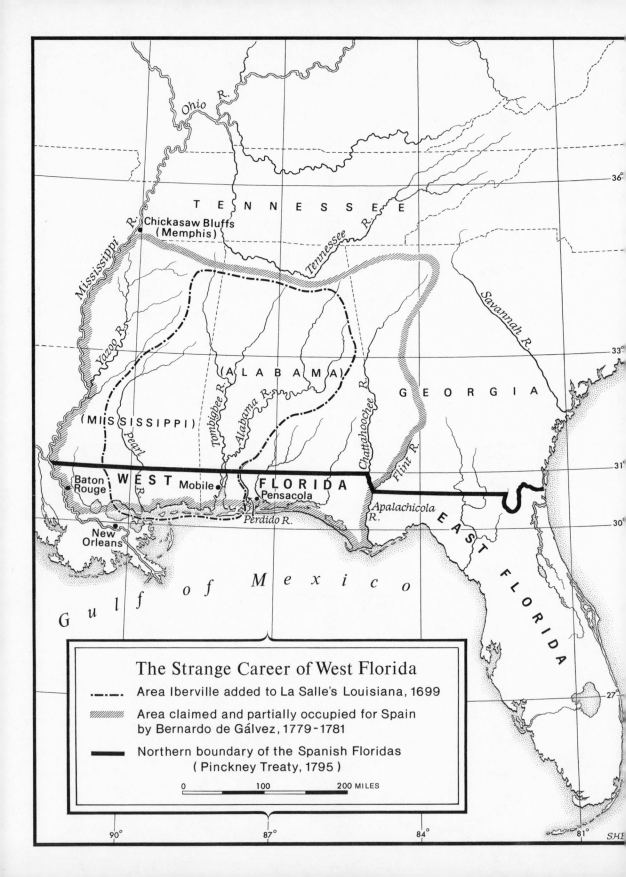

Ohio R.

Mississippi R.

T E N N E S S E E

Chickasaw Bluffs
(Memphis)

Tennessee R.

Yazoo R.

(A L A B A M A)

(M I S S I S S I P P I)

Tombigbee R.

Alabama R.

Pearl

Chattahoochee R.

G E O R G I A

Savannah R.

Flint R.

Baton
Rouge

W E S T   F L O R I D A
Mobile

Pensacola

Apalachicola
R.

E A S T   F L O R I D A

New
Orleans

Perdido R.

G u l f   o f   M e x i c o

36°

33°

31°

30°

27°

The Strange Career of West Florida

—··— Area Iberville added to La Salle's Louisiana, 1699

▨▨▨ Area claimed and partially occupied for Spain
by Bernardo de Gálvez, 1779-1781

━━━ Northern boundary of the Spanish Floridas
(Pinckney Treaty, 1795)

0   100   200 MILES

90°   87°   84°   81°

SHL

parallel, as proved by Britain's own determination in 1767. The British had set it then one hundred and forty miles north of the 31st, at the mouth of Yazoo River, to create for their Tory settlers what was known as the Natchez Strip. And there the boundary dispute rested, smoldering.

In Philadelphia in 1783, members of Congress, including the ubiquitous Thomas Jefferson, were too busy organizing the U.S. Confederation and studying the Paris treaty to consider the effect of the American Revolution on world society. All the while, the fates were at work nourishing seeds that would produce still more cataclysmic changes — seeds created by the triumph of Washington's rebels over royal autocracy. Charles III was growing old and losing his control of affairs in Spain, which he had restored to some of its former greatness. Since the death of the comte de Maurepas in November of 1781, Louis XVI could not make up his mind about anything. At Marie Antoinette's urging, he dismissed his wise minister, Jacques Necker, just as Necker's fiscal reforms were giving millions of Frenchmen some hope that the monarchy was taking steps to relieve their suffering. At a French military academy in Brienne, southeast of Paris, a small, dark and handsome boy of fourteen, Napoleon Bonaparte, a member of the Corsican nobility, was studying to become an artillery officer in the French army.

The Philadelphia congressmen hardly noticed the black clouds gathering over Europe as they worked on the treaty and struggled to compromise the conflicting demands of their quarrelsome little family of thirteen states. And it was their good luck to be spared the anxiety of foreseeing that within two decades a monstrous addition to the family would be dumped on their doorstep as a casual by-product of vicissitudes abroad.

13

Thomas Jefferson:
Land Developer

THOMAS JEFFERSON WAS A WIDOWER of forty-one years when he and his eleven-year-old daughter Patsy rode the stage from Le Havre through Rouen to Paris in 1784 to help Benjamin Franklin and John Adams in the framing of commercial treaties with France. Franklin, still incomparably wise and attractive at the age of seventy-eight, had bladder trouble. He would resign soon as minister to the king and Jefferson would be appointed by the Confederation to replace him. The Virginian would be received at Versailles on May 17, 1785, by Louis XVI, a dull young man befuddled by the conflicting advices of his absolutist queen, Marie Antoinette, and that French hero of the Revolution and firebrand for royal reform, the marquis de Lafayette. The king's chief interests in life, amid the crushing problems that he had inherited from his Bourbon forebears, were hunting and making locks. Jefferson would serve as minister to the court until President George Washington called him back to Philadelphia to be his secretary of state. That would occur following the fall of the Bastille on July 14, 1789, an event signifying the collapse of the lockmaker's bankrupt regime and concluding two centuries of mostly bad, if sometimes colorful, centralized government.

The career of Thomas Jefferson up to the time of his arrival in Paris requires some review because he would have more to do with Louisiana's destiny than anyone else — more to do with bringing its influence to bear in transforming a new weak nation into a great continental power. Many artists would portray him during the eighty-three years of his life — among them Rembrandt Peale, Thomas Sully, Jean Antoine Houdon and Saint-Mémin. Much later (1927), the Idaho steeplejack, Gutson Borglum, would carve on Mount Rushmore a huge stone Jefferson gazing in perpetual majesty past George Washington's shoulder over the South Dakota Black Hills of the Louisiana Purchase. No two of these artists have agreed on what Jefferson looked like. That was the kind of face that he had — not quite handsome, not quite ugly — blurred, in effect, as though seen in a murky mirror. He was tall, lanky, straight-up, with lean cheeks and a long neck. His eyes were hazel, his complexion ruddy, his hair turbidly reddish, his voice habitually low and confidential. He was the sort of plantation aristocrat that wore the finest of London clothes with an air of contempt for their elegance — the boots scuffed, the cravat in disarray, the broadcloth coat rumpled and dusty. His mind was as hard to define as his face. It was an instrument delicately balanced between the intuitive and the practical, between idealism and fact, modesty and egotism. Jefferson's mind reflected the paradoxes of the unique society that he was helping to form — that mixture of liberalism and conservatism, the perennial conflict of which still animates and stabilizes the American scene.

Through the years up to 1784 Jefferson brought to the art of living a wonderful zest tempered by serenity and grace. He never tried to be successful. Honors just seemed to come to him because people thought that he was naturally superior. He was not a romantic adventurer out there on the edge of the Virginia wilderness, not a rugged frontiersman as his father Peter had been. He was a country gentleman. He had never traveled further west than the Shenandoah valley across the Blue Ridge, not fifty miles from his Shadwell birthplace and his beloved Monticello, a light and airy haven that he began building to his own Italian design in 1770. That was eight years after the nearby village of Charlottesville was founded and named, with utter irrelevance, for George III's German wife. Jefferson's great pleasure was exploring in his spacious mind. He read incessantly — the sciences, arts, literature, religion, history, husbandry. His purchases of books from stores in Williamsburg, Annapolis and Philadelphia helped to keep him constantly in debt. He studied the small as well as the large — about whether bathing one's feet in cold water averted colds, about whether

Peruvian llamas might be found on the Upper Missouri, about the dimensions of the bull moose. He kept track of his private world at Monticello — the moment of sunrise, the first apple blossoms, the notes of an oriole's song. He was creative with an amateur's headlong gusto. The buildings that he would design in 1819 for the University of Virginia are among the loveliest in the United States. He liked to invent things — dumbwaiters, air conditioners, an odometer, vanishing beds, a machine for writing in duplicate. He was a fair violinist and he sang on key. He played chess without much flair. He adored women and was adored by them. If he did not actually have a love affair with Mrs. Betsey Walker in his bachelor days, as her husband accused him of doing thirty years later, it was not from any lack of interest. His enemies would charge that his grasp of financial matters, both personal and governmental, was woefully weak, and that was true. They would charge that he denounced slavery while owning one hundred and fifty slaves, and that was true too. They charged that he was an atheist, but that was incorrect. He was a deist. He believed that an all-wise god, or gods, looked after the world but that there was not a god in man's image directing affairs from an upholstered heaven.[1] He had no use for biblical fantasy or for the trimmings of organized religion.

Jefferson grew to manhood under two family influences that would affect his judgment throughout his life. One influence was contempt for the British kings Georges II and III, a submissive Parliament and undemocratic English institutions, including the right of eldest sons to inherit property and forced taxation to support the established church. The other influence was interest in Louisiana — the glorious scope and variety and promise of it in leading men to a better and freer life. The land beyond the Blue Ridge was as much a part of the environment that shaped him as his own Albemarle County. As a child he had visualized the Knights of the Golden Horseshoe crossing Swift Run Gap to "the Euphrates," and his godfather Thomas Walker exploring across Cumberland Gap. He had imagined Christopher Gist smoking the calumet with Indians on the Ohio beyond the head of the Potomac where his father had planted the Fairfax stone. As a young Williamsburg lawyer and radical member of the Virginia House of Burgesses, he had read the tales of Father Hennepin and Lahontan, of La Salle discovering the steaming mouth of the Mississippi and dying in Texas, of how Bienville had founded New Orleans and how John Law had promoted the alleged easy wealth of the Mississippi valley as backing for the commercial paper of Louis XV's Banque royale. Though

Jefferson's Declaration of Independence was concerned with castigating George III, it can be presumed that his second paragraph — ". . . the inalienable rights . . . among these Life, Liberty and the Pursuit of Happiness . . ." — was inspired in some degree because such rights seemed to him to be at work in eastern Louisiana (Kentucky and Tennessee) making small groups of pioneering Virginia farmers happy and free.

In 1779, Jefferson succeeded the fiery Patrick Henry as governor of Virginia, an event that changed the cast of his Louisiana views from the visionary and romantic to the realistic and political. He began to feel then that Spain's control of the Mississippi River through its possession of the bottleneck at New Orleans was a very great threat to the kind of United States that was forming in his mind. Jefferson was not much of a wartime governor. He was a pacifist. He had no taste or skill for raising war funds or for urging men to murder one another no matter how deeply he believed in the cause of American freedom. It was his painful task, when Oliver Pollock begged him for money so that more Spanish munitions could be sent from New Orleans to George Rogers Clark's sharpshooters at Vincennes, to have to inform Pollock that Virginia's treasury was empty. As a result, Clark could not proceed from his conquest of the fertile Illinois and Ohio part of the Northwest Territory to capture the British stronghold at Fort Detroit.[2]

Jefferson had a personal interest in Clark, who was nine years younger and a former neighbor. Clark was born near Shadwell and left Charlottesville at nineteen to become an Ohio land surveyor and a frontier leader in Kentucky. His impetuous career gave Jefferson the vicarious thrill of western adventure and exploration. Clark brought him also some understanding of the geography of the Upper Mississippi and the relation of its Indian trade to Lake Superior and Lake Michigan in the east and — less clearly — to the Missouri River and the remote Mandan Indian country in the west. At the same time, Jefferson extended his knowledge of the Lower Mississippi through his contacts as governor of Virginia with Governor Gálvez, Oliver Pollock and their agents in St. Louis, Kaskaskia and Cahokia. He perceived in Spanish Louisiana the same trade imbalance and social anarchy that Bienville and Vaudreuil had observed when the vast region was French. He found a comic unreality in reports that he received about the handful of imported Spanish officials — bored aristocrats mainly being rewarded by Charles III for services to him — attempting to rule a white population dominated by French creoles and Acadians who could not speak or read Spanish. Though the top administrative, judicial and military jobs in New Orleans and St. Louis were held by Spaniards, the work was done — or left undone — by French underlings. Spain's policy of imposing a trade monopoly on her colonies was a wry joke on the Mississippi delta. The populace had to earn a living and nobody in Spain would buy what Louisiana had to sell. The quarter of a million Indians of Louisiana persisted in their traditional preference for British cloth and hardware in exchange for their native products. New Orleans merchants supplied these British goods to the Indians illicitly, demonstrating again the tendency of people in this area of freedom to do as they pleased in bland defiance of the wishes of the home government.

Governor Jefferson was fascinated by tales that came to him about the fur trade. The tales involved the movements of traders west, resuming the march that had been stalled since the days of the La Vérendryes beyond Winnipeg. The Scots at Montreal and Michilimackinac were thriving on the business they had taken over from the French Canadians after 1763. Their brigades plied the old canoe route from Grand Portage on Lake Superior to Lake of the Woods and on through Lake Winnipeg to the two Saskatchewans and the Canadian Rockies. Their men flocked to the Upper Mississippi at least as far as the Falls of St. Anthony, from posts on Chequamegon Bay and from Prairie du Chien at the Mississippi end of the old Fox-Wisconsin canoe route from Lake Michigan. Some of them crossed the wide blue river to poach in Spanish Louisiana — up the Minnesota River and into present North Dakota, and up Iowa streams such as the Des Moines, bringing them eventually to the Upper Missouri above present Omaha, Nebraska.

Jefferson heard stories also of chaotic fur trade conditions in Louisiana. From St. Louis, various members of the Chouteau family and other Frenchmen were pushing always further up the Missouri, and also north up the Mississippi to trade with Indians both in eastside British terrain in present Illinois and Wisconsin and in the westside Spanish lands of Iowa and Minnesota. Their aim seemed presumptuous in the extreme. It was to challenge the tremendous financial power of the British by making St. Louis (with its ice-free seaport at New Orleans) the world center of the fur trade by luring to it a greater volume of pelts than the volume going to Montreal, frozen in for half the year.

Some months before Cornwallis surrendered at Yorktown in October, 1781, Jefferson retired to Monticello from public life — "forever," he declared — to gather data for his book *Notes on Virginia*. The scope of the book, written originally at the request of François de Barbé-Marbois, secretary of the French legation in Philadelphia, for the benefit of his government, would extend far beyond the Blue Ridge to describe "the most beautiful river on earth" (the Ohio), the turbulent Missouri and other west-trending streams. The book would suggest also the crucial importance to the United States of the Mississippi for transport and its bottleneck at New Orleans for trade.

As a member of Congress in 1783–1784, Jefferson became still more convinced about New Orleans when he learned that Count Floridablanca of Spain was closing the Mississippi to United States shipping, establishing river patrols, and ending the right of deposit — the right, for example, of Kentucky and Tennessee merchants to store salt pork and flour free of charge at New Orleans pending transshipment. In the Treaty of Paris of 1763, France had guaranteed this right of deposit as a permanent condition of the transfer of Louisiana to Charles III. Floridablanca was giving France special privileges on the Mississippi and in Florida as a second measure to stifle American trade. And he was claiming the east bank of the Mississippi above New Orleans not just to the disputed north boundary of the Natchez Strip at 32°28″ but on north another two hundred and fifty miles to the Chickasaw Bluffs at present Memphis — the claimed boundary running east from the bluffs to the Appalachian crest beyond present Chattanooga, Tennessee.

In addition to these ominous Spanish measures, Jefferson was hearing of strong movements among the Kentucky colonists to secede from the United States to form their own nation, or to join with Spain, or perhaps to join with French dissidents in New Orleans plotting to conquer Texas and Mexico — plots harking back to Count Peñalosa's scheme of 1684 that Louis XIV had found so attractive. The Kentuckians, and settlers in Tennessee, too, were reacting angrily to opinions expressed by New England congressmen on the theme that frontier freedom was bad for their business on the eastern seaboard. The frontier, the New Englanders were saying, should stop at the Appalachians to prevent the drawing off of cheap and docile labor from their eastern factories, stores and banks.

Floridablanca's decrees and the Mississippi were immediate concerns. But Jefferson kept an eye on the trans-Mississippi west also, and "the big salt sea" on the far side — matters brought sharply to his attention of late by two unrelated events. One of these events was the publication in London in 1778 of a book called *Travels through the Interior Parts of North America in the years 1766, 1767, 1768*. It was written by a former British army surveyor from Massachusetts named Jonathan Carver, who had spent eight years during the 1770's trying to get someone to publish his story.

The Carver book was a stirring account of Upper Mississippi exploration. It evolved from the flamboyant activities of a part-time London clubman and playwright, Major Robert Rogers, who had won fighting fame with his Rogers's Rangers at Lake George in New York and with Wolfe in the storming of Quebec. In 1766, Rogers, burning with desire to solve cosmic mysteries, proposed to King George III that he lead an overland expedition from "the Head of the Mississippi" to the Pacific coast by way of "the River called by the Indians Ouragan." Nobody knows where Rogers got the name Ouragan, the spelling of which became "Oregon" in Carver's book twelve years later.[3] Rogers's dream river and its "Bay that projects North-Eastwardly from the Pacific" would turn out eventually to be the Columbia, the legendary west-slope counterpart of the east-slope Missouri. But to Rogers the river Ouragan — reached, he said, by a thirty-mile portage from the Missouri across the Continental Divide — was just a means of getting him to the west coast. From the Ouragan's bay he would explore up the coast northward past "the Straits of Anian" to find the Northwest Passage leading back eastward to Hudson Bay.

The old Northwest Passage will-o'-the-wisp had the same allure for Rogers in 1766 that it had had for Cartier and Champlain, Walter Raleigh and Nicolet. George III turned down his proposal. However, the British government offered the equivalent of $100,000 to any explorer who found the route at his own expense. Rogers was sent to Michilimackinac as post commander and he was joined there by Jonathan Carver, who had been one of his Ranger officers in the French and Indian War. Carver, a native of Massachusetts, was fifty-six years old, a tall scarecrow of a man on the order of Ichabod Crane with a long thin mournful face. He too yearned to find the Passage as compensation for years of failure. He was overjoyed when Rogers sent him forth on a preliminary reconnaissance with a French Canadian and an Indian for company.

There was nothing novel about the scarecrow's expedition except that he was British and Britishers were still a rarity in the Upper Mississippi part of Louisiana. From Michilimackinac Carver took Marquette's route to Green Bay, the Fox-Wisconsin portage and Prairie du Chien, and then

Hennepin's route up the Mississippi as far as the Falls of St. Anthony. He and his two friends spent the winter of 1766–1767 some distance up the Minnesota, perhaps at the mouth of the Blue Earth River near today's Mankato and Pierre Le Sueur's ill-fated Fort L'Huillier.[4]

Homeward bound in the spring, Carver met a second Rogers party under Captain James Tute at Prairie du Chien and he returned up the Mississippi with that party. Tute's instructions were to ascend the Minnesota and descend the Red River of the North to pick up supplies in the Winnipeg area for the trek to the "Ouragan" and the Pacific — supplies which Rogers had promised to forward from Grand Portage. Fearing a Sioux attack on the Minnesota, Tute led his group directly to Grand Portage along Radisson's old St. Croix River trail from Lake Pepin to Lake Superior. No supplies had reached Grand Portage. The reason was that Rogers was in deep trouble because of money-making schemes alleged by his superiors to be both treasonable and dishonest. So Tute and Carver returned to Michilimackinac with no chance of claiming the $100,000 reward, without being paid for their travels, and with Carver's long face more mournful than ever.

The London publisher who took a chance in 1778 on Carver's story struck a gold mine. This first western travel book by an Englishman was a huge success (it has been reprinted forty times since in most European languages). It has been noted that Louisiana was "discovered" almost as much by writers inventing things that turned out to be true as by actual explorers. When the book reached Monticello, Jefferson must have observed that the author invented geography as effectively as Hennepin, Lahontan and Charlevoix, all of whom were represented fully in his growing library.[5] Carver's glowing prophesies about the value of Louisiana would have been of special interest to Jefferson. "There is no doubt," Carver wrote of the Falls of St. Anthony region, "that at some future period mighty kingdoms will emerge from these wildernesses, and stately and solemn temples with gilded spires reaching the skies supplanting the Indian huts." That was an apt description of today's Twin Cities.

A feature of the book was Carver's map of North America, which was based on Charlevoix and showed a central pyramid of land where most of the major rivers of North America were represented as beginning. From springs close to one another at the top of the pyramid, the Oregon (Columbia) started flowing toward the Pacific; the Colorado toward the Gulf of

Jonathan Carver, whose book on his exploits in Upper Louisiana brought the word "Oregon" into popular usage and helped prepare the way for American claims to that region. (From Carver's Travels in the Interior Parts of North America)

California; the Red River of the North toward Lake Winnipeg and Hudson Bay; the Mississippi, Minnesota and Missouri toward the Gulf of Mexico; and the St. Louis River, the mouth of which is at Duluth, Minnesota, into Lake Superior and the St. Lawrence. Carver placed his magic pyramid on the hundredth meridian near present Pierre, South Dakota, where the La Vérendryes had buried their lead plate in 1743. It stood at the north end of "the Shining Mountains," which the map shows as starting in Mexico and running north just west of the Rio Grande in the manner of the real Rockies system, but without the Canadian Rockies continuation into the arctic regions. Carver may have suppressed the Canadian Rockies unconsciously because he wanted low land up there so that the Northwest Passage could run eastward to Hudson Bay from the Pacific at "De Fonte's Entrance" — referring perhaps to the Strait of Juan de Fuca leading to Puget Sound south of Nootka Sound. The map's River Oregon ran into the Pacific at the proper actual distance south of Juan de Fuca, north of which Carver's narrow Strait of Anian ran toward Alaska, separating North America from Asia.[6]

Carver's map supplied answers to everything — to all the questions that had been bothering the world's geographers since the days of Columbus. In studying it at Monticello, Jefferson must have noticed that it made the continent much wider than he had thought it to be — more than three thousand miles from Penobscot Bay in Maine to the bay of River Oregon on the Pacific coast. This width figure was corroborated by longitude data in a book that Jefferson was reading in 1783, *A Journal of Captain Cook's Last Voyage in the Pacific*. The book, published in Hartford, Connecticut, was written by a young man from Groton, John Ledyard, who had entered Dartmouth College in 1772 to prepare for missionary work with the Indians and had left soon for the more exciting life of worldwide roaming. While in London four years later, Ledyard had signed on as a marine on Cook's famous ship *Resolution*. The ship had carried the most advanced of English and French chronometers to determine longitude on that epic voyage of 1778. Knowing the longitude of New York and that of Carver's Oregon coast (the coast that the pirate Drake had named New Albion in 1579), Cook could calculate the overland distance between the Atlantic and the Pacific.

Captain Cook, like Robert Rogers and Carver, had fought with Wolfe at Quebec and had gone on to the task of exploding the myth of a South

Pacific continent by mapping coastal parts of Australia, New Zealand and Tasmania. Ledyard's book disclosed to Jefferson how Cook exploded two more myths — those of the Northwest Passage and the Strait of Anian. He saw nothing that looked like either of them in 1778, when the *Resolution* sailed past the mouth of the Columbia River and Juan de Fuca Strait, both obscured by fog, to anchor in Nootka Sound (off present Victoria Island) and then at Cook's Inlet (off present Anchorage, Alaska). The explorer was surprised at Nootka Sound to find English hardware among the seafaring Indians there — hardware that must have reached them somehow across the Continental Divide from Lake Winnipeg trading posts. The *Resolution* continued to Norton Sound near Bering Strait until stopped by wall ice off present Nome, Alaska. Cook turned south and sent Ledyard ashore at Unalaska in the Aleutians to talk to Russian fur traders about their sea otter business and about the geography of Russia's Kamchatka Peninsula and the Asian mainland. Then the *Resolution* proceeded to the Hawaiian Islands, which Cook had named for his patron, Lord Sandwich. All the while, Ledyard and other marines had kept a lookout for Spanish warships that might have appeared to arrest Cook in response to the warning to Englishmen and to Russians that the Pacific was Charles III's ocean.[7]

In February, 1779, the captain was murdered by Hawaiians in a squabble over a stolen boat, a tragedy as senseless as the murder of Cook's Louisiana counterpart, La Salle. The sorrowing crew of the *Resolution* set sail for England by way of the Indian Ocean, with a stopover at Canton, China, to buy provisions and silks and satins. The silks and satins, Jefferson noted from Ledyard's story, were paid for with funds realized by selling a few remnant skins of sea otter that Cook had picked up from the Nootka Sound Indians in exchange for bits of brass — skins that the Indians were wearing for clothing. The Cantonese paid high prices for these greasy secondhand skins, leading to a London–Canton–Nootka Sound three-way trade that would begin operating regularly in 1785.

It has been claimed that Ledyard's account changed Jefferson overnight from a bemused expansionist into a practical worker for a continental United States. In *The Course of Empire*, Bernard De Voto has warned against such a sweeping claim, though admitting that Ledyard displayed a "continental consciousness" when he saw the Oregon coast from the deck of the *Resolution*. Ledyard wrote: "It was the first time I had been near the shores of that continent which gave me birth. . . . It soothed a homesick heart."

Whether or not Ledyard's homesickness awoke in Jefferson the ambition to acquire Spanish Louisiana for the United States, to think continentally, the book probably reminded him of the Anglo-Spanish dispute of 1770 over the use of the Falkland Islands as a supply point for ships rounding the Horn on their way to the North Pacific coast — a dispute foreshadowing a contest for the sea otter trade. And the sea otter situation implied that far more was at stake than one remote trading post. Ledyard had written that goods from eastern Canada were being carried overland by Indians to Nootka Sound in 1778. That meant that British traders would follow their goods soon across the Canadian Rockies, closing the land gap between the Atlantic and the Pacific, and blocking any continental aspirations that the new United States might have.

Fear of such British action prompted Jefferson in 1783 to ask George Rogers Clark if he would be willing to map a route overland from the Mississippi to the west coast. But Congress was not ready then to add such a project to its problems even if it had had funds for it.

When Jefferson completed his *Notes on Virginia* for François de Barbé-Marbois, he was anxious to get away from Monticello and its memories of the tragic death there of his wife Martha on September 6, 1782. He was urged to return to politics by his best friend and fellow Virginian, James Madison, who was as concerned as he was about Floridablanca's closure of the Mississippi and claims to trans-Appalachian lands north of West Florida. No matter what Jefferson was considering, Louisiana seemed to present itself as an important factor.

He had an excuse to leave home in the fall of 1783 when he was elected to Congress as a delegate from Virginia. The winter session was a trying period during which the delegates struggled futilely to agree on a philosophy of government and to deal with the hard times that followed Washington's victory at Yorktown. Jefferson's own idea of a republic drawing its powers "from the consent of the governed" was fixed. He believed that the existing Confederation of sovereign states was doomed. The states would have to assign authority to a federal government in certain areas — foreign relations, defense, revenue, western lands. Like Madison, he favored a constitution that would define federal powers. He wanted a broad-based electorate. He believed that a division of legislative, judicial and executive powers would prevent the excesses of a pure democracy.

As a southerner, he regarded the settled Atlantic seaboard north of

Virginia with suspicion. He felt that its business leaders controlled affairs in their own interest — controlled them as despotically as the aristocrats of England and the Bourbon dynasties of France and Spain controlled theirs. To break up this seaboard power, Jefferson favored the creation of an agrarian society in which every American could own land. If a man could not afford to buy land from private owners in the east, his government should help him to acquire public land in the vast and delectable spaces beyond the Blue Ridge. Jefferson argued that democracy would be strengthened and national problems solved as the west filled with independent farmers all the way from Fort Pitt and eastern Tennessee to the banks of the Mississippi. A current scheme of the British to set up a buffer Indian state between the Ohio and the Great Lakes would be thwarted. The ticklish process of persuading the tribes to sell their hunting grounds and move further west would be speeded up. The British would be forced to evacuate their military posts north of the Ohio at Detroit, Michilimackinac and elsewhere that they were holding contrary to the terms of the Peace of Paris. Ostensibly they held the posts to force the Confederation to pay public and private debts to British creditors. A second and stronger motive was to retain British control of the Upper Mississippi fur trade and to continue the illegal expansion of that trade west in Spanish Louisiana.

To Jefferson, a bright spot in the national scene of 1784 was the final cession to the Confederation by several states of trans-Appalachian lands that they had been claiming since their earliest days as crown colonies. Jefferson himself phrased Virginia's deed of cession of its Northwest Territory running north from the Ohio to Canada at Lake Superior and west to the Mississippi — an area of some 350,000 square miles that would constitute the states of Ohio, Indiana, Illinois, Michigan and Wisconsin, and half of Minnesota. It was his special pleasure to head the committee named by Congress to prepare a plan of temporary government for this magnificent property.

His first concern was to avoid George III's fatal mistake. He proposed to give the divisions of the nation's first public domain full representation in Congress by putting them on an equal political basis with the thirteen original states at the earliest possible moment. And he urged the addition of Virginia's county of Kentucky to the Northwest Territory — a proposal that he hoped would defeat the aims of those separatists in Louisville and Lexington who were claiming that powerful easterners would direct Kentucky's affairs unless Kentuckians quit the Confederation and struck out on their own or signed up with other empire plotters in New Orleans.

There was, in Jefferson's Ordinance of 1784, a clear implication that the author was thinking not merely of a plan for making the Northwest Territory an active political unit of the nation. He had in mind a plan that could be used again and again for land development as the pressure of population pushed the public domain of the United States on and on westward — through Spanish Louisiana toward Oregon and the Pacific. Congress adopted most of his provisions on April 23, 1784, but no further action was taken until three years later, when the ordinance served as the basis for the Northwest Ordinance of 1787. That legislative landmark brought limited self-government to any new territory that possessed a population of five thousand. It would be admitted to the union as a full-fledged state when the population reached sixty thousand.

As Morison and Commager put it in *The Growth of the American Republic*, the Northwest Ordinance (and its companion, the Land Ordinance of 1785) "laid the permanent foundations for the American territorial system and colonial policy, and enabled the United States to expand westward to the Pacific, and from thirteen to forty-eight states, with relatively little difficulty."

14

Four Nations: One River

JEFFERSON PUT ASIDE for the present the problems of the new republic when he reached Paris with Patsy on August 6, 1784, and lodged first near the Opéra on the rue Taibout and then, after taking over as minister to France, at the Hôtel de Langeac among the shade trees of the Champs-Elysées. He had yearned to see that land of such favorite philosophers of his as Montesquieu, Voltaire and Rousseau ever since the marquis de Lafayette had told him of its charms at Richmond in 1781. He was intrigued by the paradox of a monarchy, ruled in theory by the absolutist Louis XVI, joining its ideological opposite, the United States, to defeat England, another monarchy. He was aware that France had expected to gain by this strange alliance. But he believed that the French people were democrats at heart and would force their king to liberalize his despotic Bourbon government.

The new minister arrived in Paris too late for one anticipated pleasure — a meeting with Denis Diderot, author of the *Encyclopédie* who had died a week earlier. But he talked to the comte de Vergennes often before his death in February, 1787, and thanked him repeatedly for the Franco-American alliance of 1778, and for bringing in Spain on the rebels' side — to a degree at least — a year later. He began planning a collection of the best in French wines and he hired a Paris printer to publish his *Notes on Virginia*, which appeared in May, 1785. He set up an account with the London bookseller, Stockdale, and paid 27s. 6d. for the first of many books from Stockdale — James Cook's four-volume *A Voyage to the Pacific Ocean*, which had just been published lavishly with forty-nine plates and two engraved maps. He had several discussions with the famous naturalist, the comte de Buffon, keeper of the Jardin du Roi, and he tried to correct the octogenarian's notion that animals in the wilds of Louisiana were smaller and less interesting than their European equivalents. Soon Jefferson was speaking what he called "imperfect" French and he was seen often in his careless elegance of dress at the homes of diplomats and at the best Paris salons. At one of the salons he met the talented and beautiful English painter, Maria Hadfield Cosway, aged twenty-seven and unhappily married. He fell deeply in love with her, but the affair stopped short of taking a dangerous turn some weeks later while the two were strolling along the Seine on a golden afternoon. To impress Maria with his youth and vigor, Jefferson tried to hurdle a bench, dislocating his wrist in the process. The flaming romance seemed to suffer some dislocation also during the four painful months that were required for the wrist to repair itself. Thereafter, Maria and Jefferson were just very good friends.

Paris and the endless involutions of European politics fascinated the tall Virginian. And still Louisiana hung in his mind as he embarked on the reading of James Cook's *Voyage* and recalled that he had hoped to send George Rogers Clark from the Mississippi on an expedition overland to beat the British traders in Canada to Oregon and Clark's post at Nootka among the sea otters. One morning in 1786, he had a remarkable caller at the Hôtel de Langeac — Cook's Connecticut Boswell, John Ledyard. The ex-Dartmouth student was thirty-five years old now. He had deserted the *Resolution* in '82 and was confirmed in a career as an international wanderer, often on foot, scorning baggage of any kind and subsisting on handouts from people along the way who recognized what Jefferson called "his fearless courage and enterprise." Ledyard told Jefferson that he had come to Paris in a futile search for funds to start an American fur firm on the Pacific coast to compete with the British, Spanish and Russians, all of whom expected to find wealth out there.

Jefferson, the avid armchair explorer, asked Ledyard about his Bering Strait and Aleutian Islands adventures with Cook. Then, on a sudden impulse, he asked if Ledyard thought that he could walk across Russia from Hamburg and St. Petersburg to the Kamchatka Peninsula, "cross in some of the Russian vessels to Nootka Sound, fall down into the latitude of the Missouri, and penetrate to and through that to the United States." Ledyard leaped at the thought with wild enthusiasm. Next day, Jefferson sent a request to the empress of Russia to permit Ledyard to cross her country. When Catherine the Great condemned the plan as "chimerical" and refused permission, Jefferson gave Ledyard his blessing anyhow. On June 19, 1787, the minister reported to a friend: "I had a letter from Ledyard lately, dated at St. Petersburg. He had but two shirts, and yet more shirts than shillings. Still he was determined to obtain the palm of being the first circumambulator of the earth. He says that having no money, they kick him from place to place, and thus he expects to be kicked around the globe."

It is the world's loss that Ledyard never got around to writing the story of this phenomenal odyssey. Some months later, as he begged rides along the wind-swept caravan route toward Omsk through the treeless steppes of Siberia, Jefferson wrote dubiously of his prospects to another friend, concluding, "He is a person of ingenuity and information. Unfortunately, he has too much imagination." And then, in the spring of 1788, the Russian minister in Paris brought word to Jefferson that the epic trip had been interrupted. On February 24, Catherine the Great's soldiers caught up with Ledyard at the bleak fur-and-ivory town of Yakutsk only a thousand miles from the Sea of Okhotsk, the arm of the North Pacific where boats of the Russian fur traders could have carried him on to Nootka Sound. He had traveled on foot and by horseback, wagon and sledge six thousand miles in the past eighteen months. But he still had a long way to go to the Mississippi — some twelve thousand miles. Catherine's soldiers arrested him on spy charges and conveyed him by sledge back to the Polish border — a miserable trip of six weeks. Jefferson was far from discouraged by the news of Ledyard's failure. Instead, it inspired in him a permanent determination to promote an expedition across the continent.[1]

The problem of Mississippi transport continued to intrude on the minister's enjoyment of Paris. He worried about the arrival in Philadelphia of Don Diego de Gardoqui as Spain's new envoy to the United States. Jefferson had heard about Gardoqui in his days as governor of Virginia and he had no faith in him. He remembered that during the Revolution the father of this suave Spanish diplomat had headed a group of Bilbao exporters, Gardoqui and Sons, who had sold gunpowder to Oliver Pollock for delivery to the Americans at Fort Pitt while reportedly selling powder at the same time to the British at Pensacola, Mobile Bay, Fort Bute and Natchez.

Congress appointed John Jay to negotiate with Gardoqui over Spain's closure of the Mississippi and claims to lands far north of the 31st parallel, the disputed boundary of Spanish Florida. The confederation's secretary of foreign affairs, Jay, was a logical choice since he had spent two years in Madrid during the late war seeking funds from Gardoqui and being put off by Floridablanca. Of all those extraordinary men who created the United States, Jay was the most impeccable, the most dependable, the most conscientious, the most self-controlled, the best dressed. He was a small, handsome, reserved man with a slender figure and he moved about with great dignity. He was not so much colorless as predictable. His ancestry was Huguenot French and Dutch. He was born to wealth in New York City, attended King's College (Columbia), studied law and married Sarah Livingston of the Livingston hierarchy that had dominated New York affairs for a century with the Stuyvesants, Jays and other patriarchal families. He was about Jefferson's age and served with him through those thrilling years of the Revolution. The two men admired one another warily. If Jay had a fault it was vanity. He agreed fully with the consensus that he was a man of many parts.

Watching in Paris, Jefferson had misgivings about how the brilliant Jay would handle Gardoqui and the Mississippi talks, the outcome of which was so vital to those western frontiersmen who had to have free use of the river and of New Orleans to exist. He knew that Jay had the usual bias of the Hudson River leaders in favor of eastern commercial interests. He thought that the New Yorker was overimpressed by the amount of power that Charles III possessed in his last years. And Jefferson's pessimism turned out to be justified. After a year of work with Gardoqui, Jay received from Congress in 1786 permission to "forbear" rights for free navigation of the Mississippi and deposit at New Orleans during a period of twenty or thirty years in exchange for favorable tariff treatment for American ships — that is, New England ships mainly — in Spain's European harbors. New England ships needed Spain's business badly just then because of Britain's stringent rules to protect her own merchant marine. Gardoqui promised nothing specific about whether Spain would give up her trans-Appalachian land claims and accept the 31st parallel as the Florida border.

The one-sided terms of this proposed Jay-Gardoqui treaty was met by a furious protest in Congress and it faded away to nothing, for obvious reasons. To western farmers and to the agricultural south, the terms merely supported an old argument — that the frontiersmen ought to give their settlements back to the Indians and knuckle down to the rule of eastern manufacturers and ship owners. Jefferson, the agrarian expansionist, took the farmers' side and went beyond it. To him, the terms presented a turning point in national affairs — a point of decision on whether the United States would choose to remain a small seaboard state or to expand into a power of continental dimensions. In a letter to James Madison sent from Paris on January 30, 1787, he wrote in part:

I will venture to say, that the act which abandons the navigation of the Mississippi is an act of separation between the eastern and western country. It is a relinquishment of five parts out of eight, of the territory of the United States; an abandonment of the fairest subject for the payment of our public debts, and the chaining those debts on our own necks, *in perpetuum*. I have the utmost confidence in the honest intentions of those who concur in this measure; but I lament their want of acquaintance with the character and physical advantages of the people who, right or wrong, will suppose their interest sacrificed on this occasion, to the contrary interests of that part of the confederacy in possession of present power. If they [the frontiersmen] declare themselves a separate people, we are incapable of a single effort to retain them. Our citizens can never be induced, either as militia or as soldiers, to go there to cut the throats of their own brothers and sons, or rather, to be themselves the subjects, instead of the perpetrators of parricide. Nor would that country quit the cost of being retained against the will of its inhabitants, could it be done. But it cannot be done. They are able already to rescue the navigation of the Mississippi out of the hands of Spain, and to add New Orleans to their own territory. They will be joined by the inhabitants of Louisiana. This will bring on a war between them and Spain; and that will produce the question with us, whether it will not be worth our while to become parties with them in the war, in order to reunite them with us, and thus correct our error? And were I to permit my forebodings to go one step further, I should predict that the inhabitants of the United States would force their rulers to take the affirmative of that question. I wish I may be mistaken in all these opinions.

Jefferson was not mistaken. Even as he wrote in 1787, tens of thousands of American frontiersmen in the valleys of Kentucky and Tennessee, western Carolina and Georgia, were listening to plans of their leaders to renounce the United States that seemed to treat them like stepchildren. In its weakness and indecision, the Confederation was unable either to assert the natural right of the westerners to river navigation or to protect them from attack by Spain's Indian friends in the south and England's in the north. Meanwhile, it was a time of anxiety for First Minister Floridablanca in Madrid. Though Spain was at peace with England, he saw signs that the British fleet was threatening Charles III's empire again at a time when Spain's alliance with France could not be depended upon. Louis XVI was doing nothing to improve his wretched financial condition, and his subjects were given more and more to open expressions of contempt for him and for Marie Antoinette. Spain's position on the Mississippi, Floridablanca decided, must be strengthened before it was too late by taking advantage of the discontent of the American frontiersmen and by winning the support of the Creek, Choctaw and Chickasaw Indians. His aim would be to create a trans-Appalachian Spanish empire from Kentucky down through the disputed Natchez Strip and so on around the gulf coast of Florida. Accordingly, Floridablanca sent Don Esteban Miró to New Orleans as the new governor of Louisiana and Manuel Gayoso de Lemos as governor of the claimed Natchez lands. Both men were told to encourage conspiracies against the United States in every possible way. They were instructed also to urge the American dissidents to emigrate to Natchez and to Spanish Louisiana — the effect of which would be to build up Spain's pitifully small Mississippi population for defense against both the English in Canada and the seaboard Americans.

The need for haste was stressed in these orders to Miró and Gayoso. Floridablanca was aware that John Adams, the U.S. minister to Great Britain, was in London demanding that the English evacuate their posts in the Northwest Territory. He knew, too, that the British response to Adams was to send secret agents to Kentucky to persuade the settlers to become Englishmen again, promising to give them anything they wanted in Spanish Louisiana after its seizure by British forces. But Floridablanca believed that prompt action would avert such a calamity. There was an abundance of pro-Spanish dissenters and land speculators who would collaborate with him if they thought that collaboration would advance their promotions. The Virginia patriot, Patrick Henry, had his eye on Indian lands below Chickasaw Bluffs. John Sevier had already set up the autonomous state of Franklin in eastern Tennessee. Sevier and the wealthy William Blount held a state of

Georgia grant in the Muscle Shoals area at the big bend of the Tennessee where a canal connection with the Tombigbee River would give them an outlet on the Gulf of Mexico at Mobile. A much larger Georgia grant — the entire Yazoo River valley — was held by a splendid confidence man and ex-priest from Charleston, "Dr." James O'Fallon, and his South Carolina Yazoo Company. George Rogers Clark, whose sister married O'Fallon later, supported this project, which included a river port at Walnut Hills (present Vicksburg). Upstream, Colonel George Morgan of New Jersey was gathering settlers to install on fifteen million acres that Diego de Gardoqui had promised him in Louisiana above and below the mouth of the Ohio. This vast tract ran along the river for two hundred and fifty miles from present Perry County, Missouri, south to the mouth of the St. Francis River near what is now Helena, Arkansas. It extended westward one hundred and twenty miles into Ozark country. Morgan gave the name of New Madrid to the river port city that would handle the commerce of his tract.

These busy trans-Appalachia promoters, conspirators and separatists were inspired and guided by an arch plotter who was associated with all of them in some degree — Colonel (later General) James Wilkinson of Louisville, Kentucky, perhaps the most interesting, even engaging, rascal in American history. To some observers, Wilkinson was a complete monster — the very last word in traitors. To others, including Wilkinson himself, he was a hero — "the Washington of the West," whose masterful perfidy for and against the United States quickened the pace of the nation toward acquiring Louisiana. He was born on the smelly oyster flats of Chesapeake Bay east of the Potomac, and whatever his environment was, it produced a man who would thrive on intrigue as a way of life. At nineteen, already a captain, he took part in Benedict Arnold's unsuccessful invasion of Canada in 1776. From Arnold he learned the technique, indispensable to intrigue, of writing letters in code. One of Wilkinson's friends on Arnold's staff was an elegant and devious young man, also nineteen, from Newark, New Jersey, named Captain Aaron Burr. During the crucial Saratoga battles of 1777 against Burgoyne, Wilkinson was adjutant to General Horatio Gates, also a master plotter. After the war Wilkinson resigned from the army, married a rich Philadelphia girl, and drifted west looking for adventure. He found it at Lexington, Kentucky, in 1783, when he became a land speculator and a merchant in blankets and calico. Later, in Louisville, he faced the challenge of how to evade Floridablanca's latest decree, which excluded the Americans from trading on the Mississippi.

Whether James Wilkinson, head of the United States Army, was a scoundrel or a hero is a point historians will probably still be debating ages hence. (Portrait by Charles Willson Peale. Courtesy of Independence National Historical Park Collection, Philadelphia)

That delightfully lush Kentucky region of soft rains and bluegrass, which Jefferson's godfather, Thomas Walker, had found beyond Cumberland Gap in 1748, was by far the largest in area, the most populous and the most anti-Confederation part of trans-Appalachia. It was centered on the Kentucky River and bounded on the north by the Ohio. Wilkinson discovered that the *cédula* was only an annoyance to an operator like himself, who knew whom to bribe with Spanish gold. Contraband remained the preferred commerce of Louisiana's French creoles and of the sprinkling of Spanish bureaucrats, even as in Bienville's time. Every few months Wilkinson's flatboats, piled high with tobacco, were waved on by Floridablanca's river patrols on their way to markets in New Orleans.

Such magic impressed the Kentuckians, and they were impressed by Wilkinson's energy, his plausibility and his infectious belief that his mysterious activities were bound to make everybody rich. Soon they put him above the faded hero of Vincennes, General Clark, as their separatist leader. In this role, he took up residence in New Orleans for three months in 1787, learned Spanish, pledged allegiance to Charles III and his Catholic God, and became a good friend of Governor Miró and his staff, who found him enchanting and his bribes even more so. With the governor he worked out a plan of conspiracy to submit to Floridablanca to bring about Kentucky's secession from the United States, and to make it an ally of Spain in defending the southwest and Mexico from foreign invasion. In return for his services, Wilkinson asked to be named as Spain's sole agent in Kentucky with dictatorial power to control Kentucky commerce on the Mississippi and the immigration of its citizens to Spanish Louisiana and Florida.

Floridablanca took a long time reaching a decision about Wilkinson's plan. It was not until March of 1789 that the royal order of the Spanish Junta reached Miró in New Orleans. It was a cautious order, avoiding any hint of conspiracy against the United States. It must have been disappointing to Wilkinson. Though he was appointed Spain's secret agent in Kentucky and was granted a loan of $7,000, he was given no monopoly to control the American part of the Mississippi trade. The royal order opened the river to all Americans subject to a fifteen percent duty at New Orleans — or a six percent duty, if Miró thought that the shipper was pro-Spanish. Immigration was thrown open to any American taking the loyalty oath. Immigrants were promised liberal land grants and all the commercial privileges on the Mississippi that Spanish subjects enjoyed. And the order contained an extra inducement to the Americans — an astonishing departure from the immemorial policy of Catholic Spain. For the first time, the despised Protestants would be granted religious toleration on Spanish soil. They would be permitted to practice their heresies undisturbed, at least in Louisiana and Florida.

The caution in Floridablanca's order derived from startling international developments. One of them was changes in the U.S. government which, in Samuel Bemis's phrase, "rescued the people from anarchy." In 1786, Alexander Hamilton, a rising young New York lawyer who had fought with Washington through the Revolution, had joined James Madison in a movement to force the feeble Confederation to strengthen its authority over the governments of the thirteen states, and "to render the Constitution adequate to the exigencies of the union."[2] Washington, like Jefferson an ardent expansionist, was elected president of the Constitutional Convention in Philadelphia. As he saw it, an important exigency was the separatist conspiracies which Wilkinson, Sevier, Blount, Clark and others were said to be promoting so enthusiastically in trans-Appalachia. The new Constitution, formulated mainly by Madison and presented to Congress in September, 1788, was approved by the necessary nine states as the law of the land in June, 1789. It gave the federal government the overriding authority it needed to run the country as a nation rather than as a collection of balky cooperatives.

It was obvious to Floridablanca that these measures for a stronger United States put a crimp in his schemes to collaborate with the American frontiersmen. Of much greater concern to him was the death of his monarch, Charles III, on December 14, 1788. The king's son and successor, Charles IV, was mentally retarded if not quite an imbecile. The son tended to excuse his laziness on the grounds that he and his kingdom were Bourbon dependencies of France. His middle-aged wife, María Luisa of Parma, a narrow, violent, domineering creature, was planning to replace Floridablanca as first minister with her young lover, a twenty-two-year-old junior army officer named Manuel de Godoy, duque de Alcudia.

While Floridablanca was mourning Charles III's death, he observed with dismay the decline of the power of Charles's cousin in France. The question was whether this gentle, unstable, well-meaning Louis XVI would honor the Franco-Spanish alliance that Vergennes had arranged in 1779 in the event that Great Britain attacked Louisiana and other Spanish colonies in her pursuit of a world trade monopoly. When the French king had asked his Assembly of Notables to solve his troubles in 1787, the marquis de Lafayette had stepped up to demand that he summon the States-General — for the first time since Marie de Medici had summoned it in 1614 during the regency of Louis XIII. This body of "three estates" — nobles, clergy and commoners — became the National Assembly after the king requested, reluctantly, a constitutional monarchy similar to England's. On July 11, 1789, Lafayette presented to the Assembly a declaration of rights modeled on Jefferson's Declaration of Independence. Lafayette's presentation and the storming of the Bastille by the populace three days later marked the start of the French Revolution.

Floridablanca did not have to wait long for a test of the French alliance. While members of the States-General were meeting with Louis XVI in the spring of 1789, a tiny drama in a wildly picturesque littoral setting occurred a third of the way around the world from the splendor of Versailles. The viceroy of Mexico had sent a Spanish warship under Captain Estevan José Martínez up the California coast with orders to drive out trespassers from the Pacific Ocean. The warship may have passed, in a fog off Oregon, a Yankee clipper ship of two hundred and twelve tons called the *Columbia*, that had been sent out on its maiden voyage to China by some Boston merchants seeking a share of the new triangular northwest-coast fur trade. The *Columbia* carried sea-otter skins which its master, a Rhode Islander named Robert Gray, had picked up at Nootka Sound the previous winter.

The Martínez warship hove to in the bay at Nootka and dropped anchor near a small hut onshore, where a number of Englishmen and Nootka Indians were trading goods and furs. Three British merchant ships and one Portuguese stood in the harbor. Martínez's marines seized the trading hut, relieved the English ships of their goods and ordered them on their way. Later, the Spanish captain captured and kept several other British ships on the grounds that they were violating the sovereignty of the Pacific northwest which, he said, Spain possessed by right of discovery, occupation, and Pope Alexander VI's hoary bull of 1493. Martínez waved aside the rebuttal of the British, that Sir Francis Drake had claimed New Albion (Oregon) for Queen Elizabeth in 1579, and that Captain Cook had reasserted the claim in

*Spain and England had reached the brink of war in 1790 when the news
reached Europe that a Spanish naval captain had seized the goods of British
traders at Nootka Sound. (Reprinted from* The Westward Crossings
by Jeannette Mirsky by permission of the University of Chicago Press)

1778 when he added the Nootka region. The British declared also that
Spain had actually occupied no land on the Pacific shore north of San
Francisco Bay, where Juan Bautista de Anza had founded the Presidio and
Mission Dolores in 1776.

It took many months for the indignant British sailors to get on around
the world and back to England to report that Spain was claiming exclusive
ownership of the northwest coast. There was no immediate official clamor.
Ambassadors discussed the matter quietly over glasses of sherry and
reached no solution. News of it circulated slowly. All at once, in May of
1790, governments everywhere seemed to realize simultaneously that the
Nootka affair was of global import. At issue was the question of what really
constituted ownership of vast areas, mostly unexplored, that the nations of
Europe had annexed for little or no good reason after 1492.

Tiny Nootka was the big test case. But no nation was going to war twenty-five thousand miles from home. Instead, the test revolved mainly around Louisiana and Florida, which were vulnerable to attack and, suddenly, extremely attractive to everybody, including George III's prime minister, William Pitt the Younger. Pitt was a frail man who drank large quantities of port for his health's sake. But he was a statesman of the highest order, a gifted orator and a subtle politician. He extracted two million pounds from his stingy monarch to send the British fleet to the Gulf of Mexico and the Caribbean. Some units went to South America and the Philippines. Pitt instructed two of his army operatives, the tempestuous loyalist William A. Bowles of Maryland and John Murray Dunmore, governor of the Bahamas, to promote an independent Creek-Cherokee Indian state in Spanish West Florida. The plan for this Indian state was similar to the earlier British plan for an Indian buffer state north of the Ohio. Pitt's Canadian agent at Fort Detroit, Dr. John Connolly, was already in Louisville seeing if James Wilkinson and George Rogers Clark would drop their Spanish friends and lead their Kentuckians in the conquest of New Orleans, of Natchez, and of the Yazoo River region, with English help from Canada. Connolly stressed that after the Kentuckians conquered Louisiana and Florida, they could join the Venezuelan revolutionist, Francisco Miranda, in seizing Texas from Spain and — at long last — the fabulous silver mines of Mexico.

Floridablanca was dismayed as reports of this latest British threat at Nootka to Spain's empire poured in to him in Madrid. He sent orders to Governor Miró at New Orleans to do what he could with his single small regiment of undependable French creoles to strengthen Spanish defenses at Walnut Hills (Vicksburg) and Chickasaw Bluffs (Memphis), at Pensacola, Mobile, New Orleans and St. Louis. He appealed to Louis XVI to honor the Family Compact, though he knew that France was in turmoil with its revolution and that the powerless king could not come to Spain's aid.

In the end, Floridablanca had to give in to Pitt, precisely as had occurred in 1770, when Choiseul had refused French forces during the Anglo-Spanish controversy over the Falkland Islands. On October 28, 1790, the Spanish minister signed a humiliating convention with the English making full restitution for Martínez's acts at Nootka. The convention relinquished Spain's claim of sovereignty in the Pacific, and granted England's right to trade and settle on the northwest coast anywhere north of the Golden Gate. Pitt was satisfied. Perhaps he had an impulse to demand other things — Honduras and its lumber, for instance. But he thought it best to use restraint and resume friendly relations with Spain. George III was out of his straitjacket, having only just recovered from his unsettling temporary insanity. Pitt's world trade policy was doing well and making a dent in Britain's war debt. Though Pitt expected no British involvement as a result of the French Revolution, one never knew for sure. And, anyhow, he had achieved his objectives at Nootka. He had established the principle that to acquire territory it was necessary for a nation to occupy it, not merely to claim it.[3]

A factor in Pitt's restraint after Nootka was the statesmanship of George Washington, who had taken the oath as the first president of the United States — replacing the weak Confederation — in New York on April 30, 1789. Washington, like Jefferson, had always felt that an English Mississippi would seriously challenge the ability of the United States to survive. But he had no money in 1789 to defend against a Louisiana invasion. He had no navy, and almost no army — only 672 officers and men. But he had himself, and the international prestige that he had won by defeating Britain. He had a booming economy riding high on capital that Englishmen were eager to advance for their own profit — capital for American smugglers doing big business in the British West Indies, capital so that hundreds of Yankee skippers could enter the roaring China trade out of Boston that Robert Gray had begun.

During the Nootka crisis, Washington worked on plans to frustrate attempts by Spain in West Florida and by England north of the Ohio to set up independent Indian states — plans to be executed by trained Indian fighters like "Mad Anthony" Wayne. To strengthen these plans, he asked for the loyalty and help of the American frontiersmen whom he understood perfectly because many of them were Virginians like himself. He gave his approval when the Virginia legislature encouraged Kentucky County to go on its own and seek statehood under the provisions of the Northwest Ordinance of 1787. He approved North Carolina's similar action in freeing its Tennessee district. He made every effort to convince all these trans-Appalachia people — one hundred and forty thousand of them — that their interests were safe in the hands of the federal government and would not be tampered with by their wealthy enemies on the east coast.

Washington's handling of the western separatist leaders was supremely pragmatic. This was no time to call them traitors for conspiring against the United States — conspiring exactly as he himself had conspired against George III only a decade back, and for the same reasons. He knew that they were the ablest and most energetic men west of the Blue Ridge. Instead of forcing them into the arms of Spain or England, he sought to bring their talents under his command by appointing them to high office. William Blount was named governor and superintendent of Indian affairs in the new Southwest Territory running from Kentucky south to the disputed 31st parallel–boundary of Spanish Florida. John Sevier became a brigadier general under Governor Blount. The affable scoundrel, James Wilkinson, was commissioned a lieutenant colonel in the United States Army just as he was spending the last of the $7,000 that Governor Miró had loaned to him, and concluding agreements to receive from Spain a pension of $2,000 a year.

And Washington had frontier interests prominently in mind when he nominated Thomas Jefferson as his secretary of state in September, 1789. One purpose of this appointment of the agrarian westerner was to counterbalance his appointment of the eastern capitalist and financial wizard, Alexander Hamilton, as his secretary of the treasury. But, in the main, Washington chose Jefferson because he felt that he was the best man in America for the post. John Jay, who had handled such matters for the Confederation, could not agree.

15

———∽———

Treaty Trouble and—
Worse—Monsieur Genet

THOMAS JEFFERSON LIVED MANY LIVES during his five years as American minister in Paris. As a scientist, he combed the *Journal de Physique* and *Encyclopédie Méthodique* for items to pass on to his beloved American Philosophical Society in Philadelphia, which Benjamin Franklin had founded in 1743. He studied musical pendulums and screw propellers. He mourned the death of Pilâtre de Rozier, whose fire balloon burst into flame at six thousand feet and crashed near Boulogne in 1785. Ballooning was the rage in Paris through the 1780's and Jefferson sent data about it to members of the Philosophical Society who were ballooning above the Schuylkill. As a farmer, he bought vine shoots from Hochheim and Rudesheim with the hope of raising German white wine grapes at Monticello. He discussed love and aesthetics with Maria Cosway and with Angelica Church, the lovely sister-in-law of Alexander Hamilton, at Madame de Corny's house on the rue Chaussée d'Antin around the corner from the Opéra. He played chess with the marquis de Chastellux of the French Academy, whom he had known at Monticello. As an architect, he made at Nîmes a plaster model of the beautiful and ancient Maison-Carrée, the Greco-Roman design of which would be used for the capital of Virginia at Richmond, completed in 1792. At Washington's request, he examined the famous canal between riverheads that Louis XIV had built in Languedoc to connect the Mediterranean near

Narbonne with the Atlantic near Bordeaux. Washington was urging Congress at the time to put a canal across the Alleghenies from the headwaters of the Potomac to the Ohio and Mississippi to improve commercial ties with the discontented Kentuckians.

Jefferson wrote officially to John Jay and privately to friends like James Madison and James Monroe on the problems of selling New England whale oil and Virginia tobacco to France. He wrote of the Russo-Turkish crisis, Morocco's declared war against England, the Dutch revolt against Austria, the Barbary Coast pirates, the turbulence in Prussia under Frederick William II, the controversy between the pope and the king of Naples, and the decay of Spain, where Queen María Luisa and her Manuel de Godoy were pushing the liberal royalist Floridablanca out of power.

The American minister noted the continuing corruption of the nobility at Versailles, the archaic political views of the comte d'Artois, the king's brother, and the tendency of Louis XVI to drink a bottle of champagne and go hunting whenever a national crisis arose. He observed open court scandals such as that of the notorious bishop of Autun, born Maurice de Talleyrand-Périgord, whose illegitimate children were said to be scattered around Paris like chestnuts. One of them, a boy produced by the comtesse de Flahaut, would turn up later as Napoleon's aide-de-camp.[1] Jefferson had heard of Talleyrand — small, lame, brilliant, ambitious — through mutual friends, the marquis de Lafayette and Condorcet, the philosopher and revolutionist.

During the terrifying summer of 1789, the American minister saw many demonstrations against the king in the Place Louis XV. He tended to blame Marie Antoinette for the nation's woes. "This angel," he would write in his autobiography, "as gaudily painted in the rhapsodies of Burke, with some smartness of fancy, but no sound sense, was proud, disdainful of restraint, indignant at all obstacles to her will, eager in the pursuit of pleasure, and firm enough to hold to her desires, or perish in the wreck. Her inordinate gambling and dissipations, with those of the comte d'Artois, and others of her *clique*, had been a sensible item in the exhaustion of the treasury, which called into action the reforming hand of the nation. . . . I have ever believed that, had there been no Queen, there would have been no revolution."

All the while, Jefferson studied European trends for their bearing on the chances of winning an open Mississippi and of getting the British out of

Fort Detroit and the rest of the Northwest Territory, keystones in his emerging dream of a continental United States. He did not share the views of eastern capitalists that Floridablanca's easy immigration policy would empty their factories of cheap labor and make Spain's Louisiana empire a threat to the United States. Of Colonel Morgan's proposed New Madrid colony below St. Louis, he wrote, "While this measure weakens somewhat the United States for the present, it begins our possession of that country considerably sooner than I had expected, and without a struggle." He had a similar view toward those American speculators who were being lured to the Yazoo River region above Natchez. "I wish a hundred thousand of our inhabitants," he said, "would accept the invitation. It will be the means of delivering to us peaceably what may otherwise cost us a war." His feeling derived from his conviction that no American pioneer with gumption enough to tame the wilds of Louisiana could ever become a loyal Spanish subject, subservient to the Catholic religion, to Spain's frustrating regulations and to an economy dedicated to paying for the extravagances of royalty. If these pioneers settled in Louisiana, they would be looking soon for ways to break away from Spain.

Of course Jefferson recognized the other side of the coin — the problem of keeping such independent people loyal to the United States. On May 26, 1788, he wrote from Paris to his friend John Brown, not knowing then that Brown was one of James Wilkinson's conspirators:

Your removal from Carolina to Kentucky was not an indifferent event to me. I wish to see that country in the hands of people well disposed, who know the value of the connection between that and the maritime States, and who wish to cultivate it. I consider their happiness as bound up together, and that every measure should be taken, which may draw the bands of union tighter. It will be an efficacious one to receive them into Congress, as I perceive they are about to desire. If to this be added an honest and disinterested conduct in Congress, as to everything relating to them, we may hope for perfect harmony. The navigation of the Mississippi was, perhaps, the strongest trial to which the justice of the federal government could be put. If ever they thought wrong about it, I trust they have got to rights. I should think it proper for the western country to defer pushing their right to that navigation to extremity, as long as they can do without it tolerably; but that the moment it becomes absolutely necessary for them, it will become the duty of the maritime States to push it to every extremity, to

245

which they would their own right of navigating the Chesapeake, the Delaware, the Hudson, or any other water. A time of peace will not be the surest for obtaining this object. Those, therefore, who have influence in the new country, would act wisely to endeavor to keep things quiet till the Western parts of Europe shall be engaged in war. Notwithstanding the aversion of the courts of London and Versailles to war, it is not certain that some incident may not engage them in it. England, France, Spain, Russia, Sweden and Denmark will all have fleets at sea, or ready to put to sea immediately. Who can answer for the prudence of all their officers? War is their interest.

By October of 1789, Jefferson was ready for a vacation far from the bloody uproar of Paris in the struggle for control of the French government between nobility and clergy on one side and a mélange of reformers on the other — reformers ranging from middle-class constitutional monarchists and moderate republican Girondists to the Paris mob of extreme Jacobin revolutionaries under Robespierre and Danton. Jefferson had had both of his daughters, Patsy and eleven-year-old Polly, with him for two years. He thought that they should resume their lives in their peaceful home environment of Virginia. The three sailed from England by way of Le Havre on October 22 and landed at Norfolk on November 23. As they were riding toward Monticello, a courier brought Jefferson his first news that Congress had approved Washington's nomination of him as secretary of state.

He had not wanted this task of virtually creating the structure and policies of a difficult post. What he had wanted was to retire after a few months more in Paris to spend the rest of his life as a country gentleman raising crops and manufacturing nails, and "putting up and pulling down" his buildings at Monticello as an amateur architect. He kept President Washington waiting for his acceptance and it was not until late March of 1790 that he got to his state department desk in New York, which had been the nation's capital since 1784 but which would be replaced soon by Philadelphia. He put Monticello out of his mind and found himself caught up soon in the fascination of the current international scene — and no wonder. He arrived at the start of catastrophic events that would remake the Western world and bring success to the feeble and fumbling United States far beyond the hopes of its leaders — success built on the distress of Europe that would reach a climax with Napoleon's fall in 1815.

Jefferson's concept of what the aims of the United States should be contained grandiose elements — a fur trade larger than Canada's, discovery of an overland route up the Missouri to John Ledyard's Oregon, the greater participation of Yankee ships in the West Indies and in the China trade with Nootka Sound. But the focus of his perspective was La Salle's Louisiana, which he knew now to be larger than all of western Europe with a variety of soil, climate and topography that would appeal to every kind of agrarian temperament. To him, the American experiment in republican government would triumph because of the dynamic quality of a society of free farmers west of the Blue Ridge. Their initiative and industry would bring strength to the limited potential of the maritime states. The example of the Kentucky region's filling up in a decade proved to him that the rest of eastside Louisiana would fill up also with the end of restraints imposed by Spain on the Mississippi and by England north of the Ohio. He knew that these restraints were artificial and temporary because they were not supported by massive migrations of people.

Through the spring and summer of 1790, Jefferson watched the Anglo-Spanish controversy over Nootka Sound and studied rumors of British plans for war and for an invasion of Spanish Louisiana. Perhaps this embroilment would give him a chance to use American neutrality as a bargaining tool to dislodge the two belligerents from their trans-Appalachian positions. For seven years, both Spain and England had refused to discuss their positions seriously and had neglected to send diplomats to the United States of high enough rank to negotiate treaties. To activate the English, Jefferson offered neutrality, though he could not say what stand the Americans would take if British troops tried to advance from Fort Detroit toward New Orleans through the American Northwest Territory. He assured Lord Grenville, however, that the army which Washington hoped to send against hostile Ohio Indians had no intention of invading British Canada.

In August, the secretary of state suggested to Spanish officials that the angry Kentuckians could not be prevented from taking part in the British invasion of Louisiana if that seemed necessary to them to win free navigation of the Mississippi for their flatboats and a free port near its mouth for the transfer of their produce to seagoing ships. At the same time, he asked the French to persuade their Spanish ally to grant this perennial American request. But none of these attempts to play one country against the other succeeded in 1790. And, in October, the threat of an Anglo-Spanish war vanished when Spain capitulated on the Nootka matter. Shortly thereafter,

Spain and England, the bitterest of foes for centuries, began a pretense of being friends and allies in their mutual concern over anti-monarchist developments in France.

Meanwhile, Jefferson had to contend with troublesome side issues. After President Washington appointed Alexander Hamilton as his secretary of the treasury, he named another Revolutionary War aide, General Henry Knox, as secretary of war. Both these men stood for everything that Jefferson abhorred — a centralized government ruled by a business elite; admiration for England and its monarchy; a national debt and credit structure; contempt for the masses, farmers especially; interpretations of the U.S. Constitution so loose as to vitiate its function as protector of states' rights. The resulting feud between Hamilton, the eastern capitalist, and Jefferson, the agrarian strict constructionist, would evolve into the two faces of the American political system — Federalists and anti-Federalists, Republicans and Democrats, conservatives and liberals. When Jefferson averred that the three greatest men in history were Sir Francis Bacon, Sir Isaac Newton and John Locke, Hamilton had his reply ready: "The greatest man was Julius Caesar."

Hamilton and Knox loved to meddle in Jefferson's department. In private talks with a British diplomat, George Beckwith, Hamilton hinted that a joint British-American attack on New Orleans was conceivable. While Jefferson's chargé in Madrid, William Carmichael, was struggling to make a good impression there, General Knox ordered one of his army officers at Kaskaskia, Lieutenant John Armstrong, to explore in mufti the Missouri River from its mouth to its unknown source. Fortunately, the Spanish did not get wind of this blatantly expansionist move and Armstrong lost his appetite for his secret mission on the outskirts of St. Louis.

Going into 1792, Jefferson was not pleased to learn that Queen María Luisa and her protégé, Manuel de Godoy had finally dismissed Floridablanca from the first ministry and had put him in jail for safekeeping. Floridablanca was at least familiar and predictable. In Louisiana, James Wilkinson's friend, Governor Miró, was replaced by a compulsive doer, Héctor, baron de Carondelet, the ex-governor of San Salvador. Carondelet spoke no English, knew nothing of Louisiana's complicated affairs, refused to take advice, and believed that precipitate action was the best policy. He noted that his agent Wilkinson, inherited from Miró, was busy preparing to fight Ohio Indians with General Anthony Wayne. With Kentucky already admitted to statehood and Tennessee well on the way, the various Wilkinson-inspired conspiracies seemed to be dying on the vine. In place of them, the new governor went to work to strengthen Spain's alliances with the Creeks, Chickasaws and Choctaws. The watchful Jefferson perceived that this effort was designed to keep the American frontiersmen out of western Florida and out of the disputed Natchez-Yazoo country along the Mississippi west and south of the Tennessee.

The political crisis in France that Jefferson had thought would end quickly with the establishment of a limited monarchy, moved on and on to chaos and anarchy. A climax came in August, 1792, with the overthrow of the king and the moderate Girondists by the fanatic revolutionary Commune de Paris of Robespierre and Danton. An epidemic of national insanity and pathological hatred of everything Bourbon followed. Louis XVI and Marie Antoinette, both about thirty-eight years old, rode in carts to the guillotine, where they accepted a grisly public dying with courage and composure. Somewhat later, their ten-year-old son Louis Charles, the dauphin, was said to have died in a windowless dungeon of the Paris Tour du Temple of dampness, filth, bad food, loneliness and the sadism of his keepers. The destruction of the king and queen, not for their sins but for their symbolism, would bring reaction and ruin to the revolutionary cause.[2] An immediate effect of the king's death on January 23, 1793, was to plunge Robespierre's democracy nine days later into war with Great Britain and Holland, and then with Britain's unwilling ally, Spain, and also with Portugal, Prussia and Austria. This totally unforeseen start of Napoleon's rise to power was far more of a European diversion than Jefferson had wanted for the United States so that it could survive its growing pains and win its objectives in the west.

An odd aspect of Louis XVI's regime was the tendency of many members of court society to wind up in the United States during the process of adjusting their lives politically for survival. After the fall of the Bastille, the wily Talleyrand, bishop of Autun, had proclaimed himself a "patriot" and "chaplain of the Revolution." He resigned as bishop in 1791, urged the sale of church properties, joined the moderate National Assembly and went to London to seek British neutrality from his friend William Pitt. The declaration of war by the French Republic against England after Louis XVI's execution wrecked Talleyrand's London mission and also his standing with Robespierre's government. He was expelled from England and fled to Philadelphia, where he spent the next thirty months studying the American scene and awaiting developments which would allow him to return to French politics.

Another Frenchman in the United States was the famous Versailles botanist, André Michaux, who held dangerous republican views. He went to New York in 1785 with a royal commission, and bought a plantation near Charleston, South Carolina, which served as a base for studies in North American flora. The studies took him to the Bahamas, the swamps of Florida, the Carolina Appalachians, and even to Hudson Bay. The Hudson Bay trip merely whetted his appetite for an even greater adventure. Having heard of the scientific interests of the American Philosophical Society, he went to Philadelphia and proposed to the directors a trek up the Missouri and on across the Continental Divide to the Pacific.

His proposal was passed along to Jefferson, who was instantly enthusiastic. Unlike General Knox's impolitic reconnaissance out of St. Louis, this one could be described as purely scientific. Jefferson raised a thousand guineas for Michaux's expenses, including gifts from President Washington and Alexander Hamilton. One of Jefferson's young army friends, Meriwether Lewis, whom he had known in Charlottesville since Lewis's birth, heard of the plan and pleaded to make the trip. Jefferson turned him down because he was only eighteen and lacked scientific training.

In January of 1793, Jefferson drew up for Michaux a remarkable letter of instruction "for exploring the western boundary." The letter showed the growth of Jefferson's geographical knowledge since the failure of his scheme to send George Rogers Clark westward twelve years earlier. It showed also how strong his continental aspirations had become. The letter read:

Sundry persons having subscribed certain sums of money for your encouragement to explore the country along the Missouri, and thence westwardly to the Pacific Ocean, having submitted the plan of the enterprise to the directors of the American Philosophical Society, and the society having accepted the trust, they proceed to give you the following instructions:

They observe to you that the chief objects of your journey are to find the shortest and most convenient route of communication between the United States and the Pacific Ocean, within the temperate latitudes, and to learn such particulars as can be obtained of the country through which it passes, its productions, inhabitants and other interesting circumstances. As a channel of communication between these States and the Pacific Ocean, the Missouri, so far as it extends, presents itself under circumstances of unquestioned preference. It has, therefore, been declared as a fundamental object of the subscription (not to be dispensed with) that this river shall be considered and explored as a part of the communication sought for. To the neighborhood of this river, therefore, that is to say, to the town of Kaskaskia, the society will procure you a conveyance in company with the Indians of that town now in Philadelphia.

From thence you will cross the Mississippi and pass by land to the nearest part of the Missouri above the Spanish settlements, that you may avoid the risk of being stopped.

You will then pursue such of the largest streams of that river as shall lead by the shortest way and the lowest latitudes to the Pacific Ocean. When, pursuing those streams, you shall find yourself at the point from whence you may get by the shortest and most convenient route to some principal river of the Pacific Ocean, you are to proceed to such river, and pursue its course to the ocean. It would seem by the latest maps as if a river called Oregon, interlocked with the Missouri for a considerable distance, and entered the Pacific Ocean not far southward of Nootka Sound. But the society are aware that these maps are not to be trusted so far as to be the ground of any positive instruction to you. They therefore only mention the fact, leaving to yourself to verify it, or to follow such other as you shall find to be the real truth.

You will in the course of your journey, take notice of the country you pass through, its general face, soil, rivers, mountains, its productions — animal, vegetable and mineral — so far as they may be new to us, and may also be useful or very curious; the latitudes of places or material for calculating it by such simple methods as your situation may admit you to practice, the names, numbers, and dwellings of the inhabitants, and such particulars as you can learn of their history, connection with each other, languages, manners, state of society, and of the arts and commerce among them.

Under the head of animal history, that of the mammoth is particularly recommended to your inquiries, as it is also to learn whether the Lama or Paca of Peru, is found in those parts of this continent, or how far north they come.

The method of preserving your observations is left to yourself, according to the means which shall be in your power. It is only suggested that the noting of them on the skin might be best for such as may be the most important, and that further details may be committed to the bark of the paper-birch, a substance which may not excite the suspicions among the Indians, and little liable to injury from wet or other common accidents. By the means of the same substance you may perhaps find opportunities, from time to time, of communicating to the society information of your progress, and of the particulars you shall have noted.

When you shall have reached the Pacific Ocean, if you find yourself within convenient distance of any settlement of Europeans, go to them, commit to writing the narrative of your journey and observations, and take the best measure you can for conveying it thence to the society by sea.

Return by the same, or some other route, as you shall think likely to fulfill with most satisfaction and certainty the objects of your mission, furnishing yourself with the best proofs the nature of the case will admit of the reality and extent of your progress. Whether this shall be by certificates from Europeans settled on the western coast of America, or by what other means, must depend on circumstances. Ignorance of the country through which you are to pass, and confidence in your judgment, zeal and discretion, prevent the society from more minute instructions, and even from exacting rigorous observance of those already given, except, indeed, what is the first of all objects, that you seek for and pursue that route which shall form the shortest and most convenient communication between the higher parts of the Missouri and the Pacific Ocean.

It is strongly recommended to you to expose yourself in no case to unnecessary dangers, whether such as might affect your health or your personal safety, and to consider this not merely as your personal concern, but as the injunction of science in general, which expects its enlargement from your inquiries, and of the inhabitants of the United States in particular, to whom your report will open new fields and subjects of commerce, intercourse, and observation.

While Michaux was discussing his proposed continental journey with Jefferson, a young Girondist in Paris named Edmond Charles Genet was being ordered to Philadelphia by Robespierre to serve the French Republic as minister plenipotentiary to the United States. Genet had not always been a revolutionist. He was brought up in court at Versailles as a liberal royalist. His father had served under Choiseul in Louis XV's foreign office. Young Genet's sister Henrietta was first lady of the bed chamber of Marie Antoinette. Another sister, Julie, was cradle rocker for the infant dauphin. With these friends of the queen to protect him, Genet did not hesitate to express his liberal views on economic reform before the States-General in 1789. The reactionary comte d'Artois had him fired from the foreign office but his sisters got him a better job in the French embassy at St. Petersburg. There, according to his biographer, Meade Minnigerode, Genet won the praise of Catherine the Great by defending the French Revolution in her presence. The empress sent him a gift of diamond knee buckles — and dismissed him from Russia. From then on, Genet made an art of shifting steadily and ardently leftward in his support of whatever revolutionist was top man in France for the moment. He became a close friend of the English radical Tom Paine, who told him a great deal about democracy in the United States and taught him to speak vernacular English.

These lessons were most helpful to "Citizen" Genet when he arrived in Charleston on April 8, 1793, gorgeously attired in gold epaulets, satin waistcoat and flowered cravat. His conveyance was the French warship *Embuscade* — aptly named since its purpose was to ambush and capture English merchant ships for sale in American ports as prizes of war. He was welcomed with hysterical warmth by Charleston residents who found in him a super-hero in the triumph of freedom over royal tyranny. He was also a creature of romance, for the story spread over the land that he had headed a Girondist plot to save Marie Antoinette from the guillotine by hiding her in his cabin on the *Embuscade*. He was supposed to have tried to hide the little dauphin too.[3] But his chivalry was said to have been foiled at Brest by the alertness of Robespierre's secret police.

From Charleston, Genet rode slowly north by stagecoach, receiving the plaudits of the populace at every hamlet. The triumphal tour was climaxed on May 17–18 in Philadelphia by wild demonstrations of joy and attempts by the Americans to sing the year-old revolutionary song "La Marseillaise."[4] Excitement was heightened by the presence in the capital of a waxworks model of the guillotine. People could watch in happy horror as the big knife fell and Louis XVI's wax head dropped while his wax lips seemed to turn blue. President Washington received this flamboyant new minister coldly, having just issued a proclamation of neutrality forbidding his countrymen to take active sides in the current struggle of republican France against the coalition of England, Spain and Holland.

As Genet's behavior became more and more arrogant, Jefferson found himself in a difficult position as a friend of France, opposing the pro-British sentiments of Alexander Hamilton and General Knox. For a time, Jefferson defended the minister in cabinet meetings, expressing hope that the hatred of the French government for royalist Spain might become useful as a threat to persuade Spain to open the Mississippi to free navigation. But complete disillusionment set in late in May. Jefferson realized then that public adulation had gone to the thirty-year-old Frenchman's head. It had led Genet to regard the United States virtually as a province of France obliged to follow French leadership in a vast uprising of the masses against the kings and aristocrats of Europe and Britain's domination of the seven seas.

Brushing aside Washington's neutrality proclamation of April 22, Genet began bringing prize ships into Delaware Bay and arming privateers manned by American citizens to capture more British and Spanish prizes. When President Washington remarked that this violated American sovereignty, Genet wrote angry letters to the Philadelphia and New York papers. He gave Jefferson the impression that he would go before Congress to demand that Washington abide by the terms of the Franco-American alliance of 1778. He asked the U.S. Treasury to pay off some of its war debt to France in advance. He needed the money, he said, to finance his immediate objective, which was to free Louisiana and Florida from Spain, and Canada from England. He told Jefferson on July 5, 1793, that he had persuaded André Michaux in Charleston to put off his Missouri River trip to the Pacific for the American Philosophical Society. Instead, he was sending Michaux to Louisville to build military barges and to commission Kentucky's leaders as French generals with orders to recruit armies of liberation totaling three thousand men and to lead them in crusades against tyranny up and down the Mississippi. Genet added that George Rogers Clark had already accepted a commission as "Major General of the Independent and Revolutionary Legion of the Mississippi," and so had Clark's brother-in-law, James O'Fallon.

Genet asked Jefferson to recommend his Louisiana liberation plan to the governor of Kentucky, Isaac Shelby, and to identify Michaux officially as a French consul to conceal his military activities. After conquering the Mississippi, France and her Kentuckians would liberate South America with the assistance of the Venezuelan Francisco Miranda, and then go on to the conquest of British India. In the meantime, Genet declared, French marines would seize the Spanish half of Santo Domingo to serve as a base for capturing Jamaica and the rest of the British West Indies. With both the Caribbean and the Gulf of Mexico transformed into French lakes, La

Salle's dream of a circular imperialism would be achieved at last — from Montreal and the Great Lakes down and out the Mississippi through the French West Indies and back again to France.

By the end of July, 1793, with Americans divided into factions for and against Genet and with the British issuing orders to imprison American sailors and seize American ships working with the enemy, Jefferson had to admit that Genet was about to entangle the United States in the Anglo-French war. Washington's cabinet met on August 1 and 2 and agreed unanimously to ask France to recall him. Robespierre, the extreme Jacobin, was glad to do so when he got the request in September. He had never had faith in this royalist-turned-Girondist and he had deplored of late Genet's expressed contempt for Washington's authority and his failure to forward needed war supplies to France. Robespierre's actual notice of recall did not reach Philadelphia until after January 1, 1794. That was the date of Jefferson's retirement as secretary of state to resume — "permanently" — the life of a country gentleman at Monticello. In his place, Washington appointed another ex-governor of Virginia, Edmund Randolph. While Genet awaited his order of dismissal from Paris he continued to function for a time as French minister, fuming and fretting but committing no more obnoxious acts. When his replacement, Joseph Fauchet, arrived with Robespierre's instructions to return Genet to France under arrest, Washington refused to extradite him out of kindness to save him from the guillotine. The ex-minister had sold his Philadelphia house and was finding peace and happiness where he could do no harm — raising ducks on a small Long Island farm.[5]

During 1794, the general war in Europe created a pattern of anxiety that gave the United States its great chance to resolve by peaceful means its problems west of the Blue Ridge — problems that Jefferson believed were repressing the nation's natural growth and weakening his agrarian ideal. There was the anxiety of Manuel de Godoy, twenty-seven years old now and a master at putting things off in his management of Spain as he followed his infatuated queen and her half-witted husband in their restless circuit of royal residences — Aranjuez in spring, San Ildefonso in summer, San Lorenzo in the fall, and Madrid at any season. In June, Godoy's agents in Philadelphia reported to him that President Washington appeared to be considering an alliance with Great Britain that might be aimed at seizing Louisiana and Florida. He worried also about reports from New Orleans

To Spain's chief minister, Manuel de Godoy, Louisiana was merely a chip in an international poker game. (Portrait by Goya. Courtesy of Real Academia de Bellas Artes de San Fernando, Madrid)

that the Creeks and Chickasaws from Florida were attacking settlers in Georgia and Tennessee with such brutal abandon that American counter-measures seemed likely. Godoy had become disillusioned with his unnatural Anglo-Spanish alliance. Its effect, he found, was to keep the Spanish busy fighting the French on land while England toiled to destroy the French navy. Without the traditional Franco-Spanish naval partnership, Spain would not be able to protect her colonies from eventual seizure by the British. But Godoy had a plan to prevent this disaster. When Robespierre went to the guillotine in July of 1794, presaging the return of France to a government of law and order, the Spanish minister sent his agents to Paris to start arranging what amounted to a resumption of the old Bourbon family pact against England.

While Godoy worried in Spain, the British foreign minister, Lord Grenville, worried in London. To Grenville, the Genet farce had a serious aspect. It showed that France, fired by republican patriotism, wanted to get back Louisiana from Spain in a new challenge of England's hegemony and as a source of raw materials for the reviving French army and navy. Grenville was acutely conscious of the anti-British feeling on the American seaboard caused by British harassment of American ships and sailors. He knew that the frontiersmen of Kentucky had become equally opposed to his government when they learned that the English lieutenant governor in Upper Canada, John Graves Simcoe, had rebuilt Fort Miami at the head of the Maumee in the Northwest Territory as a defensive outpost of Fort Detroit and as an encouragement to the old barrier state plan of the Ohio Indians. The Kentuckians were joining General Anthony Wayne's army which — as Grenville learned later — was about to subdue the Indians and to destroy their barrier state in Ohio once and for all.

Lord Grenville's concern about these developments was obvious to the impeccable John Jay when he arrived in London on June 12, 1794, as Washington's minister "plenipotentiary" — meaning that Jay was empowered to negotiate a treaty along lines prepared by Jefferson before he resigned as secretary of state. Up to then, the British had been notorious for their contemptuous frigidity toward officials of their former colonies. This time Jay found himself being received warmly by George III and Queen Charlotte. Furthermore, Grenville showed interest in his mission, which was to convince the British that Congress was apt to declare war on Britain if Britain did not end its harassment of American shipping and its occupation of forts in the Northwest Territory and elsewhere.

For weeks Grenville was cooperative though deeply involved in the war of England and her European allies against France. By September 13, the Englishman had agreed to a plan for the payment of debts which the colonists had owed to English merchants at the time of the revolution, and for the placing of British trade with the United States on a most-favored-nation basis. Grenville agreed also to evacuate by June 1, 1796, Fort Detroit, Michilimackinac and all other posts on American soil. By holding on to these posts after the Anglo-American peace treaty of 1783 as collateral for the payment of debts, England had retained her rich Indian and fur trade out of Montreal, more than half of which came from the Northwest Territory and from the adjoining areas of Spanish Louisiana across the Upper Mississippi.

Grenville had several reasons to abandon the northwest posts in addition to his wish to keep the United States neutral in the European war. Loss of fur country would be mitigated by Jay's acceptance of Grenville's proposal to permit the British to trade freely with the Indians and to maintain warehouses anywhere in the evacuated U.S. territory. Because of his expectation that the Americans under General Wayne would defeat the Ohio Indians, Grenville believed that some loss of fur terrain was inevitable in any case. Wayne's victory had already occurred, of course, at Fallen Timbers on August 20, 1794. Removal of the Indians from Ohio would open that fertile region to rapid American settlement, driving out the beaver and ruining the region as a fur producer.[6]

In hindsight, the debate over boundaries separating the Northwest Territory from Canada and from Spanish Louisiana was the crucial part of the Jay-Grenville negotiations. The boundary agreed on in 1783 through the Great Lakes to Lake Superior's Grand Portage and along the Rainy Lake canoe route to "the northwest corner of the Lake of the Woods" was clear enough. The bone of contention was the continuing line described as running "west" from "the northwest corner" to the source of the Mississippi — a line that seemed to give to the British the same right of access to the Mississippi as that enjoyed by the Americans. But in 1794, Grenville was aware that that part of the boundary agreed upon in 1783 did not exist because the source of the Mississippi was known by then to be somewhere deep in American terrain to the south — at least one hundred miles south — not west, of the Lake of the Woods. As a consequence, Grenville argued that the whole U.S.–Canada boundary had to be moved south from the Lake of the Woods to fulfill the river access commitment.

Neither of the negotiators knew enough about western geography to appreciate fully what was at stake in their discussions. Grenville suggested two new boundaries. One of them would run from Sault Ste. Marie through the middle of Lake Superior to its west end at present Duluth, Minnesota, and then on "west to Red Lake River" which he had been told was an east branch of the Mississippi. Such a line was impossible since the Red Lake River is a branch of the Red River, which flows north into Lake Winnipeg. Grenville's alternative line started at the 45th parallel of latitude far to the east on the St. Lawrence near Montreal and ran due west through what is now the middle of southern Ontario, across Lake Michigan near the present Ludington ferry, and then through Upper Michigan and mid-Wisconsin to the confluence of the St. Croix River and the Mississippi just below present

St. Paul, Minnesota. From thence, his proposed line ran due north to Rainy Lake.

According to Samuel F. Bemis in his classic *Jay's Treaty*, either of these boundaries suggested by Grenville would have turned over to England more than thirty thousand square miles of American property including what proved to be some of the world's most valuable deposits of iron and copper. Dr. Bemis added: "If such a line had been granted, it would have placed the starting point of the boundary to be drawn westward in the future to the Pacific much farther south, perhaps so as to make over to Canada the greater part of the present states of Minnesota, North Dakota, Montana, Idaho and Washington, regions of incalculable potential value and economic consequence." The historian had in mind also that the 45th parallel strikes the Pacific coast south of the Columbia River valley, the lure of which would cause the epic westward movement of the 1840's over the Oregon Trail.

As a matter of principle, John Jay, who had prepared the draft of the treaty of 1783, stood firm against Grenville's alternatives. He denied that the 1783 treaty implied a British right of access by land to the Mississippi, even though England had claimed the right of free navigation as a carry-over from her treaty with France at the end of the French and Indian War. Jay had on his side an English boundary tradition. It began with an article in the Treaty of Utrecht of 1713 calling for an Anglo-French commission to decide on a line west of the Great Lakes to separate the grant that the English had made to Hudson's Bay Company from La Salle's Louisiana. The English members of the commission had put the line along the 49th parallel. France had never accepted that line. The La Vérendrye family had explored and claimed for France vast areas north of it. But, Jay pointed out, after the transfer of westside Louisiana from France to Spain in 1763, British mapmakers made a habit of marking the 49th parallel on their maps as though it were the official boundary between Canada and Spanish Louisiana.

In the end, Jay and Grenville signed on November 19, 1794, what came to be called Jay's Treaty, the terms of which were virtually the same as those agreed upon in September. It was a historic document — Great Britain's final acknowledgment of American sovereignty over a vast and priceless domain stretching north from the Ohio to Canada, and west from the Appalachians to the Mississippi. However, the matter of where the boundary should run beyond the northwest corner of the Lake of the Woods was left for a joint commission to determine at some unspecified later date. And the signers agreed to keep the treaty secret pending the outcome of the European struggle.

Even while Jay was toiling away on Downing Street, President Washington was looking for another minister plenipotentiary to put pressure on Spain for a similar treaty to clear up the old sovereignty problems of Mississippi navigation and of boundaries south of the Ohio along lines which Jefferson had prepared while he was secretary of state. The time was propitious. Manuel de Godoy and his king and queen needed the friendship of the Americans just then. Their royalist offensive against the forces of the government that had executed Louis XVI had failed. The republican French had crossed the Pyrenees and were threatening to descend on Madrid from the Ebro River. Godoy's English allies had been driven out of Toulon on the Mediterranean by the still unknown protégé of Robespierre and artillery expert, Napoleon Bonaparte, aged twenty-four, who had been promoted to general by the National Convention in Paris.

President Washington could not use his regular minister in Madrid to negotiate a settlement because of Spanish protocol in the matter of rank. For more than two years that minister, William Short, who had been Jefferson's close friend and private secretary in Paris, had been pressing Godoy to do something. Short, a diplomat of great skill and patience, was the American minister at The Hague as well as at Madrid. He was a Virginian and a charter member of Phi Beta Kappa from William and Mary College. But neither his two ministries nor his Phi Beta Kappa key ranked him high enough to be permitted in the same room with their Royal Highnesses Charles IV and Queen María Luisa. Washington offered the treaty assignment to "the retired" Jefferson and to Patrick Henry, both of whom declined. So the president settled on his regular minister in London, Thomas Pinckney, who had fought under General Gates in the Revolutionary War and had served as governor of South Carolina. Pinckney, an attractive, worldly man, had grown up in England and had traveled extensively in Europe as an Oxford undergraduate and as a law student at the Inner Temple.

Pinckney delayed his arrival in Madrid until June 28, 1795, at the urging of John Jay, who thought it wise to keep the Spanish guessing as to the contents of Jay's Treaty as long as possible before its ratification by the

U.S. Senate. And Pinckney realized before July of 1795 ended that Godoy was as eager to negotiate — in his own slow way — as Jay had found Grenville to have been a year earlier. The sly William Short seems to have persuaded the Spaniard that Jay's Treaty implied the existence of an Anglo-American military *entente* that could be dangerous to Spain's interests in Louisiana and Florida if friction should arise between Spain and Great Britain. Such friction, Godoy knew, was apt to arise when Grenville learned of Godoy's latest secret diplomatic maneuver — a masterpiece. On July 22, 1795, he had ended the royalist alliance with Britain and made one instead with Spain's deadly enemy up to then, republican France. In drawing up this Treaty of Basel the French had pressed hard in effect, for Genet's objective of 1793; they demanded the retrocession of Louisiana from Spain to France. Godoy refused but gave them a sop — the Spanish half of Santo Domingo, so that the old West Indian stopover on the voyage from Europe to New Orleans would be entirely French.

Bit by bit, Pinckney won his points during the weeks of August and early September. A major triumph was Godoy's reluctant acceptance of the 31st parallel as the U.S.–Florida boundary, eastward from the Mississippi to the Chattahoochee, and on from there to the Atlantic, as the Florida-Georgia boundary runs today. By that article, Godoy gave up the Natchez–Yazoo River region and the other lands of present Mississippi and Alabama — the trans-Appalachian empire that Bernardo de Gálvez had claimed for Spain by conquest during the American Revolution (see the map on page 212). Godoy conceded also an entrepôt provision reading as follows:

His Catholic Majesty will permit the Citizens of the United States for the space of three years from this time to deposit their merchandise and effects in the Port of New Orleans and to export them from thence without paying any other duty than a fair price for the hire of the stores, and his Majesty promises either to continue this permission if he finds during that time that it is not prejudicial to the interests of Spain, or if he should not agree to continue it there, he will assign to them on another part of the banks of the Mississippi an equivalent establishment.

And still Godoy quibbled with Pinckney over small points. He argued for instance, that since the middle of the Mississippi was the boundary between the United States and Louisiana, any craft crossing the line was trespassing — until Pinckney convinced him that if boats moved at all they

261

John Jay's treaty of 1794 forced England to belated recognition of U.S. sovereignty over lands won during the American Revolution. (Portrait by Joseph Wright. Courtesy of The New-York Historical Society)

As Jefferson's minister plenipotentiary, Thomas Pinckney won important boundary concessions in West Florida. (Portrait by John Trumbull. Courtesy of the Yale University Art Gallery)

had to move with the bends of the channel from one side of the river to the other. Godoy wasted more time dragging the American around to various royal residences to accommodate the social schedule of the king and queen.

At last, the affable Pinckney decided that he had been affable long enough. On October 24, he asked for his passports, the delivery of which would signify that negotiations had failed. The very next day Godoy agreed to everything and got out carriages for Pinckney and William Short to use on the thirty-mile ride to the village of San Lorenzo, where the gloomy El Escorial palace rose against the slopes of the Guadarrama range. There, on October 27, Pinckney and Godoy signed the paper that would be known to some thereafter as Pinckney's Treaty, to others as the Treaty of San Lorenzo. After the signing, Godoy informed the two Americans that he was sending orders to Governor Carondelet in New Orleans for the removal of all Spanish troops from garrisons in the ceded lands within six months of the treaty's ratification. He did not reveal, however, that he had instructed Carondelet to continue paying a pension of $2,000 a year to James Wilkinson, Spain's adviser on American affairs and perennial promoter in Kentucky of a pro-Spanish separate state. Wilkinson, who had just been appointed to take over from the British at Fort Detroit, was soon to be named top general of the United States Army in the west following the death of Anthony Wayne.[7]

16

The Tightrope Walkers

THE HANDSOME MANUEL DE GODOY, duque de Alcudia, was the toast of European society through the 1790's, and not merely because he managed to keep the queen of Spain as his mistress and the king of Spain as his best friend. Before Godoy reached the age of thirty he was in total charge of every department of the Spanish government, including the Council of the Indies, which handled Louisiana and other parts of New Spain.[1] He worked at his jobs and applied a maturing, if limited, intelligence to them. He thought of himself as a realist who met the handicap of Spain's military weakness by upholding the time-honored prestige of her royal house and maintaining the balance of power in the bitter and perennial rivalry between France and England.

Godoy's star soared when he wrecked England's set of military alliances — the so-called First Coalition — by negotiating the Treaty of Basel during the summer of 1795. By its terms, Spain ended her unnatural association with England, and France resumed her traditional place by the side of Spain. Prussia defected from the coalition also, and so did Austria in 1797, which meant that England would have to bear the brunt of the Anglo-French contest for the next five years. Charles IV rewarded Godoy for the Treaty of Basel by creating in his honor a title of titles, the Prince of Peace. This was a crashing bit of irony since the treaty worked well to advance the war plans of the little artillery expert, General Napoleon Bonaparte, who had been performing miracles in southern France. With Spain now a friend of France instead of a foe, the French army of the Pyrenees was free to start an offensive in Italy.

In October, 1795, Bonaparte hurried to Paris to serve on the military staff of the comte de Barras in putting down a royalist insurrection against the republican Convention. Barras's next step was to move the Convention away from its republican ideals into a bourgeois government called the Directoire headed by himself and four other "regicides" — republican politicians who had distinguished themselves by sending Louis XVI to the guillotine. Barras was so impressed by Bonaparte's "whiff of grapeshot" victory over the royalist rebels on the rue Saint-Honoré that he married him off to one of his favorite mistresses, a wealthy French creole from Martinique, Marie Joséphine Rose Tascher de la Pagerie, whose husband, the vicomte Beauharnais, had been beheaded during the Terror. As a member of the salon set of Paris intellectuals, Joséphine regarded the Corsican as her social and mental inferior but had hopes that he would amount to something. Two days after the marriage, Barras made Bonaparte commander of all the French armies and sent him south to direct the conquest of Italy. Bonaparte took with him his oldest brother, Joseph, a lazy, acquisitive man who would play a peculiar part later in the Louisiana Purchase.

The Directoire, torn by factions of republicans and royalists, began to sink into chaos and anarchy. The only thing that held it together was the surging popularity of Bonaparte as a result of his Italian victories and the quantities of plunder that he was shipping back to Paris. Tales spread of his thrilling plans — a protective girdle of French-controlled European states, seizure of Malta, of Egypt, even of British India. To bolster the Directoire, the comte de Barras recalled Charles Maurice de Talleyrand, at the suggestion of the novelist Madame de Staël, from his exile to serve as minister of foreign affairs. Talleyrand had spent two and a half years in Philadelphia, where he had come to admire the economic and political potential of Spanish Louisiana but had had little chance to exercise his talents as a lady's man. The young and beautiful Madame de Staël seems to have been exactly what he needed. Soon after he took office in July, 1797, Madame de Staël's husband retired from Paris to Stockholm and sued his wayward wife for divorce.

For a time the Prince of Peace did not realize how much his Treaty of Basel had contributed to the rise of Bonaparte. Godoy could congratulate himself that Spain, as an ally of France, was able to resist efforts that the

French had been making for years to recover westside Louisiana on their own bargain terms. Not that Godoy cared about his lemon of a province. His attitude toward it was starkly pragmatic. He had none of the emotional involvement of La Salle, of Marquette, of Bienville. He refused to be concerned with the beauty of the Mississippi valley, its vastness and variety, its exotic Indian society, the excitement of its exploration, the benefits that its wealth might bring to humanity. To him its value was strategic — a buffer protecting the silver mines of northern Mexico from attack by the British. Those mines plus the sugar and molasses trade of the West Indies produced most of the twenty-five million dollars of annual revenue from New Spain that Godoy spent to pay the cost of supporting his expensive royal family.

In all other respects, Louisiana was a troublesome liability that Godoy would be glad to return to France — at a proper price and with guarantees that the French would continue to maintain it as a buffer. The cost of owning the province was staggering. Its imports far exceeded its exports. The king's fiscal agent in Mexico City was spending the equivalent of $800,000 (U.S.) a year on its civil and military establishment against revenues netting barely $100,000. The deficit was made up by a Mexican subsidy.[2] Its armed force was a farce — a single regiment of a thousand men divided among a dozen garrisons between Mobile and St. Louis, plus eleven small river patrol boats that were expected to guard the whole Mississippi. The cost of feeding, housing and preserving the health of a soldier in Louisiana was five times higher than in Spain. And how could Godoy be expected to protect such an immense terrain? As he said, "You can't lock up an open field."

Here was a Spanish empire with nothing Spanish about it except a handful of civil servants, army officers, priests and nuns, and the distinctive Spanish architecture that they had brought to New Orleans where most of them lived. Provincial officials had never been given the resources to make a real attempt to colonize the Mississippi valley, partly perhaps because the authorities back in Madrid feared that their Catholic colonists might become heretics in Louisiana's undisciplined environment. The polyglot non-Spanish majority conspired incessantly to get free of Charles IV. The population increased much too slowly. The total number of Europeans in Louisiana came to no more than twelve thousand, concentrated mainly in the Mississippi delta area below the mouth of the Red River. This figure must have struck Godoy as pathetic compared to the two hundred thousand

Americans who had poured into Kentucky since the end of the Revolutionary War, and the one hundred thousand in Tennessee.

Godoy was aware that the nerve center of Louisiana's business was in New Orleans, where the chief activity was still smuggling — not just local smuggling but international. The area around the delta capital with its bays, lagoons and bayous was a paradise for dealers in contraband that passed from the ports of Europe and the United States to those in the Gulf of Mexico and the Caribbean. Feeble attempts by the Spanish intendant to stop this evasion of paying royal duties wound up in futility. The cure was worse than the disease. If the citizens of New Orleans could not smuggle for their living they would face bankruptcy and starvation.

The energetic Governor Carondelet was somewhat less pessimistic than Godoy about the future of the province. But Carondelet's hopes of forming a Creek and Choctaw Indian alliance in West Florida were waning and there was no sign that his sly pensioner, General Wilkinson, was luring any Kentuckians away from the United States to become loyal Spaniards. St. Louis, which was supposed to replace Montreal as the hub of the American fur trade, was far from achieving Pierre Laclède's original purpose. The trade of its hundred fur merchants had grown little in the past decade — in contrast to ominous reports reaching Carondelet of British advances on both the Upper Missouri and the Upper Mississippi. An early report had come from a French Canadian, Jacques d'Eglise, who had poled his pirogues in 1790 fifteen hundred miles up the Missouri from St. Louis to several Mandan and Minnetaree villages at the mouth of the Knife River (in present North Dakota above Bismarck). D'Eglise had found a Frenchman named Menard living there who said that he worked for British traders who sent their goods from Canada to the Knife River villages along the old Assiniboine and Souris rivers route. Menard had added that many other Britishers circulated in the region from Michilimackinac and Grand Portage using the old Lake Michigan and Superior water routes to reach the Mississippi. From thence they trespassed westward in Spanish Louisiana to the Upper Missouri by way of the Minnesota River or the Des Moines.

D'Eglise's report induced Governor Carondelet to take measures to reassert Spanish claims to the Upper Missouri drainage and to force a diversion to St. Louis of the illicit British trade with the Indians. A further measure amounted to a reopening of the old Anglo-Spanish argument about who owned Nootka Sound. The governor would challenge England's claim to the Pacific northwest by establishing an overland route from the Upper

Missouri across the Rockies to the Pacific.[3] In October, 1793, he formed a royal "Company of Explorers of the Upper Missouri" and promised them a reward of $3,000 if they managed "to reach the South Sea." That first company consisted of nine French Canadians led by a St. Louis school-teacher, Jean-Baptiste Truteau. It was much too small to cope with the problems of Missouri River travel and the hostility of Sioux and Arikara Indians. The party got only a few miles into present South Dakota beyond the mouth of the Niobrara. A second expedition of thirty-three men left St. Louis in August, 1795, under James Mackay, a naturalized Scotsman who had spent years with the North West Company in Canada on the Qu'Ap-pelle branch of the Assiniboine. The Dakota and other Indians were still hostile and stopped Mackay's advance near the present Nebraska–South Dakota line.

During 1797, the frustrated Mackay floated down the Missouri to St. Louis with his men to report the failure of his mission. But his two-year trek had brought some positive results, including data about the Yellowstone branch of the Missouri and a description from the Indians of a large stream of unspecified length flowing to the Pacific from the Continental Divide near the source of the Missouri high in the Rockies. Most of the news that Mackay sent to Carondelet and to Godoy was information that they had too much of already — more disturbing facts about many British posts at river points throughout Upper Louisiana.[4]

In the meantime, Godoy watched the approach of a new phase of the Anglo-French war in which Spain would be involved on the French side. That contingency, combined with the British threat on his buffer province, prompted him to offer to give Louisiana — and the problem of defending it against the British — back to France in exchange for Santo Domingo and property in Italy. A secret treaty of retrocession was actually signed on June 27, 1796, but the Directoire refused to ratify it on the grounds that Godoy's price was too high.[5]

The Prince of Peace was disappointed but not discouraged. He would wait for a more propitious time and try again to unload Louisiana. He had learned to be patient while following his king and queen around to all those palaces.

While Manuel de Godoy teetered on his tightrope, Thomas Jefferson teetered on his, facing many of the same problems emanating from Europe that Godoy faced. In addition, Jefferson had to resolve strong divisions of opinion on domestic issues among his own countrymen. We saw him last retiring "forever" after the Genet affair to the quiet joys of farming at Monticello. We meet him again in December, 1796, when he became vice president of the United States under the presidency of his old comrade in revolution, John Adams of Massachusetts. It was this 1796 election that fused American politics into a two-party system of Federalists and Republicans, of conservatives and liberals. The election itself, for the last time, was by simple majority of the electors of the sixteen state legislatures, high man to be president and number two the vice president. John Adams received seventy-one votes; Jefferson sixty-eight; Thomas Pinckney, the hero of Pinckney's Treaty, fifty-nine; and Aaron Burr, thirty.

As Dumas Malone has explained, Jefferson had nothing whatever to do with bringing about his election to the vice presidency. It was managed with his reluctant consent by Republicans who convinced him that the cause of American freedom was doomed without his leadership against the diehard Federalists. His supporters included his old Virginia friends James Madison and James Monroe; the Swiss-born Albert Gallatin of Pennsylvania; George Clinton, the perennial governor of New York; its chancellor, Robert R. Livingston; and the elegant and persuasive ex-senator from New York, Aaron Burr, who had become a power up and down the Hudson in spite of his devious political and financial maneuvers. John Adams, Alexander Hamilton and John Jay were leading Federalists. We have noted that their party stood for a strong central government, an electorate of aristocrats on the order of England's, federal assumption of state debts, and a loose way of interpreting the Constitution to increase federal powers in relation to those of state legislatures. Its members were ardently pro-English and supporters of the business interests of the northeastern states. Many Federalists looked with loathing on the Jefferson-inspired Northwest Ordinance of 1787, by which an uncontrollable wilderness like Kentucky, ruled by undisciplined ruffians who never took a bath, could send two senators to Congress with power equal to that of senators from New England. The Republicans took stands exactly opposite to those of the Federalists. They were ardently pro-French, guardians of states' rights and supporters of the idea that the federal government could assume no authority not specifically granted to it by the Constitution. They defended the interests of the agricultural south and the trans-Appalachian west. They were pledged to defend also the new

Mississippi Territory, planned for 1798, that would run from the Tennessee line down the Mississippi to the boundary of Spanish West Florida at the 31st parallel.

The election of Adams occurred in spite of protest meetings and riots throughout the nation following Washington's belated proclamation in February, 1796, of that Federalist instrument, Jay's Treaty. Ignoring the treaty's favorable boundary provisions for the northwest, the Republicans denounced it for failing to protect American sailors from British impressment on the high seas, for denying compensation for slaves that the British had carried off during the Revolution, and for giving British fur traders the same privilege as Americans to move freely on the Mississippi and in the Northwest Territory. Jefferson called it "an infamous act, which is nothing more than a treaty of alliance between England and the Anglomen of this country against the legislatures and people of the United States."

But Adams won the presidency, and most of his cohorts construed his victory as meaning that the general public supported the Federalist point of view. While Jefferson, the pro-French pacifist, denounced the militant Hamilton for proposing to join forces with what Jefferson called "the harlot England" in a campaign to seize Spanish Louisiana and the Floridas, relations between France and the United States deteriorated into an undeclared maritime war. The French, claiming that Jay's Treaty worked to the advantage of the British, captured American ships and sailors as ruthlessly as the British did.

In a break with Hamilton, President Adams agreed with Jefferson that it was unthinkable for the United States to be at war with its old ally in revolution. He sent three commissioners to Paris to relax the tension through talks with Charles Maurice de Talleyrand, who represented Bonaparte and the expiring Directoire. Of course, peace with France was the last thing that Hamilton and his circle wanted in 1797–1798. They punished the president for what they called his anti-British stand by virtually taking over his administration, helped in the process by Talleyrand's customary carelessness in matters of morality.

Instead of dealing directly with the three Americans, Talleyrand sent three nameless agents to dicker with them in secret rendezvous — agents known later as Messieurs X, Y and Z. The mysterious trio proposed some respite from maritime seizures in exchange for a U.S. loan to Bonaparte and a bribe of $240,000 to be paid to Talleyrand to reward him for getting

Bonaparte to approve the treaty. An enraged Adams told members of Congress about "the XYZ Affair" in April of 1798 and found himself joined by them in bipartisan condemnation of Talleyrand's tactics. Even the stoutest Francophiles — friends that Talleyrand had made during his exile in Philadelphia — sank deeper into melancholy when the gossip reached them that the former bishop of Autun had fathered still another babe in an indiscreet manner. This one was said to be by the wife of Talleyrand's predecessor as foreign minister for the Directoire, Charles Delacroix. The babe, christened Ferdinand Victor Eugène, would be famous in time as Eugène Delacroix, one of the greatest of French painters.

But Hamilton and his Federalists pressed their advantage too far during the height of anti-French feeling over the XYZ Affair. They were able to push measures through Congress in total contradiction to the spirit of the American Revolution. The first of these measures was the Naturalization Act, which aimed at suppressing foreign-born Republican leaders like Albert Gallatin by requiring fourteen years of residence in the United States instead of five for admission to citizenship. The Alien Act was passed next by Congress, giving arbitrary powers to the president to expel foreigners who displeased him. And then came the Sedition Act — a monstrous blow at freedom of expression by making it a high crime for people to campaign against federal laws.

A strong reaction developed. It was led by Jefferson and his Virginians, and by their Republican friends beyond the Appalachians — those frontiersmen who were still inspired by the feeling of freedom and opportunity that they had known ever since the Revolution had opened the wide open spaces of the west to them. Both the Kentucky and Tennessee state legislatures framed resolutions denouncing the Alien and Sedition acts. The nation generally approved Jefferson's phrasing of the Kentucky resolutions, denying the constitutionality of the acts and declaring that the federal government had no right to exercise such broad powers. As a result, the acts were repealed, and the Republicans triumphed in the presidential and vice-presidential elections of 1800, though not by much. Jefferson and Aaron Burr won over John Adams and C. C. Pinckney. Two events in the year before the election favored the Republicans. One was the death in December, 1799, of the greatest Federalist, George Washington, whose endorsement had always been a boon to his party. A second event was the removal of the XYZ issue by the signing of the Convention of 1800 (Treaty of

Morfontaine) in September. When ratified, some months later, the convention restored diplomatic relations between the United States and France and released the United States from military commitments to France contained in the Franco-American alliance of 1778.

A very strange thing happened in this election. Though two parties were listed on the ballots, separate ballots for president and vice president were not provided in the voting for state electors. By pure accident, the Republican candidates, Jefferson and Aaron Burr, who were running harmoniously for the first and second offices in that order, each received seventy-three votes, throwing the choice between the two into the U.S. House of Representatives. The House was dominated by Federalists. And so the president of the United States was chosen not by the triumphant Republicans but by the defeated Federalists. On top of that strangeness was the way that the House voted — half for Jefferson, half for Burr, through thirty-five ballotings during February of 1801. On the thirty-sixth ballot, the deadlock was broken by the abstention of several Burr supporters, at the urging of a Federalist leader. The Federalist leader was, of all people, Jefferson's arch foe for two decades, Alexander Hamilton. He argued that Jefferson was less obnoxious to him than Burr, whom Hamilton compared to Rome's infamous conspirator Catiline.

Looking backward to the vice presidency of Jefferson for a moment, it cannot be claimed that he exerted himself unduly through the stormy years of the Adams administration. He rarely appeared in Philadelphia before the capital was moved to the damp and humid village of Washington in 1800. He spent most of the period at Monticello tinkering, sniffing, feeling, musing, gazing in rapt admiration at the Blue Ridge. He was in his mid-fifties now, but little changed in appearance from the tall, hazel-eyed, straight-up aristocrat with the careless air who had gone to Paris to replace Benjamin Franklin as U.S. minister. There was a majestic serenity about the way his mind worked. He could fume one minute at the eccentricity of the planet and marvel the next at the beauty of a moon's rainbow falling in his meadow on a summer evening, and go on to hours of speculation on why the American Indians had so many languages. He was always at peace with himself whether fuming or marveling or speculating. His world was a jigsaw puzzle composed of a myriad of fascinating pieces. He knew that some pieces were more important than others but to him each was endowed with universality and had its place in the final solution.

His political views had not changed in twenty years because the conditions on which he had based them remained the same. A key condition was that France and England still battled for world supremacy, and were apt to keep on battling for many years. Their preoccupation with their contest was serving to protect the new nation from interference with its development — a substitute for the army and navy that Alexander Hamilton demanded. It was a sound substitute in combination with neutrality and the phenomenal gains in the U.S. population — from two million people in 1776 to five million by 1800. As more people poured out over the wilderness, worthless land was transformed into valuable real estate.

Jefferson believed more than ever that freedom of the individual was the essential element of good government and a good society. He believed that farmers on their own land were the freest of men and so it followed that a nation of farmers was superior to a nation of merchants and artisans who tended to be enslaved and corrupted by the tyranny and materialism of money. Farmers needed more space as they became more numerous, more prosperous and more set in their democratic convictions. That was why he believed that possession of Louisiana and everything beyond it — eventually — all the way to the Pacific would be necessary to complete development of the ideal republic that he had had in mind when he wrote the Declaration of Independence. For the present, he thought of Louisiana as a region where Indians east of the Mississippi could go if they found themselves unable to corrupt their heritage by becoming farmers in the manner of white men. West of the Mississippi they could resume their own way of life as the white settlers — "advancing compactly as we multiply" as Jefferson would put it — ruined their eastside hunting grounds and compelled them to sell their lands.

But these views on expansion in the future and Indian removal were private views. Jefferson's public policy on western affairs was to maintain the status quo as determined by Pinckney's Treaty — continued free navigation of the Mississippi and the right of deposit at New Orleans. To disclose grandiose dreams for the further west would stiffen the backs of the Federalists at a time when he needed to keep them reasonably amenable to the pacific tenor of his management of European relations. The president-to-be took a calm view of the separatist movements that General Wilkinson and others were still presumed to be promoting among the frontiersmen. Jefferson argued that the blood and economic ties with the east of those rugged Protestants were too strong for them to seriously consider joining forces in Louisiana with Spanish Catholics to help pay for the rococo love life of Manuel de Godoy and Queen María Luisa.

He was far more disturbed by fresh news of British advances that had come to light with the abortive Spanish expeditions out of St. Louis. Such penetration of the American Northwest Territory and of the Upper Missouri showed that "the harlot England" had not been discouraged by the fort-evacuation requirement of Jay's Treaty from continuing to plan conquest of all the country around and west of the Great Lakes. Those far-flung trading posts combined with Mackenzie's crossing of Canada to the Pacific in 1793 were obvious steps by the British to outflank the Americans and to close the territorial gap between the Upper Missouri and Oregon.

And Jefferson had more reason, after his election as president, to suspect the worst of England. Reports came of a western trek that was made in 1797–1798 by a twenty-seven-year-old employee of Mackenzie's North West Company named David Thompson.[6] Jefferson could not have known then of course that this Thompson would become the greatest of English explorers in the west — the equal of immortals like La Salle and Pierre de La Vérendrye. Born near London in 1770, Thompson was apprenticed at age fourteen to the Hudson's Bay Company and learned the harsh realities of the wilds when he traveled out of Hudson Bay as far as the Canadian Rockies near present Calgary. He had a passion for exploration and mapping which was not appreciated by his company. In 1797, he transferred to the North West Company and was assigned at once to mapping its posts west of Lake Superior, to survey the unofficial boundary, the 49th parallel, between Canada and Louisiana west of Lake of the Woods, and to map a trail from Lake Winnipeg up the Assiniboine and Souris rivers to the Mandan villages on the Upper Missouri.

Thompson spent ten months roaming the prairies of Minnesota and Dakota, during which his small party survived a frightful winter and murderous Sioux in a circuit of four thousand miles. He corrected mistaken ideas about the Red River of the North and he moved up the diminishing Mississippi beyond Leech Lake through a labyrinth of wild-rice waterways to what he supposed was the source of the Mississippi at Turtle Lake near today's Minnesota resort town of Bimidji. Thompson's calculations of latitude for Turtle Lake at 47°38″ and roughly at longitude 95 blasted for good the Treaty of Paris myth that the Mississippi began west of the Lake of the Woods at or near the 49th parallel.[7] As he was returning to Grand

Portage on Lake Superior he met Alexander Mackenzie, who praised his discoveries and promised that funds for much more western exploration would be made available to him.

The United States, Jefferson must have thought early in 1801, could use an exploring David Thompson or an Alexander Mackenzie of their own. But his immediate worry was the strong rumor that Godoy had managed to cede Louisiana to France at last. Possession of the province by a weak Spain was endurable. French ownership, particularly of New Orleans, was an entirely different matter. Jefferson made no bones about his horror at what had happened to France after the fall of the Directoire in 1799 and Bonaparte's rise to dictatorship as First Consul. Bonaparte's plans, or at least a theory of them, were widely known. First he would seek a truce with England, having failed to advance on British India. He would stop plundering Europe and devote his talents to recovering the American empire that France had lost to England in 1763. The French Canadians of Quebec would be urged to free the St. Lawrence of British despotism. Bonaparte's navy, combined with Godoy's, would dominate the Gulf of Mexico and a French canal would be built across Panama to the Pacific. Then the First Consul's soldiers would occupy New Orleans, using Santo Domingo as a supply station. Since that beautiful Caribbean island had been seized recently by the black ex-slave, Toussaint L'Ouverture, Bonaparte would precede his drive on New Orleans by sending a force to Santo Domingo to destroy Toussaint's power.[8]

With two threats on his mind — the cession of Louisiana to France and the British thrust westward — the new U.S. president took care to select a cabinet of tried and true friends to support him in meeting what had assumed for him the proportions of a national crisis. He nominated James Madison for secretary of state, Albert Gallatin for the treasury, Henry Dearborn of Maine for war, Levi Lincoln for attorney general. As his private secretary he chose a young family friend from Charlottesville, Lieutenant Meriwether Lewis, who knew a great deal about western affairs from years of army service with General Anthony Wayne and James Wilkinson. These appointments were expected. But the last was a surprise to the Republican fraternity. As minister to France, charged with the awesome task of managing the unmanageable Bonaparte, Jefferson named a man with no diplomatic experience whatever, Chancellor Robert R. Livingston of New York.

17

The Chancellor's Great Adventure

PRESIDENT JEFFERSON was taking something of a chance on the talent for diplomacy of his minister plenipotentiary, Robert Livingston. But he knew that the appointment was pleasing to nearly all members of both parties in New York State. The chancellor was an example of those curious paradoxes in American society, then as now — the ultraconservative liberal, the law-and-order revolutionist, the plutocrat defending the rights of paupers. He was born in New York City in 1746 and baptized into the Church of England as heir to the most entrenched of dynasties along the broad and luminous Hudson River. His great-grandfather had married into the landed Schuyler and Van Rensselaer families, to which the landed Beekmans were added. Robert R. married Mary Stevens of the landed New Jersey Stevenses. By 1801, Livingston, as First Lord of the Manor, headed a tribe of twenty-five or thirty Livingston families whose wealth and influence touched every part of the commercial, social and political life of New York and New Jersey. The famous Federalist John Jay, whom he detested, was married to his cousin Sarah Livingston. As the chancellor prepared to leave for Paris, a Pennsylvania portrait painter named Robert Fulton, who would be marrying Livingston's cousin Harriet, was already there telling Bonaparte's engineers of his plans to build a steamboat. Fulton would call the boat the *Clermont* in honor of Livingston's beautiful thirteen-thousand-acre estate in Dutchess County one hundred and ten miles above New York City.

Livingston had served in both Continental Congresses and was on the committee with Jefferson that drafted the Declaration of Independence. He began his twenty-four-year term as chancellor (secretary) of New York State in 1777, lived with James Madison in Philadelphia as a revolutionist in 1779, and spent a year as secretary of foreign affairs for the Confederation. He was, in short, one of these illustrious men who created the United States. He backed George Washington for president but quit the Federalists when Washington failed to put him in his cabinet. After 1792, he retired from active politics to enjoy the good life of Dutchess County and to play a quiet role as a Jefferson Republican and an admirer of revolutionary France.

This dry continuity gives no hint of his flavor — his genially implacable air of authority, his immense self-confidence, his Jefferson-like interest in all manner of things including pretty women, his desire to be something more than vastly rich and fashionably respectable. His qualifications to serve as minister to France appeared to be so-so. Though he read French easily, he did not speak it well because he was a bit deaf and unable to pick up its subtle music. But he would prove to have the same warm response to Frenchmen and French life that Jefferson had had. Livingston's self-confidence was such that he could look forward to meeting the awesome First Consul with unconcern. On this line, George Dangerfield wrote in his inspired biography of the chancellor: ". . . Livingston had another, a somewhat peculiar advantage, when it came to dealing with the impassive disdain of a grand seigneur like Talleyrand: He simply did not conceive that any man was a finer social specimen than himself."

The chancellor's departure for Paris was delayed through the summer until after Jefferson received, in the fall of 1801, Bonaparte's ratification of the Convention of 1800. Meanwhile the rumors that Manuel de Godoy had retroceded Louisiana to Bonaparte had resolved into something close to certainty. The truth behind the tales was that the retrocession had been agreed upon by the second Treaty of San Ildefonso on October 1, 1800. It was confirmed in more detail by the Treaty of Aranjuez on March 21, 1801. Three properties were involved in these two secret treaties. Spain would give up Louisiana to France, and also the duchy of Parma, on the Po drainage northwest of Bologna, which Bonaparte's army had occupied in 1796. The duque de Parma was Charles IV's son-in-law, and also his nephew — a mark of that touching concern of the Spanish Bourbons to keep everything in the family. To compensate the nephew for the loss of Parma,

Robert R. Livingston was spectacular proof that in this strange United States a man could be a republican and an aristocrat at the same time. (Portrait by John Vanderlyn. Courtesy of The New-York Historical Society)

Bonaparte would give to him that most glittering of Italian jewels, Tuscany, with its glamorous cities of Florence, Pisa and Siena. Tuscany would be reorganized in a Spanish dominion called the kingdom of Etruria, an ancient and honored name.

It should be understood that Bonaparte's interest in acquiring Louisiana as his first step in recovering all of La Nouvelle-France came to a head as a result of his great victory on June 14, 1800, over the Austrians at Marengo. That victory would bring on the collapse of England's second coalition (with Austria, Russia and Naples) against France. It gave Bonaparte the power to force a maritime truce on Britain while he went ahead with plans to ship an army and colonists to New Orleans by way of Santo Domingo. As for Manuel de Godoy, he was very glad to exchange his profitless province at last for the wealth and culture of Tuscany. And he was pleased to exact an oral promise from Bonaparte that France would not transfer the property to any other nation without offering it first to Spain.[1] Though Talleyrand, negotiating for Bonaparte, pressed hard for the inclusion of East and West Florida in the cession, Godoy refused flatly, explaining that the coastlands of Florida and Texas symbolized the ancient authority of the Spanish king over the Gulf of Mexico, as decreed by the papal bull of 1493. Talleyrand accepted Godoy's refusal sympathetically, reserving only the right to discuss the matter later. He had his own good reasons for his restraint. Article Three of the Treaty of San Ildefonso read:

His Catholic Majesty promises and engages to retrocede to the French republic, six months after the full and entire execution of the above conditions and stipulations relative to His Royal Highness, the Duke of Parma, the colony or province of Louisiana, with the same extent that it now has in the hands of Spain, and that it had when France possessed it, and such as it ought to be after the treaties subsequently entered into between Spain and other states.

The phrase that Talleyrand's lawyers had put into this article contained the words "the same extent that it [Louisiana] had when France possessed it." The Frenchmen were well aware that the strategic part of the Florida coastland — West Florida and the Mobile Bay region extending above Lake Pontchartrain toward the Mississippi — had been added to La Salle's original Louisiana by Iberville in 1699. The village of Mobile had been the seat of the French provincial government of Louisiana from then until 1722, when Bienville had moved it to New Orleans and had accepted, unhappily, the Perdido River as the boundary between French Louisiana and Spanish Florida east of it (see the map on page 212). To Talleyrand, those words meant that West Florida had been part of French Louisiana in 1762 "when France possessed it," regardless of the transfer of West Florida later — to England in 1763 and to Spain in 1783. At the proper time, he concluded, France would have an excuse to occupy West Florida as part of the retrocession of Louisiana agreed upon by Spain at San Ildefonso.[2]

The First Consul tried to keep news of the treaty from getting out. For one thing, Charles IV had not yet signed it pending the performance of French promises involving Tuscany. Moreover, Bonaparte did not want his possession of the province to complicate his truce talks with the English who, of course, still had dreams of possessing Louisiana themselves. Actually, the English heard about the retrocession early, and passed a version of the Treaty of Aranjuez along to the American minister in London, Rufus King, who sent it in November, 1801, to Secretary of State Madison in Washington. That was about the time of the departure from Brest of Bonaparte's expedition to Santo Domingo to crush the rebellious Toussaint L'Ouverture and his half-million blacks. The initial French force consisted of twenty thousand men and thirty ships commanded by Bonaparte's brother-in-law, General Charles Leclerc.

It was about the time also of the arrival at the Breton port of L'Orient of Robert Livingston with his wife, two daughters, their husbands and their personal servants. "The Chancellor," George Dangerfield has written, "had fortified himself against the rigors of an autumnal voyage by bringing with him not only the usual mountain of luggage, but also a quantity of live-stock — poultry, pigs, sheep, and a cow and calf — while his carriage was lashed to the quarterdeck where it served as a parlor for the four ladies." For a week and more the French countryside was entertained as the fascinating equipage of the new U.S. minister trundled up the road along the Loire from Nantes and on to Paris. The American legation was on the rue Tournon across the Seine from the Tuileries palace, where Bonaparte was in residence, and not far from Talleyrand's office on the rue de Bac. Livingston, at fifty-five years a tall imposing man with a firm, light step, was surprised and pleased to be met at the legation by the marquis de Lafayette and by François de Barbé-Marbois, an old friend of his in Philadelphia during the American Revolution, for whose instruction on western America Jefferson had written his *Notes on Virginia.*

Bonaparte had appointed Barbé-Marbois in February to be his minister of the public treasury. He was Livingston's age — a small, spry career bureaucrat from Metz who had gone so far in his love of the United States as to visit the Oneida chief Grasshopper on the Mohawk in 1784 and to devise a scheme there for diverting the British fur trade in the Northwest Territory from Montreal to Albany. He had also courted and married a Philadelphia debutante half his age named Elizabeth Moore, conducting his amour in slang English taught him by John Adams's teen-aged son, John Quincy. After Barbé-Marbois's service at the French legation in Phila-delphia, Louis XVI sent him in 1785 as his intendant to Santo Domingo, where he noted the problems of doing business with the smugglers of New Orleans, and where he watched with dismay the developing island revolu-tion arising from abominations practiced on the black slaves by the rich French planters. Barbé-Marbois was not Talleyrand's equal in changing political colors to suit the times. Robespierre imprisoned him in 1793 as a royalist émigré. Later the Directoire exiled him to French Guiana for two years, also for his absolutism. In 1800 Bonaparte, who had become thor-oughly absolutist himself by then, brought him home to help with his finances and to advise him on what to do about Toussaint L'Ouverture.

Robert Livingston hoped that Barbé-Marbois would help him to ap-proach the unapproachable dictator. In Paris, the American began the great adventure of his life by studying James Madison's instructions for meeting the crisis of retrocession. He found the instructions somewhat deflating since parts of them were copies of instructions that Madison had sent to his ministers in Madrid and London — suggesting that Livingston was merely being kept informed of what was going on in the more important posts. Also, the instructions betrayed a wariness, as though the Virginia Republican did not quite trust the ex-Federalist from New York to handle his assignment in a way that would be approved by those Jeffersonians of the west and south who doubted the ability of any easterner to do anything right.

Livingston had his first meeting with Bonaparte's foreign minister on December 5, and rather enjoyed treating him with the same lofty disdain that the small, obese and limping Talleyrand displayed toward him. During their talk, the Frenchman denied what everybody knew — that a treaty of retrocession had been concluded if not entirely resolved. And Talleyrand took pains to stress that he, not Bonaparte, was in charge of the Louisiana matter. Next day, the marquis de Lafayette arranged for Livingston and his family to watch the First Consul, garbed in a red coat splattered with gold braid, in the Tuileries courtyard reviewing his guard astride the big white horse that he had ridden at Marengo. The horse, Livingston decided, was no great shakes. He had handsomer horses at Clermont. And the big horse was out of proportion to the neat little Corsican sitting on top of him. In the Audience Room of the Tuileries after the review, Talleyrand presented Livingston to Bonaparte. The conversation, relayed by interpreters, was reported to have gone like this by Madame de Staël in *Dix années d'exil:*

BONAPARTE: "You have been in Europe before, Monsieur Livingston."

LIVINGSTON: "Non, mon général."

BONAPARTE: "You have come to a very corrupt world."

At that point, according to Madame de Staël, Bonaparte turned to Talleyrand with a bleak smile and said to him: "Explain to Monsieur Livingston that the old world is very corrupt. You know something about that don't you, Monsieur Talleyrand?"

The American minister found himself warming to Bonaparte — his artlessness, his courtesy, his grace of movement, his appealing air of sadness and loneliness. Livingston began to hope that, given time, he could bring the Louisiana-Florida question directly to him — that he could break through the dense protocol that Talleyrand maintained to protect his own power as a bribe-taking intermediary. Knowing Bonaparte's hatred of democrats, Livingston played the role of an aristocrat — a natural role for New York's First Lord of the Manor. He refurbished the rue Tournon legation to give it regal sumptuousness in contrast to the drab British legation. Guided socially by Barbé-Marbois and by Pierre du Pont, an old friend of Jefferson's, he attended balls and banquets and salons where he might meet politicians close to the First Consul.[3] He picked up gossip about the army that General Victor was assembling at Dunkerque on the Straits of Dover to take to New Orleans as soon as Charles IV signed the retrocession treaty. He bought a cocked hat and a winged collar to ride suitably attired in a wolf hunt organized by Bonaparte's eldest brother, Joseph Bonaparte. When the Peace of Amiens was announced in March, Livingston feted it as a French victory over Britain, though he saw it was only an armistice that could not last. The basic issue — Britain's refusal to give France a fair share of world trade — remained. Hearing that General Leclerc's wife Pauline, who was Bonaparte's sister, was suffering from the humidity of Santo Domingo, Livingston offered her the town house in New York of his brother Edward, who was mayor of the city, or Clermont, if she preferred. Pauline declined, which may have saved the proper Livingstons in Dutchess County some embarrassment since Pauline was whispered to be the mistress of a number of celebrities, including Bonaparte himself.

Through the spring of 1802, Livingston mulled over Jefferson's objectives in view of the retrocession. They had crystallized of late into grandiose aims — the outright purchase from France of the island of New Orleans and both Floridas, and the acceptance by France of the Mississippi as the boundary between Louisiana and the United States. To finance the purchase, Jefferson was prepared to suggest that the United States take these properties in exchange for the payment by France of the claims of American shipowners totaling some five million dollars (twenty million livres or so) against French privateers who had plundered the American ships in periods of war with England between 1793 and 1800. Livingston was perplexed as to how to help the president to achieve his aims under the restraints imposed by Madison's instructions. Though the chancellor was the president's minister plenipotentiary, the secretary of state had given him no authority to negotiate. But late in May Livingston received a message that was quite different from Madison's vague dispatches. It was dated at Washington on April 18, 1802, and it came from President Jefferson himself. It was a private letter that would not be made public for three decades. Livingston saw in it a preeminent state paper — an historic acknowledgment of the willingness of the United States at last to take its place as a world power.

The letter opened with the words, "The cession of Louisiana and the Floridas by Spain to France works most sorely on the United States." It went on to describe "a new epoch in our political course" and to pledge a complete reversal of Jefferson's policy of pacifism and Franco-American amity. The letter continued:

There is on the globe one single spot, the possessor of which is our natural and habitual enemy. . . . The day that France takes possession of New Orleans, fixes the sentence which is to restrain her forever within her low-water mark. It seals the union of two nations which, in conjunction, can maintain exclusive possession of the ocean. From that moment, we must marry ourselves to the British fleet and nation. We must turn all our attention to a maritime force, for which our resources place us on very high ground; and having formed and connected together a power which may render reinforcement of her settlements here impossible to France, make the first cannon which shall be fired in Europe the signal for the tearing up any settlement she may have made, and for holding the two continents of America in sequestration for the common purposes of the united British and American nations.[4]

In this conditional shift by Jefferson from his pacifism, Livingston found an end to his perplexities about his mission. Jefferson's letter meant that if New Orleans was transferred to France, the United States would seize the river capital with British help the moment war resumed in Europe. The chancellor felt that he could go ahead on his own now. He could ignore Talleyrand's dictum that the retrocession could not be discussed because it was not yet "resolved." He could dispense with protocol by approaching Bonaparte directly. Livingston had Jefferson's plain statement of what he didn't want to happen. The statement contained the moral, if not official, authority for Livingston to proceed as he thought best.

At the outset, what he thought best was to avoid the issue entirely by convincing the First Consul that possession of Louisiana would be of no value to France as a colony and would bring on an Anglo-American alliance that would hold France "forever within her low-water mark." During July, the chancellor prepared a long essay for the edification of Bonaparte — a blunt memoir that went far beyond the pale of standard diplomacy. Its title was "Whether it will be advantageous to France to take possession of Louisiana?" Its refrain reached a climax in an uncompromising "No!" after a rising crescendo of Louisiana horrors through twelve thousand words stressing slave insurrections, Indian attacks, wholesale death by malaria, smuggling bandits and troop desertions. The author had twenty copies of his report printed and he distributed them to Talleyrand and other insiders like Barbé-Marbois and his wolf-hunt friend Joseph Bonaparte, any one of whom might feel inclined to read it to the First Consul.

The essay was frank. France, it averred, had too many colonies already. She had no people or capital to spare to take on another province as hopelessly difficult and costly as Louisiana. England could colonize successfully due to her skill in creating capital by the tasteless mass production of goods — a talent France lacked because of her high cultural standards. Only black slaves could work in Louisiana's unhealthy climate. But slaves were expensive and it took ten years to teach them how to raise rice. Though Santo Domingo could use Louisiana timber, it would be unwise for the islanders to stop their current practice of buying timber from the northern states. If they did so, the liquor-loving Americans would switch from rum to domestic hard cider causing a collapse of the Santo Domingo molasses market. Merchants in France could not sell their goods in Kentucky through New Orleans because Kentuckians got what they needed from Philadelphia — except French wine, which would spoil from the heat in transit up the Mississippi. Livingston plunged on to commit a maximum in heresy. French cognac, he wrote, could not compete with Kentucky's home-made peach brandy "which, with age, is superior to the best brandy of France." As for shipping French farmers to colonize Louisiana, he predicted that they would cross the river soon to the United States where land was cheaper and already cleared "owing to the dexterity of American woodsmen who have been educated to use the ax, and acquired that strength in the muscles of the arm which is unattainable by men who have been brought up in other employments."

Some weeks later, Joseph Bonaparte told the chancellor that he had discussed the memoir with his brother who had made no comment. Since nothing seemed to have been accomplished, Livingston toiled on, often through the night, producing more long essays, cogent and unofficial, and then changed to other tactics. He decided to bypass Talleyrand entirely and to rely on Joseph Bonaparte to present his ideas. Again and again he urged this Bonaparte to keep the friendship of the Americans by restoring Louisiana to Spain in exchange for New Orleans and the Floridas which would go to the United States for their spoliation claims against France. Late in October, Joseph caught him off guard by asking casually whether the United States would prefer to have the Floridas or Louisiana? He had no idea what prompted the question. Reporting it to Jefferson, Livingston wrote on October 28: "I told him that there was no comparison in their value, but that we had no wish to extend our boundary across the Mississippi, or give color to the doubts that had been entertained of the moderation of our views; that all we sought was security, and no extension."

But the seed of Joseph's thought took root in Livingston's mind.

Perhaps he related the question to what he knew of Jefferson's secret dream of pushing on west. In the meantime, he made an attempt at bribery, knowing that Joseph Bonaparte, like Talleyrand, was not above that approach. The Bonaparte family, Livingston said to him, might come a cropper in France some day. If that occurred, would members of the family like to retire to vast private estates of their own in New Orleans and the Floridas? Such sanctuaries could be arranged now if France gave the United States jurisdiction over those lands.

Joseph was not interested.

Well then — and here the expansionist seed in Livingston's mind burst into flower — would Joseph ask the First Consul what he thought of selling all of Louisiana north of the Arkansas to the United States? The French would retain full rights of river navigation and they could build their own international port at Léon across the Mississippi from what would then be the U.S. port of New Orleans. This plan, Livingston argued, would please the western Americans. It would please the king of Spain because it would preserve the traditional wilderness barrier that protected his Mexican treasures from the British in Canada. And it would prevent the formation of an Anglo-American alliance.[5]

That program did not appeal to Joseph either.

As the new year of 1803 began, the elder Bonaparte informed Livingston that their private talks must cease. He must resume official relations with Talleyrand because the latter was beginning to complain. It was all most discouraging. The chancellor had nothing to show for many months of nerve-wracking, unauthorized, undercover maneuvering to get the dictator to recognize the growing power of the United States and to put his mind on the matter of giving up New Orleans and the Floridas. The great man seemed totally absorbed in planetary designs, having moved a giant step on his way to becoming Emperor Napoleon when he was named consul for life in August with the right to choose his successor. Yet Livingston saw small clouds gathering in the glorious Napoleonic sky. The British were still clinging to the island of Malta in violation of the Treaty of Amiens. The word was out that Charles IV had finally signed, on October 15, the Treaty of San Ildefonso conveying Louisiana to France whenever her officials were ready to accept it. But he had declined to give up either of the Floridas, though Bonaparte — or Napoleon as his monarchist admirers were beginning to call him — offered to add Parma to the new Spanish kingdom of

Etruria. Travelers from Santo Domingo talked of widespread yellow fever and debauchery that were destroying General Leclerc's army. A new black uprising there had followed Leclerc's attempt to restore slavery, and his arrest and deportation to France of Toussaint L'Ouverture while pretending to be his friend.[6] The ships of General Victor's expeditionary force to occupy Louisiana were bottled up at Hellevoetsluis near Rotterdam. That could mean that British naval units in the Straits of Dover were watching them and that the brief Peace of Amiens was about over.

And what, the chancellor wondered, was this talk of trouble in New Orleans?

As we have seen, any semblance of stable government in Louisiana ended in the early 1750's with the governorship of the marquis de Vaudreuil. After that, French governors, intendants and judges were theoretically in charge until General O'Reilly took over, and then there was a succession of Spanish officials, liberally salted in minor jobs with French creoles, German creoles, and even Americans such as Governor Gálvez's friend Oliver Pollock. What saved the Spanish province from the dishevelment of pure anarchy was the orderly, if largely illicit, commerce flowing down to New Orleans from the St. Louis and Ohio regions. With the debut in 1798 of New Orleans, by the terms of Pinckney's Treaty, as a port where upstream shippers could park their goods duty free pending transfer to seagoing craft, the river trade had increased hugely. Produce to the annual value of nearly three million dollars floated down from the American states of Kentucky and Tennessee, from Mississippi and Indiana territories, and from the soon-to-be-sanctioned state of Ohio. Another million dollars' worth came from St. Louis and the Spanish villages below it — Ste. Genevieve, Arkansas Post, Natchitoches and the rest.

The right of deposit specified by Pinckney's Treaty had a life of three years. When that time expired, Charles IV had an option to extend it or to assign to shippers "an equivalent establishment" for deposit "on another part of the banks of the Mississippi." The official in charge of deposit was Juan Ventura Morales, a native of Málaga who had been the intendant at New Orleans since 1796. He was not responsible to the provincial governor but only to the viceroy in Mexico City. Morales had nothing particular to distinguish him for better or for worse. He was just the usual resentful underpaid Spanish bureaucrat far from home who took no more gratuities from the shippers than necessary to subsist on his measly salary. When the three-year right-of-deposit period ended, he applied to the king for permission to close the depot if he thought it wise. Apparently he did think it wise. Many American shippers in the spring of 1802 withdrew from Morales the courtesy of gratuities and began to use the deposit privilege as a cover for large-scale smuggling, especially of Spanish gold and silver. When the intendant asked them to mend their ways they denied his authority, telling him what everyone knew — that New Orleans was not Spanish any longer because Manuel de Godoy had given it to the French.

During July, Charles IV shipped off to Morales his permission to end the right of deposit. On October 16, ironically the day after the king conveyed Louisiana to France, the intendant posted his notice that he was closing the New Orleans depot. Morales did not bother to inform the aged and decrepit provincial governor, Manuel de Salcedo, of his action, and he did not assign an alternate depot as required by Pinckney's Treaty. The shippers from the western states who read the notice that day reacted quickly. Within hours, their couriers were hurrying north toward Natchez and Nashville to complain to the governors of Tennessee and Kentucky about what Spain — or was it France? — had done to their treaty rights, and to demand a U.S. declaration of war against somebody.[7]

18

Bonaparte Makes Up His Mind

THE SMALL TEMPEST OF AMERICAN PROTEST in New Orleans over the suspension of the right of deposit by Intendant Morales became a national tornado when the news reached Washington in mid-November. The war-hawk Federalists blew even harder than the Republican governors of the western states. There was jubilance in the outcries of Alexander Hamilton, who found new hope for his dying party if he could persuade the furious frontiersmen in the Ohio country to desert Jefferson and his policy of anti-British, weak-kneed pacifism. Senator Ross of Pennsylvania began work on a resolution demanding that Congress raise an army of fifty thousand men at once and appropriate a war fund of five million dollars to be used in seizing the ceded New Orleans from France.

Thomas Jefferson, having endured political slander over his ancient love affair with Betsey Walker and his alleged current liaison with his pretty slave girl, Sally Hemmings, pretended to be calm.[1] His December message to Congress — Hamilton called it "a lullaby" — contained only fifty words about the retrocession, and no words at all about the closure. But the president was disturbed by the embarrassing position in which the closure placed him. Morales had acted at the worst possible time. Jefferson was not ready for martial action against Spain or France, as called for by Hamilton and Ross. Though he knew that General Leclerc had failed to subdue the blacks of Santo Domingo and that the Peace of Amiens was growing shakier by the hour, the "first cannon" that he had mentioned to

Robert Livingston in his bellicose letter of April 18 had not yet been fired in Europe as a signal "to marry ourselves to the British fleet" and to move on New Orleans.

The reports from Livingston seemed to show that Bonaparte was still all-conquering. His prefect, Pierre Clément Laussat, was expected to leave Holland for New Orleans soon with General Victor's occupying force to receive Louisiana from Charles IV's Governor Salcedo. But Jefferson tended to accept Livingston's opinion that the First Consul's affairs were at a precarious balance. The president believed that they would tilt to his advantage — that the United States would be able to preserve its peace and neutrality and come to terms with France on the purchase of New Orleans and the Floridas — if he could keep the war-hawk Federalists under control for just a while longer.

He had things in his favor. The first twenty months of the Jefferson administration had brought domestic serenity and blooming confidence in the future of the country, only mildly marred — until the closure occurred — by the prospect of a French Louisiana. Many Federalists in Congress, even many western Republicans, did not want the distraction of a war with France and Spain for all their clamor about the illegal closure and retrocession. Peace was pleasant. Nearly every American had visions of getting filthy rich — eastern manufacturers, southern planters, Kentucky farmers, Tennessee land developers, and swarms of Mississippi boatmen floating a record volume of produce down to the gulf. Contributing to business confidence and national unity was the healthy state of government finances. Jefferson could report in his December message to Congress that the year's external duties had produced enough revenue to pay eight million dollars of principal and interest on the public debt, with four and a half million dollars left over for current expenses. The message implied that continued wise management — that is, no war spending — would result in retiring the public debt entirely in a few years as sales of public lands increased in the new territories of Mississippi and Indiana and elsewhere. Revenue from such sales would be seriously curtailed if war came to the Mississippi valley.

Through the Christmas holidays of 1802, Jefferson plotted to stalemate the martial Federalists, always with the astute advice of his best friend, James Madison. It was easy to induce the marqués de Casa Yrujo, the Spanish minister, to denounce publicly the closure of deposit at New

Rembrandt Peale made this portrait of Jefferson when the president was sixty-two years old, some months after Congress ratified the Louisiana Purchase treaty. (Courtesy of The New-York Historical Society)

James Monroe was too upright a man to let his antipathy to Robert Livingston interfere with the paramount business of buying Louisiana. (Portrait by Rembrandt Peale. Courtesy of Brown Brothers, Sterling, Pennsylvania)

Orleans. Jefferson and Yrujo were closely allied gastronomically by their common interest in truffles and how to prepare them. Besides, Yrujo's wife, Sally, was the daughter of the Republican governor of Pennsylvania, Thomas McKean. Somehow Madison managed to convince some war-hawks and also the French chargé d'affaires, L. A. Pichon, that Jefferson's pacifism was only skin deep. Pichon was advised to warn the First Consul that he should think twice of the consequences before making a foe of the United States by occupying New Orleans.

The president's plotting concluded with a master stroke. Early in January, he nominated his Virginia neighbor and onetime law student, James Monroe, as envoy extraordinary and minister plenipotentiary to work with Livingston in Paris and with Charles Pinckney, the American minister in Madrid, "in enlarging and more effectually securing our rights and interests in the river Mississippi and the territories eastward thereof." Monroe, who was forty-four, had been one of the youngest of the revolution-ary patriots and had just concluded his third term as governor of Virginia. He was a phenomenon in human affairs, being a man without discernible faults — wise, upright, moral, modest, and statesmanly. He was much too kind to have a sense of humor. His background was classically American. His father was a Fauquier County carpenter who taught him Latin at the home hearth when he was a small child and later sent him trudging many miles to school with gun in hand to replenish the family larder if a deer appeared.

Jefferson was entirely sincere when he told Monroe that "the future destinies of the Republic" would be determined by his success in Paris. But the nomination had a strong political slant. Monroe was enormously popular with all those living west of the Blue Ridge. For a decade and more he had championed their struggle for free navigation of the Mississippi and the right of deposit. He had opposed violently the proposed bartering away of western interests during the Jay-Gardoqui talks of 1785, and he had de-plored Jay's Treaty of 1794. His prestige in the west, Jefferson knew, was so great that the frontiersmen would curb their martial impulses when they found that Monroe was being sent abroad to seek a pacific solution to the New Orleans–Florida question. There were subtle added considerations. Monroe's partnership with Livingston would counteract the dislike of the westerners for the New Yorker who, they felt, was just another eastern aristocrat on the order of their public enemy number one, John Jay. And one thing more. Monroe had served as minister to France in the mid-1790's and had been recalled by Washington because, as a Jefferson democrat, he had refused to stand up in Paris for Jay's Treaty. The recall had hurt him deeply and he could be counted on this time to do his very best to show that Washington had made a mistake.

Jefferson's several stratagems were too much for the war-hawks. The congressional committee report of January 12, 1803, might have been written by the president himself. It authorized "the Executive to commence, with more effect, a negotiation with the French and Spanish Governments relative to the purchase from them of the island of New Orleans, and the provinces of East and West Florida." It continued, "It must be seen that the possession of New Orleans and the Floridas will not only be required for the convenience of the United States, but will be demanded by their most imperious necessities. The Mississippi and its branches, with those other rivers above referred to, drain an extent of country, not less, perhaps, than one-half of our whole territory, containing at this time one-eighth of our population and progressing with a rapidity beyond the experience of any former time, or any other nation. The Floridas and New Orleans command the only outlets to the sea, and our best interests require that we should get possession of them." The report stressed the peaceful intentions of the United States but hinted that war was possible, and so was a fighting alliance with England. It closed with "the Committee have no information before them, to ascertain the amount for which the purchase can be made, but it is hoped that, with the assistance of two million dollars in hand, this will not be unreasonable."[2]

Congress adopted the report by the overwhelming majority of two to one. On January 13, the Senate approved sending Monroe to Paris. These favorable actions convinced Jefferson that it was politically safe at last to give the nation some inkling of his secret continental dreams. His veiled method of revelation was to propose the same transcontinental exploration that he had discussed with George Rogers Clark in 1783, with John Ledyard in 1788, and with André Michaux in 1793. Those discussions had come to nothing. This time he was prepared to put the scheme through. During 1802, he and his young private secretary, Captain Meriwether Lewis, had spent many evenings enjoying vicarious travel while poring over masses of books, maps and reports on Louisiana that Jefferson had been collecting since the start of his Paris residence.

The president's perspective as a geography student would have seemed naïve to politicians like Manuel de Godoy and Talleyrand, who saw the world's divisions as resembling so many pieces on a chessboard that they hoped to move correctly to give them more personal power, wealth and pleasure. Jefferson's approach was romantic and selfless — the pure wonder of the aesthete and scientist, overpowered by the beauty and variety and promise of every mile of land as he followed Marquette through the great Mississippi valley, La Salle to his nemesis deep in Texas, the Mallets to Santa Fe, the La Vérendryes trailing over the purple vastness of the northern plains to the foot of the mysterious Rockies. And more clearly than ever he saw the whole glowing empire of Louisiana as indispensable to the onward march of freedom that was bringing millions of Americans to their heart's desire.

These were philosophical musings. The president's practical aim was to send a party overland under the leadership of the twenty-eight-year-old Lewis from St. Louis to the coast of Oregon by way of the Missouri. In his study, Jefferson had learned much from James Mackay's notes on the Yellowstone. The notes had given him a vague idea as to what lay across the Continental Divide beyond the source of the Missouri. More information came from Alexander Mackenzie's recent book on his trek to Bella Coola Bay in 1793 and on David Thompson's roamings west of Lake Superior. As the president studied, his sense of urgency increased with the issues of closure and retrocession and with his awareness that Britain still hoped to expand southward to the Upper Missouri from Canada.

On January 18, 1803, Jefferson sent his "confidential message recommending a western exploring expedition" to Congress. Its true purpose — military and expansionist — was to find a route to the Pacific that would be useful if a contest developed with Britain or France for control of the continent. But he befogged that purpose with a cloud of verbiage about how to bring the Indians of the west to white man's ways through government trading posts, and about the virtues of "enlarging the boundaries of knowledge, by undertaking voyages of discovery, and for other literary purposes." The message closed on a less altruistic note: "The appropriation of two thousand five hundred dollars, 'for the purpose of extending the external commerce of the United States,' while understood and considered by the executive as giving legislative sanction, would cover the undertaking from notice, and prevent the obstructions which interested individuals might otherwise previously prepare in its way."

Congress approved this recommendation for what future generations would know as the Lewis and Clark Expedition. The Washington envoys of France, Spain and England seemed to approve it too. They agreed to issue passports to Jefferson's explorers which would permit them to cross their lands when necessary during their "literary" trip.[3]

Every man has a day in his life blacker than all the others. That day for Robert R. Livingston could well have been Thursday, March 3, 1803, when he received a copy of the congressional authorization "to commence, with more effect, a negotiation" to buy New Orleans and the Floridas. With the authorization was a letter from Secretary of State Madison dated January 18 containing these lines:

In deliberating on this subject [of the purchase] it has appeared to the President that the importance of the crisis called for the experiment of an extraordinary mission; carrying with it the weight attached to such a measure, as well as the advantage of a more thorough knowledge of the views of the Government, and the sensibility of the people than could be otherwise conveyed. He has, accordingly, selected for this service, with the approbation of the Senate, Mr. Monroe, formerly our Minister Plenipotentiary at Paris, and lately Governor of the State of Virginia; who will be joined with yourself in commission extraordinary to treat with the French Republic; and with Mr. Pinckney in a like commission to treat, if necessary, with the Spanish Government. . . . Mr. Monroe will be the bearer of the instruction under which you are jointly to negotiate.

Madison's letter mentioned the president's "undiminished confidence" in Livingston, and there was a hint, to soften the blow further, that Monroe's appointment had been made to sooth domestic tempers. No matter. To Livingston, the plain fact was that Madison, his old housemate in Philadelphia during the Revolution, and the president threatened to rob him of his chance for glory. For fourteen months, he had been bombarding Bonaparte with ever more importunate essays and letters and verbal messages saying why France should renounce the retrocession — or else sell New Orleans and the Floridas to the United States while honoring the American spoliation claims. By social adroitness, including a diplomatic flirtation with the British ambassador, Lord Whitworth, he had induced Talleyrand, Joseph Bonaparte and Barbé-Marbois to bring him into personal contact with the First Consul. And now Madison was sending Monroe to share the fruits of his toil at a time when his efforts seemed about to be crowned with success. Livingston's bitterness was compounded by Madison's description of him as "the ordinary representation of the United States" in contrast to Monroe's sonorous title of "envoy extraordinary and minister plenipotentiary."[4] And it was clear who would be regarded in Paris as top man in the new negotiating team. Monroe was "the bearer of instructions" — that is, he was entrusted with the symbols of authority to act.

It was intolerable. Here was a cloud over Livingston's hopes that he might emerge from the rut of being merely the hereditary First Lord of the Manor. He had been counting on the triumph of his Paris mission as a one-man affair to demonstrate his intrinsic worth. It would put him in line for any highest honor — the governorship of New York, say, or the vice presidency of the United States — and vice presidents seemed to go on to the presidency. But this dual negotiation would reduce the scale of his achievement immeasurably. And so he had only one course to follow. He must push on without authority from Madison to come as close as he could to fulfilling the president's objectives before the envoy extraordinary arrived in Paris.

If Livingston was worried about this unorthodox procedure he could argue that it was for the good of his country. He knew how to get along with the First Consul, as one aristocrat got along with another. He was duty-bound to use his social advantage before that thorough man of the people, James Monroe, turned up to add a jarring note. Of course the chancellor was aware that Monroe might have a social advantage of his own. Monroe's teen-aged daughter, Eliza, was a student at Madame Campan's Seminary in nearby Saint-Germain. Her best friend there was Joséphine Bonaparte's daughter, Hortense de Beauharnais. It seemed quite possible that Hortense's stepfather knew and liked Eliza and looked forward to meeting her father and his wife Elizabeth, whom Parisians had called "La Belle Américaine" during his ministry.[5]

Livingston guessed correctly that he had a few weeks in which to operate before Monroe would appear. All through March news unfavorable to retrocession poured into the rue Tournon. Livingston was sure that François de Barbé-Marbois was reporting to Bonaparte the efforts of Senator Ross to mobilize American opinion against the French take-over of Louisiana. As minister of the public treasury, Barbé-Marbois did not try to conceal from Livingston his anxiety about the state of French finances and the growing weakness of the French navy. And he confirmed reports that General Victor's force off Holland would not set sail for New Orleans just yet; it was being reassigned to guard duty on the English Channel. That change pointed to war with England, the imminence of which was made clear by an ominous incident on March 12. As Livingston described that day:

I broke off this part of my letter to attend Madame Bonaparte's drawing-room, where a circumstance happened of sufficient importance to merit your attention. . . . After the First Consul had gone the circuit of one room, he turned to me, and made some of the common inquiries usual on those occasions. He afterwards returned, and entered into a further conversation. When he quitted me, he passed most of the other Ministers merely with a bow, went up to Lord Whitworth, and, after the first civilities, said: "I find, my Lord, your nation wants war again." L. W.: "No, sir, we are very desirous of peace." First Consul: "You have just finished a war of fifteen years." L. W.: "It is true, sir, and that was fifteen years too long." Consul: "But you want another war of fifteen years." L. W.: "Pardon me, sir, we are very desirous of peace." Consul: "I must either have Malta or war." L. W.: "I am not prepared, sir, to speak on that subject; and I can only assure you, citizen First Consul, that we wish for peace."

Through the rest of March, the American minister pressed variations of his old theme on Bonaparte and Talleyrand — the theme that the best course for France was to sell New Orleans and the Floridas to the United States, or to give up retrocession. He offered a new idea — to make a free port of New Orleans — and he increased stress on the need for the First Consul to acknowledge American spoliation claims of twenty million livres. And he asked that France honor officially the terms of Pinckney's Treaty on the right of deposit (actually the royal order countermanding Morales's closure had just been dispatched from Madrid to New Orleans.)[6] At last, on Easter Sunday, April 10, with the gardens of the Champs-Elysées in full spring bloom and the church bells pealing reminders of the Resurrection, Livingston learned that Monroe's ship had reached Le Havre on Good Friday after a month's rough voyage. Mr. and Mrs. Monroe were spending Easter with Eliza at Saint-Germain. They could be expected in Paris on Tuesday. The chancellor spent most of his Easter writing Secretary of State Madison to show him how thoroughly he had set the stage over the past

This engraving by Richomme after A. Gérard's painting has been called the best likeness of First Consul Bonaparte during the period when Livingston was trying to persuade him to sell Louisiana.
(Courtesy of Tutt Library, Colorado College)

year for the coming dual negotiations. Between the lines of his letters was the inference that the envoy extraordinary would have an easy time in Paris because Jefferson's objectives had all but been won by "the ordinary representation."

Livingston did not know how strong his case was becoming. Even as he scratched away, three French officials were holding a momentous discussion a few miles west of the rue Tournon in Louis XIV's old palace at Saint-Cloud. The subject was what to do about Louisiana. One of the three was Napoleon Bonaparte, thirty-three years old, neatly elegant, dark-skinned, boyishly intent, imperious. Another was the aging Denis Decrès, his minister of the marine, who had fought in Virginia with the marquis de Lafayette during the American Revolution. The third was François de Barbé-Marbois, minister of the public treasury, who probably knew more about the United States and its leaders than any other European. He knew also about Santo Domingo, New Orleans, the Floridas, and their relation to the economy and politics of the Gulf of Mexico. Talleyrand, the minister of foreign affairs, was not present. Neither was Joseph Bonaparte. The First Consul, for reasons of his own, did not want just then to hear their views, which followed Talleyrand's old line of using New Orleans as a springboard for the reconquest of La Nouvelle-France as it had been before the French and Indian War.

The conference had been called because Bonaparte had reached a crisis in his spectacular career. He had come to regard himself as the great idealist whose destiny was to save all people from the tyranny of British commercialism. He believed that, as things stood, merchants in London, backed by the British navy and the British colonial system, dictated the price of the world's goods and the rates of exchange. Hardly anybody anywhere — from India and China to Africa to New York to St. Petersburg to Oregon — could sell anything without paying tribute to the British monopoly, which used the tribute steadily to increase Britain's domination of the seven seas. This was the background of Bonaparte's problem on Easter Sunday: the problem of whether to challenge Britain by going ahead with his — and Talleyrand's — plan for a rival colonial empire of his own in Louisiana, or by establishing absolute control over the economy of the Continent.

The crisis had been precipitated early in January by a tragedy. The First Consul had learned then that his brother-in-law, General Leclerc, had died of what we would call malaria, in Santo Domingo. His sister Pauline had survived. Most of Leclerc's army of more than twenty thousand men had been destroyed by the disease or by Toussaint's fighting blacks. The remnant of the French force had barely managed to escape from the island and sail for home, leaving a huge amount of armament and many ships behind them.[7]

After this disaster, Bonaparte had to decide whether he could spare enough ships and money to order General Victor on his way from Holland to occupy New Orleans. If he gave up retrocession — that is, if he declined to accept Louisiana from Spain — he could start planning an assault on Malta as an alternative anti-British action. But the loss of Santo Domingo forced him to consider still another course. "I think," he said abruptly to Decrès and Barbé-Marbois at the start of their Easter conference, "of ceding Louisiana to the United States. They only ask of me one town in Louisiana. But I already consider the colony as entirely lost." He added, in words startlingly like those in Livingston's essays, "It seems to me that in the hands of this growing power, it will be more useful to the policy and even to the commerce of France, than if I should attempt to keep it."

Through the day and into the night the discussion went on. Bonaparte listened mainly. Many years later, Barbé-Marbois, at the age of eighty-three, wrote down his recollection of what each of the two ministers had said. The gist of what he remembered follows:

Barbé-Marbois: "We should not hesitate to give up Louisiana which is about to slip from us anyhow. War with England is inevitable. Shall we be able with very inferior naval forces to defend the province against that power? This conquest would be still easier to the Americans. The province is scarcely inhabited. You have not fifty soldiers there. Where are your means of sending garrisons thither? Can we restore fortifications that are in ruins, and construct a long chain of forts upon a frontier of four hundred leagues? The French have attempted to form colonies in several parts of the American continent. Their efforts have failed. The English, patient and laborious, do not fear the solitude and silence of newly settled countries. The Frenchman, lively and active, requires society. He is fond of conversing with his neighbors. He willingly enters on the experiment, but at the first disappointment, quits the spade or ax for the chase. Do not expect from Louisianans any attachment for your person. They render homage to your fame, but their love is reserved for those whom they regard as the authors of their happiness. They have lost the recollection of France. On learning that they are to become French again, they would say to one another, 'This change will not last longer than the others.' "

Denis Decrès: "We should keep Louisiana. We are still at peace with England. It would be unwise to abandon, for fear of a doubtful danger, the most important establishment that we can form out of France. If peace is maintained, giving it up cannot be justified. To retain it would be a great boon to our commerce and navigation. There can be no marine without colonies; no colonies without a powerful marine. The political system of Europe is only preserved by a combined resistance of many against one. This is as necessary with respect to the sea as to the land. It does not become the First Consul to fear the kings of England. France, deprived of her navy and her colonies, is stripped of half her splendor, and of a great part of her strength. Louisiana can indemnify us for all our losses. There does not exist on the globe a single port susceptible of becoming as important as New Orleans. The Mississippi does not reach there till it has received twenty other rivers, most of which surpass in size the finest rivers of Europe. The climate is the same as that of Hindostan. The navigation around the Cape of Good Hope to the Indies has changed the course of trade from Europe. What will be its direction if at the isthmus of Panama a simple canal should be opened to connect the one ocean with the other?[8] Louisiana will be on this new route, and it will then be acknowledged that this possession is of inestimable value."

The conference ended with nothing decided, and the three men retired for the night at the Saint-Cloud palace. At daybreak, Barbé-Marbois was called to Bonaparte's room to read to him some messages that had just arrived from the French embassy in London. They described frantic preparations for war with France that were being made all over England. As the small and sleepy minister finished reading, Bonaparte seemed suddenly to take a stand. He would, he declared, have to have Malta. At the same time he would guard against an Anglo-American alliance by taking steps to keep the friendship of the United States.

Then, as Barbé-Marbois recalled it, he said, "The English wish to keep Malta for ten years. This island, where military genius has exhausted all the means of defensive fortification to an extent of which no one without seeing it can form an idea, would be to them another Gibraltar. To leave it to the English would be to give up to them the commerce of the Levant, and to rob my southern provinces of it. They wish to keep this possession, and have me immediately evacuate Holland. Irresolution and deliberation are no longer in season. I renounce Louisiana. It is not only New Orleans that I will cede. It is the whole colony without any reservation. I renounce it with the greatest regret. I direct you to negotiate this affair with the envoys of the United States. Do not even await the arrival of Mr. Monroe. Have an interview this very day with Mr. Livingston. But I require a great deal of money for this new war against England. For a century France and Spain have been putting out for improvements in Louisiana, for which its trade has never repaid them. The cost of all these things is justly due us. But I will be moderate, in consideration of my need to sell. But keep this to yourself. I want fifty million francs [$9,380,000], and for less than that sum I will not treat."

The Barbé-Marbois memoir has the First Consul continuing, "Perhaps it will be objected that the Americans may be found too powerful for Europe in two or three centuries. But my foresight does not embrace such remote fears. Tomorrow you shall have full powers. Neither Mr. Monroe nor his colleague is prepared for a decision which goes infinitely beyond anything that they are about to ask of us. Begin by making them the overture, without any subterfuge. You will acquaint me, day by day, hour by hour, of your progress. The cabinet of London is informed of the measures adopted at Washington, but it can have no suspicion of those which I am now taking. Observe the greatest secrecy, and recommend secrecy to the Americans. They have not a less interest than yourself in conforming to this counsel. Keep in touch with M. de Talleyrand who alone knows my intentions."

By mid-Monday morning, Barbé-Marbois was back at the French treasury making notes on how best to deliver momentous news to Livingston. He had hoped to see him that day but his courier brought back word from the rue Tournon that the chancellor was tied up with Talleyrand and with preparations to receive the Monroes. One thing worried the Frenchman a little. As he was leaving Bonaparte, he had expressed regret that the retrocession of Louisiana had caused so much anti-French feeling in the United States. To this the First Consul had replied, "Well, you have charge of the treasury. Let them give you one hundred millions of francs, and pay their own claims and take the whole country."

In a matter of minutes Bonaparte had more than doubled his price. Barbé-Marbois thought that one hundred and twenty millions seemed a lot to ask of an infant nation barely fourteen years old.

19

Fait Accompli

ON MONDAY MORNING, April 11, Robert Livingston received a request from Talleyrand asking him if he could come at once to his rue du Bac office. Such importunity was unusual. It was not the habit of the foreign affairs minister to deign to make Livingston feel necessary to him. Talleyrand had a reason, of course, having just learned that Barbé-Marbois had been picked by Bonaparte to conduct the Louisiana negotiations. Talleyrand intended to keep his hand in anyhow, though it was obvious that the First Consul had replaced him because of his propensity for demanding bribes, as in the XYZ Affair. And perhaps Bonaparte had suspicions about the secret talks that Talleyrand and Joseph Bonaparte had been having with Lord Whitworth as to how much England would pay them if they persuaded the First Consul to keep Louisiana and let Britain keep Malta.[1]

As the chancellor walked to the French foreign affairs office through the April morning he reviewed once more Jefferson's aims to acquire New Orleans and the Floridas. Talleyrand surprised him by receiving him promptly. His manner was almost cordial, if a bit preoccupied. After the customary handshake, Livingston heard Talleyrand saying casually, "Would the United States be interested in buying all of Louisiana?"

One can assume that the chancellor was at least baffled. Was Talleyrand serious and, if not, what did he have in mind? In his letter to Madison written later that day Livingston stated:

> I told him no; that our wishes extended only to New Orleans and the Floridas; that the policy of France should dictate (as I had shown in an

official note) to give us the country above the river Arkansas, in order to place a barrier between them and Canada. He said, that if they gave New Orleans the rest would be of little value; and that he would wish to know "what we would give for the whole." I told him it was a subject I had not thought of; but that I supposed we should not object to twenty million francs, provided our citizens were paid. He told me that this was too low an offer; and that he would be glad if I would reflect upon it, and tell him tomorrow. . . . He added, that he did not speak from authority, but that the idea had struck him.

On Tuesday morning, Livingston welcomed the Monroes at the legation and helped them to get settled in lodgings nearby. In the afternoon, the two envoys reviewed Madison's instructions of March 2, authorizing them to buy any part or all of New Orleans and the Floridas at a top price of $9,380,000 (fifty million francs). Madison had valued the U.S. dollar at 5.45 "livre tournois" or 5.33 francs. The total of American spoliation claims against France, left blank in the instructions, was understood to be not less than $3,750,000 (twenty million francs). Madison based his valuation — or undervaluation — of the real estate on rumors sent to him by Livingston and by Pierre du Pont that Bonaparte had offered Charles IV the equivalent of forty-eight million francs for the Floridas. The secretary of state estimated that New Orleans was worth four times as much as the Floridas. West Florida was twice as valuable as East Florida.

All well and good. So, in view of Talleyrand's strange question on Monday, how much was the westside vastness of the Mississippi valley, *plus* New Orleans, worth? As Livingston and Monroe went into dinner with the legation staff on Tuesday night, they concluded that Louisiana's value should be no concern of theirs. They could wonder about it but they had no authority to do more than that. At dinner, Livingston happened to catch a glimpse of Barbé-Marbois strolling — almost skulking — in the legation garden. The chancellor sent his secretary and son-in-law, Robert L. Livingston, to invite the Frenchman in for coffee and to meet Monroe. Barbé-Marbois appeared and wasted no time revealing that he, not Talleyrand, would represent the First Consul in the upcoming negotiations. Then he took Livingston aside and murmured that something of critical importance had occurred at Saint-Cloud on Sunday. The chancellor must come and discuss it with him that very night.

After Monroe left the legation to retire, the two old friends met like conspirators at the French treasury. In a high state of excitement, Barbé-Marbois repeated everything that Bonaparte had said to him on Sunday about his decision to sell Louisiana. He went on to urge Livingston to hurry up and buy the province before war broke out. Otherwise, Britain would seize New Orleans with naval forces from Jamaica, not only as a maneuver against France but against the United States also — a step in England's old plan of westward expansion to tie up with British Canada and her foothold in Oregon. Livingston began to feel something of Barbé-Marbois's excitement when the Frenchman repeated Bonaparte's remark, "Let them give you one hundred millions of francs, and pay their own claims, and take the whole country." That was the moment when the chancellor realized what was happening here — that the Monroe-Livingston mission to buy a paltry if strategic seventy-five thousand square miles of coastal sands was vanishing beneath the tidal wave of this monstrous new proposal involving a region at least as large as the United States. Though this meeting in the dead of night was clandestine and unofficial, he had to recognize that Bonaparte was making a firm offer to sell Louisiana for $22,500,000, which included the cost of paying the American claims of up to $3,750,000. In other words, he and Monroe were being asked to buy an empire on their own responsibility without authority from their government in Washington and without time to get that authority. Not next month or next summer, but right now before war broke out.

Perhaps for the first time in his life, the imperturbable prince of Dutchess County found himself struggling to keep cool. He was seeing suddenly with Jefferson's eyes Jonathan Carver's "stately temples" rising above the Falls of St. Anthony, Bourgmond's golden plains, the languorous Acadian country west of New Orleans, and, most of all, the great river and its branches unifying the wilderness and waiting for future generations of Americans to push on west and enjoy their bounty. Such visions brought upon him a terrible itch to buy. He did not regard Bonaparte's price of one hundred and twenty million francs as particularly high considering, as Barbé-Marbois put it, "the extent of the country, the exclusive navigation of the river, and the importance of having no neighbors to dispute you, no war to dread." He kept thinking how Jefferson's secretary of the treasury, Albert Gallatin, had collected twelve and a half million dollars in revenue for the

United States during 1802 without half trying, with a much larger collection expected in 1803. He estimated that, under American control, New Orleans alone would produce port duties of several millions annually. He recalled Jefferson's refrain — that it was far cheaper to buy land at almost any price than to go to war for it.

But the chancellor's long, fleshy face filled with an expression of pain as he told the sympathetic Barbé-Marbois about the dire poverty of the United States and denounced Bonaparte's price as "exorbitant." He declined to state a price of his own on the grounds that he could do so only in concert with his colleague Monroe. But his French friend was determined to get some sort of commitment. "If," Barbé-Marbois pleaded, "you would name sixty million francs and pay the American claims of twenty million more I would try to see how far this would be accepted." Eighty million francs was $15,000,000. Quite a comedown from Bonaparte's $22,500,000! Livingston responded moodily that the new sum was "greatly beyond our means and might cause the overthrow of Jefferson's government and the triumph of the pro-British faction in Congress. Would not the few millions acquired at this expense be too dearly bought?" Barbé-Marbois replied, "But try, then. See if you can not come up to my mark."

They parted at midnight. Livingston could not think of sleeping. Instead he went to work at the legation writing a report to Madison on his conversation with Barbé-Marbois. One object of the report was to outline these important new proposals. The other was to make it quite clear that they had been initiated without the aid of James Monroe. The report concluded in part:

Thus, sir, you see a negotiation is fairly opened, and upon grounds which I confess I prefer to all other commercial privileges; and always to some a simple money transaction is infinitely preferable. As to the quantum, I have yet made up no opinion. The field opened to us is infinitely larger than our instructions contemplated; the revenue increasing, and the land more than adequate to sink the capital, should we even go the sum proposed by Marbois; nay, I persuade myself, that the whole sum may be raised by the sale of the territory west of the Mississippi, with the right of sovereignty, to some Power in Europe, whose vicinity we should not fear. I speak now without reflection, and without having seen Mr. Monroe, as it was midnight when I left the Treasury Office, and is now near 3 o'clock. It is so very important that you should be apprized that a negotiation is actually opened, even before Mr. Monroe has been presented, in order to calm the tumult which the news of war will renew, that I have lost no time in communicating it. We shall do all we can to cheapen the purchase; but my present sentiment is that we shall buy. Mr. Monroe will be presented to the Minister [Talleyrand] tomorrow, when we shall press for as early an audience as possible from the First Consul. I think it will be necessary to put in some proposition tomorrow: the Consul goes in a few days to Brussels, and every moment is precious.

Though the negotiation was indeed "fairly opened," its monumental import was in comic contrast to the disharmony of the negotiators. There was the First Consul, at sharp odds with his foreign minister, who had weapons ready to harpoon Barbé-Marbois if the treasury official trespassed much further on Talleyrand's domain in the Louisiana matter. There was Livingston seeing his great ambitions being destroyed by Monroe's appearance. There was the high-minded envoy extraordinary, acutely aware of the chancellor's pique and yet determined to do what he had been sent to do — that is, to negotiate well as chief of this mission so that Jefferson could point with pride to his achievements to impress the voters of Kentucky and Tennessee. Perhaps if transatlantic telephones had existed in April of 1803 to complicate things more, the Louisiana Purchase would never have come to pass. As it was, Livingston and Monroe confined their complaints about each other to very private letters to Secretary of State Madison, who would not receive them for a month or six weeks. Thus Monroe implied in his letter of April 15 that the chancellor was blocking his immediate presentation to Bonaparte to deny him the prime diplomatic status that came with presentation — the status Livingston already enjoyed. Monroe wrote further:

I was informed on my arrival here by Mr. Skipwith [Fulwar Skipwith, the American consul general in Paris] that Mr. Livingston, mortified at my appointment, had done everything in his power to turn the occurrences in America, and even my mission, to his own account, by pressing the Government on every point with a view to show that he had accomplished what was wished without my aid; and perhaps also that my mission had put in hazard what might otherwise have been easily obtained. His official correspondence will show what occurred prior to my arrival & sufficiently proves that he did not abstain even on hearing that I was on my way, from topics intrusted to us jointly.

The chancellor got in a few licks of his own when he wrote Madison two days later:

On the 14th I called upon Mr. Monroe to present him to the Minister [Talleyrand]. Before we went we examined our commission, in which there are two circumstances with which I am not satisfied. . . . The first is that I have not the same rank in the commission with Mr. Monroe. It is important that I should be thought to stand as well as with our Government as any other person. If so, my age, and the stations I have held entitle me not to have had any other person placed above me in the line I have filled. The second is, that the commission contains power only to treat for lands on the east side of the Mississippi. . . .

Several paragraphs later, Livingston touched on the presentation matter:

No notice has been given of Mr. Monroe's reception; and I am not without my fears that he will not be received before the usual diplomatic day, which will not be till the 15th [of May] and, before that time, the Consul will probably go upon his tour to Flanders. Mr. Monroe, having been compelled, when here, to be well with the party [Federalist] then uppermost, and who are now detested by the present ruler, it will be some time before they know how to estimate his worth; and Talleyrand has, I find, imbibed personal prejudice against him, that will induce him to throw every possible obstruction in his way, that he can do consistently with their own views.

But the negotiations moved along at a fair clip in spite of the feuding. Monroe soon found himself sharing Livingston's enthusiasm for buying the whole tract. On Friday, April 15, the Americans placed with Barbé-Marbois the same offer of twenty million francs (plus twenty million more to pay the American claims) that Livingston had suggested to Talleyrand on Monday. As the hours passed, both men seemed to forget personal differences in their absorption with the part that they were playing in the course of history. On Saturday, before lunching with the Second Consul, Jean-Jacques, duc de Cambacérès, the two bargainers showed their growing interest by deciding to raise their bid to the maximum of fifty million francs that Madison had

*Though the Louisiana Purchase treaty was dated April 30, 1803,
the signatures were not actually affixed until May 2. When
André Castaigne made this painting of the signing a century later,
he placed the principals in Napoleon's study with Rigaud's portrait
of Louis XIV as a background. As Livingston signs the treaty,
Monroe is beside him shaking hands with Barbé-Marbois
(Courtesy of Brown Brothers, Sterling, Pennsylvania)*

stipulated in authorizing them to buy New Orleans and the Floridas. That sum they hoped, might appeal to Bonaparte because it was the value that he was said to have put on the kingdom of Etruria when he gave it to the duke of Parma in exchange for the retrocession of Louisiana. Barbé-Marbois turned up after lunch and agreed to take their fifty-million bid to Bonaparte at Saint-Cloud on Sunday, though he expressed doubt that the First Consul could be budged off his price of eighty million francs.

No response on the bid came from Saint-Cloud on Sunday, but the Americans were not concerned. "Thus we stand at present," Livingston wrote to Madison, "resolving to rest upon our oars." The time for resting was fortuitous. Monroe had never quite recovered from his rough March crossing of the Atlantic. Now he went to bed for a while, confining his activity to conferences with Livingston. For the next ten days, the chancellor brought to Monroe's bedside a series of terms for a treaty of sale that were suggested by Barbé-Marbois if and when an agreement on price could be reached. On Saturday afternoon, April 27, Monroe felt well enough to take to a sofa in the parlor of his lodgings to meet with Livingston and Barbé-Marbois. After an hour or so of polite jockeying, the French minister left with them a projected treaty that, he said, Bonaparte would sign. The Americans spent Sunday revising its articles on commerce and spoliation claims to fit their ideas. The two bickered at some length over boundary questions but, as Monroe said, "we must not lose time." In the end they agreed that the exact boundaries of what they proposed to buy must remain imprecisely defined as in the Treaty of San Ildefonso of 1800 — "the same extent that Louisiana had when France possessed it." There would be plenty of time later on to argue with England about the disputed northern boundary, with Spain about where Louisiana ended and Spanish Texas began somewhere between the Red River and the Sabine. As for the western boundary, Jefferson's young explorer, Meriwether Lewis, would soon be charting a point on that boundary line along the crest of the Rockies as he journeyed overland to strengthen the tenuous U.S. claim to Oregon. And West Florida? Well, for the present the less said about who owned it — Spain? France? — the better. If Talleyrand considered it to be part of the original French Louisiana, so did Monroe and Livingston.

Next day, Monday, April 29, the Americans called on Barbé-Marbois in his office at the Treasury. Perhaps they were excited, or apprehensive, or just too tired to feel anything after weeks of strain. The three men talked of this and that, rustled papers, pondered. And suddenly, incredibly, the whole affair was settled. Monroe described what happened in his journal:

We proposed to offer 50. millions to France & 20. on acct. of her debt to the citizens of the U States, making 70. in the whole. On reading that article he [Barbé-Marbois] declared that he would not proceed in the negotiation on a less sum than 80. Millions, since it would be useless as the Consul had been sufficiently explicit on that point; Indeed he assured us that his government had never positively instructed him to take that sum, but that as he had told the Consul it was enough, that he would ask no more, and to which he understood the Consul as giving his assent, he Mr. Marbois had thought himself authorized to accept & propose it to us, but that he could not proceed unless we agreed to give it. On this frank and explicit declaration on his part & after explaining to him the motive which led us to offer that sum we agreed to accede to his idea & give 80. millions.

So that was that. On Tuesday, the thirtieth, a "Treaty of Purchase between the United States and the French Republic" was approved by "R. R. Livingston, James Monroe, and Barbé-Marbois." By its terms, the United States agreed to accept "the Colony or Province of Louisiana, with the same extent that it now has in the hands of Spain, and that it had when France possessed it" just as soon as France received it formally from Spain. The cash price to be paid was sixty million francs ($11,250,000). In addition, the U.S. Treasury obligated itself to pay a maximum sum of twenty million francs ($3,750,000) including interest to satisfy the individual spoliation claims of American citizens against France as each of these claims came to be adjudicated and certified by a three-man American claims board.

With the purchase of an empire all but achieved, Livingston and Monroe could resume suspecting one another. For weeks the envoy extraordinary had been foiled, seemingly by "my colleague," in his wish to be presented to the First Consul. On their way back to the rue Tournon from the April 29 talks, Livingston had promised to inform Talleyrand that Monroe was well again and in shape to meet Bonaparte at last. "To guard against accidents, however," Monroe noted acidly in his journal, "I wrote the minister to that effect, and a note to my colleague to request him to call for me as he went to the house of the minister. Just as I was ready to visit the minister my colleague returned from him & informed me that it was arranged that I should be presented next day, that is on the first of May."

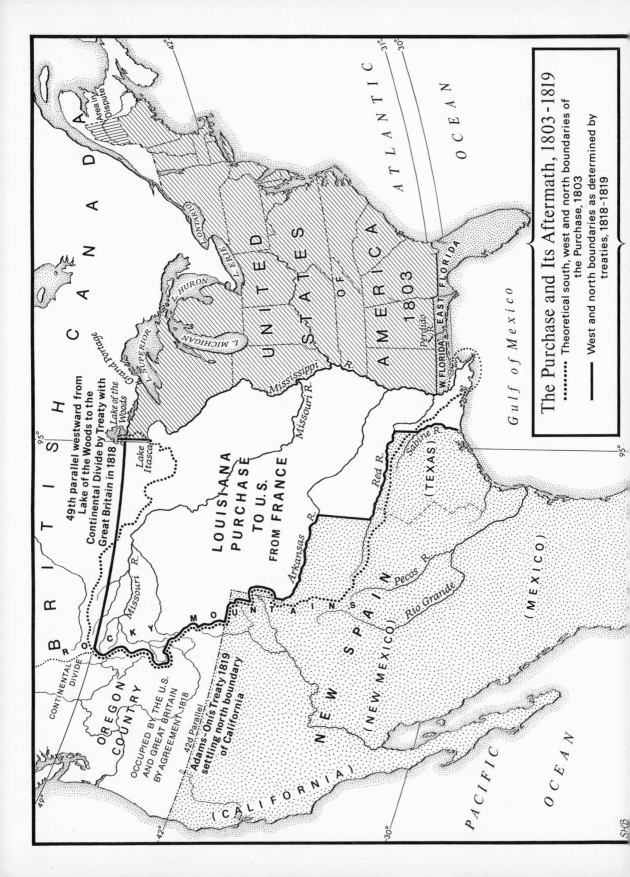

The Purchase and Its Aftermath, 1803–1819

.... Theoretical south, west and north boundaries of the Purchase, 1803

——— West and north boundaries as determined by treaties, 1818–1819

ATLANTIC OCEAN

Gulf of Mexico

PACIFIC OCEAN

BRITISH CANADA

Area in Dispute

UNITED STATES OF AMERICA 1803

L. SUPERIOR
L. HURON
L. MICHIGAN
L. ERIE
ONTARIO

Mississippi R.
Missouri R.

W. FLORIDA   EAST FLORIDA
Perdido R.

LOUISIANA PURCHASE TO U.S. FROM FRANCE

49th parallel westward from Lake of the Woods to the Continental Divide by Treaty with Great Britain in 1818

Lake of the Woods

Grand Portage

Lake Itasca

CONTINENTAL DIVIDE

OREGON COUNTRY

OCCUPIED BY THE U.S. AND GREAT BRITAIN BY AGREEMENT, 1818

42d Parallel

Adams-Onis Treaty 1819 settling north boundary of California

(CALIFORNIA)

R O C K Y   M O U N T A I N S

Arkansas R.
Red R.
Sabine R.
Pecos R.
Rio Grande

NEW SPAIN

(NEW MEXICO)

(TEXAS)

(MEXICO)

95°
42°
31°
30°

SHB

The presentation took place as scheduled — a purely social occasion.[2] Next day, May 2, the three negotiators actually signed the Louisiana Purchase treaty. The First Consul signed its ratification by France on May 22 (five days after Britain's declaration of an embargo on French commerce and the resumption of the Anglo-French war). Bonaparte began at once spending his sixty million francs in advance on futile preparations to invade England. The cash payment of the sixty millions was arranged in the late fall of 1803 through the issuance to Bonaparte of U.S. six percent stock that could not be redeemed for fifteen years. The First Consul sold this stock (face value, $11,250,000) to the Dutch banking house of Hope and Company and the British house of Baring at a discount of 87½ per each $100 unit. As a result, Bonaparte received in cash only $8,831,250 for the million square miles of Louisiana, as against his total price of $15,000,000. In those days, as in these, international bankers occupied a realm high above international politics. Nobody thought it odd that a British firm should be advancing money to France to invade Britain.[3]

The very day in April that the Americans in Paris were buying Louisiana, President Jefferson in Washington was writing a letter to an old friend, Dr. Hugh Williamson, to explain what he had achieved by his patience toward Spain on the heated closure issue. "Although I do not count with confidence on obtaining New Orleans from France for money, yet I am confident in the policy of putting off the day of contention for it. . . . In the meantime, we have obtained by a peaceable appeal to justice, in four months, what we should not have obtained under seven years of war, the loss of one hundred thousand lives, an hundred millions of additional debt, many hundred millions worth of produce and property lost for want of market, or in seeking it, and that demoralization which war superinduces on the human mind." Early in June, Jefferson felt the first faint throb of a fantastic hope when he read Livingston's letter of April 11 to Madison reporting Talleyrand's odd question about buying *all* of Louisiana. And then, on July 3, messages and treaties from Livingston and Monroe, dispatched in triplicate with couriers from Le Havre and Bordeaux and London for safety's sake, began pouring into the White House to give the president an Independence Day full of joy beyond his imagining. How, he must have asked himself, could so much have happened to the United States in the twenty-seven years that had passed so rapidly since he wrote the

Declaration? In particular, why, as Dumas Malone put it, "this epic-making agreement with France . . . owing to a concurrence of extraordinarily fortunate circumstances?"

Through the weeks that followed at Monticello, Jefferson took stock of the situation in between his usual bird-watching, flower-sniffing and stargazing. He had consoling statistics at hand. How large was France? Two hundred thousand square miles, perhaps. How large was Charles IV's Spain? Nearly the same. How large were the British Isles? Half the size of France. How large was the Louisiana Purchase? A million square miles probably. At fifteen million dollars for the whole, what did that come to per square mile? Fifteen dollars — or a bit more than two cents an acre. And what was Albert Gallatin netting in his recent sales of U.S. public land? Around a dollar an acre. No wonder those British and Dutch bankers thought the United States was a good credit risk!

Of course Jefferson had problems. The purchase treaty and two conventions had to be ratified by the Senate, and the U.S. stock issue approved by the House. The deadline for ratification was October 30. The stock had to be on a frigate bound for the Tuileries eighteen days after the transfer ceremony in New Orleans. Livingston was sending frantic warnings to Madison that Bonaparte was beginning to regret the transaction and might try to void the treaty. The Spanish minister, the marqués de Casa Yrujo, Jefferson's fellow student of truffles, was claiming — and rightly — that the First Consul had promised in 1800 not to sell Louisiana without Spain's permission, and anyhow France did not own the province because she had not yet completed the Tuscany terms of the retrocession. Madison dismissed Yrujo's complaints on the grounds that the United States had nothing to do with arrangements between Spain and France.

These domestic matters were worrisome but supportable. Having lived vicariously beyond the Blue Ridge since childhood, the president knew the political nervous system of western expansion as he knew that of his own lanky body. He almost enjoyed the anguished protests of the bitter-end Federalists in New England denouncing the cost of the purchase (eight hundred and sixty-six wagon loads of solid silver weighing four hundred and thirty-three tons!). In *Jefferson the President: First Term* Dumas Malone quotes the comments of a Boston journalist: "We are to give money of which we have too little for land of which we already have too much." This "unexplored empire, of the size of four or five European kingdoms," would destroy the balance in the Union. "A great waste, a wilderness, unpeopled with any beings except wolves and wandering Indians" could be cut up into numberless states.

But the Bostonian was in a minority. Most Americans of both parties praised the event, and their enthusiasm grew as they realized its implications. There was a sectional timbre to some of the cheering. The New Yorkers were proud that their Chancellor Livingston single-handedly had brought the purchase to pass. The southerners and westerners were proud that *their* hero, James Monroe of Virginia, was the man who really made it happen.[4]

Nothing demonstrated more clearly the dualism of the composite American, that elastic talent to resolve conflicting points of view, than Jefferson's handling of the constitutional issue. Having opposed for many years, as a strict constructionist, Hamilton's doctrine of implied powers, he maintained staunchly in 1803 that the Constitution did not permit Congress or the executive to buy a million square miles of a foreign country and to make full-fledged American citizens of its residents. But when it came to doing something that he thought had to be done, he bent his mind around to accepting the inevitable, even if it involved what he regarded as profligate legal behavior. In a letter to his Kentucky friend, Senator John Breckinridge, he wrote on August 12, 1803:

This treaty must of course be laid before both Houses, because both have important functions to exercise respecting it. They, I presume, will see their duty to their country in ratifying and paying for it, so as to secure a good which would otherwise probably be never again in their power. But I suppose they must then appeal to *the nation* for an additional article to the Constitution, approving and confirming an act which the nation had not previously authorized. The Constitution has made no provision for our holding foreign territory, still less for incorporating foreign nations into our Union. The executive in seizing the fugitive occurrence which so much advances the good of their country, have done an act beyond the Constitution. The Legislature in casting behind them metaphysical subtleties, and risking themselves like faithful servants, must ratify and pay for it, and throw themselves on their country for doing for them unauthorized, what we know they would have done for themselves had they been in a situation to do it. It is the case of a guardian, investing the money of his ward in purchasing an important adjacent territory, and saying to him when of age, I did this for your good; I pretend to no right to bind you; you may disavow me, and I must get out of the scrape as I can; I thought it my duty to risk myself for you. But we shall not be disavowed by the nation, and their act of indemnity will confirm and not weaken the Constitution, by more strongly marking out its lines.

Though young Senator John Quincy Adams asked for an amendment permitting the purchase and for a referendum within Louisiana, Congress had no use for such "metaphysical subtleties." Jefferson did not mention a constitutional issue in his message of October 17 to the Senate and House. Three days later the Senate ratified the purchase treaty by the large majority of 27 to 7. The House approved the stock issue to Bonaparte 89 to 23.[5]

Meanwhile Jefferson went ahead with plan after plan to develop the new empire — for surveys of the Mississippi between the Falls of St. Anthony and the mouth of the Ohio, for a fifteen-day express mail service from Washington to New Orleans by way of Nashville and Natchez, for more inducements to persuade eastside Indians to cross into Louisiana. He informed Tennessee officials that the Tombigbee was virtually their river down to Mobile and the gulf because West Florida would soon be occupied by the United States even though Charles IV was denying that it had been part of the 1800 retrocession of Louisiana to Bonaparte. Plans for Meriwether Lewis's trek to the Pacific were far advanced. Lewis was in Cahokia near St. Louis signing up recruits and buying equipment for the journey up the Missouri in the spring. The president was pleased to find that Lewis had chosen for his co-commander Captain William Clark, with whom Lewis had fought Indians in Ohio under General Anthony Wayne. Clark was the younger brother of Jefferson's neighbor in Albemarle County, George Rogers Clark, the great western hero whom Jefferson had hoped to send to Oregon in 1783.

Spanish Minister Yrujo suggested that Charles IV's soldiers might resist the American occupation of New Orleans. But Jefferson knew that that was pure bluff, having received word that Spain's force in the delta area numbered only three hundred demoralized men, half of whom were either sick or in jail. On November 1, the president sent orders by way of his new Nashville express route to his reliable governor of Mississippi Territory,

*The French and Spanish of New Orleans were silent but
Americans cheered joyously as Governor Claiborne
and General Wilkinson received Lower Louisiana from
Bonaparte's prefect, Monsieur de Laussat.*
(*From Ripley Hitchcock's* The Louisiana Purchase)

William C. C. Claiborne, and to his unreliable-but-indispensable chief of staff, General James Wilkinson. Their task as U.S. commissioners was to accept Lower Louisiana from Bonaparte's prefect, Pierre Clément de Laussat, who had turned up in March to prepare the populace for the arrival of General Victor and his occupying force from Holland — the overdue force that would never arrive.

Laussat was an old-style Jacobin with a lot of Edmond Genet's tactless arrogance and bumptious energy. The French creoles despised him and feared that in his republican zeal he might free their black slaves, who outnumbered the native whites in the delta area three to one. The Ursuline nuns believed that the prefect was a heretic. Most of them left the old Ursuline convent in New Orleans to find sanctuary in Havana under the rule of His Catholic Majesty Charles IV. The unhappy creoles were unhappier still in August, when they learned that Laussat would not be around much longer — that the United States would receive Louisiana from the French as soon as the French received it from the Spanish. To the creoles, such a transfer meant, among other disasters, that the twangy American version of English would become the official language in place of their melodious tongue. And they feared that attempts would be made to substitute American law and New England morality for the charming and careless ways that New Orleans had enjoyed since the first masked balls and absinthe socials of the marquis de Vaudreuil era.

These were minor complaints. New Orleans had been a city with no country to love for too long to be tragic about another change of nationality. That of Wednesday, November 30 — from Spain to France — was a glum affair, but chiefly because it rained cats and dogs and the unpaved streets were rivers of sewage and garbage. At high noon in the Cabildo, Prefect Laussat joined the Spanish commissioners, Governor de Salcedo and the marqués de Casa Calvo, followed discreetly by Intendant Morales, like Banquo. The ancient Salcedo, as decayed as his regime, handed Laussat the keys to the local forts and tottered out on the balcony to tell the several thousand drenched spectators in the Place d'Armes below that they were released from obedience to Charles IV. A cannon boomed dully as the Spanish flag came down and the French flag went up. But, as the American consul, Daniel Clark, reported to Jefferson later, "Except for the cannon not a sound was heard. The most gloomy silence prevailed and nothing could induce the crowd to express the least joy or give any sign of satisfaction on the occasion."

Next day, Laussat set December 20 as the date of the transfer from France to the United States, which meant that France would actually own Louisiana for only twenty days. The announcement hardly seemed to call for a celebration, but the populace decided to have one anyhow, with the street dancing lasting until dawn. The ceremony in the Place d'Armes on the twentieth followed the formula of that on November 30 except that Daniel Clark arranged a noisy claque of Americans to counter the apathy of the French and Spanish as Laussat presented Lower Louisiana to Claiborne and Wilkinson on Bonaparte's behalf. During the flag ritual, the pulley stuck briefly as Old Glory went up the pole. Of this event, Laussat was alleged to have said later, "It stuck there half way up as though ashamed to find itself replacing the French colors to which it owed its glorious independence."

For reasons of economy, the French prefect devised much simpler arrangements for the three-way transfer of Upper Louisiana. He appointed Captain Amos Stoddard, the U.S. post commander at Cahokia opposite St. Louis, to represent Bonaparte in receiving the region from the Spanish Lieutenant Governor Dehault de la Suze. President Jefferson had already asked Stoddard to represent the United States, which would give the young Massachusetts officer a rare experience — the simultaneous receiving, as a Frenchman, and the bestowing on himself, as an American, of an immense Spanish terrain.

The event occurred in the log village of St. Louis on March 9, 1804. In its rustic way the ceremony was far more colorful than the New Orleans rites. A happy crowd of four hundred fur traders in buckskin and Indians in breechclouts with their wives and children stood around the small government house on the low bluff above the great brown river. Auguste Chouteau, co-founder of St. Louis, was there, and his half-brother Pierre, both of whom had been helping Captain Meriwether Lewis to plan his transcontinental trek by telling him all they knew about the Missouri as far west and north as the Mandan Indians. Lewis was Jefferson's representative at the transfer. As he entered the government house with Captain Stoddard, cannon boomed at the Spanish fort on the hill and continued booming while Governor Dehault read his proclamation from the porch of the house:

Inhabitants of Upper Louisiana:

By the King's command, I am about to deliver up this post and its dependencies.

The flag under which you have been protected for a period of nearly thirty-six years is to be withdrawn. From this moment you are released from the oath of fidelity you took to support it.

The fidelity and courage with which you have guarded and defended it will never be forgotten; and in my character of representative, I entertain the most sincere wishes for your perfect prosperity.

DEHAULT DE LA SUZE

Thus, after nearly three centuries, the dreams of many men came to nothing at St. Louis — the selfish dreams of de Soto and Coronado, the noble dreams of Marquette and La Salle, the brave hopes of Bienville and the La Vérendryes. For most of these men, Louisiana had held the promise of a happier world with freedom and justice for all. Their failure was a result of complex causes, including the failure of royal absolutism to produce progressive government, the obsession of the kings of Spain and France with the petty affairs of Europe, and the dynamic effects of English liberalism on England's American colonies. As the end came with the governor's proclamation, there may have been present a few thoughtful Frenchmen and Spaniards who shed a tear or two. But spectators such as Captain Stoddard, Meriwether Lewis and the rising Chouteau family could have felt only joy standing at this gateway of a new empire as young and glowing as their own aspirations.

If ghosts stood beside them watching the transfer they could have been those of Peter Jefferson and George Washington recalling the excitement that they themselves had felt seven short decades before looking west with the same hopes from the crest of the Alleghenies.

Epilogue

THE TWELVE YEARS following the Louisiana Purchase brought one international crisis after another, each of which reduced the power and the will of Europeans to resist President Jefferson's intent to add the Floridas to his new empire and to strengthen the weak claim of the United States to Oregon. The crises included Britain's great naval victory over the French and Spanish fleets off Trafalgar in 1805, the shift of the Spanish people to England's side against France when Napoleon put his brother Joseph on the Spanish throne in 1808, and successive insurrections in Spain's American colonies starting with Venezuela in 1810. The era ended with Andrew Jackson's crushing defeat of the overconfident British near New Orleans in January, 1815, and Napoleon's downfall at Waterloo three months later.

These were coming events. When Jefferson got the glorious news of the Purchase on July 3, 1803, he went to work at once to make Louisiana an active part of the union and to determine its boundaries. While his Federalist opponents accused him of unconstitutional conduct and of being "As despotic as a Turk," he persuaded Congress to create the Territory of Orleans, with his friend William C. C. Claiborne as governor. It consisted of the lower, well-populated two hundred and fifty miles of the Purchase, the tropical part from the 33d parallel on down to the gulf. Eight years later, it would become the State of Louisiana, extending eastward into West Florida as far as the Pearl River, and including the Baton Rouge area on the Mississippi. The wild remainder of the Purchase, from the 33d parallel north some twelve hundred miles to the disputed boundary of Canada, was set up briefly as the District of Louisiana, attached to Indiana Territory, before becoming the Territory of Louisiana ("Missouri" after 1812 to avoid confusion with the State of Louisiana), with the capital at St. Louis. As its first governor, Jefferson appointed the ubiquitous James Wilkinson, who continued as commander-in-chief of the U.S. Army.

Along with these administrative arrangements, the president drew up instructions to guide James Monroe as his minister in London and as his envoy extraordinary in Madrid to settle boundaries and acquire the Floridas. Jefferson maintained, of course, that West Florida was part of the Purchase, having been French property when Louis XV gave Louisiana to Spain in 1762. For bargaining purposes, Jefferson argued that Spain's province of Texas between the Rio Grande and the Red River at Natchitoches was part of the Purchase too, having been formerly French by reason of La Salle's colony at Matagorda Bay in the 1680's.

He knew that Monroe would shape his diplomacy to counter the geopolitical stands on North America held by European officials. The Spanish still claimed the Pacific coast north from California all the way to Russian Alaska, even though Spain had admitted England's right to trade there by the Nootka Sound Treaty of 1790. England claimed that same Oregon country from the Pacific coast east to the Continental Divide. Spain and England both ignored the claim of the United States to at least some of Oregon based on Captain Gray's discovery of the mouth of the Columbia in 1792. In the Spanish view, the province of New Mexico extended northwest from Santa Fe and the Upper Rio Grande deep into the Mississippi drainage basin of the Louisiana Purchase. How far northeast varied from Spaniard to Spaniard. The minimum spread of New Mexico was as far as the Arkansas, the maximum as far as the Missouri. The Santa Fe traders had never penetrated eastward any great distance because the Comanche Indians guarded their country with something like a religious fervor. The Spanish knew that the Red River divide in the west would seem to be the logical boundary between New Mexico and Louisiana, as it was traditionally the boundary in the east between Texas and the Natchitoches area. That was why Spanish mapmakers, who had no idea where the Red ran west of the Great Raft, sent it shooting north on their maps rather than west — a strategy that tended to enlarge New Mexico.

James Monroe's diplomacy in 1806–1807 accomplished very little but

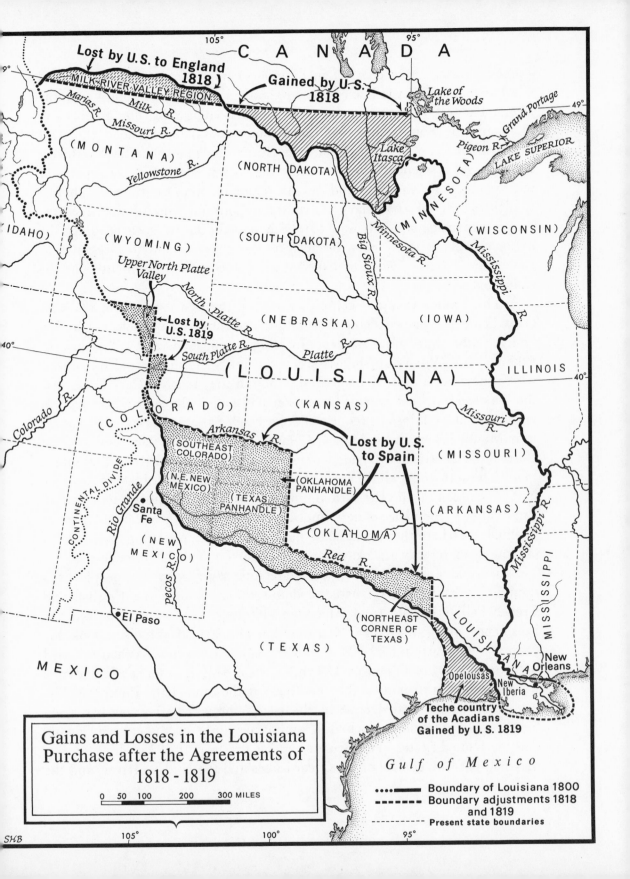

Gains and Losses in the Louisiana
Purchase after the Agreements of
1818 - 1819

0   50 100   200   300 MILES

Lost by U.S. to England 1818
MILK·RIVER VALLEY REGION
Gained by U.S. 1818

C A N A D A

Lake of
the Woods

Grand Portage

Pigeon R.

LAKE SUPERIOR

Lake
Itasca

Marias R.

Milk   R.

Missouri   R.

(M O N T A N A)

Yellowstone   R.

(NORTH DAKOTA)

(MINNESOTA)

(WISCONSIN)

(IDAHO)

(W Y O M I N G)

(SOUTH DAKOTA)

Big Sioux R.

Minnesota R.

Mississippi R.

Upper North Platte
Valley

North Platte R.

(NEBRASKA)

(I O W A)

Lost by
U.S. 1819

South Platte R.

Platte   R.

(L O U I S I A N A)

ILLINOIS

Colorado   R.

(C O L O R A D O)

(KANSAS)

Missouri R.

Arkansas   R.

Lost by U.S.
to Spain

CONTINENTAL DIVIDE

(SOUTHEAST
COLORADO)

N.E. NEW
MEXICO)

(OKLAHOMA
PANHANDLE)

(MISSOURI)

Rio Grande

Santa
Fe

(TEXAS
PANHANDLE)

(OKLAHOMA)

(ARKANSAS)

Pecos R.

(NEW

MEXICO)

Red   R.

Mississippi R.

El Paso

(NORTHEAST
CORNER OF
TEXAS)

L O U I S I

M E X I C O

(T E X A S)

A N A

New
Orleans

Opelousas

New
Iberia

Teche country
of the Acadians
Gained by U. S. 1819

Gulf of Mexico

••••••• Boundary of Louisiana 1800
‒ ‒ ‒ ‒ Boundary adjustments 1818
          and 1819
–––––– Present state boundaries

105°

100°

95°

SHB

Jefferson found great comfort in the enormous success of the Lewis and Clark expedition to the Pacific coast by way of the Missouri and Columbia rivers. The trek westward — from the Mandan villages in 1805 and back to St. Louis in 1806 — shattered the mystery that had shrouded the west through ages of mythology about the Strait of Anian and the Northwest Passage. As a scientist, the president was entranced by Lewis's reports of new plants and animals, and by his chart of the Continental Divide, Louisiana's western boundary, nearly three thousand miles up the Missouri. As an expansionist, Jefferson saw the expedition as spearheading the nation's push to the Pacific because of the strong claim to Oregon that Lewis and Clark had established by wintering at the mouth of the Columbia.

That exploration was complemented by the two journeys of a young army lieutenant named Zebulon Montgomery Pike, one of them northward and the other into the southwest. In 1805–1806, General Wilkinson sent Pike and his soldiers up the Mississippi from St. Louis to find its source, which they didn't quite manage to do, though they reached Cass Lake near the Turtle Lake that David Thompson had called the source in 1798. A year later, at Wilkinson's request, Pike ascended the Arkansas to its source near Mount Elbert in the highest Colorado Rockies, and then moved south close to the Continental Divide looking for the elusive Red River that ought to have been there by all the logic of theoretical geography. Instead the Pike party stumbled on the Rio Grande in New Mexican territory (today's San Luis valley). Spanish soldiers appeared and hauled them off as spies to Chihuahua, where they spent some months in jail before being escorted out of New Spain by way of Texas to the American outpost Natchitoches.[1]

In 1808 a weary and aging Jefferson, revered by his people even though his Embargo Act had failed miserably to force the English and French belligerents to treat American shipping with respect, passed the presidency along to James Madison, his best friend. Madison took his country reluctantly into the War of 1812 against England. When it ended with the Treaty of Ghent on December 24, 1814, Louisiana's boundaries were as much in dispute as they had been at the time of the Purchase. The Treaty of Ghent settled none of the issues for which the war had been fought — impressment, blockades, boundaries in the north between Canada and the United States. The British had set fire to part of Washington but they had not won control of the Great Lakes and the Hudson River, and the news was soon out that Andrew Jackson's frontiersmen had driven Sir Edward Packenham's veterans of the Napoleonic wars from the field of Chalmette below New Orleans. This victory did great things for American morale and convinced the English finally and forever that what they had lost in 1783 was lost for good.

With the War of 1812 and Napoleon out of the way, the long-pending Florida and boundary problems could be tackled optimistically. The American who tackled them was John Quincy Adams, eldest son of the second president of the United States. Adams was the American minister to London in September, 1817, when President James Monroe ordered him home to Washington to clear up the problems as his secretary of state. Adams was a perfect choice. As a child in Philadelphia, in addition to teaching Barbé-Marbois how to speak English, he had listened at length to Jefferson's views on western expansion and on the importance of Oregon and the Columbia to the nation's ocean-to-ocean future. Thereafter, he had worked in American legations abroad from his fourteenth year on. When he took over the state department in Monroe's administration, he was fully aware of Britain's new respect for the United States, and he instructed his envoys in London and Paris, Richard Rush and Albert Gallatin, to press hard for decisions on the northern line and on who was sovereign in Oregon.

The Anglo-American talks dragged on into the fall of 1818. At first Britain's commissioners proposed to put the boundary along the 49th parallel west from the northwest corner of the Lake of the Woods, but no further west than the Continental Divide in the Rockies. Rush and Gallatin said no. Then the British suggested running the 49th on west over the divide until it hit the Columbia River, and then south and west down the Columbia to its mouth at the site of the winter post of Lewis and Clark. That was no good either (Secretary Adams had warned his envoys not to give any part of the Lower Columbia to the British). But agreement was reached on October 20 — the Convention of 1818. Its Article III made the 49th parallel from Lake of the Woods west to the Rockies the northern border of the United States. The Oregon country beyond, with no boundaries specified, would be subject to joint Anglo-American occupancy for a period of ten years, open to the citizens and ships of both countries exclusively. That proviso put a very large American foot in the Oregon door.

While Rush and Gallatin were working on the Canadian line in London, Adams was working in Washington with the Spanish minister,

*Though John Quincy Adams was the son of the Federalist president John Adams,
he was an ardent Jeffersonian when President Monroe made him secretary of state
charged with settling the boundaries of the Purchase and acquiring Florida.
(Portrait by John Singleton Copley. Courtesy of the Museum of Fine Arts, Boston)*

Luis de Onís y Gonzales, to reach agreement on far more complicated matters. One of them was the American demand to buy the Floridas. The United States had occupied West Florida long since as far east as the old French boundary at the Perdido River. In the spring of 1818, Andrew Jackson's soldiers, without official sanction, seized East Florida as well on the grounds that Spain had failed to prevent her Florida Indians from attacking American settlers in Georgia. A separate matter was the setting of boundaries in the southwest and west between Louisiana and Spanish Texas and New Mexico. Related to that was Adams's task of persuading Onís to limit Spain's domain west of the Continental Divide — Spanish California — to a northern boundary short of Oregon. To Adams, that would become crucial in view of the Anglo-American agreement to the exclusive joint occupancy of Oregon.

Soon after Jackson's conquest of Florida, Adams decided that the time had come for a general showdown with Onís. Spain's bargaining position was pitifully weak. England had lost interest in supporting her as an ally after Napoleon's downfall. Spain was exhausted by her efforts to control her revolting colonists south of the Rio Grande. Adams had assurances in the summer of 1818 that Onís was prepared to give up the Floridas if the United States would assume spoliation claims of American citizens against Spain to a maximum of five million dollars. What remained to be settled were the boundaries in the west — Onís trying to move them eastward from New Mexico as far as possible into the Louisiana Purchase, and Adams resisting strenuously, though ready to give up Texas and even some of Louisiana if Onís would give up Oregon in addition to Florida.

For six months, the American and the Spaniard shuffled their boundaries back and forth on the latest map of North America — the map of the Philadelphian John Melish, published in June, 1816, and "improved to the 1st of January 1818." The Melish map was far from accurate, but it was good enough to enable the negotiators to formulate and sign the Adams-Onís Treaty of February 22, 1819. This historic document gave the Floridas to the United States for the payment of five million dollars in claims. It made a permanent boundary for Louisiana, as between Spanish property and that of the United States, using the Sabine River north from the Gulf of Mexico, the Red River west to the 100th meridian, and the Arkansas to its source. From the source of the Arkansas, the Louisiana line ran due north to the 42d parallel, and then due west to the Continental

Divide — in present Wyoming. In accepting this sixteen hundred miles of Louisiana boundary, Onís came around to accepting also Adams's demand that the 42d parallel from the Continental Divide to the Pacific serve as the boundary between California and the Oregon country.

Though these boundaries cost the United States some territory, as the map on page 323 shows, they cleared of dispute the entire width of present Wyoming and Montana to provide access from St. Louis through the Louisiana Purchase to Oregon. That width of access, Adams believed, was more than enough to insure American ownership of Oregon eventually.[2]

With the passage of time, the Louisiana Purchase emerges as a happening that had as much to do with forming the national character and creating the United States of today as the Declaration of Independence and the American Revolution. The brightness and wonder of it has a dark side — the tragedy that came to the original inhabitants, the Indians, caught in the flood of settlers from the east whose aspirations were beyond administrative control. The newcomers crossed the Mississippi by the millions, driving the natives before them until no room remained for them to carry on the kind of civilization that they had spent centuries developing. The new Americans did not mean to be deliberately cruel and unjust. Their habits of mind had evolved from the repressive governments and economic systems of Europe, where the fruits of the earth could be won only by ruthless acquisitiveness and driving ambition at the expense of those less aggressively animated.

It took time, trial and error, science and invention, for the settlers to transform La Salle's wilderness into today's domesticated thirteen states — all of the nineteenth century and most of this one. Through those years, the magnificent empire that Napoleon surrendered for fifteen million borrowed dollars has poured forth its bounty from generation to generation. And yet it is a young empire still, its resources barely scratched, its possibilities largely undeveloped, its promise as infinite as when Jefferson yearned to possess it for freedom's sake. That is one reason why so many modern pioneers of late have been packing up their families to leave behind the congestion and clamor and struggle of older and bigger communities to find happier times in the wide spaces between the Mississippi and the Continental Divide.

CHAPTER NOTES,
SOURCES,
APPENDIX,
AND INDEX

Chapter Notes

1

Phantom River

1. Cleve Hallenbeck, an able analyst of historical routes, wrote in his biography of Cabeza de Vaca (1940) that from Galveston Island the four wanderers reached and ascended the Colorado River of Texas to present Austin, dipped south to the San Antonio area, returned to the Colorado as far as Big Spring, crossed to the Pecos, the main tributary of the Rio Grande, and ascended it north to the Carlsbad-Mescalero Pass area of eastern New Mexico, then trudged south to El Paso, Texas, north again up the Rio Grande and west over the Continental Divide to the Gila River and on south from the southeast corner of Arizona to Compostela. These first Europeans in the American West followed popular Indian trails most of the time, setting the style for all those who came after them — trails that they could count on to provide facilities for survival, just as motorists today follow highways with gas stations and motels along the way.

2. The legend of the golden Seven Cities began long before Columbus and derived from the yearnings of Europeans for a happier place than where they were. During the Middle Ages, the Seven Cities were in "Antillia," an imaginary Catholic heaven in the Sea of Darkness. The name is echoed in the Antilles group of Caribbean islands. When John Cabot, the Genoese who grew up in Venice, explored for England in 1497, he sought the Seven Cities on land somewhere west of Ireland on his way to find Asia. He ran into Newfoundland instead. The Florentine Giovanni da Verrazano had the Seven Cities in mind as he explored the North Atlantic coast for France from Florida to Labrador in 1524. Herbert E. Bolton in his *Coronado* (1949) explains how the Spanish conquerors of Peru and Mexico placed the Seven Cities north of Mexico City in a valley called Cibola. This Cibola turned out to be the valley of the Zuni River south of Gallup, New Mexico. The Spaniards under Coronado found only six

331

"cities" — ordinary villages of the Pueblo Indians. One of them, Zuni, thirty miles south of Gallup, is as much alive today as it was in 1540. Eighteen miles further south is the ruin of Hawikuh, the city that Coronado saw first. The Spanish word *cibola* means "bison." The phrase "Plains of Cibola" applied in the old days not to the Seven Cities valley of the Zuni River but to the buffalo country of New Mexico, Texas, Oklahoma and Kansas.

3. The small bright stream that Coronado found in Palo Duro Canyon was formed by the junction of Palo Duro and Tierra Blanca creeks. It constitutes the main, the Prairie Dog Town, fork of the Red River, which flows east 1,360 miles, partly along the Texas-Oklahoma border, through the cities of Texarkana, Shreveport, Natchitoches and Alexandria — Indian villages in Coronado's day — to reach the Mississippi below Natchez. The other Red River, "of the North," only a third as long, is used as a boundary too, between Minnesota and North Dakota, and one would think that it was in the Mississippi drainage, since it starts a hundred miles south of the Mississippi's source at Lake Itasca. It isn't, though. It flows into Hudson Bay by way of Lake Winnipeg.

Coronado's Red River has always been a troublesome boundary because of its habit of changing course drastically during floods. Its name derives from the rich red color of the region's soil, as shown dramatically in the walls of Palo Duro Canyon, part of which forms the largest state park in Texas. The historic JA Ranch is in the same canyon, a huge spread founded in 1876 by the frontiersman Charles Goodnight and his backer, the Irish nobleman John Adair, whose relatives operate it still. Coronado named the canyon Palo Duro (hard wood) because of its cover of juniper and piñon. Perhaps he invented the name Llano Estacado (stockaded or palisaded plain) to apply to portions of eastern New Mexico and the Texas Panhandle because of the spectacular escarpment that he saw above him as his army approached this vast uplift from the Pecos River valley. Herbert E. Bolton feels that the American name of the area, Staked Plains, is an incorrect translation of the Spanish Llano Estacado. He calls the idea that Coronado staked out his Texas Panhandle route to keep from getting lost "an engaging folk tale."

The ultimate source of the Red River beyond its feeder streams at Palo Duro Canyon escaped discovery until 1852, when Captain Randolph B. Marcy tracked it down. Today, his route can be followed from Canyon, Texas, near Palo Duro by driving eighty miles west through the windmill ranchlands along the course of Tierra Blanca Creek, and then, at the crossroads of Bellville, just inside the New Mexico line, five miles south on a back road to a deserted village called Hollene. The village contains a forlorn cemetery, a ghostly dance hall, a false-front store with doors and windows gone, and a teetering gas pump — a perfect example of the thousands of western villages destroyed by changing times. In a field of the old Escadaba Ranch adjoining Hollene is a waterhole containing the rusty remains of a 1941 Ford. That is where the Red River is said to start.

4. The visit of de Soto has not been forgotten by the present inhabitants of Caddo Gap. The town is a pretty Deep South sort of place, full of magnolia and dogwood and dominated by a big square white house with a widow's walk on top. There is a statue of a Tula Indian chief, arm raised in a gesture of defiance. It was erected in 1936 by the De Soto Expedition Commission and its plaque asserts that Caddo Gap was indeed de Soto's western terminus. The mountains in the west rise two thousand feet above the gap and they look almost as impassable as the Continental Divide in Colorado. The gap is on the Caddo River, a hangout for bass, crappie and fishermen. Perhaps de Soto's men caught some fish as they retreated down it to winter on the Ouachita.

In contrast to Caddo Gap, Coronado's Quivira is as flat as a table — a high, dry region swept by strong winds. Tradition places the straw villages near Coronado Heights, a picnic spot above the delightful Swedish outpost of Lindsborg, Kansas. It is in the center of the Smoky Hill River wheat and sorghum belt and is totally Swedish, with Swedish craft shops, a Swedish Bowl, a Swennson Street, a Swedish Crown Smorgasbord Restaurant, a Svensk Hyllningsfest, a Svensk Conditori, a Birger Sandzen Gallery featuring the Swedish sculptor Carl Milles, and Swedish gables on the Swedish stone walls around the residences.

Not far from Lindsborg, in the Rice County courthouse at Lyons, carved figures are displayed representing Coronado's helmeted soldiers and skullcapped priests. One museum case contains "the Coronado Stone," twenty inches long and twelve inches wide, which a farmer claimed to have dug up in 1941; it bore the date, in Spanish, of August 3, 1541. Experts on artifacts do not take it seriously because somebody reported that he saw the farmer studying a Spanish dictionary in the local library just before the find. Also displayed at the courthouse are metal bits that Smithsonian archaeologists say could have been chain-mail links dropped by the Chosen Thirty. In 1965–1966, experts from the Smithsonian investigated thirty Rice County sites and identified them as remnants of Quiviran Basket Maker villages. The prehistoric Quivirans raised corn, used clay pots, and bore other resemblances to the Pueblo culture of the Upper Rio Grande. Near one site west of Lyons there is a monument to Father Juan de Padilla, who was with Coronado in Quivira. Padilla returned there a year later to start a mission and was killed by the Quivirans. Thereafter, the Indians had the kingdom pretty much to themselves until the 1860's, when settlers like the Lindsborg Swedes began to arrive.

5. Explorers underestimated the width of North America for ages, partly because of their incorrect, wishful interpretation of what the Indians tried to tell them about geography. In 1633, Captain Thomas followed Indian directions and sailed up the Delaware River expecting to come out on the Mediterranean Sea in four days. His hopes were dashed at the Delaware Water Gap. His Indian informant had directed him toward Lake Erie — no Mediterranean, to be sure, but still a considerable sea of ten thousand square miles. Originally, the Strait of Anian and the Northwest Passage were the same myth — until the Spanish moved the strait's supposed location southward nearer the latitudes of the gulfs of Mexico and California. The idea of the Northwest Passage to northern Asia began at least as early as 1500 when the Portuguese Gaspar Corte-Real entered Davis Strait east of Hudson Bay and south of Baffin Bay. Thereafter, Northwest Passage searchers pushed further and further into arctic waters. Actual proof that Asia and North America were separate continents came in 1741, when the Dane Vitus Bering, probing eastward from Russia, discovered Bering Strait between the Chukchi Peninsula and Alaska. But none of the thousands of Northwest Passage searchers probing westward made it as far as Bering Strait until 1903–1906 when the Norwegian Roald Amundsen got through from Baffin Bay in a tiny sloop, the *Gjoa*. Practically, this Northwest Passage remains unconquered. In the summer of 1969, Standard Oil paid $40,000,000 to send the 115,000-ton icebreaking tanker *Manhattan* from Davis Strait through Lancaster Sound and Melville Sound to the North Slope oil fields of Alaska. In the eighty-day, 11,000-mile trip, the huge ship had all kinds of trouble and an extended debate began on whether the voyage had proved anything.

6. Today, the highway from Nicolet's Baie des Puans (Green Bay) ascends the enchanting Fox River valley past Lake Winnebago and Muir Memorial Park through a rolling fertile land dotted with huge dairy barns. Just short of the town of Portage,

Wisconsin, a little park marks the source of the Fox. An abandoned canal runs on to the Wisconsin River at Portage. The canal covers the mile or so over which Indians and Canadian *voyageurs* carried their birch-bark canoes from the St. Lawrence to the Mississippi watershed.

A note on fur-trade terms: Nicolet was a *coureur de bois*, a French-Canadian businessman who wandered far into the wilds to exchange his wares for the beaver of the Indians, often without buying a license from the king's bureaucrats in Quebec. His employees, the men who handled his canoes and gear, were his *voyageurs*, a word which refers also to French travelers by water in general.

7. The Canadian village of Trois Rivières was founded by Champlain in 1634 at the junction of the St. Lawrence and two channels of the St. Maurice. It produced many French explorers but it is just another ugly factory town today, wrapped in the choking vapors of its paper mills.

8. The three-hundredth anniversary of the issuance of the Hudson's Bay Company's charter to Prince Rupert and his friends occurred on May 2, 1970. Rupert would have been pleased if he could have foreseen the future of his little log trading post on James Bay, an arm of Hudson Bay. In 1970, the great company known universally in Canada as "the Bay" reported annual sales of better than half a billion dollars. Writing at the time of its tercentenary, D'Arcy O'Connor explained in the *Wall Street Journal* how the eighteen original "true and absolute Lordes and Proprietors" were granted a monopoly by Charles II for the exploitation of what came to one and a half million square miles of Hudson Bay drainage. The Bay firm expanded its monopoly beyond the drainage and over the Continental Divide to the Pacific by the time of its famous merger in 1821 with its Montreal rival, the North West Company. In 1869, most of the Bay's land was taken over by the Canadian government and the Bay went into other fields, including oil, wholesale tobacco, and retail stores serving Indians and Eskimos in remote places. But it has not abandoned its original fur trading from its 137 posts spread through the Far North. In concluding his article, O'Connor wrote that Queen Elizabeth visited the Bay's Winnipeg headquarters in 1970 and collected the sovereign rent from the company "as stipulated in its 300-year charter. The rent: two elk and two black beavers."

Incidentally, Hudson Bay is not as far from England as one might suppose. Its main port, Churchill, is nearer Liverpool than New York is.

2

The Mist Rises — a Little

1. I am summarizing here several paragraphs on the office of *intendant* in France during the seventeenth and eighteenth centuries that begin on page 124 of Walter D. Edmonds's *The Musket and the Cross* (1968).

2. There were five semisedentary allied tribes of Iroquois — Mohawks, Oneidas, Onondagas, Cayugas and Senecas. They comprised two thousand warriors at most,

living in farming villages mostly along the Mohawk River south of Lake Ontario in central New York. After they began to get guns from Dutch traders at Fort Orange on the Hudson in the 1630's, they became the most powerful and belligerent of eastern Indians. During the next twenty years, they shot or cut to pieces or burned or ate or scattered members of four other Iroquoian tribes — Eries and Neutrals around Lake Erie; Hurons and Tionontati in the Ottawa-Ontario area west of Montreal. They caught and killed numbers of individual French villagers whom they caught off guard in the woods and they murdered several Jesuit missionaries working among them. But they had an aversion to eating Europeans, believing that their flesh would be unappetizing because they ate so much salt. The Iroquois were consistently pro-English and anti-French in war and in the fur trade for more than a century after their Ticonderoga battle with Champlain and his Indian allies in 1609. They blocked many French efforts to occupy the Ohio country and were always a threat even on the Upper Mississippi. But their numbers were reduced by their own constant warfare and psychopathic desire to dominate. Their League of the Iroquois ceased to terrorize the East by the time of the American Revolution.

3. French Catholics in La Salle's youth were divided in two parties. The "Gallican" Catholics (Rouen was predominantly Gallican) gave the French monarch semidivine authority, denied the pope temporal power and restricted his religious authority. The "ultramontane" or "papal" Catholics adhered to the medieval tradition that the pope had the last word in all things.

4. A prime purpose of the Society of Jesus from the 1550's on was to combat Protestant heretics by the militant strengthening of Catholicism and the power of the pope in Europe, Asia, Africa and the Americas. Jesuit priests, who first appeared on the St. Lawrence in 1625, were inspired by the spectacular success of their order in the vast South American territory of Spanish Paraguay, where a handful of Jesuits ruled absolutely over 114,000 Indians in fifty-seven villages. The Canadian Jesuits dreamed of creating a similar theocracy but were thwarted by the militancy of the Iroquois, the advent of royal government with the growth of the fur trade, and the coming of rivals such as the Recollets (Franciscans) and the Sulpicians.

5. While in the West Indies, Columbus found the word *canaoa* (boat) in common use and he may have noticed its curious resemblance to the French *canot*. The birch-bark canoe was developed by Indians in the northern birch zone of North America. This graceful craft solved the problem of travel on the St. Lawrence and the Great Lakes, and it was a great factor in the rapid advance of the French from the Atlantic inland to their Mississippi empire from the north while the English were stalled behind the Appalachians and the Spanish were checked by the stormy Gulf of Mexico. All through the seventeenth century and later, the birch-bark canoe was by far the best means of wilderness travel. On the Mississippi drainage south of the birch zone, water travel was hampered by the labor of building rafts or hollowing out logs by burning to make the heavy, clumsy dugout canoes. Horses were useless overland because they could not get through the thick woods and marshes of the East or over the mountains until trails were improved in the eighteenth century. Out west, Indians in the Rockies began using Spanish horses from the Upper Rio Grande around 1680. Horses were the perfect mode of transport for the western environment but they did not bring a new and better way of life to the Plains Indians until the middle 1700's.

6. Jolliet's exploration of Lake Erie in 1669 completed the discovery by Frenchmen of all the Great Lakes. Talon's deputy, Simon François Daumont, sieur de Saint-

Lusson, appeared at Sault Ste. Marie on June 14, 1671, and took possession, in the name of Louis XIV, of those Great Lakes "bounded on the one side by the seas of the North and of the West, and on the other by the South Sea." Saint-Lusson's party totaled fifteen Frenchmen, including Jolliet. Delegates from fourteen Indian tribes witnessed the elaborate ceremony.

7. October is the month of months to enjoy the Marquette country by car — one of the nation's most beautiful regions. Minneapolis is a good starting point. A highway runs from there up the wide, pulsing St. Croix River through the vivid woods to Taylor Falls and across to Lake Court Oreilles where the Chippewas treated their French gods, Radisson and Groseilliers, so reverently, and on to Chequamegon Bay on Lake Superior at Ashland. The site of Father Allouez's St. Esprit is near there and so is the marker showing where Radisson's little fort with its burglar alarm of bells stood. The eastering road follows the deep blue immensity of Lake Superior through the restful town of Marquette to Sault Ste. Marie, still the hub of the northern lake area. Huge locks control the rapids connecting Lake Superior and Lake Huron and in the locks one finds enormous freighters loaded with Lake Superior lumber bound for foreign ports. Marquette's grave is at St. Ignace southward from Sault Ste. Marie. Near St. Ignace is Mackinac Island and its marvelous relics of a century of Anglo-French struggle to own that part of the world. From St. Ignace, the highway crosses the five-mile Straits of Mackinac Bridge and runs along Lake Michigan to Frankfort, where big auto ferries make it over to Green Bay in three hours. Michigan is a very big lake and it is usually riled up with whitecaps and big blue waves. Looking at the waves, one understands why Marquette and other canoeists kept close to shore in case of a storm.

8. Of the meaning of the calumet, Father Hennepin wrote in his *Description de la Louisiane* (1683): "Such a pipe is a safe conduct amongst all the allies of the nation who has given it; and in all embassies the calumet is carried as a symbol of peace, the savages being generally persuaded that some great misfortune would befall them if they should violate the public faith of the calumet."

3

The Paths of Glory . . .

1. It was the settler Charles Hoag who coined the word "Minnehapolis" in 1852 by combining *minnehaha*, the Sioux word for "laughing water," with the Greek *polis* (city). The *h* disappeared soon. What is now Hennepin Avenue Bridge began in 1854 as a graceful suspension bridge from the west shore of the river to Nicollet Island, where it joined a span between the island and the east bank. The two bridges formed the first of all Mississippi crossings. Though Hennepin's sixteen-and-a-half-foot Falls of St. Anthony (he made them fifty feet high) had none of the majesty of his other scenic wonder, Niagara Falls, they were the only falls anywhere on the Mississippi.

I have purloined these facts practically word for word from Lucille M. Kane's excellent book *The Waterfall That Built a City* (St. Paul, 1966). It explains how the falls began to turn gristmills and sawmills for Fort Snelling soldiers as early as 1821. After 1857, they became the power basis for the huge lumber and milling industries in Minneapolis. The falls tumbled over a limestone sheath that began to disintegrate under the higher pressures that were created for the waterwheels. In 1869, the falls seemed to be going out and so the limestone sheath was protected by the kind of overlying apron that conceals them today. After 1890, hydroelectric power began to replace waterwheel power, a process that was completed in 1960, when the last waterwheel stopped turning.

2. Hennepin's name, Lac des Pleurs, did not survive. Duluth had two brothers Pepin in his party and their name came to be applied soon to Lake Pepin.

3. On the whole, Hennepin's views of American Indians were more tolerant than those of many white critics who followed him. These critics have tended to ignore the fact that every shocking practice of the "savage" red man has its parallel — often in a more extreme form — in the practices of "civilized" white men, up to and including polygamy, absurd pomp, theft, cannibalism, scalping, human sacrifice, mass murder and fornicating in public.

4. Among other Hennepin memorials in Minnesota there are two at Mille Lacs, namely, Father Hennepin State Memorial Wayside Park, and a second Hennepin Island. And we noticed Hennepin Street when we stopped at Little Falls some hundred miles up the river from the Falls of St. Anthony to visit Charles A. Lindbergh State Park and the charming clapboard house where the flyer grew up.

But Daniel Greysolon has received some belated recognition of late. Way back in 1928, the will of Albert L. Ordean of Duluth left a sum that eventually accrued to $77,000 for the purchase of a "fine artistic statue of Sieur Du Lhut." The commission went to the controversial cubist sculptor Jacques Lipchitz. His non-cubist bronze figure of Duluth wearing an Indian jacket, plumed hat and long curls was unveiled on November 5, 1965, at the Duluth campus of the University of Minnesota. Lipchitz's symbolic presentation was called "grotesque" and worse by some critics at the time. But my expert informant, James Taylor Dunne, chief librarian of the Minnesota Historical Society in St. Paul, reports that "affection for the statue has replaced the original dislike." Partly as a result of the statue furore, Mr. Dunne went to France and visited the lovely Loire valley village of Saint-Germain-Laval, where Duluth was born, just west of Lyons and south of Roanne. With the help of Dr. A. Boel of Roanne, Mr. Dunne found much new data on Duluth's life, including his family background, a Duluth portrait, and the date of his birth, 1636. His paper on the subject is on file at the St. Louis County Historical Society in Duluth.

5. That name, La Fleuve Colbert, was about to expire, like the great Jean-Baptiste Colbert himself (he died in 1683). Though his fiscal policies, his expansion of the royal navy and merchant marine, and his promotion of modern industry were the making of Louis XIV, he found his counsels ignored in the end. But he had the satisfaction of seeing his son, the marquis de Seignelay, replace him as minister of marine and of colonies.

6. The garden suburb of Metairie in western New Orleans bears the name of Jacques de la Metairie, La Salle's notary public at Fort Frontenac. La Salle had brought him along as legal witness to his Mississippi discoveries. The naming of English Turn will be explained in due course.

7. A delicious compulsion can seize the traveler following the trail of a great explorer like La Salle. His discovery trail of 1682 can be picked up on the Illinois river at the small town of Utica, where his big Indian village stood. Starved Rock State Park, site of his second fort, is just across the river. Downstream below Peoria is the forlorn site of Fort Crèvecoeur with its stairway of two hundred and three steps on the woody left bank above the railroad tracks. The stone marker at Crèvecoeur bears this inscription:

In
1680
Upon This Spot Stood Fort Crèvecoeur
Built from the Plans of Robert
de la Salle. Here was centered the
Hope of Louis XIV
for a broader empire of the French
on American Soil
From here in 1680 went forth
La Salle on his heroic march of
1500 miles to Fort Frontenac
and in 1682 also from here
to the great task of the
Exploration of the Mississippi
River

Below Crèvecoeur near the junction of the Illinois and the Mississippi is Pere Marquette State Park, a pleasant place full of croquet players and sailboaters with a McAdams Peak overlook from which one can see the creamy striated bluffs on the west side of the big river. Lewis and Clark Park is on the river's edge just south of the uproar and ugliness of Alton, Illinois. At this park in spring one can watch the Missouri pouring mud and trees into the Mississippi just as Marquette and La Salle found it to be doing. Continuing south for nearly a thousand miles on roads paralleling the Mississippi, the traveler passes the incoming Ohio; La Salle's Fort Prudhomme on its Third Chickasaw Bluff short of Memphis; Clarksdale, Mississippi, where de Soto crossed the river; and the mouths of the Arkansas and Red rivers. Below the crescent of New Orleans, the Mississippi delta road ends in misty flats a few miles above Head of Passes not far from the spot where La Salle is presumed to have read his proclamation. The spot is marked by a rather handsome white-spired monument to La Salle erected in 1967 by Plaquemine Parish.

4

. . . Lead But to the Grave

1. The idea of seizing the Santa Barbara mines from a Mississippi base was a wild one. We know now that these mines were high in the Sierra Madre Occidental at the headwaters of Conchos River in Chihuahua Province, at least two thousand

miles by land and water from the mouth of the Mississippi. On today's highways, Santa Barbara is eight hundred and fifty miles from the mouth of the Rio Grande at Brownsville, Texas, by way of Saltillo and Monterrey.

2. Of La Salle's hopes for La Rivière aux Boeufs, Henri Joutel wrote in his journal words that appeared in English as "Perceiving that the water of the River where we were roul'd down violently into the Sea, he fancy'd that it might be one of the Branches of the Mississippi and propos'd to go up it, to see whether he could find any Tokens of it, or the Marks he had left, when he went down by Land to the Mouth of it."

3. On an esplanade of Washington Avenue in the cotton plantation town of Navasota, Texas, stands a bronze statue of La Salle by Frank Teich as he may have looked at the age of forty-three just before his murder in the Navasota area.

4. Some historians believe that in December of 1684 La Salle deliberately led his three ships past the mouth of the Mississippi, knowing that it *was* the Mississippi, because he was more concerned with getting closer to the Rio Grande on the Texas coast so that he could launch an attack on the Santa Barbara mines. In his *Franco-Spanish Rivalry in North America*, Henry Folmer has written, "Had he remained faithful to his original plan of founding a colony on the Mississippi, La Salle would probably not have ended his life in tragic failure. The colonial rivalry between his country and Spain ensnared La Salle into an adventure of conquest that was no longer suited to his times." I find nothing in the voluminous record of La Salle's career to justify even a suspicion that there was such a mine-seizing priority in his mind. It seems much more likely that La Salle failed because he and Beaujeu mistook the mouth of the Mississippi for Apalachicola Bay. When La Salle realized at Matagorda Bay that he had missed the mouth that he had found in 1682, Beaujeu claimed that it was too late for him to go back hunting for it. The long delay, Beaujeu said, had run his *Le Joly* short of the supplies needed to return to civilization. As it turned out, Beaujeu seems to have steered *Le Joly* enough out of her homeward way to identify the lost mouth in passing.

La Salle's interest in the Santa Barbara mines was an expedient interest, fitting the king's preoccupation with mineral wealth. Probably La Salle meant to do something about seizing Mexican mines later, if all went well with the Mississippi colony in the Baton Rouge area.

It should be noted that the remarkably thorough documentation of the La Salle period derives chiefly from the long and patient toil of Pierre Margry, the curator of archives for the ministry of marine and colonies in Paris. In 1842, Margry began copying out in his own cramped hand official correspondence pertaining to affairs in La Nouvelle-France. Francis Parkman did research in Paris in 1869 and 1872 and became fascinated with this material, which Margry guarded rather carefully at first. In *The Journals of Francis Parkman*, Mason Wade, the editor, has written, "Parkman's acquaintance with Margry had ripened into friendship through correspondence, and the latter produced a long birthday ode in honor of the American historian who had hymned 'les beaux actes de notre histoire.'" But Margry was still unwilling to let Parkman use his La Salle collection; and Parkman found that many essential documents had been withdrawn from the archives by the collector-curator. The best that Parkman could obtain from Margry was authorization to offer the rights of publication to the former's Boston publishers. But when Parkman returned home, he found Boston in flames; and since the business section of the city was nearly wiped out by the great fire of November 17, no Boston firm was inclined to undertake what at best would be a bit of philanthropic publishing. Parkman went to work creating a lobby for a congressional appropriation for the publication of Margry's documents, with the help of O. H. Marshall and Charles Whittlesey. Eventually, the lobby included Senator George Frisbie Hoar, General James Garfield and William Dean Howells. Its efforts were crowned with success and in 1878 the first three volumes of *Découvertes et établissements des Français* were published. (See the Sources for Chapter 4.)

5

Iberville's Mardi Gras

1. In his memoir of this trip Tonty gives the year as 1685 but it took place actually in 1686. Tonty, usually a cautious fellow, proposed on this trip to return to Montreal from the mouth of the Mississippi by hiking overland three thousand miles around the north shore of the Gulf of Mexico and up the Atlantic coast to New York, and on up the Hudson River and across Lake Champlain to the St. Lawrence. He would have done it, too, but his men refused to hike with him so they all returned to Starved Rock by canoe up the Mississippi.

2. The site of this earliest mission, San Francisco de los Tejas, is reached by driving seven miles south of Weches on state route 21, and then one mile west on a dirt road.

3. The modern approximation of Captain de León's El Camino Real runs from Mexico City through San Luis Potosí, Saltillo, and Monclova into Texas at Eagle Pass (San Juan Bautista) and on through San Antonio, Austin, Bryan, Crockett, Nacogdoches and St. Augustine to Los Adais Historical Park and Natchitoches, Louisiana.

4. If Duluth had had his choice, he would have stayed out there in the cool, clear beauty of the Lake Superior wilds to the end of his days, but the gout got him in 1697 and he had to spend a miserable and luxurious old age in Montreal, where he died on February 21, 1710. The trader Jacques de Noyon is said to have wintered at Rainy Lake in 1688 and to have got along to Lake of the Woods a year later in his search for a Northwest Passage. But the portages were so complex and difficult that no European tried it again for a generation. A modern account of this historic canoe route is presented in *Portage into the Past* by J. Arnold Bolz (1960).

5. *La crosse* was the name French traders and priests gave to the Iroquois game of *baggataway* because the racquet used to throw the ball resembled a bishop's staff, or crozier. By Perrot's time, the game was being played as far west as the Mississippi. The sort of Indian entertainment lavished on Perrot and on Radisson and Hennepin before him, was practiced by many tribes right up through the nineteenth century. A

typical case was the treatment of the baron de Lahontan by three Green Bay tribes in the 1680's. Lahontan described what happened:

They began with congratulating my arrival, and after I had return'd them thanks, fell a singing and dancing one after another, in a particular manner, of which you may expect a circumstantial account when I have more leisure. The Singing and Dancing lasted for two hours, being seasoned with Acclamations of Joy and Jests, which make up part of their ridiculous Musick. After that the Slaves came to serve, and all the Company sat down after the Eastern fashion, every one being provided with his Mess, just as our Monks are in the Monastery-Halls. First of all four Platters were set down before me in the first of which there were two white Fish only boil'd in Water; in the second, the Tongue and Breast of a Roe-buck boil'd; in the third two Woodhens, the hind Feet or Trotters of a Bear, and the Tail of a Beaver, all roasted; and the fourth contain'd a large quantity of Broth made of several sorts of Meat. For Drink they gave me a very pleasant Liquor, which was nothing but a Syrrup of Maple beat up with Water. The Feast lasted two Hours; after which I intreated one of the Grandees to sing for me; for in all the Ceremonies made use of among the Savages, 'tis customary to employ another to act for 'em. . . . Next day and the day after, I was oblig'd to go to the Feasts of the other two Nations, who observ'd the same Formalities.

6. Some Frenchmen used their religion as a weapon in King William's War. Francis Parkman told how Jesuit priests in the Acadia region converted the Abenaki Indians to Catholicism and then fired them up for battle against the English by assuring them "that Jesus Christ was a Frenchman, and his mother, the Virgin, a French lady; that the English had murdered him, and that the best way to gain his favor was to revenge his death."

7. Only two of the three major and many minor passes carrying the Mississippi ten miles or so from Head of Passes into the Gulf of Mexico are used today by seagoing ships. Pilottown near Head of Passes is a sandbar settlement on stilts with two camps, one for bar pilots taking ships into the gulf, and one for river pilots taking them upstream to New Orleans and Baton Rouge. Louisiana State has a wildlife station on Iberville's Pass a Loutre. Hodding Carter, in *Lower Mississippi* has told how the shallow depth of even the largest passes, South and Southwest, were dangerous for ocean craft through much of the nineteenth century. There seemed to be no way to deepen the channels until 1879, when Captain James B. Eads designed and built jetties of willow, piling and stone that produced a thirty-foot-deep channel through South Pass. The Eads method was used later on Southwest Pass so that Texas-bound ships could get through that channel safely. The Eads jetties still keep the depth of the channels at thirty feet as compared to the twelve-foot depth of Iberville's time.

8. Dr. Coxe had very large ideas, though he could not have known fully how large they were. He had bought recently a royal grant issued by Charles I in 1627 to Sir Robert Heath, giving him possession of the Carolina coast from 31° to 36° north latitude — Savannah, Georgia, say, north almost to Winston-Salem, North Carolina — and extending westward to the Pacific. The grant was called "Carolana" and Coxe sent a Colonel Welch to explore it overland from the Carolinas in 1698. Welch claimed to have followed English trade routes across the lower Appalachians through the Chickasaw country to the Mississippi near the mouth of the Arkansas.

9. Bénard de La Harpe, the French explorer, had another idea of what occurred at English Turn when he wrote of the incident twenty years later. As La Harpe got it, "Captain Ben" (Banks) asked Bienville if this river was the Mississippi. Bienville

replied that it was a different stream entirely, so Captain Ben turned his boat around and departed to find the real thing. La Harpe wrote also that one of "Captain Ben's" Huguenots proposed privately to Bienville that he would bring four hundred families of Carolina Huguenots to colonize Louisiana as repatriated Frenchmen if Louis XIV would permit it. Bienville sent the proposal to Versailles. The king's reply was a flat "No." He had a genius for missing golden opportunities where Louisiana was concerned.

10. The dates of these expeditionary sailings to and from Louisiana were as follows: Iberville's second fleet, consisting of the new forty-six-gun frigate *Renommée* and the cargo boat *Gironde*, left La Rochelle on October 17, 1699, and anchored in Biloxi Bay on January 8, 1700. Iberville set sail May 28, 1700, on the return voyage, arriving in France in August, 1700. The *Renommée* was used again on his third and last expedition (with the *Palmier*), which reached Pensacola harbor in December, 1701. Iberville arrived at Mobile Bay in February, 1702, left for France on March 31, and was back at La Rochelle in mid-June, 1702.

6

Chaos in Paradise

1. In his book *The Minnesota*, Evan Jones reports that no trace of Le Sueur's Fort L'Huillier remains near the Blue Earth–Minnesota junction. However, in 1907, a nearby farmer, William Mitchell, dug up seventeen headless skeletons on his place. Local historians believe that they are the bones of Sioux Indians killed by a band of Foxes who were jealous of their trading activities with Le Sueur. The explorer's name is immortalized by Le Sueur County below Mankato and by Le Sueur town where the Mayo Clinic brothers originated. The town of St. Peter near Le Sueur was so named because the Minnesota was once called the St. Peter — Le Sueur's La Rivière St. Pierre.

7

Noble Swindler

1. L'Acadie, or Acadia — meaning "fertile land" in Micmac — was the French name for the large region that the English called Nova Scotia in 1621. Through the seventeenth century the French and English struggled to possess L'Acadie — a land which then included part of the Penobscot Bay area and present New Brunswick. The Treaty of Utrecht gave to England what now constitutes Nova Scotia — the former L'Acadie less New Brunswick across the Bay of Fundy north of it and the Penobscot Bay region to the west. By the treaty's terms, France retained Cape Breton Island. This provision gave French Canada and its St. Lawrence settlements some, but not enough protection against English naval attacks.

2. Commander St. Denis was still at Natchitoches, and still smuggling discreetly, when he died in 1744. He is well remembered by the languid, wisteria-perfumed town that he created, a beautiful French-feeling place with fine old homes, some dating from Louisiana Purchase days, and galleries of "iron lace" along Front Street above the grassy banks of the Cane River, which is a sort of overflow channel of Red River. Natchitoches is pronounced "Nak-it-tish" — sometimes "Nak-uh-tush." A plaque on McClung's Drug Store off St. Denis Street is marked "Saint Denis Tomb." The plaque explains that the Chevalier Louis Juchereau de Saint-Denis was born in Quebec on September 17, 1767, and died at Natchitoches on June 11, 1744 — "A gallant soldier of France, explorer of Louisiana, and trader with the Indians, founder of Natchitoches in 1714, commandant of the Poste de Natchitoches 1720 to 1744." The tree-shaded site of his Fort St. Jean-Baptiste is on Jefferson Street. A boulder on the Northwestern State College campus marks the spot where St. Denis's home stood.

Spain's frontier outpost, Los Adais, that St. Denis knew so well, can be reached from Natchitoches by driving fifteen miles west almost to Robeline — actually a segment on the old El Camino Real to the Rio Grande and Mexico City. Near Robeline, one turns right on a little back road of red gravel (route 485) half a mile to a cleared knoll among very tall pines full of screaming blue jays. The Presidio de Nuestra Señora del Pilar de los Adais was built on the knoll in 1721 to protect the nearby San Miguel de Linares mission from the Indians and the French. From this Spanish frontier bastion one can continue west thirty-five miles to the Sabine River. The Sabine, a narrow twisting channel in a wide bottomland, would become the boundary between the United States and Spanish Texas.

3. Sometime when you are in Paris and bored with the ordinary tourist fare, take a stroll from the Place Vendôme, where John Law's mansion stood, eastward down the rue de Rivoli past the Louvre on the way to the Bastille, where the outspoken Cadillac spent some unhappy days for telling the truth about Louisiana. Half a mile beyond the Louvre you reach the handsome Gothic Tour Saint-Jacques and here you turn north (left) and walk up the Boulevard de Sébastopol a couple of blocks to the rue des Lombards, which is called, like its London namesake, after the Lombard usurpers who operated here. Just around the corner off the rue des Lombards is the rue Quincampoix, looking today just as full of cutthroats as it must have looked when Law's Banque générale was the short street's main building. In his *Eighteenth-Century France*, Frederick C. Green has given us a classic picture of the rue Quincampoix in 1719:

Imagine the scene in this narrow malodorous thoroughfare on a broiling July day. Penned in between the chains which are stretched across either end of "la rue" is a screaming, sweating throng in which every rank is represented. The brokers of kings huckster with powerful porters from the markets who by sheer brute force have succeeded in fighting their way into the offices of the company and have run panting from the rue Vivienne to dispose of stock. An enterprising hunchback lends his hump as a desk and makes a fortune of a hundred and fifty thousand *livres* in this strange fashion. The proprietors of houses in the street let their rooms for what they care to ask, and a poor cobbler who for years had plied his craft in a flimsy little shack finds wealth overnight by the simple expedient of fitting it up as an office. The adjacent restaurants are packed with fashionables, some amusedly watching the scene, others issuing orders to their perspiring brokers. Scullions become "carriage folk" and coachmen ride inside their own equipages. One *nouveau riche* absentmindedly jumps up behind his own coach and to his astonished servant explains angrily that he is just seeing whether the carriage will bear another postilion. All over the country vehicles of every sort are booked up for months ahead, for all France is moving towards "the street."

4. In translation Law's epitaph reads:

Here lies that famous Scot,
A peerless mathematician
Who, by the rules of algebra,
Sent France to the poorhouse.

8

The Frustrations of Bienville

1. Two students of Bourgmond, Henry Folmer and Gilbert J. Garrahan, S.J., have agreed that Fort Orléans was built in the broad, fertile bottomland of the Missouri five or six miles south of the present railroad town of Carrollton. Folmer puts it "near present Cranberry Island, close to the village of the Missouris." Father Garrahan puts it "above the mouth of Wakenda Creek on the north bank of an island opposite the Missouri village." Carrollton is on U.S. 24, seventy-five miles east of Kansas City.

2. Poor Sergeant Dubois! In her marriage contract, the practical Daughter of the Sun inserted a clause giving her the right to have her husband beheaded if he failed to meet her specifications in the performance of his conjugal duties. Back home on the Mississippi, after a reasonable test period, she concluded that he had indeed failed, and that was the end of Sergeant Dubois.

3. This "Côte des Allemands" began in 1719–1722 with a German settlement on the west bank of the Mississippi at Lucy, near present Edgard. From there it extended gradually up and down the river and on both sides of it in what are now St. Charles and St. James Parishes from Hahnville to Donaldsville. German names are numerous in the white-tombed cemeteries scattered among the fields of sugarcane bordering the river.

9

Approach to the Rockies

1. In an article based on the Mallet brothers' journal in *The Colorado Magazine* (September, 1939), Henry Folmer gave the names of the eight explorers who left the mouth of the Niobrara on May 20, 1739, as Pierre and Paul Mallet, Michel Beslot,

Joseph Bellecourt, Manuel Gallien, Philippe Robitaille and Louis Morin (all described as "creoles of Canada") and Jean David "of Europe." Folmer deduced that the eight rode south to reach the Platte River near Loup Fork on June 2, the Big Blue River near Osceola, Nebraska, on June 14, the Republican River between Superior and Red Cloud on June 17, the north fork of the Solomon River near Harlan, Kansas, on June 19, and the Solomon's south fork (near Stockton where they lost seven horses) on June 20. They continued southwest across the plains of western Kansas to the Saline River west of Hays on June 22, the Smoky Hill River on June 24, and Walnut Creek near Ness City. They reached the Arkansas River near present Garden City, Kansas, on June 30 — a point seventy miles upstream from Coronado's crossing of the Arkansas near Ford, Kansas, in 1541. The Mallets' route on up the Arkansas and then south over Raton Pass would become the mountain division of the Santa Fe Trail in the 1820's. The distance they traveled from the Niobrara to Santa Fe was around seven hundred and fifty miles.

Folmer's English translation of part of Bienville's report on the Mallets that he sent to Versailles, dated April 30, 1741, reads, with bracketed editorial notes:

Monsieur: Last March arrived here four Canadians returning from Santa Fe, capital of the New Kingdom of Mexico, where they had been by way of land, without having informed anyone of their plan. We have been as much surprised as pleased by this discovery which might become a very important factor for the colony. The Company of the Indies has made heavy expenses in order to find out about the Spanish territories. It had a fort constructed on the Missouri [Fort Orléans] where it had fifty men in garrison and the company counted on this to make an important trading post of it. It procured honors and rewards for M. de Bourgmont who had undertaken this discovery [of a Santa Fe route] and who failed, as several others have failed before him. The strangest aspect of it is that M. de la Harpe, who undertook the discovery by way of Red River and the Arkansas did not succeed any better. It seems nevertheless, from the [Mallet] journal that a branch of this river [the Canadian] flows from the Spanish territories and that one can ascend this river as far as a distance of forty leagues [one hundred and ten miles] from Santa Fe. It is even probable that there are other branches which come even nearer [the source of the Conchas River branch is only seventy miles from Santa Fe]. It is true that this trade will offer great difficulties because of the distance; nevertheless, when it will be possible to go by water it will not be more difficult to send a convoy there every year when the waters are high than it is to go to Illinois.

2. In September, 1721, the French Jesuit scholar, Pierre François-Xavier de Charlevoix, arrived in Quebec to collect all available data about La Nouvelle-France. Most of these facts and rumors could have been obtained from experts on the scene like Governor Bienville but the Versailles bureaucrats, including the comte de Toulouse, who sponsored Charlevoix's fact-finding trip, distrusted their colonial officials and felt that their reports might cover up skulduggery. In the spring of 1721, Charlevoix began a long tour, which included Montreal, Fort Detroit, Michilimackinac, Green Bay, Kaskaskia, Natchez, New Orleans and Biloxi. At its end, he tended to accept the baron de Lahontan's fictional Long River and prevailing fantasies about the River of the West and the Western Sea. He accepted also the notion that the Mississippi, Missouri, Minnesota and Red rivers began in the same height of land. But on the whole, his *Histoire et description générale de la Nouvelle-France* was a fine piece of work and vividly written. Charlevoix created the phrase "The Missouri seems to enter the Mississippi like a Conqueror," which is just about right.

3. The site of this large Fort St. Charles, lost for a century and more, was found and excavated in 1908 by historians and Jesuit priests from the Winnipeg

suburb of St. Boniface. Bones unearthed from the site of the fort's chapel are believed to be those of Jean-Baptiste de La Vérendrye and others in his party, who were massacred by the Sioux in 1736. The fort's site is on Magnusson Island in the remote Northwest Angle State Forest of Minnesota near a wilderness village called Penasse, the most northerly point in the United States excepting Alaska. The island used to be mainland until the water level of the Lake of the Woods was raised in modern times. There are no roads to Penasse. It is a trip of fifty miles or so from Warroad, Minnesota, across the Lake of the Woods, by boat in summer, by dog sled or wind sled in winter. It can be reached also from Rainy River at Baudette, Minnesota — a somewhat longer boat trip.

4. La Vérendrye's departure from Fort La Reine for the Mandan villages was the fifth time that a major European party approached the Louisiana heartland by back doors, so to speak, instead of taking boats directly up the Mississippi from the Gulf of Mexico. Coronado's Chosen Thirty went into central Kansas on horseback from the Upper Rio Grande, de Soto from Florida and northern Mississippi. The Marquette and La Salle canoe parties entered from Lake Michigan.

5. In *The Course of Empire*, Bernard De Voto traced the rumor of white-skinned, blue-eyed Mandan Indians back to a "wholly fictitious English pamphlet" published in 1583 to support English claims to North America against those of Spain. The pamphlet asserted that the New World was not discovered by Columbus in 1492 but by a Welsh prince named Madoc, who planted three thousand Welsh colonists somewhere in the land in 1170. These colonists bred with the Indians and gave Welsh words to Indian tongues but retained their whiter skins during migrations westward which, the pamphlet explained, resulted in the Ohio Mound Builders civilization and that of the Aztecs and Mayans in Mexico. From this basis, the fable was improved through the years. The Ohio Welsh Indians lost a great battle near the Falls of the Ohio, and fled to and up the Missouri leaving a trail of artifacts — Welsh mounds, Welsh-smelted metal, Welsh-style pottery. When the English began looking covetously westward across the Mississippi, they improved their fable again. The Pawnee Indians, or the Padoucas, the rightful owners of French Louisiana, were surely Welshmen. When French traders reported that the Pawnees and Padoucas were not white-skinned enough, the English fabulists moved their expatriate Britishers further up the Missouri, and so they became Mandans. Though the La Vérendryes noticed a few Mandans with light skins, blue eyes and blond hair, they attributed it simply to variations from the norm common to all Indians. Most Welshmen, De Voto pointed out, are not blond and blue-eyed anyway, but black-haired and dark-eyed.

6. The Missouri is notorious for changing its channel. It is quite possible that it trended southwesterly from the Mandan village when Louis-Joseph put his compass on it in 1738. According to his astrolabe, the village's latitude (Bismarck) was 48° 12″ — which is about the actual latitude of Minot, North Dakota, one hundred miles north. Bismarck's latitude is 46° 48″.

7. Before Louis-Joseph discovered the Saskatchewan, many French Canadians believed that the river was an outlet of Lake Winnipeg and that it flowed west to the Pacific as a Strait of Anian or an arm of the Western Sea. The belief derived from Cree descriptions of how the Saskatchewan freezes and thaws in early spring. In thawing, the water sometimes spreads over the top of the ice far beyond the river

banks, creating a sea-like appearance even to movements resembling a tidal ebb and flow. And when the water backs up behind blocks of ice, it actually runs west.

8. In 1741, when the younger Pierre de La Vérendrye returned to Fort La Reine from a brief visit to the Mandans, he brought with him two horses, the first ever seen in the vast northland west of Sault Ste. Marie. In his fine study *The Indian and the Horse*, Frank Gilbert Roe shows how the Spanish settlers on the Rio Grande brought Arabian horses with them from Mexico City in 1600. The nearby Ute Indians and Jicarilla Apaches began using them for transport as early as 1660. A map in Roe's book by Francis Haines implies that the pack-train horses and mules used in 1714 by Louis Juchereau de St. Denis for smuggling in East Texas had come down there from Santa Fe, rather than up from Mexico. In their northward dispersion, horses appeared first west of the Continental Divide, reaching the Snake Indians as early as 1690 and the Nez Percé of western Montana and Idaho by 1710. Their spread from Santa Fe northeast into the Great Plains followed a course in reverse to the route of the Mallets from the Niobrara to Raton Pass and Taos. As we have seen, Bourgmond and du Tisné found the Pawnees using horses in 1719. By 1740, the Arikaras, Teton Sioux and others on the Upper Missouri were using them. Horses, so useless for travel in the eastern woodlands, were beautifully adapted to the grassy spaces and shallow rivers of the plains. They brought a change in the life of the western tribes as great as the change brought by the automobile to all mankind after 1900. It was the use of horses that allowed small bands of badly armed Indian warriors to hold out against the entire United States Army with all its modern armament during the Indian wars of 1860–1890.

9. To people pained by the frantic pace of superhighway travel, following the explorations of the La Vérendryes by car is a return to the leisurely motoring one knew a generation back, and particularly pleasant if the trip west from Montreal to the Big Horns is made in late spring or early fall. In Quebec and Ontario, historical signs dot the route to Sault Ste. Marie, starting with the La Salle plaque at his Lachine Rapids as one leaves the St. Lawrence and moves up the Ottawa through terrain as enticing and as French as the Loire valley. West of Sault Ste. Marie, the road swings around Lake Superior, often close to the north shore through picturesque places like Wawa and Nipigon, with moose strolling on the outskirts. Thunder Bay is the new 1970 name for La Vérendrye's Fort Kaministiquia (the white-capped river roars down to Superior like thunder). The road continues through the Quetico woods of graceful birch and spruce across the low St. Lawrence–Hudson Bay divide to Rainy Lake and on to the paper-mill town of Fort Francis. At Pither's Point there a plaque marks the presumed site of La Vérendrye's Fort Pierre (1731). This is pre-Cambrian Shield terrain, unsuited for farming but fine for timber, and full of lakes like jewels sparkling in the forest. From Fort Francis, the road runs along the Rainy River and north through the eastern fringes of Lake of the Woods to Kenora, a dull modern name for what was colorfully called Rat Portage Post in fur-trade days.

At Kenora, the eastern channel of the dramatic Winnipeg River heads for Lake Winnipeg, but the road leaves the old canoe route and the woods of Ontario too, running into the Manitoba prairie. Fort Rouge (1738) stood at the junction of the Red River and the Assiniboine in the heart of Winnipeg, capital of Manitoba. The site of the first Fort Maurepas (1734) is said to be in an oak grove six miles north of Selkirk on the west bank of the Red, and not far from the superb reconstruction of the Hudson's Bay Company's Lower Fort Garry (1831). In Portage-la-Prairie, fifty miles west of Winnipeg, a cairn at the city's water-treatment plant marks the site of

La Vérendrye's Fort La Reine (1738). A model of the trading post is displayed in the Fort La Reine Museum on the main highway. The portage implied by the city's name ran from the Assiniboine River northward to Lake Manitoba. Canoeing traders used the lake to arrive eventually at the mouth of the Saskatchewan to the Nelson River leading to English posts on Hudson Bay.

The La Vérendryes' three-hundred-mile trail from Fort La Reine to the Mandan villages can be approximated by driving up the Assiniboine to Brandon, on south through Turtle Mountain Provincial Park to Rugby, North Dakota, and then angling down the flat and peaceful Souris River wheat country to Velva. The wind blows constantly. Every farmhouse is protected against it by windbreaks of Chinese elms and Caragana trees. People at the Velva post office can direct one fifteen miles or so northeast to a deserted wheat village on the Great Northern Railway called Verendrye — the sole place name in the entire upper plains country of the United States memorializing the family who discovered it. Verendrye is a pretty village, a victim of changing rural ways of living. Its empty buildings — three groceries, a bank, a garage, a restaurant, pool hall, farm equipment store — are well kept up, as though the owners expect things to start humming again at any moment. In 1925, a most imposing granite globe-shaped monument was placed in a field a mile away by the Great Northern at a cost of $25,000. The globe, surprisingly, does not honor the La Vérendryes, suggesting the reluctance of Anglos to face the fact that Frenchmen, not Englishmen, were the pioneer explorers of the west. Its legend reads: "David Thompson, Geographer and Astronomer, passed near here in 1797 and 1798 on a scientific and trading expedition. He made the first map of the Country which is North Dakota and achieved noteworthy discoveries in the Northwest."

Years ago, a Verendrye National Monument existed on the Missouri River near Sanish, west of Verendrye. It marked the site of a village which, some historians believed, was the Mandan village that the La Vérendryes visited first on their 1738 trip. This Sanish monument site lies beneath the waters of Garrison Reservoir now. The pain of its loss was eased when it was decided by later historians that the flooded Sanish site was that of a Hidatsa, not a Mandan, settlement. The first Mandan village of the La Vérendryes, they said, is fifteen miles east of Bismarck and is called Menoken. It can be found by turning left (north) off Interstate 94 at the modern Menoken town sign and then immediately right on the frontage road running east along the Interstate. At the first public road, one turns left off the frontage road and drives north a few hundred feet to a stone gatepost and a narrow unkempt lane leading through the weeds a hundred yards to a stone summerhouse with log rafters and a metal plaque inside. The plaque reads: "Menoken Indian Village Site has been designated a Registered National Historic Landmark. U.S. Department of the Interior, 1964." The site itself is a pleasant grassy clearing in the woods above the deep ravine of Apple Creek with depressions here and there where the Mandans' dome-shaped houses, bastions and a defensive moat were said to have been and with a hillock on the far side.

Louis-Joseph de La Vérendrye's journal of his year-long trip with his brother François in 1742–1743 is so imprecise that students cannot agree on his route. Some say that the four explorers went up the Yellowstone to view the Absaroka Range of the Rockies near present Billings, Montana. In *The Course of Empire* Bernard De Voto puts them no further west than the Black Hills of South Dakota. The present author favors the Big Horns route as presented by Francis Parkman in *A Half Century of Conflict* and by Antoine Champagne in *Les La Vérendrye et Le Poste de l'Ouest*. This thousand-mile route seems to fit Louis-Joseph's directions, distances, elapsed time and Indians encountered much better than the others.

To follow it very roughly by car, one drives west from Bismarck to Belfield, North Dakota, south on U.S. 85 to Bowman, west to Baker, Montana, and south again over the loneliest of ranch roads through Ekalaka to Broadus, and on south up the Powder River to the Big Horns at Sheridan and Buffalo, Wyoming. From Buffalo, one drives southeast on more rambling, dusty, Wyoming ranch roads to reach the Cheyenne River in the pastoral terrain around Hot Springs, South Dakota, and so on to Pierre, the state capital.

The Historical Museum of the Memorial Building in Pierre is the owner of one of the great relics of western history — the actual lead plate that Louis-Joseph de La Vérendrye buried on the hillock above the Arikara village and marked with a cairn. The plate, eight and a half inches long and six and a half inches wide, bears his name, that of the marquis de Beauharnois, and the date of the plate's burial, March 30, 1743. It was found on the hillock on Sunday, February 17, 1913, by a child named Hattie Foster, who noticed it sticking out of the ground, showed it to the other children with whom she was playing, and tossed it aside. One of them, George O'Reilly, picked it up and took it to his father, William O'Reilly, who sold it later to the State Historical Society for $700. In 1933, the Historical Society and the Fort Pierre Commercial Club dedicated a monument to the Vérendryes three miles north of Pierre at the spot where the plate was found.

10. In a belated gesture of thanks, Louis XV promoted Pierre de La Vérendrye to the rank of captain in 1746 and awarded him the Cross of St. Louis in May, 1749. He died that same year in Montreal (December 5, 1749) and was buried there in the chapel of Ste. Anne de Notre Dame. His three sons continued trading out of the posts they had created west of Lake Superior and exploring up the Saskatchewan well into the 1750's. With the fall of Montreal in 1760, the fruits of all their discoveries fell to the British and their fur companies.

After leaving New Orleans, Jean-Baptiste Le Moyne de Bienville chose to spend his long retirement in France rather than in his native Montreal. He lived in peaceful obscurity until his death in Paris at the age of eighty-eight on March 7, 1768.

10

The Westering English

1. One of the last of trade expeditions from French Louisiana to New Mexico occurred in 1752, when Jean Chapuis and Louis Feuilli left Fort Chartres with a pack train of nine horses along a route similar to the later Santa Fe Trail. They got as far as the Pecos mission just short of Glorieta Pass. Here they were arrested, taken to Santa Fe for questioning and then shipped to Mexico City and to Spain to serve sentences for violating New Spain's old ban on foreign traders. Thereafter, general knowledge of the few trails that had been used between the Mississippi and Santa Fe was lost until the trails were rediscovered early in the nineteenth century

by exploring Americans. An unusual route from Texas to Santa Fe was pioneered in 1787 by a French employee of the Spaniards, Pedro Vial, who trailed his way from San Antonio north to the Wichita Falls area, and then straight through the very hostile lands of the Comanche Indians by way of the Red and Canadian rivers to the Pecos mission and the capital. Five years later, Vial and two companions, at the behest of the New Mexican governor, traveled from Santa Fe to St. Louis and back. Some students claim that the Santa Fe Trail had its real origin in this round 1792–1793 trip. Others deny it, saying that too much of Vial's route was along the Canadian River rather than along the Arkansas River part of the Santa Fe Trail.

2. Why did it take so long for explorers to start pushing inland toward the Mississippi from the west coast of North America? As a rule, the lure of trade or gold was what impelled people to explore. When Sir Francis Drake sailed his pirate ship up the California coast in 1578 as far as New Albion (Oregon), he found no commercial reason to explore inland, and neither did Sebastián Vizcaíno when he discovered Monterey Bay in 1602. Thereafter, while Europeans thronged to the east coast of North America and ships plied trade routes from the Orient past the Sandwich Islands (Hawaii) to Acapulco in Mexico, the west coast was left entirely alone until Vitus Bering discovered Alaska for Russia in 1741 and Russian traders moved steadily southward down the coast developing Indian trade. Spain regarded the Russians as trespassers, claiming the west coast at least as far north as Juan de Fuca Strait — the big bay that leads to Puget Sound and present Seattle. To block the trespassers, the Spanish would begin colonizing and setting up missions in California, first at San Diego in 1769, and at Monterey a year later. Then the Englishman, Captain James Cook, would sail up the west coast in 1778 looking for an outlet that might be the Northwest Passage from Hudson Bay or Lake Superior. He would land on today's Victoria Island at a bay called Nootka Sound a bit north of Juan de Fuca Strait.

And so, with Spain, England and Russia finding Indian trade on the west coast, things would be shaping up for an argument from 1778 on.

3. According to Justin Winsor in *The Mississippi Basin*, at least two of Céloron's lead plates have turned up. One of them was found at the turn of the century protruding from the Ohio River bank near the mouth of the Muskingum. The boys who found it melted most of it down for bullets. The remaining fragment is owned by the American Antiquarian Society at Worcester, Massachusetts.

4. As commander of the Poste de l'Ouest, replacing the Vérendryes, Jacques Le Gardeur de Saint-Pierre sent Joseph-Claude Boucher, chevalier de Niverville, from Fort La Reine to seek a route to the Pacific by way of the Saskatchewan to the Rockies and down the western side by its equivalent stream to the ocean. Saint-Pierre knew that the more benign Upper Missouri must have a similar equivalent stream leading to the Pacific but the Upper Missouri was off limits to Frenchmen because it was thought to begin near the source of the Rio Grande in Spanish New Mexico. Niverville's second assignment was to build a fort up the Saskatchewan to win the business of Indians who were taking their furs to the English at Hudson Bay. Niverville fell ill and got no further than the mouth of the Saskatchewan but his men pushed on and built Fort La Jonquière (1751) near the forks of the Saskatchewan. The Hudson Bay English, hearing about this fort, sent Anthony Henday to investigate it, and to keep their Indian suppliers of furs in line. Henday went far beyond

the forks of the Saskatchewan almost to present Calgary in sight of the Canadian Rockies. He discussed business with several Blackfeet tribes out there but without success. The French and Indian War put a stop to any further western exploration by anybody, English, French or Spanish, until the late 1760's.

11

France Loses an Empire

1. The state of Illinois has contributed wonderfully through its park system to the instruction of travelers in the history of that salubrious part of French Louisiana surrounding the mouth of the Ohio River. A restoration of the last Fort Chartres rises on the flats bordering the Mississippi four miles north of Prairie du Rocher. A plaque explains that this stronghold was constructed in 1753–1756 at a cost of about $40,000. It was regarded at the time as "the most commodious and best built fort in North America." It could house four hundred soldiers, though its usual garrison was half that number. It became English property by the Treaty of Paris in 1763 but French troops stayed on there until October 10, 1765, when the English arrived and renamed it Fort Cavendish. It was abandoned and destroyed in 1772.

Fort Kaskaskia State Park lies some twenty miles below Fort Chartres on the Kaskaskia River near the site of the original French village of Kaskaskia which the Jesuit, Gabriel Marest, founded in 1702–1703. Fort Kaskaskia was built during the French and Indian War to protect the village. The French destroyed it in 1766 to prevent its use by the British. Fort Kaskaskia State Memorial is a small brick building on Kaskaskia Island, formed by loops of the Mississippi. It contains the church bell from France which Louis XV gave to Kaskaskia village in 1741. No bridge serves the memorial in Illinois. It can be reached by car from the Missouri side of the river.

The log Cahokia Court House State Memorial just south of East St. Louis was built about 1737 and may be the oldest building in the Illinois country. It occupies the site of Cahokia village founded in 1699 by missionaries from the Seminary of Quebec. The word Cahokia means "wild geese" in the language of the Illinois Indians. Before St. Louis was founded in 1764, Cahokia had a French and Indian population of three thousand and was the commercial center of Upper Louisiana.

Fort Massac State Park, on the right bank of the Ohio near Metropolis, Illinois, marks the site of Kerlérec's Fort Massiac. The British did not use it after their conquest of the region but it became a popular stopping place for American soldiers and traders during and long after the Revolution. Somewhere along the way, the letter "i" was dropped from the French Massiac name. Preliminary work has been done to restore the fort.

2. Not long after the fall of Montreal to the British, Louis XV recalled Governor Kerlérec to Paris and put him in the gloomy-looking state prison and fortress,

the Bastille, for some months of "admonitory correction" as punishment for Louisiana's poor showing during the French and Indian War. For people of Kerlérec's class, a period spent in the Bastille could be quite an agreeable experience. The food was good, visitors were allowed, and there was space for games and exercise. The emerging prisoner was feted by his friends, who felt that incarceration carried a certain amount of prestige.

3. The Mississippi River has a total drainage area of 1,240,000 square miles, or more than one-third the area of the United States, Alaska excepted. This was the Louisiana area claimed by La Salle for France in 1682. Of the total, some 240,000 square miles constitute the area lying on the east side of the river which includes the drainage of the Ohio River and its tributaries (202,000 square miles), and smaller streams such as the Illinois, Wisconsin and St. Croix. The eastside drainage covers most of the states of Ohio, Indiana, Illinois, Tennessee and Kentucky and important parts of Mississippi, Alabama, Wisconsin and Minnesota. The very much larger westside (Louisiana Purchase) drainage of a million square miles ends at the Continental Divide in the Rocky Mountains. It holds the states of Missouri, Arkansas, Iowa, North and South Dakota, Nebraska and Oklahoma and most of Louisiana, Colorado, Wyoming, Kansas, Montana and Minnesota. The northeast corner of New Mexico is part of this westside drainage also.

4. The Iberville route did fail as an alternate exit from the Mississippi to the gulf, though British engineers tried for ten years to make a workable channel of the upper eight miles through the swampy debris of canebrakes, cypress logs and tropical undergrowth. In seasons when the Mississippi flowed high, some ships managed to get through to Amite River and Lake Pontchartrain, though their masts got tangled with low-hanging live oaks and strings of Spanish moss. Meanwhile, English land speculators in the Mississippi River part of West Florida below the site of present Vicksburg, Mississippi, built a road along the Iberville route to the Amite River, from where they could continue by boat through Lake Pontchartrain to Mobile (see the map on page 86). But for the most part these pioneers used the Mississippi past New Orleans to reach the gulf under the free passage rights that they had received from the duc de Choiseul. They made no secret of their purpose to eliminate New Orleans as the commercial capital of the Mississippi valley. As a starter, the British army built Fort Bute in 1764 at the mouth of the Iberville and the English colonists founded a village there called Manchac to challenge the supremacy of New Orleans.

5. Longfellow's long narrative in hexameter verse about the beautiful Evangeline Bellefontaine was inspired by a talk that the author had with his friend Nathaniel Hawthorne and a Salem clergyman named Reverend Horace Conolly. Hawthorne had heard Evangeline's story from Conolly. The novelist did not want to use the story himself and urged Longfellow to have a go at it. The poet spent more than a year putting it together. Newton Arvin in his *Longfellow* explains that some of the descriptions were derived from John Charles Frémont's government reports of his western explorations which appeared in the mid-1840's. One of Frémont's guides was the French creole Basil Lajeunesse, a name Longfellow borrowed to apply to the father of Evangeline's lover. *Evangeline* was a sensational success. The opening line, "This is the forest primeval. The murmuring pines and the hemlocks" still brings nostalgia to older readers who do not mind the fact that pines and hemlocks were rare in the Acadian farming area. They recall the poem's account of how "that maiden of

seventeen summers" in her Norman cap and blue kirtle married the sturdy Gabriel Lajeunesse, lost him in the confusion of their forced exodus from the Bay of Fundy, and embarked later on a lifelong, continental search for her lover. Her trek took her down the Mississippi by way of the St. Lawrence, Lake Erie and the Ohio — always just a few days behind Gabriel. She left the Mississippi near the mouth of the Iberville in 1765, probed into Bayou Plaquemine and the Atchafalaya and then reached the higher and drier Teche region west of New Orleans "with its prairies and forest of fruit-trees; they who dwell there have named it the Eden of Louisiana." But Evangeline was on the wilderness trail again soon, seeking Gabriel in Natchitoches, in the Oklahoma Ozarks, in Upper Michigan, and, finally, in Philadelphia, where she found him at last as he lay dying of old age in an almshouse.

The poor woman did not do her searching in vain. The memory of her incredible constancy is kept bright by descendants of the original "cajuns" on the Teche around New Iberville, St. Martinsville (Atakapa), Breaux Bridge and Opelousas. The prosperous descendants bear no resemblance to their simple and illiterate ancestors. The most modern of helicopters and pontooned planes buzz overhead servicing the oil and gas lagoons. But the air of the Teche is still langorous and romantic with the perfume of honeysuckle and cape jessamine. At St. Martinsville one visits the Acadian House Museum, Evangeline Museum, Evangeline Oak and Evangeline Statue. Restaurants everywhere specialize in superb jumbo shrimp, crayfish and brisquette of beef with horseradish. At Lafayette, the library of the University of Southwestern Louisiana has a priceless collection of Acadian source material.

12

Spain Gets a Lemon

1. Some writers believe that the Quebec Act of 1774 gave Frenchmen of the province that separatist yearning and feeling of special identity that their descendants display with such vigor and pride today — not a homeland French identity but a French-Canadian one that harks back to the qualities and heroism of natives like Louis Jolliet and the sieur d'Iberville. Even in late years, statesmen from France visiting Canada have found no particular rapport with the Quebec French. In *The Westward Movement*, Justin Winsor suggested that the Quebec Act and the un-English privileges that it bestowed on the French Canadians derived from General James Murray, who became Quebec's first English governor in 1764 and who reported to Parliament that the British then in Canada "were the meanest and most immoral people he ever saw while the French Canadians were frugal, industrious and moral, and had become reconciled to English rule." Murray proposed to annex "the region lying beyond the Alleghanies" to Quebec province so that the "moral" French Cana-

dians would settle it and exclude the "immoral" and troublesome English colonists who were passing west from the Atlantic seaboard.

2. Father Escalante and his party of less than a dozen men crossed the Continental Divide from the Rio Grande drainage to that of the Colorado near Abiquiu, New Mexico, some one hundred and fifty miles southwest of the nearest point of the Arkansas River drainage in Louisiana. But the route, described in modern terms, can concern us because of the beauty and excitement of it. From Santa Fe, it moved north through Abiquiu into the Rockies at Pagosa Springs, Colorado, west to Durango and Mesa Verde National Park, and then rambled north through Cortez and Telluride to Montrose, Colorado, and over Grand Mesa to Debeque on the Colorado River. The fathers crossed Douglas Pass to Rangely, Dinosaur National Park, Vernal (Utah) and Utah Lake south of Salt Lake City. Their return trek took them south past what are now the delightful Mormon towns of Cedar City and St. George and eastward to Page, Arizona, at the foot of Glen Canyon Dam. They crossed the Colorado at a point ("Crossing of the Fathers") now deep beneath Lake Powell. From there they wound their way back to Santa Fe via the stunning desert country of the Hopi and Navajo Indian reservations. They were gone from July, 1776, to January 2, 1777, and they traveled two thousand miles in all.

3. Oliver Pollock was not one to be daunted by adversity. After his release from prison in Havana he kept pushing his claims against the Congress and was awarded $90,000 in December, 1785. He did not receive the money for six years but the award had the effect of restoring his standing as a top trader who knew how to get around the maze of Spanish regulations. By the early 1790's he was back in New Orleans on his way to wealth again as agent for the Reed and Forde firm of Philadelphia merchants. Before Pollock died in 1823, Congress and the state of Virginia reimbursed him for all the sums that he had advanced on their behalf for supplies during the Revolution.

4. As of 1783, the several limits of exploration by Europeans west of the Mississippi line included that of the French Mallet brothers in 1739 to the southern Rockies (Sangre de Cristo Range) and Santa Fe via the Arkansas River; that of the La Vérendrye brothers via Winnipeg and the Souris River to the Big Horns spur of the central Rockies at present Sheridan, Wyoming, in 1742–1743; and that of Boucher de Niverville in 1751 from Fort La Reine up the Saskatchewan at least to the western boundary of present Saskatchewan province. Niverville worked for Jacques Le Gardeur de Saint-Pierre who succeeded the La Vérendryes at the Poste de l'Ouest before his meeting with young George Washington at Fort Le Boeuf near Lake Erie in 1753.

There was no Spanish westering to speak of after Cabeza de Vaca's transcontinental trek in the 1530's and de Soto's Arkansas trip in 1541 and Escalante's to Utah in 1776. Only one Englishman had done any major exploring in Canada before the La Vérendryes and Niverville. His name was Henry Kelsey, and he was nineteen years old at the time. He made a trip from York Factory of the Hudson's Bay Company to Lake Winnipeg, the lower Saskatchewan and perhaps the lower Assiniboine River in 1690–1692. The next Englishman to push farther into Canada was Anthony Henday, also of Hudson's Bay Company. He examined the North and South Saskatchewan and Red Deer rivers in 1754 on a journey that brought him to the foot of the Canadian Rockies west of Calgary, the first European of certain record to see them. After Henday, there was no new British westering up to 1783, so the theoretical limit of British exploration then was the east slope of the Canadian Rockies. The man who would change the limit drastically in another decade, Alexander Mackenzie, had already arrived in Canada from Scotland to enter the fur trade.

13

Thomas Jefferson: Land Developer

1. During the Thomas Jefferson period of the Louisiana story I have relied heavily for material on the remarkable life of Jefferson written by a great American scholar, Dumas Malone. The first volume, *Jefferson the Virginian*, appeared in 1948. It was succeeded by *Jefferson and the Rights of Man* (1951); *Jefferson and the Ordeal of Liberty* (1962); *Jefferson the President: First Term, 1801–1805* (1970); and *Jefferson the President: Second Term* (1974). For their insights on the Jefferson period, I found these books as enthralling as Francis Parkman's series on the development of French Canada.

2. Even though short of funds, Clark managed to build Fort Jefferson in 1779 along lines suggested by the governor. The fort served as a strategic stronghold on the Mississippi twelve miles below the mouth of the Ohio near present Wickliffe, Kentucky. It was a factor in preventing the British and their Indian allies from driving south from Detroit during the Revolutionary War to seize control of the whole Mississippi valley.

3. A passage in *Oregon* of the American Guide Series (Portland, 1940) explains that the word "Oregon" is probably derived from the Santee Dakota word *oragan*, meaning a birch-bark dish. Carver states in his book that the Sioux gave him the name. It was popularized and perpetuated in 1817 when William Cullen Bryant used it in his somewhat gloomy poem "Thanatopsis," which advises one to take comfort in the beauties of nature as one approaches his "eternal resting-place." Bryant wrote:

> *Take the wings*
> *Of morning, pierce the Barcan wilderness,*
> *Or lose thyself in the continuous woods*
> *Where rolls the Oregon, and hears no sound,*
> *Save his own dashings.*

Though the Boston skipper, Robert Gray, entered and named his river Columbia, after his ship, in May, 1792, the "Oregon" designation hung on for many years and then was applied to "the Oregon country," comprising all the land from the Rockies to the Pacific and from Spanish California northward to Alaska.

4. In November, 1766, Carver came upon a great limestone cave a dozen miles below the mouth of the Minnesota River (in present St. Paul, Minnesota). Some months later, he watched a Sioux burial ceremony on the bluff above the cave in what is known today as Indian Mounds Park near Carver Lake. Carver's Cave used to be a tourist attraction but, like Father Hennepin's Falls of St. Anthony upstream, it has bowed to "progress" and vanished from public view.

5. Jefferson's love of books was fully developed by 1783 when, according to Dumas Malone, he listed 2,640 volumes in his Monticello library. He had six thousand and more when the library was bought by Congress in 1815 to replace the government library that was lost in the burning of the Capitol the year before. This Jefferson Library was the nucleus of the present collections of the Library of Congress. In the 1950's, the government published a catalogue in five volumes, *The Library of Thomas Jefferson*, superbly compiled by E. Millicent Sowerby. Jefferson did not record when and where he bought many of his books but Miss Sowerby's bibliography contains a great deal of information about his purchases and about the authors. The present writer was astonished to find that every one of the seventeenth- and eighteenth-century source books used in his Louisiana research — Joutel, Marquette, Radisson and the rest — had been owned by Jefferson.

6. Carver, a poor businessman, received no benefit at all from his book. He died penniless in London in 1780, reportedly of starvation and of worry over the alcoholism of his second wife. He was buried in the potter's field in London. For four decades after his death, his daughters and several speculators sought official confirmation for what was called the Carver Grant. It consisted of ten thousand square miles of land in Wisconsin and Minnesota that Carver said had been given to him by two Sioux Indian chiefs on May 1, 1767. The grant ran from the banks of the Mississippi easterly for one hundred miles. It extended from the Falls of St. Anthony south to the mouth of Chippewa River at the foot of Lake Pepin. The Reverend Dr. Samuel Peters was the last "owner" of the grant, which he called "Petersylvania." Its validity was denied finally by the U.S. government in 1825.

7. The Spanish king had been pushing his Pacific claims steadily north up the California coast ever since 1769, when his Franciscan priests founded the San Diego mission. In 1773, his seamen under Juan Pérez were instructed to sail to the Strait of Anian "at sixty north latitude" — at the Mount St. Elias border of Alaska. They reached the Queen Charlotte Islands and turned back to anchor briefly in Nootka Sound on August 7, 1773. Two years later the Spaniards in two ships under Pérez, Bruno Heceta and Bodega y Cuadra made landings on the present Washington coast in sight of Mount Olympus and in the vicinity of today's Sitka, Alaska. As Heceta and Pérez returned south past Nootka Sound they discovered, on August 17, 1775, a large bay at 46° 17″. They named it Assumption Bay and they surmised that it must be "the mouth of some great river, or some passage to another sea." It was actually the mouth of the Columbia.

14

Treaty Trouble — and Worse — Monsieur Genet

1. A detailed and moving account of Ledyard's incredible career can be found in Jeannette Mirsky's *The Westward Crossings*. After hiking back to Paris from the Polish border he told friends that he planned to go to Kentucky to prepare for a

crossing to "the South Sea" from St. Louis. But a profitable trek was offered to him in London by Sir Joseph Banks, who hired him to make a three-year journey from Cairo to the source of the Nile and on to the head of the Niger for the African Association. Cairo turned out to be the end of Ledyard's long, long trail. He died of a sudden fever there in 1789, aged thirty-eight. He was, Miss Mirsky wrote, "a bright arrow that missed its mark."

2. Alexander Hamilton was born in 1757 on the British isle of Nevis in the Caribbean under circumstances that some of his political enemies made much of. Technically, he was a bastard, having been conceived while his French Huguenot mother, Rachel Fawcett, waited to be divorced from her estranged Danish husband. The divorce, issued in 1759, forbade her to marry her lover, James Hamilton, a Scottish merchant. Thereafter, the two were accepted in Nevis as entirely married and they enjoyed the highest social standing. Family misfortunes caused young Alexander to be dependent on relatives and friends. His brilliance was so apparent that they sent him to New Jersey for an education and then to New York, where he entered King's College in 1774. He became a firebrand rebel at once and won General Washington's admiration as an artillery captain. In 1777 he became Washington's private secretary with the rank of lieutenant colonel. He married into the prominent Schuyler family of New York shortly before becoming Colonel Hamilton and leading troops with success in the battle at Yorktown. Through the 1780's he practiced law and served with distinction in Congress.

3. The Nootka convention of 1790 was so vague that a second convention had to be drawn up and signed in 1794. By its terms, Spain retained rights in the Nootka area while acknowledging British sovereignty and limiting her own northward claims to the top of present California. After all the hullabaloo, Nootka Sound never amounted to much as a trading post.

15

Treaty Trouble — and Worse — Monsieur Genet

1. Court gossip of the 1780's had it that the mother of this Adélaïde, the comtesse de Flahaut, got her start in life as one of a number of teen-aged mistresses of Louis XV. When she became an adult and therefore too old to interest the king she married a leading member of the Farmers-General whose control of Virginia tobacco purchases gave Jefferson so much grief. Adélaïde was eighteen when she married the comte de Flahaut, who was fifty-four. The gossips said that she married Flahaut with the understanding that she could have a young lover if one turned up. The man who turned up was "the charming little abbé, Talleyrand."

2. With the overthrow of the French monarchy in August, 1792, the family was imprisoned in the gloomy Tour du Temple, which stood near the present Place de

la République. From this building, Louis XVI was carted past his Tuileries palace to the guillotine in the Place Louis XV (Place de la Concorde). Marie Antoinette was held in the Temple until August 1, 1793, when she was moved to the Conciergerie, a prison in the Palais de Justice near Notre-Dame cathedral. She was executed on October 16, 1793. One of the royal children, Marie-Thérèse Charlotte, was kept in the Temple until 1795, when she was exchanged by convention officials for republican prisoners abroad. In 1799 she married her first cousin, the duc d'Angoulême, son of Louis XVI's brother, the comte d'Artois.

The falling-knife machine for "humane" decapitation, called *la guillotine* during the Revolution, had been used for centuries in Europe. Its promoter, Dr. Guillotin, was a member of the Constituent Assembly in 1789.

3. The little dauphin, Louis Charles, duc de Normandie, became the titular king of France, Louis XVII, after the execution of his father. The official date of his death was June 8, 1795, with burial in the Paris cemetery of Sainte-Marguerite. However, rumors of his escape from the Temple began about the time of Genet's departure for South Carolina. A deaf mute was allegedly substituted for him. The rumors became a legend that lives on and on. More than forty "lost dauphins" have turned up, including Eleazar Williams, a white orphan child who was picked up by an Iroquois band while he was bathing in Lake George, New York. Williams became a missionary and then an Iroquois chief named Onwarenhiiaki. The great French naturalist, Jean Jacques Audubon, whose *Birds of America* was inspired by his extensive Mississippi River travels, was born in the same year as the dauphin and was living during the French Revolution in La Vendée, a province from which many royalists escaped to the United States. Audubon's origins were obscure. When he settled down at the Falls of the Ohio in 1808 the story got started — and followed him all his life — that *he* was Louis XVII. The most famous "lost dauphin" was fictional, the snake oil salesman in Mark Twain's *Huckleberry Finn*. He was run out of town by an irate mob and found sanctuary on the Mississippi raft of Huck and his black friend Jim. To give himself stature, the old faker conded to Huck, "Yes, my friend, it is true. Your eyes is lookin' at this very moment on the pore disappeared Dauphin, Looy the Seventeen, son of Looy the Sixteen and Mary Antonette — the rightful King of France." Huck and Jim were so impressed that they waited on His Majesty hand and foot from then on. Mark Twain was careful to be accurate in making his lost dauphin seventy years old at the time of his story (the mid-1850's).

4. This stirring national anthem, "La Marseillaise," was put together in an hour or so on April 24, 1792, by a French captain of engineers, Claude Joseph Rouget de Lisle, who knew a little something about music but not much. It got its name from the fact that it was sung with tremendous enthusiasm by republican troops heading for Paris from Marseilles. It was improved harmonically through the years by several French composers, but the melody and words were de Lisle's.

5. At the age of thirty-one, Genet had had enough excitement to last him for the rest of his days and he decided to drop politics as a career and turn instead to being a social success. In 1794 he married Cornelia Clinton, daughter of George Clinton, governor of New York. Three children were born to them at Jamaica, Long Island, and three more near Albany, to which they moved in 1800. After his wife's death in 1810, he married Martha Brandon Osgood, daughter of Washington's first postmaster general. When Napoleon became ruler of France as First Consul he invited Genet to come home but Genet refused. He had become a naturalized American citizen by then and had gone full circle in his political views, supporting the French

royalists once more. Before his death in 1836, he worked on prison reform and invented a lifeboat for barges on the Erie Canal.

André Michaux, whom Genet diverted from the chance of becoming the first European to reach the Pacific via the Missouri, reached Louisville, Kentucky, on September 16, 1793, to recruit Genet's liberation army. He delivered the minister's military commission to George Rogers Clark, learned of Genet's impending recall, and called a halt to the liberation project. He returned east by way of Cumberland Gap and the Shenandoah valley, arriving in Philadelphia on December 12, 1793. He lost Jefferson's support because of his connection with Genet but continued his botanical studies in the United States for some years. As he was returning to France in 1797, he lost all his North American collections in a shipwreck. He died in Madagascar in 1802.

6. General Wayne followed up his great victory a year later by persuading twelve Indian tribes of the Great Lakes–Ohio region to set up boundaries between their hunting lands and those available to U.S. settlers. By this Treaty of Greenville of August 3, 1795, signed near present Muncie, Indiana, the Indians gave up three quarters of the present state of Ohio plus sixteen small areas such as Vincennes, Detroit, and the site of Chicago for ten thousand dollars' worth of annuities. Wayne died at Erie, Pennsylvania, on December 15, 1796, while taking over Great Lakes posts evacuated by the British.

7. Although Thomas Pinckney performed admirably in Spain, Pinckney's Treaty was really the work of William Short, following Jefferson's instructions. Short was the victim of the common tendency of society to credit achievements to people of the highest rank associated with them rather than to those underlings who bring them about. Short was deeply hurt by the failure of his government to give him plenipotentiary rank. After riding back to Paris with Pinckney he resigned from the foreign service, ending a long term as the first U.S. "career" diplomat. Much later, during the last months of Jefferson's second term as president, Short was nominated U.S. minister to Russia. Anti-administration forces in the Senate prevented approval of the nomination.

16

The Tightrope Walkers

1. New Spain, one of the four viceroyalties of Charles IV's colonial empire, consisted in 1795 of some three million square miles of property. Mexico and Louisiana each contained roughly a million square miles of this total. The supreme administrative and fiscal center of New Spain was in Mexico City but Louisiana's ordinary affairs were directed from the captaincy-general in Havana. Besides Mexico and Louisiana, the viceroyalty included California, New Mexico, Texas, the Spanish West Indies and the two Floridas. California, the newest province, was barely twenty years old. It functioned to block the advance of the British and Russians down the Pacific coast, and as an experiment by Franciscan missionaries to convert the Indians

of the province to Catholicism. Naval officers at the provincial capital of Monterey reported to the viceroy on fur trade developments in the Oregon country, such as the discovery and naming of the Columbia River by Captain Robert Gray of Boston in 1792.

East of California and tied tenuously to it by dangerous desert trails was New Mexico, comprising today's New Mexico and Arizona. Most of its ten thousand Spanish settlers prospered modestly in the dreamy isolation of its multi-colored Upper Rio Grande valley. Their business was exploiting on their haciendas the Pueblo Indians in the environs of Santa Fe, Albuquerque and Taos — exploitation patterned on that of Spain's aristocrats over the peasants at home. These New Mexican overseers supplied horses and gear to the nomadic Indian tribes who had adopted the horse as a revolutionary way of life throughout the vast plains of Louisiana. After Governor Anza defeated the Comanches in 1779, the Comanche barrier that had blocked traffic from Santa Fe eastward through the Upper Canadian and Red River valleys was not quite as dangerous as it had been.

Cuba was the dominant island property of New Spain after Godoy's Treaty of Basel gave Spain's half of Santo Domingo to France. East and West Florida were, except for villages at Mobile, Pensacola and St. Augustine, uninhabited coastal wastelands. The West Florida port of Mobile was nominally Spanish under the direction of Governor Carondelet in New Orleans, but it operated at the behest of its foreign traders, particularly after 1795 when Americans from the Muscle Shoals area of the Tennessee shipped their produce to the gulf on the Tombigbee and Alabama rivers and demanded the same right of deposit at Mobile that Pinckney's Treaty gave to American shippers at New Orleans.

The several states of Mexico ran north from Panama to the Rio Grande. From thence the province of Tejas (Texas) stretched north to the Sabine River and beyond to the divide between the Sabine and Red rivers. It can be recalled that Spain denied La Salle's claim to Texas by sending in soldiers and priests in 1690–1693, and then occupying it for good in 1716 as far north as the low Sabine–Red River divide. France honored that vague divide boundary when the War of the Quadruple Alliance ended in 1720. Before the French ceded Louisiana to Spain in 1762, the latter had maintained a presidio at Los Adais, the village capital of Texas on the divide near the Natchitoches trading post in French Louisiana. The cession had made the border presidio unnecessary and the Texas capital was moved from Los Adais south to San Antonio. Texas in the 1790's was almost as wild as it had been when La Salle set up his tragic colony at Matagorda Bay. The sprinkling of Spaniards, two thousand at most, lived in San Antonio and Nacogdoches, and near the Indian towns of the Trinity and Brazos River valleys. The mere size of Texas served to protect the land approach to Spain's mines in Mexico. For Texans, civilization began at Natchitoches on the Red River, where the French creoles were making money raising sugar cane. The old trading post was tied by road to New Orleans by way of Opelousas and Attakapas (today's St. Martinsville) — the romantic Teche region populated by Acadians, to which were added a few royalist refugees from Paris.

2. Arthur Preston Whitaker states in *The Mississippi Question, 1795–1803* that in the year 1797 Charles IV spent $795,662 on Louisiana against revenues of $537,-869. But the revenues included a subsidy of $453,064 supplied by the viceroy of Mexico, apparently in recognition of the value of Louisiana to Mexico as a buffer.

3. Fables of geography die hard. Carondelet favored an expedition up the Missouri partly because he held to the century-old notion that the source of the Missouri was near the source of the Rio Grande and the Rio Grande was supposed to start near

Santa Fe. The governor's proposed overland route, therefore, could be expected to connect both New Orleans (via St. Louis) and Mexico City (via Santa Fe) to the North Pacific coast!

4. Mackay had taken along with him a young Welshman, John Evans, as his cartographer. Evans had been commissioned by Mackay back in England to check the lingering legend that the Mandans were the Welsh descendants of the pre-Columbian Prince Madoc. Though Evans slipped by the Sioux to Knife River and got back safely to Mackay's camp, he found, as Pierre de La Vérendrye had found, that the Mandans were not light-colored enough to be Welsh.

5. The real reason that the Directoire failed to ratify the 1796 treaty of retrocession seems to have been that the comte de Barras hoped to get Louisiana for nothing. In November, 1796, one of Bonaparte's generals, Victor Collot, arrived in St. Louis to examine the province as a preliminary to occupying it (he was under the delusion that the Louisiana French would be delighted). Collot picked up Carondelet's belief that the Missouri was the best overland route to the Pacific. The general concluded also that part of the Missouri route would serve French forces in a move on Santa Fe. Collot's reconnaissance was supposed to be secret but news of it got out and was used by the Federalists to bolster their anti-French views.

6. The president learned details of David Thompson's exploration and of Mackenzie's transcontinental trip in 1801 after the publication in London of Mackenzie's book, *Voyages on the River St. Lawrence and through the Continent of North America to the Frozen and Pacific Oceans.*

7. David Thompson erred in his supposition that Turtle Lake was the source of the Mississippi, but not by much. The actual source would be found in a few decades thirty-five air miles southwest of Turtle Lake at Lake Itasca. Turtle Lake is a hundred miles south of the 49th parallel.

8. Toussaint, one of the greatest of black heroes, rose out of slavery first as foreman of other African slaves on a French plantation in Santo Domingo and later as leader of all the island's slaves who were freed by the French National Assembly in 1791. He took the surname L'Ouverture — "the opening" — signifying his success in defeating the plantation owners and the English force that they brought in to help them. In 1797, when Toussaint was fifty, Bonaparte appointed him governor of the island. One year later, Toussaint called himself "the Bonaparte of Santo Domingo" and declared the island to be independent of France under his dictatorship.

17

The Chancellor's Great Adventure

1. Though Manuel de Godoy enjoyed a sort of sabbatical during 1799 and part of 1800, he retained the king's confidence and his foreign policies prevailed. Bona-

parte's promise not to alienate Louisiana without Spain's consent was reaffirmed in July, 1802, by General Gouvion-Saint-Cyr, speaking for the First Consul.

2. In establishing priorities, Talleyrand could have said that the Treaty of Fontainebleau awarding French Louisiana to Spain was signed on November 3, 1762, at which time West Florida was an administrative unit of Louisiana. The Treaty of Paris, in which both Spanish East Florida and French West Florida were given to England, was signed on February 10, 1763.

3. Pierre Samuel du Pont de Nemours, like the marquis de Lafayette, had supplied Thomas Jefferson with inside information on French political trends for many years. He was the father of Eleuthère Irénée du Pont who in 1802 founded the famous gunpowder factory on Brandywine Creek near Wilmington, Delaware. E. I. du Pont de Nemours & Company still seems to be going strong on the same old Wilmington stand.

4. President Jefferson's letter to Mr. Livingston follows in full:

Washington, April 18, 1802.

The cession of Louisiana and the Floridas by Spain to France, works most sorely on the United States. On this subject the Secretary of State has written to you fully, yet I cannot forbear recurring to it personally, so deep is the impression it makes on my mind. It completely reverses all the political relations of the United States, and will form a new epoch in our political course. Of all nations of any consideration, France is the one which, hitherto, has offered the fewest points on which we could have any conflict of right, and the most points of a communion of interests. From these causes, we have ever looked to her as our natural friend, as one with which we never could have an occasion of difference. Her growth, therefore, we viewed as our own, her misfortunes ours. There is on the globe one single spot, the possessor of which is our natural and habitual enemy. It is New Orleans, through which the produce of three-eighths of our territory must pass to market, and from its fertility it will ere long yield more than half of our whole produce, and contain more than half of our inhabitants. France, placing herself in that door, assumes to us the attitude of defiance. Spain might have retained it quietly for years. Her pacific dispositions, her feeble state, would induce her to increase our facilities there, so that her possession of the place would be hardly felt by us, and it would not, perhaps, be very long before some circumstance might arise which might make the cession of it to us the price of something of more worth to her. Not so can it ever be in the hands of France: the impetuosity of her temper, the energy and restlessness of her character, placed in a point of eternal friction with us, and our character, which, though quiet and loving peace and the pursuit of wealth, is high-minded, despising wealth in competition with insult or injury, enterprising and energetic as any nation on earth; these circumstances render it impossible that France and the United States can continue long friends, when they meet in so irritable a position. They, as well as we, must be blind if they do not see this; and we must be very improvident if we do not begin to make arrangements on that hypothesis. The day that France takes possession of New Orleans, fixes the sentence which is to restrain her forever within her low-water mark. It seals the union of two nations, who, in conjunction, can maintain exclusive possession of the ocean. From that moment, we must marry ourselves to the British fleet and nation. We must turn all our attention to a maritime force, for which our resources place us on very high ground; and having formed and connected together a power which may render reinforcement of her settlements here impossible to France, make the first cannon which shall be fired in Europe the signal for the tearing up any settlement she may have made, and for holding the two continents of America in sequestration for the common purposes of the United British and American nations. This is not a state of things we seek or desire. It is one which this measure, if adopted by France, forces on us as necessarily, as any other cause, by the laws of nature, brings on its necessary effect. It is not from a fear of France that we deprecate this measure proposed by her. For however greater her force is than ours, compared in the abstract, it is nothing in comparison of ours, when to be exerted on our soil. But it is from a sincere love of peace, and a firm persuasion, that bound to France by the interests and the strong sympathies still existing in the minds of our citizens, and holding relative positions which insure their continuances, we are secure of a long course of peace. Whereas, the change of friends, which will be rendered necessary if France changes that position, embarks us necessarily as a belligerent power in the first war of Europe. In that case, France will have held possession of New Orleans during the interval of a peace, long or short, at the end of which it will be wrested from her. Will this short-lived possession have been an equivalent to her for the transfer of such a weight into the scale of her enemy? Will not the amalgamation of a young, thriving nation, continue to that enemy the health and force which are at present so evidently on the decline? And will a few years' possession of New Orleans add equally to the strength of France? She may say she needs Louisiana for the supply of her West Indies. She does not need it in time of peace, and in war she could not depend on them, because they would be so easily intercepted. I should suppose that all these considerations might, in some proper form, be brought into view of the Government of France. Though stated by us, it ought not to give offense; because we do not bring them forward as a menace, but as consequences not controllable by us, but inevitable from the course of things. We mention them, not as things which we desire by any means, but as things we deprecate; and we beseech a friend to look forward and to prevent them for our common interest.

If France considers Louisiana, however, as indispensable for her views, she might perhaps be willing to look about for arrangements which might reconcile it to our interests. If anything could do this, it would be the ceding to us [of] the island of New Orleans and the Floridas. This would certainly, in a great degree, remove the causes of jarring and irritation between us, and perhaps for such a length of time, as might produce other means of making the measure permanently conciliatory to our interests and friendships. It would, at any rate, relieve us from the necessity of taking immediate measures for countervailing such an operation by arrangements in another quarter. But still we should consider New Orleans and the Floridas as no equivalent for the risk of a quarrel with France, produced by her vicinage.

I have no doubt you have urged these considerations, on every proper occasion, with the government where you are. They are such as must have effect, if you can find means of producing thorough reflection on them by that government. The idea here is, that the troops sent to St. Domingo, were to proceed to Louisiana after finishing their work in that island. If this were the arrangement, it will give you time to return again and again to the charge. For the conquest of St. Domingo will not be a short work. It will take considerable time, and wear down a great number of soldiers. Every eye in the United States is now fixed on the affairs of Louisiana. Perhaps nothing since the revolutionary war, has produced more uneasy sensations through the body of the nation. Notwithstanding temporary bickerings have taken place with France, she has still a strong hold on the affections of our citizens generally. I have thought it not amiss, by way of supplement to the letters of the Secretary of State, to write you this private one, to impress you with the importance we affix to this transaction. I pray you to cherish Dupont. He has the best disposition for the continuance of friendship between the two nations, and perhaps you may be able to make a good use of him.

5. As far as the records go, Livingston was the first American official to suggest that it might be a good idea for the United States to acquire property at once west of the Mississippi. It is permissible to speculate that he chose the region north of the Arkansas because he knew about Jefferson's interest in the Missouri as the most promising overland route to the Pacific and as the key to the far-western fur trade. George Dangerfield, who made a most penetrating study of Livingston's motives for his biography, feels that the chancellor made his north-of-the-Arkansas suggestion entirely on his own. "He was," Dangerfield said recently, "an *inveterate* projector."

6. Toussaint L'Ouverture put himself in Leclerc's custody in May, 1802, was sent off to France on June 10, and was imprisoned at Joux, near Besançon. He died there on April 27, 1803.

7. George Dangerfield has revealed in his Livingston biography that, until recently, Bonaparte was believed to have persuaded Charles IV to order the closure of New Orleans so that France could use the right of deposit as a bargaining point after the retrocession of Louisiana. However, Dangerfield has written, "a bundle of documents discovered some twenty-five years ago in the Archivo Histórico Nacional shows that the order to Morales was nothing more or less than a Spanish reprisal against American smuggling, and against lack of consideration shown to Spanish sailors in American ports."

18

Bonaparte Makes Up His Mind

1. Jefferson really did display distinctly amorous feelings for Betsey Walker in 1768 when he was a twenty-five-year-old bachelor. Betsey was twenty-one at the time and married to John Walker, who happened to be off in the wilds somewhere on government Indian business. In 1805, the president confessed to his secretary of the navy, Robert Smith, that "when young and single I offered love to a handsome lady. I acknowledge its incorrectness." Millions of words have been written to prove and deny that during his term of office the president fathered four children by the black girl Sally Hemings. It seems to be true that several of Sally's children resembled him, especially Madison Hemings, born in 1805, who claimed years later that he actually was the president's son. It is, of course, a wise child who knows his own father. In *Jefferson the President: First Term*, Dumas Malone examines the allegations in some detail (Appendix II: "The Miscegenation Legend").

2. The committee's report was slyly written to fit the case if France sold New Orleans and its western part of Florida to the United States. To make this western part larger than it ever had been as a French property, the report put its eastern boundary at the Apalachicola River, which was in Spanish terrain one hundred and fifty miles east of the traditional Perdido River line. Apalachicola River was the boundary that the British had used to divide their East and West Floridas from 1763 to 1783.

3. The historian Lloyd E. Worner of Colorado College has noted that even while Jefferson and Captain Lewis were planning to blaze a trail across the continent under army auspices the president was promoting the U.S. Military Academy, which opened at West Point with ten cadets on July 4, 1802. From then on for many decades, the U.S. Army was far more concerned with science and exploration than with military matters, reflecting the interests of Jefferson and the American Philosophical Society.

4. The Century Dictionary defines an envoy extraordinary and minister plenipotentiary as "the full title of a minister of the second grade, next in dignity to an ambassador." In Jefferson's time, Livingston's title of "minister resident" or "minister plenipotentiary" was regarded in Paris as a step lower than "envoy extraordinary." But Madison wrote Livingston that in his opinion "the characters of Minister Plenipotentiary and Envoy Extraordinary are precisely of the same grade."

5. The youthful friendship of Eliza Monroe (later Mrs. George Hay) and Hortense de Beauharnais lasted throughout their lives, even after Hortense became the desperately unhappy queen of Holland as the unloved wife of Louis Bonaparte, Napoleon's younger brother. Hortense's son, Charles Louis Bonaparte, tried to overthrow Louis Philippe in 1836 and was exiled to New York. Later Charles Louis became emperor of France as Napoleon III.

6. The American uproar over Morales's closure of the right of deposit at New Orleans did not last long because ways were soon found by the rule-despising citizenry to get around it. By February, 1803, Morales himself had concocted legal evasions. Pedro Cevallos, the Spanish minister of foreign affairs, had issued orders to "tolerate" the right of deposit. The right was restored without fanfare on May 17, 1803.

7. The failure of Leclerc's army of twenty thousand men to defeat a rabble of illiterate black slaves defending their villages recalls other disasters that have come to ultramodern military forces trying to achieve victory in an environment for which their tactics and equipment were not designed — the fiasco of the U.S. Army in Vietnam, for example. After the death of Leclerc and the defeat of his successor, Rochambeau, the blacks found a new leader, Jean-Jacques Dessalines, to replace the dead Toussaint L'Ouverture. The independence of Santo Domingo under the name of Haiti was declared on January 1, 1804.

8. As things turned out, the French Panama Canal Company under Ferdinand de Lesseps did its best from 1879 on to build for Louisiana's benefit (and the world's) the "simple canal" that Decrès had in mind across the Isthmus of Panama. After ten years of trying, marked by corruption and extravagance of mammoth proportions, the company went bankrupt. Other failures followed before the "simple canal" was finally completed under U.S. government auspices at a cost of $366,650,000. The first ocean steamer went through on August 3, 1914.

19

Fait Accompli

1. George Dangerfield, in his Livingston biography, cites C. D. Yonge, the British historian, as writing in 1868 that Lord Whitworth, the British ambassador, offered Joseph Bonaparte upwards of one hundred thousand pounds if he would persuade the First Consul to keep the peace. Yonge wrote that Whitworth raised the bribe to two

million pounds when the higher-priced fixer, Talleyrand, joined in the talks which were said to have taken place from mid-March through April.

It could be inferred that these bribes induced Joseph to change from Livingston's ally in the retrocession issue to his opponent. In any case, the matter led to a famous tale of fraternal conflict, told by Bonaparte's younger brother Lucien, who had negotiated some of the Louisiana-Tuscany arrangements with Manuel de Godoy in 1801. The date of the conflict was April 7, 1803, the morning after the First Consul attended the first Paris performance of *Hamlet* by the French actor Talma. Joseph and Lucien were admitted to the consular bathroom where Bonaparte luxuriated in perfumed water and sniffed snuff from his snuffbox. Joseph and Lucien began berating Napoleon for his proposed sale of Louisiana to the United States. Soon, Joseph lost his temper completely, advanced to the edge of the marble tub and announced over Bonaparte's parboiled body that the sale was unconstitutional and would prompt him to seek his brother's overthrow. At that point, Napoleon rose dripping and screamed, "Thou, my enemy? Look, Sir Orator of the clubs, I would dash you to earth as I do this snuffbox." In dashing the snuffbox to the floor, the most powerful man on earth slipped and fell in the tub, deluging Lucien and Joseph with perfumed water and causing the terrified valet to drop the towel and faint dead away. "That," Lucien wrote in his memoir, "ended this hot discussion on which the fate of a colony was concerned, and out of which nothing came, except a little greater haste in the execution of his calamitous plan — the sale of Louisiana for a few millions, destined to be applied to an insensate strife against Europe." Six weeks later, the First Consul expelled Lucien Bonaparte from France for refusing to marry the widow of the duke de Parma, Charles IV's son-in-law who, you may recall, had received the kingdom of Etruria in exchange for the retrocession of Louisiana.

Lucien Bonaparte was not the only brother to displease Napoleon with marital missteps during this period. On November 4, 1803, President Jefferson wrote Livingston that the twenty-year-old youngest Bonaparte, Jerome, had just married Elizabeth Patterson of Baltimore, daughter of "the wealthiest man in Maryland, perhaps in the United States." The president added, "The effect of this measure on the mind of the First Consul is not for me to suppose; but as it might occur to him *prima facie*, that the Executive of the United States ought to have prevented it, I have thought it advisable to mention this subject to you." When Napoleon learned of this marriage he deplored it and had it annulled in 1805 by imperial decree. But, in the meantime, a son had been born to the couple in England, Jerome Napoleon Bonaparte, who became the founder of the famous Baltimore line of Bonapartes. Jerome's grandson, and Napoleon's grandnephew, Charles Joseph Bonaparte, a Harvard-educated lawyer, was secretary of the navy under Theodore Roosevelt, and also Roosevelt's attorney general.

2. Of his presentation to the First Consul, Monroe wrote in his journal on May 1, 1803:

I accompanied my colleague to the Palace of the Louvre, where I was presented by him to the Consul [who] observed that he was glad to see me. "Je suis bien aisé de le voir." "You have been here 15 days?" I told him I had. "You speak French?" I replied "A little." "You had a good voyage?" Yes. "You came in a frigate?" No, in a merchant vessel charged for the purpose. Col. Mercer was presented; says he "He is Secretary of legation?" No but my friend. He then made enquiries of Mr. Livingston & his secretary how their families were, and then turned to Mr. Livingston & myself & observed that our affairs should be settled.

We dined with him. After dinner when we retired into the saloon, the First Consul came up to me and asked whether the federal city grew much. I told him it did. "How many inhabitants has it?" It is just commencing, there are two cities near it, one above, the other below, on the great river Potomack, which two cities, if counted with the federal city would make a respectable town, in itself it contains only two or three thousand inhabitants. "Well; Mr. Jefferson, how old is he?" Abt. sixty. "Is he married or single?" He is not married. "Then he is a *garçon.*" No, he is a widower. "Has he children?" Yes, two daughters who are married. "Does he reside always at the federal city?" Generally. "Are the publick buildings there commodious, those for the Congress and President especially?" They are. "You the Americans did brilliant things in your war with England, you will do the same again." We shall I am persuaded always behave well when it shall be our lot to be in war. "You may probably be in war with them again." I replied I did not know, that was an important question to decide when there would be an occasion for it.

3. Some patient accountant has put the final price for Louisiana at $27,267,622 (about four cents an acre) after the payment of admissible spoliation claims and interest. The English and Dutch bankers permitted principal payments to begin in 1812 instead of 1818 as designated in the treaty. Principal payments to redeem the whole stock issue were completed in 1823.

4. The present author tends to feel that Livingston did have the purchase of Louisiana all but arranged before the envoy extraordinary arrived in Paris, though sympathizing with Monroe's point of view. The who-did-it issue was very much alive all through 1803. As late as November, the chancellor was writing Madison: "But he [Monroe] unfortunately came too late to do more than assent to the propositions that were made to us, and to aid in reducing them in form." The New Yorker actually altered the dates of some reports to back his priority. The Federalists supported Livingston against Jefferson's westerner, Monroe, claiming that the chancellor's August, 1802, memorial influenced Bonaparte to sell the province. To this the Republican *National Intelligencer* replied on July 11: "Mr. Livingston's merit may have been great. Far be it from us to impair it. But his merit consists, not in standing alone, but in carrying into effect the will of those he represented."

James Monroe presented his stand in a letter of May 25 to the senators of Virginia. The letter read in part:

I consider this transaction as resulting from the wise & firm tho' moderate measures of the Executive and Congress during the last session. Without those measures we should not have acquired Louisiana. . . . The decision to offer us the territory by sale was not the effect of any management of mine, for it took place before I reached Paris; nor of my Colleague or it would have taken place sooner: Being postponed until my arrival in France or indeed till the mission was known, is full proof that it was the result of the causes above mentioned & of these only. . . . Personally I pretend to nothing but zeal & industry after I got here, a merit which is equally due to my colleague. . . . It is proper to add that I expect no misrepresentation from my colleague & that I am happy to have it in my power to bear testimony in the most explicit manner in favor of his zealous sincere & diligent cooperation thro' the whole of this business.

President Jefferson watched the long debate with amused nonpartisanship. In a private letter of July 11 to General Horatio Gates, he wrote: "I find our opposition is very willing to pluck feathers from Monroe, although not fond of sticking them into Livingston's coat. The truth is, both have a just portion of merit; and were it necessary or proper, it would be shown that each has rendered peculiar services, and of important value. These grumblers, too, are very uneasy lest the administration should share some little credit for the acquisition, the whole of which they ascribe to the accident of war."

Livingston seemed to survive very well his disappointment over being forced to share honors with Monroe. He was pleased on January 4, 1804, when Barbé-Marbois and other French friends in Paris gave him a gala testimonial dinner at the Hôtel de Fleury on the Left Bank. He ended his diplomatic career on May 26, 1805, when he and his entourage sailed from Nantes for New York. He resumed life as a gentleman farmer on his Clermont estate in Dutchess County, winning distinction as a promoter of gypsum in fertilizer and as the author of a popular handbook, *Essay on Sheep*. He financed Robert Fulton in the development of Fulton's revolutionary steamboat, which began running from New York to Albany in 1807, using the paddle-wheel principle that Fulton had developed in Paris, with Livingston's help, in 1802. The First Lord of the Manor died at Clermont in 1813.

James Monroe left Paris in July, 1803, to serve as U.S. minister in London. A year later he joined Charles Pinckney in Madrid in an unsuccessful attempt to buy the Spanish Floridas. Back in London, he spent two hectic years trying to convince the British that their impressment of American sailors and their blockades to drive Napoleon's ships from the high seas would lead to war — the war that Congress declared against Britain on June 18, 1812. Monroe served as President Madison's secretary of state and secretary of war before becoming president himself in 1816.

5. After Senate ratification of the purchase treaty and congressional approval of payment arrangements, the amendment issue died of anemia, which had the effect of establishing a precedent for the principle of implied powers in the U.S. Constitution and elasticity to meet changing conditions. As might be expected, those who voted against the purchase of Louisiana included Senators James Hillhouse and Uriah Tracy of Connecticut, William Plumer and Simeon Olcott of New Hampshire and Timothy Pickering of Massachusetts.

Epilogue

1. Zebulon Pike had his chance to solve two geographical riddles, the source of the Mississippi and the source of the Red River, but they were so difficult to find that he may be forgiven for his failure. The source of the Mississippi was sixty miles from Cass Lake at the end of a labyrinth of little and big lakes, the sorting out of which baffled explorers after Pike for a quarter-century. The source was discovered on July 13, 1832, by a remarkable ethnologist named Henry Rowe Schoolcraft, who was supposed to be on a peace mission to the Chippewa and Sioux Indians that had been authorized by Andrew Jackson's secretary of war, General Lewis Cass. Schoolcraft and his escort of soldiers and Indian guides threaded their way to the source (the Indians called it Elk Lake) by way of Cass Lake and Lake Bimidji. Schoolcraft called the source Itasca, a name which he formed out of the Latin *veritas* and *caput* ("truth" and "head"), using the last two syllables of one and the first syllable of the other. Today's Itasca State Park is one of the most interesting in the nation. Lake Itasca, 1,478 feet above sea level, is 2,552 miles from the Gulf of Mexico. If you are curious why the Missouri flows so much faster than the Mississippi, compare the latter's fall of 1,478 feet with the Missouri's fall of 6,560 feet in its flow of 2,950 miles to St. Louis from its ultimate source at Red Rock Pass in southwestern Montana.

In Pike's day, the Red River was supposed to rise in the same height of land as the Arkansas and the Missouri — in the Continental Divide of the Rocky Mountains. Actually, the Red River rises in the Texas Panhandle — in the height of land separating the Red River drainage from that of the Pecos branch of the Rio Grande. The Red's official source is in the Palo Duro Canyon (near Canyon, Texas) that Coronado and his Chosen Thirty visited in May, 1541, on their way to Quivira. It is no wonder that Pike failed to find it by moving due south from the Arkansas headwaters some three hundred miles northwest of Palo Duro. Major Stephen Long and his explorers missed the Red also in 1820 after dipping south from the Arkansas across Raton Pass. The river there that they thought was the Red turned out to be the Canadian, a branch of the Arkansas. Partly because of Comanche hostility, the Upper Red and its ultimate source at the head of Tierra Blanca Creek were not mapped accurately until Captain Randolph B. Marcy led an army expedition to the area from Fort Arbuckle on the Washita in 1852.

After his Chihuahua confinement, Captain Pike (he had been promoted from lieutenant in August, 1806) was released by the Spanish from custody at the Sabine River, where the so-called Neutral Ground began — a no-man's-land fifty miles wide between the Sabine and the Red that General Wilkinson had designated by force of arms a few months earlier pending boundary settlements. As the text of this chapter shows, the Sabine became the permanent Spanish-American boundary in that Natchitoches area. Wilkinson deserves the credit for that gain of terrain, even though his Neutral Ground maneuver seems to have been made to clear himself of plotting with his old friend Aaron Burr to conquer Mexico and set up a southwest empire. Whether this empire was to have been for the benefit of Burr and Wilkinson or the United States has never been decided, but both plotters survived extended federal trials on charges of treason which were held in Richmond, Virginia. In 1812, Wilkinson resumed his army command at New Orleans and was in charge when Mobile was occupied in 1813.

2. The Anglo-American Convention of 1818 for joint occupancy of Oregon "on the north-west coast of America, westward from the Stony Mountains" was renewed in 1827. By then Russia had relinquished her coastal claims below 54–40. In 1846, because of the flow of American immigrants to Oregon, a treaty was signed fixing the boundary between American and British property at its present position, the 49th parallel. The states of Washington, Oregon and Idaho resulted from the agreement.

Sources

1

Phantom River

CONQUISTADORES: *The Journey of Coronado* by Pedro de Castañeda, translated and edited by G. P. Winship (Ann Arbor: University Microfilms, #13, 1966). *Spanish Explorers in the Southern United States, 1528–1543*, edited by F. W. Hodge (New York, 1907). *Coronado: Knight of Pueblos and Plains* by Herbert E. Bolton (Albuquerque, N.M., 1949). *Relacam* (Evora, 1557) by "a Portuguese of Elvas" who accompanied de Soto, of which an English translation was published in 1609 by Richard Hakluyt under the title *Virginia Richly Valued* (Ann Arbor: University Microfilms, #12, 1966). *Great River* by Paul Horgan, Vol. I (New York, 1954).

CARTIER and CHAMPLAIN: *A Shorte and briefe narration of the two Navigations and Discoveries to the Northwest partes called Newe France* by Jacques Cartier, translated by John Florie (London, 1580) (Ann Arbor: University Microfilms, #10, 1966). *The Course of Empire* by Bernard De Voto (Boston, 1952). *Cartier to Frontenac: Geographical Discovery in the Interior of North America in Its Historical Relations, 1534–1700*, by Justin Winsor (Boston, 1900).

GROSEILLIERS and RADISSON: Radisson's English account: *Voyages of Peter Esprit Radisson* (Prince Society ed.; New York, 1943). *The Explorations of Radisson*, from the original MS in the Bodleian Library and the British Museum, edited by Arthur T. Adams (Minneapolis, 1961). *Caesars in the Wilderness* by Grace Lee Nute (New York, 1943).

GENERAL: *In Quest of the Western Ocean* by Nellis M. Crouse (New York, 1928). *Pioneers of France in the New World* (1865) by Francis Parkman (Boston,

1897). *Mapping the Trans-Mississippi West,* Vol. I: *The Spanish Entrada to the Louisiana Purchase, 1504–1804,* by Carl I. Wheat (San Francisco, 1957).

2

The Mist Rises — a Little

TALON, COLBERT and LOUIS XIV: *The Musket and the Cross* by Walter D. Edmonds (Boston, 1968). *France under Richelieu and Colbert* by John Henry Bridges (1866; reprint edition, London, 1912).

THE JESUITS: *The Jesuits in North America* (1867) and *Pioneers of France in the New World* (1865) both by Francis Parkman (Boston, 1897).

JOLLIET and MARQUETTE: "Voyages of Marquette," in *The Jesuit Relations,* with French and English text (Ann Arbor: University Microfilms, #28, 1966).

LA SALLE and TONTY: *History of Cavelier de La Salle, 1643–1687,* by Paul Chesnel (New York, 1932). *La Salle and the Discovery of the Great West* (1869) by Francis Parkman (Boston, 1897). *Relation of the Discoveries and Voyages of Cavelier de La Salle from 1679 to 1681,* translation after Pierre Margry by Melville B. Anderson (Chicago, 1901).

FRONTENAC: *Count Frontenac and New France under Louis XIV* (1877) by Francis Parkman (Boston, 1897). Also Justin Winsor's *Cartier to Frontenac* (Boston, 1900).

GENERAL: Before starting work on this book I had the joy of reading the twelve volumes of that greatest of American historians, Francis Parkman (1823–1893), whose first work, the two-volume *The Conspiracy of Pontiac* was published in 1851. His last work, *A Half-Century of Conflict,* appeared in 1892. I envy any student of history who has this rich Parkman experience still ahead of him.

For data on the discovery of the Great Lakes, see *Lake Erie* by Harlan Hatcher (Indianapolis, 1945). The birch-bark canoe is discussed by Donald Culross Peattie in *A Natural History of Western Trees* (Boston, 1953).

3

The Paths of Glory . . .

LA SALLE and TONTY: *The Journeys of René Robert Cavelier, Sieur de La Salle,* Vols. I and II, edited by I. J. Cox (New York, 1905), as related by Henri de

Tonty, Father Zenobius Membré, Louis Hennepin, Father Anastasius Douay, Father Chrétien Le Clerc, Henri Joutel and La Salle's brother, Jean Cavelier.

LOUIS XIV: *Versailles and the Court under Louis XIV* by James Eugene Farmer (New York, 1905).

HENNEPIN and DULUTH: *A Description of Louisiana* by Louis Hennepin (1683), translated and published by John Gilmary Shea (1880) (Ann Arbor: University Microfilms, #30, 1966). *New Discovery* by Father Louis Hennepin, edited by Reuben G. Thwaites, reprinted from the second London issue of 1698 (Chicago, 1903).

GENERAL: *Découvertes et Etablissements des Français dans l'Ouest et dans le sud de l'Amérique Septentrionale (1614–1754)* by Pierre Margry, 6 vols. (Paris, 1877–78). These volumes of official French documents collected by the indefatigable Margry constitute the most important source of background information on La Nouvelle-France. *Lower Mississippi* by Hodding Carter (New York, 1942).

4

. . . Lead But to the Grave

LA SALLE COLONY: *A Journal of the Last Voyage Perform'd by Mons. de la Sale to the Gulph of Mexico, to find out the Mouth of the Mississippi River*, by Henri Joutel (published in French, 1713; translated into English, 1714) (Ann Arbor: University Microfilms, #31, 1966). "The Location of La Salle's Colony on the Gulf of Mexico" by Herbert E. Bolton, *Mississippi Valley Historical Review*, Vol. II (Sept., 1915). Also *The Journeys of René Robert Cavelier, Sieur de La Salle*, Vol. II, edited by I. J. Cox (New York, 1905).

PEÑALOSA: "New Light on Don Diego de Peñalosa" by C. W. Hackett, *Mississippi Valley Historical Review*, Vol. VI (Dec. 1919).

GENERAL: *Franco-Spanish Rivalry in North America, 1524–1763*, by Henry Folmer (Glendale, Calif., 1953). *The Journals of Francis Parkman*, edited by Mason Wade, 2 vols. (New York, 1947).

5

Iberville's Mardi Gras

SPANISH MOVES INTO TEXAS: "The Spanish Re-exploration of the Gulf Coast in 1686," edited and translated by Irving A. Leonard, *Mississippi Valley Historical*

Review, Vol. XXII (March, 1936). "History of Texas Geography" by Z. T. Fulmore, *Texas State Historical Association Quarterly*, Vol. I (July, 1897). "The Beginnings of Texas" by R. C. Clark, *Texas State Historical Association Quarterly*, Vol. V (Jan., 1902). *No Man's Land: A History of El Camino Real* by Louis R. Nardini (New Orleans, 1961).

UPPER MISSISSIPPI PIONEERS: *Upper Mississippi* by Walter Havighurst (New York, 1937). *Minnesota: A History of the State* by Theodore C. Blegen (Minneapolis, 1963). *The Fur Trade in Canada* by Harold A. Innis (New Haven, 1930).

LAHONTAN: *New Voyages in North America* by the Baron de Lahontan, from the English edition of 1703, edited by Reuben G. Thwaites (Chicago, 1905).

IBERVILLE, BIENVILLE and PONCHARTRAIN: *Lemoyne d'Iberville, Soldier of New France*, by Nellis M. Crouse (Ithaca, N.Y., 1954). Iberville's *Badine* journal, from Pierre Margry's *Découvertes*, Vol. IV. "Iberville at the Birdfoot Subdelta — Final Discovery of the Mississippi" by Richebourg Gaillard McWilliams, and "Jérôme Phélypeaux, Comte de Pontchartrain and the Establishment of Louisiana, 1696–1715," by John C. Rule, both in *Frenchmen and French Ways in the Mississippi Valley*, edited by John F. McDermott (Urbana, Ill., 1969).

6

Chaos in Paradise

BIENVILLE and LAHONTAN: see sources for Chapter 5.

SÂGEAN: "The Eldorado of Mathieu Sâgean," App. II, in *La Salle and the Discovery of the Great West* (1869) by Francis Parkman (Boston, 1897).

MISSISSIPPI VALLEY: "The Tennessee River as the Road to Carolina" by Verner W. Crane, *Mississippi Valley Historical Review*, vols. III and IV (June, 1916–March, 1917). "Projects for Colonization in the South, 1684–1732." by Verner W. Crane, *MVHR*, Vol. XII (June, 1925). *Journal of a Voyage to North America* by Pierre François Xavier de Charlevoix, reprint of the original English translation, London, 1761, edited by Louise Phelps Kellogg, 2 vols. (Chicago, 1923). "France and Louisiana in the Early Eighteenth Century" by Marcel Giraud, *MVHR*, Vol. XXXVI (March, 1950). "Explorers in the Valley" by Kate L. Gregg, *Missouri Historical Review*, Vol. XXXIX (Oct., 1944; Jan., 1945). "Early Religious Efforts in the Lower Mississippi Valley" by V. Alton Moody, *MVHR*, Vol. XXII (Sept., 1935). "Lead Mining in Pioneer Missouri," edited by Ada Paris Klein, *MHR*, Vol. XLIII (April, 1949). "The Founding of Ste. Genevieve, Missouri" by Ida M. Schaaf, *MHR*, Vol. XXVII (Oct., 1932). "France and the Mississippi Valley" by Louise P. Kellogg, *MVHR*, Vol. XVIII (June, 1931). "The Significance of the Mississippi Valley in American Diplomatic History, 1686–1890," by Richard W. Van Alstyne, *MVHR*, Vol. XXXVI (Sept., 1949).

CHARLES JUCHEREAU DE ST. DENIS: "A French Pioneer in the Mississippi Valley," by Norman W. Caldwell, *MVHR*, Vol. XXVIII (March, 1942).

PIERRE LE SUEUR: *The Minnesota* by Evan Jones (New York, 1962). *Minnesota*, American Guide Series (New York, 1938). *Minnesota: A History of the State*, by Theodore C. Blegen (Minneapolis, 1963).

7

Noble Swindler

LOUIS JUCHEREAU DE ST. DENIS: "Who was Juchereau de Saint-Denis?" by Edmund J. P. Schmitt, *Texas State Historical Association Quarterly*, Vol. I (Jan., 1898); "The Real Saint-Denis" by Lester G. Bugbee, *TSHAQ*, Vol. I (April, 1898).

JOHN LAW, ANTOINE CROZAT and the DUC D'ORLEANS: *Eighteenth-Century France* by Frederick C. Green (New York, 1964). *Money & Trade Consider'd* by John Law (London, 1720). *Law et son système des finances* by Louis A. Thiers (Paris, 1826).

TREATY OF UTRECHT, etc.: *The Rise and Fall of New France* by George M. Wrong, 2 vols. (New York, 1928).

LOUISIANA BUSINESS: "Trade Between the Windward Islands and the Continental Colonies of the French Empire, 1683–1763" by Clarence P. Gould, *Mississippi Valley Historical Review*, Vol. XXV (March, 1939). "The Development of Industries in Louisiana During the French Regime, 1673–1763," by N. M. Miller Surreu, *MVHR*, Vol. IX (Dec., 1922). "French Governors of Louisiana" by André Lafargue, *MVHR*, Vol. XIV (Sept., 1927).

8

The Frustrations of Bienville

EARLY NEW ORLEANS: *Creoles of Louisiana* by George W. Cable (New York, 1889). "The Superior Council in Colonial Louisiana" by James D. Hardy, Jr., and "Some Eighteenth Century Views on Louisiana" by Pierre H. Boulle, both in *Frenchmen and French Ways in the Mississippi Valley*, edited by John F. McDermott (Urbana, Ill., 1969).

PENSACOLA WAR, VALVERDE and VILLASUR: *Franco-Spanish Rivalry in North America, 1524–1763*, by Henry Folmer (Glendale, Calif., 1953). "Dauphin Island in the Franco-Spanish War, 1719–22" by Jack D. L. Holmes, in *Frenchmen and French Ways* cited in the previous paragraph.

BOURGMOND, DU TISNÉ and LA HARPE: *Journal historique de l'établissement des Français à la Louisiane* by Bénard de La Harpe (Paris, 1831), from La Harpe's report dated May 1, 1720. "Fort Orleans of the Missoury" by Gilbert J. Garrahan, S.J., and "Étienne Véniard de Bourgmond in the Missouri Country" by Henry Folmer, both in *Missouri Historical Review*, Vol. XXX (Oct., 1940–July, 1941). "Fort Orleans, the First French Post on the Missouri" by M. F. Stipes, *MHR*, Vol. VIII (April, 1914), "De Bourgmont's Expedition to the Padoucas in 1725" by Henri Folmer, *The Colorado Magazine*, Vol. XIV (July, 1937).

PLAINS INDIANS: *Indians of the High Plains* by George E. Hyde (Norman, Okla., 1959).

9

Approach to the Rockies

MALLET BROTHERS: "The Mallet Expedition of 1739 through Nebraska, Kansas and Colorado to Santa Fe" by Henri Folmer, *The Colorado Magazine*, Vol. XVI (Sept., 1939). For Pierre Mallet's journal, see Pierre Margry's *Découvertes et établissements des Français dans l'Amérique Septentrionale* (Paris, 1887–88), Vol. VI, pp. 455–459, 463–464, 466–468.

THE LA VERENDRYES and the MARQUIS DE BEAUHARNOIS: *Les La Vérendrye et le poste de l'Ouest* by Antoine Champagne (Quebec, 1969).

HORSES IN THE WEST: *The Indian and the Horse* by Frank Gilbert Roe (Norman, Okla., 1955).

WELSH INDIANS: *The Course of Empire* by Bernard De Voto (Boston, 1952).

10

The Westering English

LOUISIANA: *The Mississippi Basin* by Justin Winsor (Boston, 1895). *The Westward Movement, 1763–1798*, by Justin Winsor (Boston, 1897).

NEW ORLEANS: *New Orleans, 1718–1812* by John G. Clark (Baton Rouge, 1970).

LOUIS XV and MADAME DE POMPADOUR: *Louis XV: The Monarchy in Decline* by G. P. Gooch (London, 1956). *Madame de Pompadour* by Nancy Mitford (New York, 1953).

CÉLORON DE BIENVILLE (sometimes BLAINVILLE): *The Ohio* by R. E. Banta, Rivers of America series (New York, 1949). "Céloron de Blainville and French Expansion in the Ohio Valley (1749)" by George A. Wood, *Mississippi Valley Historical Review*, Vol. IX (March, 1923).

THE WESTERING ENGLISH and PETER JEFFERSON: *Jefferson the Virginian* by Dumas Malone (Boston, 1948). *The Growth of the American Republic* by Samuel Eliot Morison and Henry Steele Commager (New York, 1958).

JACQUES LE GARDEUR DE SAINT-PIERRE: *A Half-Century of Conflict* (1892) by Francis Parkman (Boston, 1897).

11

France Loses an Empire

FRENCH AND INDIAN WAR (SEVEN YEARS' WAR): *A Half-Century of Conflict* (1892) by Francis Parkman (Boston, 1897).

GOVERNOR KERLÉREC: *Les Dernières Années de la Louisiane Française* by Chevalier de Kerlérec d'Abbadie, edited by E. Guilmoto (Paris, 1904).

FORT MASSIAC and FORT CHARTRES: "New Light on Fort Massac" by John B. Fortier, and "François Saucier, Engineer of Fort de Chartres, Illinois" by Walter J. Saucier and Kathrine Wagner Seineke, both in *Frenchmen and French Ways in the Mississippi Valley*, edited by John F. McDermott (Urbana, Ill., 1969).

EAST AND WEST FLORIDA and LOUISIANE DE L'EST: *Borderland Empires in Transition* by Robert L. Gold (Carbondale and Edwardsville, Ill., 1969). "The Beginnings of British West Florida" by Clarence E. Carter, *Mississippi Valley Historical Review*, Vol. IV (Dec., 1917).

THE DUC DE CHOISEUL, LOUIS XV and CHARLES III: "The Duke de Choiseul in Anglo-French Relations, 1763–1770," by John Fraser Ramsey, *University of California Publications in History*, Vol. 17 (April, 1939). *The History of France* by M. Guizot and Madame Guizot de Witt, Vol. V (New York, 1876).

NEW ORLEANS AND GENERAL O'REILLY: "French Reactions to the Louisiana Revolution of 1768" by Pierre H. Boulle, in *The French in the Mississippi Valley*, edited by John F. McDermott (Urbana, Ill., 1965). "The Cession of Louisiana to Spain" by William R. Shepherd, *Political Science Quarterly*, Vol. XIX (Sept., 1904). "The Diplomacy of the Louisiana Cession" by Arthur S. Aiton, *American Historical Review*, Vol. XXXVI (July, 1931). *Anglo-Spanish Rivalry in North America* by J. Leitch Wright (Athens, Ga., 1971).

MISSISSIPPI RIVER and ST. LOUIS: "The Iberville Canal Project" by Douglas Stewart Brown, *Mississippi Valley Historical Review*, Vol. XXXII (March, 1946). "Auguste Chouteau, First Citizen of Upper Louisiana" by John F. McDermott in *Frenchmen and French Ways in the Mississippi Valley* (Urbana, Ill., 1969). "France and the Mississippi Valley" by Louise Phelps Kellogg, *MVHR*, Vol. XVIII (June, 1931). "Transportation and Traffic on the Ohio and the Mississippi Before the Steamboat" by W. Wallace Carson, *MVHR*, Vol. VII (June, 1920).

ACADIANS: *The Acadian Miracle* by Dudley J. LeBlanc (Lafayette, La., 1961). "A Historical Sketch of the Acadians" by Corinne Saucier, *Louisiana Historical Quarterly*, Vol. XXXIV (April, 1951). *Cajun Sketches* by Lauren C. Post (Baton Rouge, 1962). *Montcalm and Wolfe* (1884) by Francis Parkman, Vol. I (Boston, 1897). "Acadian Transients in South Carolina" by Ruth Allison Hudnut and Hayes Baker-Crowther, *American Historical Review*, Vol. XLIII (April, 1938). "The Acadians in Fact and Fiction," a classified bibliography (mimeographed) in the Stephens Memorial Library, Southwestern Louisiana Institute, Lafayette, La.

12

Spain Gets a Lemon

CHARLES III and SPAIN: *The History of Spain* by Louis Bertrand and Charles Petrie (New York, 1937).

JUAN BAUTISTA DE ANZA and ESCALANTE: *Forgotten Frontiers*, translated and annotated by Alfred Barnaby Thomas (Norman, Okla., 1932).

OLIVER POLLOCK, JAMES WILLING and GOVERNOR BERNARDO DE GALVEZ: "Financier of the Revolution in the West" by James Alton James, *Mississippi Valley Historical Review*, Vol. XVI (June, 1929). "The Loyalists in West Florida and the Natchez District" by Wilbert H. Seibert, *MVHR*, Vol. II (March, 1916). "Peter Chester's Defense of the Mississippi after the Willing Raid" by Kathryn T. Abbey, *MVHR*, Vol. XXII (June, 1935). *Anglo-Spanish Rivalry in North America* by J. Leitch Wright (Athens, Ga., 1971).

REVOLUTIONARY WAR: *Origins of the American Revolution* by John C. Miller (Boston, 1943). *The American Nation* by John A. Garraty (New York, 1966).

LOUISIANA: *The Westward Movement, 1763–1798*, by Justin Winsor (Boston, 1899).

13

Thomas Jefferson: Land Developer

THOMAS JEFFERSON (to 1784): *Jefferson the Virginian* by Dumas Malone (Boston, 1948). "The Jeffersonian Background of the Louisiana Purchase" by W. Edwin Hemphill, *Mississippi Valley Historical Review*, Vol. XXII (June, 1935).

FUR TRADE: *The Fist in the Wilderness* by David Lavender (New York, 1964). *The Fur Trade in Canada* by Harold A. Innis (New Haven, 1930). "Auguste Pierre Chouteau" and "Pierre Chouteau, Junior," by Janet LeCompte, in *The Mountain Men and the Fur Trade of the Far West*, Vol. IX (Glendale, Calif., 1972).

GEORGE ROGERS CLARK and the NORTHWEST TERRITORY: "The National Significance of George Rogers Clark" by Temple Bodley, *MVHR*, Vol. XI (Sept., 1924). *George Rogers Clark: His Life and Public Services* by Temple Bodley (Boston, 1926).

LOUISIANA AND THE MISSISSIPPI: "The Significance of the Mississippi Valley in American Diplomatic History, 1686–1890," by Richard W. Van Alstyne, *MVHR*, Vol. XXXVI (Sept., 1949). *The Mississippi River* by Julius Chambers (New York, 1910).

JONATHAN CARVER and CAPTAIN JAMES COOK: "Jonathan Carver and the Carver Grant," by Milo M. Quaife, *MVHR*, Vol. VII (June, 1920). *Three Years Travels throughout the Interior Parts of North-America for more than Five Thousand Miles* by Captain Jonathan Carver (Boston, 1797). *A Journal of Captain Cook's last Voyage to the Pacific Ocean, and in Quest of a North-West Passage between Asia and America* (Hartford, Conn., 1783) — an American edition of the original English edition of 1778.

14

Four Nations: One River

JOHN LEDYARD: *The Westward Crossings* by Jeannette Mirsky (New York, 1946).

GARDOQUI and FLORIDABLANCA: *The Spanish-American Frontier, 1783–1795*, by Arthur Preston Whitaker (Lincoln, Neb., 1927). *Louisiana Under Spain, France and the United States, 1785–1807*, edited by James Alexander Robertson (Cleveland, 1911). *Modern Spain, 1788–1898* by Martin A. S. Hume (New York, 1909).

JOHN JAY: *John Jay* by George Pellew (Boston, 1898).

JAMES WILKINSON AND THE SEPARATIST CONSPIRACIES: "James Wilkinson," by Isaac Joslin Cox, *Encyclopaedia Britannica* (1936). "Trade in Frontier Ohio" by Randolph C. Downes, *Mississippi Valley Historical Review*, Vol. XVI (March, 1930). "James Colbert and the Spanish Claims to the East Bank of the Mississippi" by D. C. Corbitt, *MVHR*, Vol. XXIV (March, 1938). "Harry Innes and the Spanish Intrigue, 1794–95," edited by Arthur Preston Whitaker, *MVHR*, Vol. XV (Sept., 1928). "The Founding of New Madrid, Missouri" by Max Savelle, *MVHR*, Vol. XIX (June, 1932).

15

Treaty Trouble and — Worse — Monsieur Genet

EDMOND CHARLES GENET: *Lives and Times* by Meade Minnigerode (New York, 1925). "The Origin of Genet's Projected Attack on Louisiana and the Floridas" by Frederick Jackson Turner, *American Historical Review*, Vol. III (Oct., 1897–July, 1898).

ANDRÉ MICHAUX: "Instructions to Andrew Michaud for Exploring the Western Boundary," in *The Writings of Thomas Jefferson*, Vol. XVII (Washington, D.C., 1905).

PINCKNEY'S TREATY: *Pinckney's Treaty: A Study of America's Advantage from Europe's Distress, 1783–1800*, by Samuel Flagg Bemis (Baltimore, 1926).

JAY'S TREATY: *Jay's Treaty* by Samuel Flagg Bemis (New York, 1923). "Jay's Treaty and the Northwest Boundary Gap" by Samuel Flagg Bemis, *American Historical Review*, Vol. XXVII (April, 1922).

16

The Tightrope Walkers

MANUEL DE GODOY: *Spain* by Richard Herr (Englewood Cliffs, N.J., 1971). *Spain* by George Hills (New York, 1970).

Missouri fur trade: "Anglo-Spanish Rivalry on the Upper Missouri" by A. P. Nasatir, *Mississippi Valley Historical Review*, Vol. XVI (Dec., 1929; Jan., 1930). *Manuel Lisa and the Opening of the Missouri Fur Trade* by Richard E. Oglesby (Norman, Okla., 1963).

David Thompson: "A Man to Match the Mountains" by Alvin M. Josephy, Jr., in *Great Adventures of the Old West* (New York, 1969).

Talleyrand: *Talleyrand* by Louis Madelin (New York, 1948).

Pre-Purchase background: *The Mississippi Question, 1795–1803*, by Arthur Preston Whitaker (Gloucester, Mass., 1962). "The Policy of France toward the Mississippi Valley in the Period of Washington and Adams" by Frederick Jackson Turner, *American Historical Review*, Vol. X (Jan., 1905).

Santo Domingo: *Santo Domingo* by Otto Schoenrich (New York, 1918).

17

The Chancellor's Great Adventure

Livingston: *Chancellor Robert R. Livingston of New York, 1746–1813*, by George Dangerfield (New York, 1960).

Barbé-Marbois: *The Man Who Sold Louisiana* by E. Wilson Lyon (Norman, Okla., 1942). *The History of Louisiana* by François de Barbé-Marbois (Philadelphia, 1830).

Leclerc: "Jefferson and the Leclerc Expedition" by Carl Ludwig Lokke, *American Historical Review*, Vol. XXXIII (Jan., 1928).

Retrocession: "Spanish Policy Towards the Retrocession of Louisiana" by Arthur P. Whitaker, *American Historical Review*, Vol. XXXIX (April, 1934).

18

Bonaparte Makes Up His Mind

James Monroe: *James Monroe* by W. P. Cresson (Chapel Hill, N.C., 1946).

OFFICIAL DOCUMENTS ON LOUISIANA: *State Papers and Correspondence bearing upon the Purchase of the Territory of Louisiana* (Washington, D.C., 1903). "Confidential Message Recommending a Western Exploring Expedition, January 18, 1803," in *The Writings of Thomas Jefferson*, Vol. III (Washington, 1905).

19

Fait Accompli

OFFICIAL DOCUMENTS ON LOUISIANA: *Annals of Congress*, Vols. 7 and 8 (1801–1805). *American State Papers*, Vol. II: *Foreign Relations*, pp. 506–572. *Territorial Papers of the United States*, Vol. IX: *Territory of Orleans*, edited by Clarence E. Carter (Washington, D.C., 1940).

LUCIEN BONAPARTE'S BATHTUB STORY: *The Louisiana Purchase* by James K. Hosmer (New York, 1902).

CONSTITUTIONAL ISSUE: *Jefferson the President: First Term* by Dumas Malone (Boston, 1970).

NEW ORLEANS AND ST. LOUIS TRANSFER CEREMONIES: *New Orleans City Guide*, American Guide Series (Boston, 1938).

HISTORY OF ST. LOUIS: *Annals of St. Louis* by Frederic L. Billon (St. Louis, 1888).

Epilogue

AMERICAN EXPEDITIONS: *The Journals of Lewis and Clark*, edited by Bernard De Voto (Boston, 1953). The *Expeditions of Zebulon Montgomery Pike*, edited by Elliott Coues, 3 vols. (Minneapolis, 1965). *Meriwether Lewis* by Richard Dillon (New York, 1965).

BOUNDARY AND FLORIDA NEGOTIATIONS: *A History of the Western Boundary of the Louisiana Purchase, 1819–1841*, by Thomas Maitland Marshall (Berkeley, Calif., 1914). *John Quincy Adams and the Foundations of American Foreign Policy* by Samuel Flagg Bemis (New York, 1949). *Boundaries of the United States and the Several States* by Franklin K. Van Zandt, U.S. Geological Survey Bulletin No. 1212 (Washington, D.C., 1966).

Appendix

1

Treaty Between the United States of America and the French Republic

The President of the United States of America, and the First Consul of the French Republic, in the name of the French people, desiring to remove all source of misunderstanding, relative to objects of discussion mentioned in the second and fifth articles of the Convention of (the 8th Vendémiaire, an 9) September 30, 1800, relative to the rights claimed by the United States, in virtue of the treaty concluded at Madrid, the 27th October, 1795, between His Catholic Majesty and the said United States, and willing to strengthen the union and friendship, which at the time of the said Convention was happily reestablished between the two nations, have respectively named their Plenipotentiaries, to wit: The President of the United States of America, by and with the advice and consent of the Senate of the said States, Robert R. Livingston, Minister Plenipotentiary of the United States, and James Monroe, Minister Plenipotentiary and Envoy Extraordinary of the said States, near the Government of the French Republic; and the First Consul, in the name of the French people, the French citizen Barbé-Marbois, Minister of the Public Treasury, who, after having respectively exchanged their full powers, have agreed to the following articles:

Art. 1. Whereas, by the article the third of the Treaty concluded at St. Ildefonso (the 9th Vendémiaire, an 9) October 1, 1800, between the First Consul of the French Republic and His Catholic Majesty, it was agreed as follows: His Catholic Majesty promises and engages on his part to cede to the French Republic, six months after the full and entire execution of the conditions and stipulations herein, relative to His Royal Highness the Duke of Parma, the Colony or Province of Louisiana, with the same extent that it now has in the hands of Spain, and that it had when France possessed

382

it; and such as it should be after the treaties subsequently entered into between Spain and other States: And whereas, in pursuance of the Treaty, particularly of the third article, the French Republic has an incontestible title to the domain and to the possession of the said territory, the First Consul of the French Republic, desiring to give to the United States a strong proof of friendship, doth hereby cede to the said United States, in the name of the French Republic, forever and in full sovereignty, the said territory, with all its rights and appurtenances, as fully and in the same manner as they might have been acquired by the French Republic, in value of the above-mentioned treaty, concluded with His Catholic Majesty.

Art. 2. In the cession made by the preceding article, are included the adjacent islands belonging to Louisiana, all public lots and squares, vacant lands, and all public buildings, fortifications, barracks, and other edifices, which are not private property. The archives, papers, and documents, relative to the domain and sovereignty of Louisiana and its dependencies, will be left in the possession of the Commissaries of the United States, and copies will be afterwards given in due form to the magistrates and municipal officers, of such of the said papers and documents as may be necessary to them.

Art. 3. The inhabitants of the ceded territory shall be incorporated in the Union of the United States, and admitted as soon as possible, according to the principles of the Federal Constitution, to the enjoyment of all rights, advantages, and immunities, of citizens of the United States; and, in the meantime, they shall be maintained and protected in the free enjoyment of their liberty, property, and the religion which they profess.*

Art. 4. There shall be sent by the Government of France a Commissary to Louisiana, to the end that he do every act necessary, as well to receive from the officers of His Catholic Majesty the said country and its dependencies in the name of the French Republic, if it has not been already done, as to transmit it, in the name of the French Republic, to the Commissary or agent of the United States.

Art. 5. Immediately after the ratification of the present treaty by the President of the United States, and in case that of the First Consul shall have been previously obtained, the Commissary of the French Republic shall remit all the military posts of New Orleans, and other parts of the ceded territory, to the Commissary or Commissaries named by the President to take possession; the troops, whether of France or Spain, who may be there, shall cease to occupy any military post from the time of taking possession, and shall be embarked as soon as possible in the course of three months after the ratification of this treaty.

Art. 6. The United States promise to execute such treaties and articles as may have been agreed between Spain and the tribes and nations of Indians, until, by mutual consent of the United States and the said tribes or nations, other suitable articles shall have been agreed upon.

Art. 7. As it is reciprocally advantageous to the commerce of France and the United States, to encourage the communication of both nations, for a limited time, in

* Article 3 is said to have been drawn by Napoleon himself.

the country ceded by the present treaty, until general arrangements relative to the commerce of both nations may be agreed on, it has been agreed between the contracting parties, that the French ships coming directly from France or any of her Colonies, loaded only with the produce or manufactures of France or her said Colonies, and the ships of Spain coming directly from Spain or any of her Colonies, loaded only with the produce or manufactures of Spain or her Colonies, shall be admitted during the space of twelve years in the port of New Orleans, and in all other legal ports of entry within the ceded territory, in the same manner as the ships of the United States coming directly from France or Spain, or any of their Colonies, without being subject to any other or greater duty on the merchandise, or other or greater tonnage than those paid by the citizens of the United States.

During the space of time above mentioned, no other nation shall have a right to the same privileges in the ports of the ceded territory. The twelve years shall commence three months after the exchange of ratifications, if it shall take place in France, or three months after it shall have been notified at Paris to the French Government, if it shall take place in the United States; it is, however, well understood, that the object of the above article is to favor the manufactures, commerce, freight, and navigation of France and Spain, so far as relates to the importations that the French and Spanish shall make into the said ports of the United States, without in any sort affecting the regulations that the United States may make concerning the exportation of the produce and merchandise of the United States, or any right they may have to make such regulations.

Art. 8. In future and forever, after the expiration of the twelve years, the ships of France shall be treated upon the footing of the most favored nations in the ports above mentioned.

Art. 9. The particular convention signed this day by the respective Ministers, having for its object to provide the payment of debts due to the citizens of the United States by the French Republic, prior to the 30th of September, 1800 (8th Vendémiaire, an 9), is approved, and to have its execution in the same manner as if it had been inserted in the present treaty; and it shall be ratified in the same form and in the same time, so that the one shall not be ratified distinct from the other. Another particular convention, signed at the same date as the present treaty, relative to a definitive rule between the contracting parties is, in the like manner, approved, and will be ratified in the same form and in the same time, and jointly.

Art. 10. The present treaty shall be ratified in good and due form, and the ratification shall be exchanged in the space of six months after the date of the signature by the Ministers Plenipotentiary, or sooner if possible.

In faith whereof, the respective Plenipotentiaries have signed these articles in the French and English languages, declaring, nevertheless, that the present treaty was originally agreed to in the French language, and have thereunto put their seals.

Done at Paris, the 10th day of Floréal, in the 11th year of the French Republic, and the 30th April, 1803.

R. R. Livingston,
James Monroe,
Barbé-Marbois

A Convention Between the United States of America and the French Republic

The President of the United States of America, and the First Consul of the French Republic, in the name of the French people, in consequence of the Treaty of Cession of Louisiana, which has been signed this day, wishing to regulate definitively everything which has relation to the said cession, have authorized, to this effect, the Plenipotentiaries, that is to say: the President of the United States has, by and with the advice and consent of the Senate of the said States, nominated for their Plenipotentiaries, Robert R. Livingston, Minister Plenipotentiary of the United States, and James Monroe, Minister Plenipotentiary and Envoy Extraordinary of the said United States, near the Government of the French Republic; and the First Consul of the French Republic, in the name of the French people, has named, as Plenipotentiary of the said Republic, the French citizen Barbé-Marbois, who, in virtue of their full powers, which have been exchanged this day, have agreed to the following articles.

Art. 1. The Government of the United States engages to pay to the French Government, in the manner specified in the following articles, the sum of sixty millions of francs, independent of the sum which shall be fixed by any other convention for the payment of the debts due by France to citizens of the United States.

Art. 2. For the payment of the sum of sixty millions of francs, mentioned in the preceding article, the United States shall create a stock of eleven million two hundred and fifty thousand dollars, bearing an interest of six per cent. per annum, payable, half yearly, in London, Amsterdam, or Paris, amounting, by the half year to three hundred and thirty-seven thousand five hundred dollars, according to the proportions which shall be determined by the French Government, to be paid at either place: the principal of the said stock to be reimbursed at the Treasury of the United States, in annual payments of not less than three millions of dollars each; of which the first payment shall commence fifteen years after the date of the exchange of ratifications: this stock shall be transferred to the Government of France, or to such person or persons as shall be authorized to receive it, in three months, at most, after the exchange of the ratifications of this treaty, and after Louisiana shall be taken possession of in the name of the Government of the United States.

It is further agreed that, if the French Government should be desirous of disposing of the said stock, to receive the capital in Europe at shorter terms, that its measures, for that purpose, shall be taken so as to favor, in the greatest degree possible, the credit of the United States, and to raise to the highest price the said stock.

Art. 3. It is agreed that the dollar of the United States, specified in the present convention, shall be fixed at five francs 3333–10000ths or five livres eight sous tournois.

The present convention shall be ratified in good and true form, and the ratifications shall be exchanged in the space of six months, to date from this day, or sooner if possible.

In faith of which, the respective Plenipotentiaries have signed the above articles, both in the French and English languages, declaring, nevertheless, that the present treaty has been originally agreed on and written in the French language, to which they have hereunto affixed their seals.

Done at Paris, the 10th day of Floréal, eleventh year of the French Republic (30th April, 1803).

ROBERT R. LIVINGSTON,
JAMES MONROE,
BARBÉ-MARBOIS

3

Convention Between the French Republic and the United States

The President of the United States of America, and the First Consul of the French Republic, in the name of the French people, having, by a treaty of this date, terminated all difficulties relative to Louisiana, and established on a solid foundation the friendship which unites the two nations, and being desirous, in compliance with the second and fifth articles of the convention of the 8th Vendémiaire, 9th year of the French Republic (30th September, 1800), to secure the payment of the sum due by France to the citizens of the United States, have respectively, nominated as Plenipotentiaries, that is to say: the President of the United States of America, by and with the advice and consent of their Senate, Robert R. Livingston, Minister Plenipotentiary, and James Monroe, Minister Plenipotentiary and Envoy Extraordinary of the said States, near the Government of the French Republic, and the First Consul, in the name of the French people, the French citizen Barbé-Marbois, Minister of the Public Treasury, who, after having exchanged their full powers, have agreed to the following articles:

Art. 1. The debts due by France to citizens of the United States, contracted before the 8th of Vendémiaire, 9th year of the French Republic (30th September, 1800), shall be paid according to the following regulations, with interest at six per cent, to commence from the periods when the accounts and vouchers were presented to the French Government.

Art. 2. The debts provided for by the preceding article are those whose result is comprised in the conjectural note annexed to the present convention, and which, with interest, cannot exceed the sum of twenty millions of francs. The claims comprised in the said note, which fall within the exceptions of the following articles, shall not be admitted to the benefit of this provision.

Art. 3. The principal and interest of the said debts shall be discharged by the United States by orders drawn by their Ministers Plenipotentiary on their Treasury; these orders shall be payable sixty days after the exchange of ratifications of the treaty and the conventions signed this day, and after possession shall be given of Louisiana by the Commissaries of France to those of the United States.

Art. 4. It is expressly agreed that the preceding articles shall comprehend no debts but such as are due to citizens of the United States who have been, and are yet, creditors of France for supplies, for embargoes, and prizes made at sea, in which the appeal has been properly lodged, within the time mentioned in the said convention of the 8th Vendémiaire, 9th year (30th September, 1800).

Art. 5. The preceding articles shall apply only, first, to capture of which the council of prizes shall have ordered restitution, it being well understood that the claimant cannot have recourse to the United States, otherwise than he might have had to the Government of the French Republic, and only in case of the insufficiency of the captors; secondly, the debts mentioned in the said fifth article of the convention contracted before the 8th Vendémiaire, an 9 (30th September, 1800), the payment of which has been heretofore claimed of the actual Government of France, and for which the creditors have a right to the protection of the United States. The said fifth article does not comprehend prizes whose condemnation has been or shall be confirmed. It is the express intention of the contracting parties not to extend the benefit of the present convention to reclamations of American citizens, who shall have established houses of commerce in France, England, or other countries than the United States, in partner-ship with foreigners, and who, by that reason, and the nature of their commerce, ought to be regarded as domiciliated in the places where such houses exist. All agreements and bargains concerning merchandise, which shall not be the property of American citizens, are equally excepted from the benefit of the said convention; saving, however, to such persons their claims in like manner as if this treaty had not been made.

Art. 6. And that the different questions which may arise under the preceding articles may be fairly investigated, the Ministers Plenipotentiary of the United States shall name three persons, who shall act from the present, and provisionally, and who shall have full power to examine, without removing the documents, all the accounts of the different claims already liquidated by the bureau established for this purpose by the French Republic, and to ascertain whether they belong to the classes designated by the present convention, and the principles established in it; or if they are not in one of its exceptions, and on their certificate declaring that the debt is due to an American citizen, or his representative, and that it existed before the 8th Vendémiaire, ninth year (30th September, 1800), the debtor shall be entitled to an order on the Treasury of the United States, in the manner prescribed by the third article.

Art. 7. The same agents shall likewise have power, without removing the docu-ments, to examine the claims which are prepared for verification, and to certify those which ought to be admitted by uniting the necessary qualifications, and not being comprised in the exceptions contained in the present convention.

Art. 8. The same agents shall likewise examine the claims which are not pre-pared for liquidation, and certify in writing those which, in their judgments, ought to be admitted to liquidation.

Art. 9. In proportion as the debts mentioned in those articles shall be admitted, they shall be discharged with interest at six per cent by the Treasury of the United States.

Art. 10. And that no debt, which shall not have the qualifications above-mentioned, and that no unjust or exorbitant demand may be admitted, the commercial agent of the United States at Paris, or such other agent as the Minister Plenipotentiary of the United States shall think proper to nominate, shall assist at the operations of the bureau, and cooperate in the examination of the claims; and if this agent shall be of opinion that any debt is not completely proved, or if he shall judge that it is not comprised in the principles of the fifth article above mentioned, and if, notwithstanding his opinion, the bureau established by the French Government should think that it ought to be liquidated, he shall transmit his observations to the board established by the United States, who, without removing documents, shall make a complete examination of the debt, and vouchers which support it, and report the result to the Minister of the United States. The Minister of the United States shall transmit his observations, in all such cases, to the Minister of the Treasury of the French Republic, on whose report the French Government shall decide definitely in every case.

The rejection of any claim shall have no other effect than to exempt the United States from the payment of it; the French Government reserving to itself the right to decide definitely on such claims, so far as it concerns itself.

Art. 11. Every necessary decision shall be made in the course of a year, to commence from the exchange of ratifications, and no reclamation shall be admitted afterwards.

Art. 12. In case of claims for debts contracted by the Government of France with citizens of the United States since the 8th Vendémiaire, 9th year (September 30, 1800), not being comprised in this convention, may be pursued, and the payment demanded in the same manner as if it had not been made.

Art. 13. The present convention shall be ratified in good and due form, and the ratifications shall be exchanged in six months from the date of the signature of the Ministers Plenipotentiary, or sooner, if possible.

In faith of which, the respective Ministers Plenipotentiary have signed the above articles, both in the French and English languages, declaring, nevertheless, that the present treaty has been originally agreed on and written in the French language, to which they have hereunto affixed their seals.

Done at Paris, the 10th day of Floréal, the 11th year of the French Republic (30th of April, 1803).

ROBT. R. LIVINGSTON,
JAMES MONROE,
BARBÉ-MARBOIS

Index